IF YOU SHOULD GO AT MIDNIGHT

IF YOU SHOULD GO AT MIDNIGHT

Legends and Legend Tripping in America

Jeffrey S. Debies-Carl

University Press of Mississippi / Jackson

The University Press of Mississippi is the scholarly publishing agency of
the Mississippi Institutions of Higher Learning: Alcorn State University,
Delta State University, Jackson State University, Mississippi State University,
Mississippi University for Women, Mississippi Valley State University,
University of Mississippi, and University of Southern Mississippi.

www.upress.state.ms.us

The University Press of Mississippi is a member
of the Association of University Presses.

First printing 2023
∞

Library of Congress Cataloging-in-Publication Data

Names: Debies-Carl, Jeffrey S., author.
Title: If you should go at midnight : legends and legend tripping in
America / Jeffrey S. Debies-Carl.
Description: Jackson : University Press of Mississippi, 2023. | Includes
bibliographical references and index.
Identifiers: LCCN 2023006028 (print) | LCCN 2023006029 (ebook) | ISBN
9781496844118 (hardback) | ISBN 9781496844125 (trade paperback) | ISBN
9781496844132 (epub) | ISBN 9781496844149 (epub) | ISBN 9781496844156
(pdf) | ISBN 9781496844163 (pdf)
Subjects: LCSH: Legend trips. | Urban folklore—United States. |
Legends—United States. | Teenagers—United States. | Supernatural.
Classification: LCC GR105 .D43 2023 (print) | LCC GR105 (ebook) | DDC
398.20973—dc23/eng/20230311
LC record available at https://lccn.loc.gov/2023006028
LC ebook record available at https://lccn.loc.gov/2023006029

British Library Cataloging-in-Publication Data available

CONTENTS

Acknowledgments vii

Part I: A Prelude to the Journey

Introduction: Of Legends and Legend Trips 3
Chapter 1: The Varieties of Ostensive Experience. 27

Part II: The Preliminal Stage

Chapter 2: Legend Telling 53
Chapter 3: Preparations and an Uncanny Journey 89

Part III: The Liminal Stage

Chapter 4: Rites and Rituals. 117
Chapter 5: Close Encounters of the Supernatural Kind 151

Part IV: The Postliminal Stage

Chapter 6: The Return 179
Chapter 7: Telling the Tale. 203

Part V: At Journey's End

Chapter 8: The Past and Future of Legend Tripping 229

Appendix: Legendary Places Visited and Events Attended 255
Notes 259
References. 271
Index 293

ACKNOWLEDGMENTS

Thanks go first, as they should, to my wife, Melissa. During the course of this work, you have accompanied me with good humor on many strange adventures to many equally strange places. I had a lot of fun, and I hope you did too. Next time, maybe we can go somewhere warmer and slightly less quirky. Maybe. Much appreciation goes also to a certain little, black cat. Although no longer with us, the idea for this project developed late one fall while taking our walks together around the yard. As your mother says, you can haunt us any time you want. Next, thanks go to the University of New Haven, which helped support a portion of this research through granting a sabbatical leave. Thanks go also to the anonymous readers, who provided useful comments and suggestions, and to Laura Vollmer for her help with the manuscript and thoughtful recommendations. Finally, many thanks to the folks at the University Press of Mississippi—especially Mary Heath, Katie Keene, and Valerie Jones—without whom this project may not have come to fruition.

Part I

A Prelude to the Journey

OF LEGENDS AND LEGEND TRIPS

> The visible creation is the terminus or the
> circumference of the invisible world.
> —RALPH WALDO EMERSON ([1836] 2008:23).

Night had overtaken the small group when they first heard a soft sound. "What was that?" one of them asked, drawing the others' attention to the subtle noise. Alarmed by something in the speaker's tone, they stood quietly for a moment, straining their ears for some clue as to the sound's origin. It was a chilly evening in the early days of spring. Small buds were just appearing on the skeletal trees, but now those were hidden deep in shadow. They huddled in the night under ranks of soaring, fragrant pine trees, with the deeper darkness of an old water tower looming at their backs.

There it was again: a sort of crunching, snapping sound like something treading on dead leaves and twigs. The group exchanged nervous glances, unable to see each other's expressions in the gloom but somehow sensing each other's agitation. "It's getting closer," another voice whispered, barely audible to the others. As if on cue, the sound came once more. Then—too quickly— it came yet again. It was repeating itself regularly now, growing louder and closer with each repetition. Voicing aloud what everyone was thinking, the first speaker softly asked, "What is it?"

Only the strange noises, now clearly identifiable as footsteps rustling the leaf litter, replied, but a range of possibilities flew rapidly through their minds. Could it be a deer? A bear? It might just be another person, but what were they doing out here at night—and were they dangerous? Then again, maybe, just maybe, it was the thing that they had come to find in the first place: something no longer living but not quite dead either. The possibility had been exciting when they first set out on their journey, but now, with the potential menace lurking unseen in the woods, that was no longer the case.

The sound was nearly on top of them now, so close that its hidden source might almost reach out and grab them, but they could still see nothing. "What should we do?" someone urgently whispered. A brief pause followed. Then, no longer whispering, came the answer that they had all been waiting to hear: "Run!"

THE STUFF OF LEGENDS AND LEGEND TRIPS

It is a familiar scenario. Change a bit here, a detail there, and the preceding story could be anyone's. This particular one happens to be mine though: a hazy memory from my college days. Chances are you have a similar memory or two. Maybe it is about that overgrown cemetery on the other side of town or the creepy, abandoned house down the street with its broken windows and gaping stare. At the very least, you have probably heard similar tales before. I did not know it at the time, but in wandering around the woods that night, I was participating in an old tradition called "legend tripping" (Hall 1973). Legends are "accounts of past happenings" (Ellis 2003:167) that are told as though they *might* be true (Dégh 2001). They are distinct from other narrative forms that claim to be true—like history—and from those that are up front about being fictitious, such as literature or fairy tales (Bascom 1965). You have probably heard many legends throughout your life. Maybe a friend once told you that the spirit of a woman who was executed for witchcraft still haunts a towering tree in the woods where the grisly deed was done. Or maybe a colleague told you a story about how, many years ago, a former coworker, down in the accounting department, heroically cussed out his jerk boss before walking off the job.

People can tell legends like these in a number of different ways. They can narrate them as a "fabulate" (von Sydow 1948:passim): a third-person account of something that happened to someone else. If the events described happened to the narrator, they might instead talk about them in the first-person as a "memorate" (von Sydow 1948:passim). Typically, narrators move freely between both forms, as they see fit, to tell the same legend with what the folklorist Linda Dégh (1969:78) calls a "dichotomous structure." Whatever form they may take, legends typically contain bizarre and even supernatural elements that shock listeners, but they also offer enough enticing detail that they cannot easily discount them (Brunvand 1981). Legends invite debate over their veracity (Dégh 2001), and often listeners are not entirely sure what to think of them. Legends are ambiguous stories that seem to stimulate a reflective ambivalence in their audiences. Upon hearing one, people might respond with conflicted feelings as it invokes both belief and doubt simultaneously. Another folklorist, Sylvia Grider, recounts a typical response from an informant discussing how her dormitory might be haunted. The young woman said, "I do not believe in ghosts. But [my friend] had me convinced and I started thinking about it" (Grider 1980:158). This statement proclaims a firm attitude of doubt and then immediately contradicts it with an equally strong expression of belief. It is not clear whether she really is "convinced" or not, and she is likely not too sure herself.

Whereas a legend is a narrative, a legend *trip* is an activity. It is a sort of quest (Tucker 2007), an attempt to find out whether a legend is actually true by investigating its claims firsthand (Hall 1980). Is there really a ghost in that empty, old house down the street? Does a band of mutants really lurk in the woods at the edge of town? Sometimes when people hear these sorts of claims, they decide to simply find out for themselves rather than rely on debate or speculation. In part, this reflects an effort to resolve some of the inherent ambiguity in legends and the irresolute feelings they engender in their audiences. In recent years, legend tripping has become increasingly popular. It has been the subject of many books and films, each claiming some degree of veracity. Perhaps most importantly, legend tripping has also been promoted by an almost endless array of "reality" television shows, like *Most Haunted, Ghost Adventures, Ghost Hunters, Finding Bigfoot, UFO Hunters, MonsterQuest,* and so forth. Taken together, these represent an undeniable cultural phenomenon, indicating increasing interest and perhaps belief in the paranormal. They signal and produce an intense interest in legend tripping as well. These shows disseminate legends, just like the more traditional mechanisms of oral communication or books, but they also disseminate legend *tripping* (Koven 2007). On any given episode, we can watch as a team of investigators catches word of some paranormal claim and sets off to investigate its validity. Sociologist Marc Eaton (2018) notes that most of the paranormal investigators he interviewed cited shows like these as the motivation for their own ghost hunting. Following closely on the tail of these televised and polished products, legend trips often appear online as well. Countless people share their experiences online through web forums and social networking sites. Viewers can even watch these adventures unfold on video-sharing sites, like YouTube, where many users upload the chronicles of their exploits for others to behold and others stream their adventures live in real time (Debies-Carl 2021).

Yes, legend tripping is certainly a familiar activity, but, outside of scholarly circles, it is also a poorly understood one. The public sphere commonly discounts it as a pointless juvenile pursuit, while it simultaneously has the capacity to create unnecessary panic among those who witness it. Moreover, it is not unusual for properties to become the unwanted target of troublesome legend trips. Loon Lake Cemetery in Jackson, Minnesota, for example, has been nearly destroyed by legend trippers investigating the grave of a supposed witch (Waskul 2016). When the nature of legend tripping is not well understood, attempts to discourage it generally make things worse. For many years, homeowners near an allegedly haunted forest in Cornwall, Connecticut, for instance, have only increased fascination with the woods by patrolling it closely for trespassers, creating an air of mystery around it (Segal 2007). Among legend trippers themselves, there is generally an uncritical acceptance and celebration of the activity without a deeper awareness of the social or psychological processes at work during the course of their adventure. At times, they may not even realize that they are investigating a legend. Moreover, many contemporary phenomena like conspiracy theories and "fake news" lack obvious red flags, such as supernatural components, that would give away their legendary nature. They, nonetheless, can inspire legend trips. In 2016, a man investigating claims of an occult child-sex-slave ring opened fire in a Washington, DC, pizzeria because he had heard legends claiming that ritual abuse was practiced there (Debies-Carl 2017).

Again, legend tripping is frequently a source of misunderstandings and conflict in society—sometimes with deadly consequences. Greater comprehension of it can help avert some of these problems, but there are also other reasons why understanding it is important. For one thing, surprising truths can be uncovered when researchers take the time to treat legends seriously. Sometimes, they reveal something objectively true at the heart of them. For example, David Hufford (1982) found just that in his investigation of supernatural assault traditions. Whatever it was people experienced in these accounts, it seemed to be universally occurring and independent of cultural tradition or psychological expectation. Of course, the truths revealed by legend do not need to take the form of objective reality. For one thing, they can also reveal quite a bit about human perception and cognition (French and Stone 2014). Moreover, folklorists have long argued that legends, regardless of whether they are true, reflect deeper social truths (Thomas 2018). Legends tell us about people's fears and hopes; they reveal who we are and who we want to be. They show us things that are hard to discuss in a more overt way. Legends about a former plantation haunted by the restless spirts of abused enslaved people or about an abandoned insane asylum where spectral patients still prowl are not just stories about the dead walking the earth. They are also signs that society is still struggling with nightmares from the past that it has not been able to put to rest (Dickey 2016b; Gordon 2008). Similarly, claims of sadistic adults poisoning Halloween candy or of shadowy conspiracies controlling the government reflect heightened concerns over the safety of children (Best and Horiuchi 1985) or the safety of democracy (Swami et al. 2011). In its capacity to capture and reflect sentiments like these, the legend is "an ideology-sensitive genre par excellence" (Dégh 2001:5).

The legends that inspire legend trips are especially important because they have the capacity to motivate action and create social change. Legend trips take time, effort, and perhaps a willingness to put up with negative social reactions. They are attempts to achieve goals that are difficult to obtain through more conventional means. Understanding those goals, therefore, also provides an understanding of the people who seek them and the social world in which they live. The legend trip offers a range of possible rewards. It promises to fulfill the desire for adventure that is missing in many people's lives, even as television and video games increase the desire for it. It provides a feeling of independence and a sense of adulthood in a society that has only vague means to otherwise mark important transitions. It offers a sense of significance, importance, and mystery as its participants engage in a quest for the uncanny that hides from the every-day world and the light of day. It also promises to solve some of those same mysteries, proffering tantalizing answers to the "big questions," like whether life continues after death or whether humanity is alone in the universe. The legend trip, thus, acts as a mirror, reflecting our own image back at us. There is much to learn from examining that image carefully, but it is also a funhouse mirror. When we look at our reflection, we may not be greeted by the self-image we expect to find there, and we may not like what we see.

For all these reasons, years later, I find myself investigating legends once again, albeit from a considerably different perspective.

PERSPECTIVES ON LEGEND TRIPPING AND THE SUPERNATURAL

When it comes to supernatural phenomena, research consistently shows that belief is the norm. After all, most Americans consider themselves to be religious (Jones and Cox 2017). Most religions, of course, endorse the reality of at least some supernatural entities and concepts, like angels and gods or heaven and eternal life after death. A report from the Pew Research Center (2018) based on 2017 data indicates that 90 percent of Americans believe in God. These believers vary considerably in exactly how they conceptualize God, but they are in agreement in terms of a spiritual character to that being or force. It is the remaining 10 percent—the nonbelievers—who are out of the ordinary.

There is an even more fascinating pattern pertaining to "paranormal" beliefs than conventional religion. "Paranormal beliefs" refer to beliefs in any phenom-enon that neither mainstream religion nor science endorses (Bader, Mencken, and Baker 2010; Goode 2000). The Chapman University Earl Babbie Research Center (2017) survey of American fears reports that paranormal beliefs are quite common despite the absence of institutional endorsement. For example, 52 percent of Americans believe that "places can be haunted by spirits," 26 percent believe that "aliens have come to Earth in modern times," and 16 percent believe that "Bigfoot is a real creature" (Earl Babbie Research Center 2017). According to this survey, nearly three quarters of Americans hold at least one of the seven paranormal beliefs measured.[1] It is the nonbelievers, again, who are unusual.

The study of supernatural and other anomalous phenomena, like those encountered on legend trips—including related religious experiences—has long been of interest to investigators spanning a wide range of fields, including folklore, sociology, psychology, anthropology, and religious studies to name just a few examples. Over the years, different researchers have advocated for distinct perspectives on the supernatural: different ways they think it should be examined. While these are often presented as competing points of view, I think they are more usefully applied to legend tripping as complementary components of a more comprehensive approach toward understanding supernatural encounters. This is because each offers a distinct way of interpreting the supernatural, each with its own advantages and disadvantages as well as its own insights and blind spots. Together, they can help achieve a more complete understanding and appreciation for what is admittedly a more complex subject than any single perspective alone can provide.

One prominent perspective highlights the role of culture in experiencing and interpreting the supernatural. Called variously a "constructivist" (Bush 2012) or "cultural-source" (Hufford 1982) perspective, it argues that people experience phenomena that they have come to believe in through enculturation and, conversely, that they will not experience these things in a way that they have not been taught or otherwise come to expect. In other words, as Wayne Proudfoot (1985:223) argues regarding religious experiences, "a person identifies an experience as religious when he comes to believe that the best explanation of what has happened to him is a religious one." Thus, a group's beliefs, values, and customs inform how its members will perceive and interpret otherwise ambiguous stimuli. For example, someone who believes in visions of the Virgin Mary is more likely to interpret a peculiar discoloration on the side of a building as the manifestation of her image and, therefore, as proof of her existence than someone who holds no such belief (Goode 2000).

This constructionist approach suggests that supernatural phenomena are important to study and understand whether they are actually real or not. One reason for this is because beliefs have consequences, regardless of the accuracy of those beliefs. As sociologist James McClenon (2001:62, emphasis original) proposes, we "need not assume that anomalous events are real, merely that what people *perceive* as real have real effects on their belief and behavior." Moreover, studying these beliefs can reveal important lessons about the people that hold them or the cultures where they are found (Thomas 2018).

An important element of the constructionist perspective pertains to cross-cultural diversity of experiences. Cultures can differ greatly from one another in terms of what they teach and expect of their members (Benedict [1934] 2005). Thus, if culture is the cause of supernatural experiences, then expectations regarding the supernatural should vary as well. If this is true, people across cultures should experience the supernatural in markedly different ways. For example, many cultures feature accounts of ghostly encounters with visible apparitions. According to one study, these are almost completely missing in ghost encounters drawn from Jewish cultural contexts (Moreman 2013). In a similar vein, another study finds that Icelanders, because of a rich cultural tradition involving speaking to the dead, are more likely to believe in apparitions and to report seeing them (Haraldsson 1985). More dramatically, the Tiv in West Africa have no tradition of the dead being able to return at all, whether visually or audibly (Bohannan 1966). Meanwhile, a comparison of good-luck superstitions between American and Japanese athletes also reveals interesting cross-cultural differences (Burger and Lynn 2010). While both groups endorse various superstitions, Americans tend toward greater superstitious tendencies. Perhaps even more interesting is the finding that Americans believe their rituals might be able to help individual athletes improve their performance whereas Japanese athletes—who come from a culture that places greater emphasis on the group—believe the practices help the team as a whole.

There is considerable variation among researchers in this tradition regarding what stance should be taken toward the veracity of supernatural beliefs. On the one hand, some constructionists criticize the possibility of the supernatural since a cultural cause makes it erroneous. In the philosophy of religion, for example, Proudfoot's (1985) highly influential work argues that culture is the real cause of experience, and therefore, independent, supernatural causes are invalid. The folklorist Lauri Honko (1964) applies a similar approach, suggesting that cultural values and norms are simply mapped onto ambiguous stimuli.

Other constructionist scholars argue for an "objective" approach. This means that researchers should "not attempt to evaluate, accept, or reject the content of religious belief . . . under study" (McGuire 1997:7). Sometimes, this is predicated on the idea that humanistic and social-scientific methodologies are incapable of testing the reality of supernatural claims: "No survey we administer or interview we conduct will prove God's existence or nonexistence. No amount of fieldwork will grant us a picture into heaven" (Bader et al. 2010:11). Others maintain this approach because, they argue, the reality of the supernatural just doesn't matter one way or the other given its cultural importance. Folklorist Jeanie Banks Thomas (2018:35), for example, states that she is "not much interested in debunking [claims, but rather] more intrigued by what a story can say about the culture from which it comes." She argues that "whether the supernatural is real is not especially germane to these [supernatural] stories" (Thomas 2018:49).

Others maintain an approach somewhere in between these positions. Sociologist Erich Goode (2000), for instance, agrees that the cultural dynamics of belief are the most important dimensions of supernatural phenomena that researchers must investigate. However, the actual truth of those beliefs matters too, albeit in a secondary way, since this actually has implications for those very dynamics. The process that leads a group of people to believe in something that is not true could vary quite a bit from a process that leads to truth. In fact, that process is likely all the more interesting to study precisely *because* it is not based on mere facts alone. If a group believes gravity causes objects to rise into the air, that would be far more interesting to examine than a group that feels gravity behaves in a more conventional, downward manner.

Overall, constructionist approaches excel at uncovering the meanings behind experiences and beliefs. They are especially useful, in this regard, in that they can help explain why some experience and beliefs vary cross-culturally or even why two people might interpret the same stimulus differently. Of course, no perspective is perfect, and there are limits to constructionism's utility. One issue to consider pertains to the objective version of this perspective. This directs researchers to remain respectful of beliefs by not judging their accuracy, but some scholars have asked how far researchers can take that neutrality when they encounter inaccurate beliefs that are also potentially dangerous. Goode (2000) provides the example of Holocaust denial, and other examples come readily to mind, like conspiracy beliefs, which in some cases have motivated shootings and other violent behavior (Debies-Carl 2017).

And emphasizing the cultural construction of the less problematic beliefs or their symbolic meanings can also be inadvertently insulting and demeaning due to their etic nature. People who are personally interested in the supernatural—such as the paranormal investigators that Eaton (2018) studies—tend to be very interested in its reality, whether they come at it from the perspective of a believer, a skeptic, or somewhere in between. Failing to weigh in on this issue can unintentionally disparage these beliefs by appearing to not take them seriously one way or the other. According to Meredith B. McGuire (1997:7), who nonetheless advocates this approach, neutrality can make people uncomfortable because they "find their cherished beliefs and practices dispassionately treated as objects of study."

One last potential problem to consider in regard to constructionist perspectives on the supernatural is that of an infinite regress: If supernatural experiences are caused by cultural beliefs in general, where do the latter come from? Discussing this problem, one observer asks, "If my belief that I see a tree is an inference from a prior belief, from what belief is that prior belief inferred? ... It seems that at some point we have to start with a belief not inferred from any other" (Bush 2012:109).

Objections like these are partly addressed by another perspective on the supernatural called "perennialism" (Stace 1961) or "experiential source theory" (Hufford 1982; Hufford 2001). This general approach considers the veracity of beliefs—the experiences that give rise to them—rather than focusing on solely symbolic or cultural interpretations. For example, Hufford gives the humorous example that the reason he believes there is a computer on his desk is because he sees the computer there, not because American culture values computers or because they might symbolize scholarship or similar activities. Without accounting for the experience itself, any symbolic interpretation "would be at best incomplete, at worst incoherent" (Hufford 2001:39). In regard to super-natural experiences, this perspective argues that some of these have a common, rational basis in real, universal experiences, just like ordinary beliefs do (Stace 1961). In other words, perennialists argue that real, objective stimuli of some sort can cause beliefs and that, therefore, these beliefs are rational and under-standable, regardless of whether the beliefs themselves perfectly represent whatever external stimuli caused them.

As I noted above, constructionism argues that variation in cross-cultural beliefs results in cross-cultural variations in supernatural experiences. This variation, in turn, suggests a cultural source for the experience. Perennialism, conversely, argues that if some portion of an experience is based on an exter-nal reality, then that same portion should be consistent cross-culturally. This consistency would then indicate an underlying unity of experience reflecting an objective stimulus that operates independently of culture. One study, based on a content analysis of memorates, finds consistent content and structure in cross-cultural accounts of supernatural experiences with things like apparitions and out-of-body experiences (McClenon 2000). A review of the research on mystical experiences similarly finds that these seem to occur cross-culturally (Wulf 2000). Summarizing a perennialist approach toward these, one scholar states, "Beneath the particular differences among experiences of Krishna, Mary, and nirvana lies a deeper, more fundamental aspect of the experience: a sense of the sacred, according to some, or of the numinous, or something along those lines" (Bush 2012:104). Likewise, a fairly stable cross-cultural pattern is evident in descriptions of a phenomenon called—among other things—the "old hag" (Hufford 1982). This is characterized by a sense of sudden paralysis and dread, while the victim seems to be fully awake in bed and aware of their environment. Whatever the cause of these experiences, perennialism suggests that cause is real, not determined by culture, and that it is accurately described by those who encounter it.

In considering the possibility of universal experiences, two things are impor-tant to note. First, for perennialists, a "universal" experience does not mean everyone has a given type of experience, but rather that it can happen to anyone in any culture regardless of whether they believe in it or, indeed, have ever even heard of it (Moreman 2013). For example, whereas everyone everywhere dreams, not everyone will ever have a lucid dream, in which they are conscious of the fact they are dreaming. Nonetheless, lucid dreaming seems to appear for some people in any given population regardless of cultural background (Mota-Rolim et al. 2020). Second, while this perspective predicts that the experiences themselves will contain universalities, it makes no such claim about how people will interpret these experiences. All experiences, supernatural or otherwise, might be interpreted somewhat differently across cultures, but cultural belief itself is not responsible for *causing* these experiences. Although experience and interpretation cannot be completely disentangled, the latter are more subject to cultural influence and, therefore, cross-cultural variability (Stace 1961).

Unlike constructionism, then, perennialism explores the veracity of experiences directly. By doing so, it attempts to respect witnesses by treating them as rational and capable observers rather than remaining agnostic and focusing on cultural implications (Hufford 1982; Hufford 2001). It also potentially solves constructionism's infinite-regress problem by tracing beliefs to a specific source (i.e., experience) rather than merely pointing to other beliefs. Of course, this perspective is not without its own problems. First, while demonstrating consistency in experiential reports is a relatively straightforward task, proving an experience is independent of culture or other shared information is another matter entirely. For example, cross-culturally occurring alien-abduction experiences could be reactions to an objective experience, but they could also be informed by globally available accounts in the media and popular culture (Appelle, Lynn, and Newman 2000). There is also considerable criticism over many claims of cross-cultural consistency themselves, suggesting that the consistent component of these experiences tends to be quite vague once variations are ruled out. For instance, although near-death experiences (NDEs) seem to be universal, even something as basic as the experience of a dark tunnel leading into light is not a universal feature of them. Indigenous peoples from Australia, North America, and Pacific islands rarely report experiencing these elements in their NDEs (Kellehear 1993). Examples like these can call into question exactly how "universal" a universal experience really is if all that remains are vague sensations once specific components are ruled out due to variability.

One further challenge to perennialism remains. Even when cross-cultural patterns, independent of shared cultural influence can be established, there is an alternative explanation aside from shared experience: the shared humanity of those experiencing it. While cultures differ, humans everywhere share a common psychological heritage. Thus, psychological perspectives represent a third way of interpreting supernatural experiences. Psychologists have been interested in anomalous experiences since the early days of the discipline (Blum

2006; Cardeña, Lynn, and Krippner 2000). There are many different, specific approaches to psychology, including developmental, behaviorist, cognitive, clinical, psychobiological, evolutionary, and many more. Given this diversity, there is considerable disagreement among psychologists over exactly how to interpret supernatural experiences. However, all share a general tendency to emphasize the role played by individual-level processes.[2] In this case, it is not necessarily an external stimulus that is the stable source of experiences but rather commonalities of human perception and cognition. Psychologists usually agree that anomalous experiences are a normal part of human psychology (Irwin 2009). Although psychopathology can certainly play a role in generating them, it is the exception rather than the rule. In fact, explanation typically takes the form of simply applying normal and known "psychological explanations of non-paranormal phenomena when attempting to explain ostensibly paranormal phenomena" (French and Stone 2014:16).

In considering how human psychology could contribute to paranormal experiences in this way, Christopher French and Anna Stone (2014) provide the example of back masking. The processes that lead people to perceive hidden messages in songs played backwards are very similar to those that might cause them to perceive ghostly voices in recordings (i.e., electronic voice phenomenon). In both cases, human brains are excellent at perceiving patterns in ambiguous stimuli, even when there really is no pattern. There is very little consistency in what people actually hear unless they have already been told what to expect. The psychologist Stuart Vyse (1997) provides a somewhat different example of how normal processes—like operant conditioning—can explain paranormal thinking in terms of superstitions. Operant conditioning is a universal process through which people learn things. If you ever struggled with opening a stubborn lock or getting a leaky faucet to turn off properly, you likely first tried wiggling it around at random. Eventually, you might have hit on just the right angle that seemed to do the trick, and from then on, you would purposely attempt to replicate that movement to get the same result in the future. Vyse points out that a similar learning process accounts for much of what an individual knows and usually works quite well. However, it "sometimes goes awry, adapting our actions to contingencies that are not really there" (Vyse 1997:200). This is the case, for instance, for many lucky charms. If your team happens to win a game on a day you wear a particular shirt, you might come to associate the two. Whether the pattern learned through operant conditioning is accurate or inaccurate, once the association is forged, it is very difficult to unlearn, even when subsequent attempts to apply it fail. Hauntings might similarly reflect psychological processes. In one study, subjects are instructed to walk around allegedly haunted locations and note any unusual experiences or feelings they have (Wiseman et al. 2003). They report these most frequently in the same places earlier witnesses had. The researchers conclude that prior knowledge could not account for this consistency, but supernatural explanations were not needed either. The subjects' reports closely correlate with something that is very real nonetheless: environmental conditions, such as lighting effects and magnetic fields, that affect their perception.

Like the perennialist perspective, psychology usually adopts the position that taking anomalous experiences seriously requires testing their veracity rather than reading their symbolic meanings alone. Again, exceptions to the rule certainly exist. Hufford (1982) criticizes early psychoanalytic psychologists for being particularly prone to a symbolic reading of anomalous experiences without any regard for testing experiential claims or even their own theories, while simultaneously assuming there was no objective truth to these experiences. Today, psychologists are much more likely to be of the opinion, as French and Stone (2014:7) argue, that research is necessary to determine whether alleged paranormal "forces actually do exist" and, regardless of the results, that this effort should improve understanding of how the mind works and "reveal a great deal about what it means to be human." Their approach to claims is the same approach that, ideally, all sciences advocate toward any claim, be it paranormal or otherwise: that is, open-minded doubt that is willing to examine evidence, wherever it might lead. Here, the point is "to distinguish between what is genuinely paranormal and what just looks like it on the surface" (French and Stone 2014:17). In this way, psychologists hope to steer a safe course between excessive reductionism, on the one hand, and uncritical credulousness, on the other (Cardeña et al. 2000).

Like the other perspectives I have considered, psychological perspectives have their limitations. Despite improvements over the years, there remain some tendencies toward reductivism and "*post hoc* scientific rationalization" that Hufford (1982:166) pointed out so many years ago. Developing a *possible* explanation for an experience is not the same as actually explaining it. Second, while psychology has unlocked many mysteries of the mind, there are still many anomalous experiences that are neither fully explained nor well understood, such as synesthesia, out-of-body experiences, and mystical experiences (Cardeña et al. 2000). While psychology inevitably must play some role in all human experience, it is not necessarily the sole cause of these experiences. Finally, *individual* psychology alone can also be reductive in the sense that it is not well suited for explaining how *groups* of people experience the supernatural. For this, one last perspective is necessary.

Whereas psychological approaches emphasize the role of internal, individual level processes, social approaches prioritize what happens when two or more people get together and influence one another. Likewise, although social and cultural perspectives often accompany one another, by "social," I mean the actual interaction of specific people in real time rather than the broader, more abstract realm of culture, where countless people interact indirectly and build traditions over time (Geertz 1973). One of sociology's early giants, Émile Durkheim ([1912] 1995), maintains that, under the right conditions, the only thing that is really necessary to induce a sense of the supernatural is the presence of other people in a conducive setting. In one of the first works to specifically examine paranormal phenomena from a social perspective, Andrew Greeley (1975) exhorts his colleagues to study the social factors—those beyond the strictly individual level—that facilitate or inhibit supernatural experiences and beliefs.

Numerous studies illustrate how social processes can facilitate paranormal experiences. First, even simply noticing a stimulus in the environment that is worthy of consideration as supernatural in character can be a collaborative activity. Rachael Ironside (2017) examines this process through an analysis of recorded paranormal investigations. Individuals alert each other to possible stimuli, like sounds or feelings, through head tilts, body shifts, and similar cues. When others notice these cues, they quickly search for the source. This collective attention serves as evidence that there really is something to be noticed in the environment since everyone else is paying attention to it (Cialdini 1993). In everyday life, people can usually spot such stimuli quickly and easily. In paranormal investigation, a clear-cut apparition would be easy to collectively notice too. However, supernatural encounters are usually much more subtle and vague (Waskul 2016). Indeed, Ironside (2017) finds that there doesn't necessarily have to be an objective stimulus at all. Participants can simply draw each other's attention to empty space, and its very emptiness implies a nonmaterial source for their collective attention. The result is a feeling of uncanniness, validated by shared perception.

Just as perception can be altered by social processes, so, of course, can interpretation. Based on participant-observation research with a group of ghost hunters, Eaton (2018) finds social dynamics play a significant role in the group's identification of anomalous events and their later determination that these were supernatural in origin. After one member of the group falls to the ground during an investigation, the team compares observations. They argue over some details and collaborate other parts of each other's accounts. Ultimately, it is not just the objective features of the event that affect their interpretation but also this discussion and other social factors. For instance, members of the group with more status have greater say in deciding what happened simply because of their ranking in the group.

A range of similar studies reveal social patterns and social influences in the realm of supernatural experience. Numerous studies find that a range of sociodemographic features—like age, education, race, and social class—predict the likelihood that a person might experience these phenomena (e.g., Bader et al. 2010). When it comes to believing claims of encounter or sharing them with others, social factors matter too. Alain L. Patry and Luc G. Pelletier (2001) find that people are more likely to believe a UFO report from a friend than from the media or popular culture. They are also more likely to report their own experiences to friends than to the media or authorities. As illustrated in studies like these, one of the advantages of a social perspective is that it provides another mechanism, like perennialist approaches, to account for supernatural experiences that cannot be explained by cultural norms and expectations or that might even run *counter* to them. Rather than requiring an external encounter however, here participants can generate it themselves through interaction. They can also modify their perception of actual stimuli through this process. Another advantage is that social processes illuminate how groups of people can appear to experience the same thing—whether in error or not—without having to resort to vague claims, like mass hallucination (Hufford 2001). That being said, this perspective cannot necessarily shed light on the nature of that stimulus itself. Moreover, social perspectives that focus on group interaction are not so well suited for situations where people experience the supernatural when they are by themselves, although they can still apply to the discussion that follows later.

Again, each of the above perspectives has its respective strengths and weaknesses. One perspective does not necessarily invalidate another in its entirety but can instead help to construct a more complete and nuanced understanding of anomalous experiences, like those found on legend trips. For these reasons, in this study, I adopt a synthetic perspective that considers each of these points of view as well as the various ways they might interact. Legend trippers are typically responding to *something* in their environment. Their perception of that stimulus is part of a psychological process that occurs in a social context. Later interpretation of that perception occurs through further social interaction and may be guided by cultural resources. It is my hope that this consideration of multiple perspectives will encourage discussion and debate and discourage the assumption that a single perspective is the only accurate one.

INVESTIGATING LEGEND TRIPS

A vast number of researchers have examined legend tripping over the years. Their cumulative efforts have resulted in a fascinating array of insights into an equally fascinating phenomenon. In this book, I offer five main contributions to this body of work. First, I provide a comparative analysis of scores of legend trips to look for overall patterns rather than extrapolate from a single case study. These include cases drawn from previous scholarly reports and over one hundred new cases that I investigated in person as well. Second, I examine new data from multiple sources—especially the internet and television—to supplement the literature's traditional emphasis on interview data. Third, throughout this study, I incorporate relevant scholarship from a range of disciplines with something to say about legend tripping. This approach takes advantage of multiple points of view to extend our understanding of the phenomenon and, hopefully, to encourage further interdisciplinary inquiries. Fourth, I include cases beyond hauntings and curses—where the usual emphasis lies—to expand the concept of legend tripping. This enlarges the scope of what counts as legend tripping while simultaneously asking what differences might arise across different types of legends. Fifth, and finally, I synthesize the existing literature and integrate it with my new findings to provide a comprehensive introduction to and update of legend-tripping research that does not require readers to examine and compare the vast number of original sources that make up the existing scholarship. To make my approach clear, it is worth elaborating on these contributions.

To begin with, again, the comparative nature of my study is something of a departure from previous work. Researchers have conducted studies on legend trips for several decades. The majority of these works take the form of detailed case studies to understand the activities and motives of the people who have gone to investigate a specific site. There are now a great many of these studies available. Taken altogether, these inquires have provided enough insight into the subject matter that it is now possible, even necessary, to conduct a more comparative analysis across multiple legend trips. This serves to distinguish what is true for legend tripping *in general* from what is unique to specific cases. What common legend characteristics promote legend tripping? Do all legend trips really share a common structure? What patterns are there to the types of activities legend trippers engage in on site? Is a legend trip really a rite of passage or is it something else? I address these questions, and many more like them, throughout the following pages. This comparison has allowed me to discover more nuanced patterns for each component of legend trips, to provide revisions to the overall structure of these activities, and to contribute many entirely new findings as well, which are not possible to extrapolate with confidence from a single case.

Some of the cases I compare are drawn from previous reports, but my study is also based on over six years of original data collection. I investigated scores of new cases to determine what they had in common. This included extensive fieldwork as well as exhaustive analysis of textual and video accounts of legend trips found both online and off. In acquainting myself with these legends and legend trips, it quickly became apparent that reading or watching videos about them would not be enough. Instead, I decided that I would need to visit the setting of some of these narratives in person. Soon enough, "some" became "many," and fieldwork became a major component of the project. I found myself looking for legendary places wherever I could. I have spent many nights in allegedly haunted inns, prowled cemeteries full of the restless dead, trekked into remote woodlands where strange creatures are said to dwell, and scanned the skies over odd places where UFOs have been spotted. Some of the places I have visited are well known, some only famous among those living nearby, and others obscure even among locals. Some are abandoned and neglected, while others are well used and pristine. Overall, I tried to include a wide representation of different types of legendary places in my itinerary. A complete list of these is presented in the appendix. Some types of places, however, seem better represented among legends than others. I consider the characteristics of places that tend to accrue legends throughout the book, particularly in chapter 2.

In the process of visiting these sites, I developed a general approach that I like to think of as a sort of "reflexive ethnography." This term can mean many things, but minimally it requires that "the researcher must see as an insider and think as an outsider" (Berg and Lune 2012:205). To this end, I tried to take on the roles of both researcher *and* legend tripper while simultaneously considering how each role might inform the other. This mixed perspective, while challenging, is well suited to a reflexive approach since the former requires a specific attitude toward the data: an "internal dialogue" in which the researcher constantly reviews what they have learned and how they have come to learn it. This means that the researcher "actively constructs interpretations of experiences in the field and then questions how these interpretations actually arose." The ideal result is reflexive knowledge or "information that provides insights into the workings of the world *and* insights on how that knowledge came to be" (Berg and Lune 2012:205, emphasis original). Ethnographers wear many hats. A reflexive approach adds to that complexity.[3]

For any particular field visit, I first set out to learn about the location's associated legendry by reading about it, watching videos on it, and studying online discussions. Upon traveling to the site, I examine the physical layout or architecture (cf. Dickey 2016b). When people are present, if appropriate, I chat with them or casually observe their activities. I do not interfere with them though, either directly or indirectly. For example, I do not engage in formal interviews or obtrusive observation. Often, no one is present in some of the more remote places, but even then, I can examine the physical evidence of human activity: those traces of erosion or accretion that mark where people have been and what they did while there (Webb et al. 1973). For example, signs of wear on particular pathways, vandalism, litter, and the like can reveal quite a bit about human activity even when the humans responsible for these signs are absent. Donald H. Holly and Casey E. Cordy (2007) use a similar approach in their study of legend trips to the graves of alleged vampires in Rhode Island. Commenting on this approach, they note that, "an archaeological approach to legend landscapes is apt to reveal a wider range of activities and visitors than one that relies solely on direct research with informants." This is because "people who come and go in the middle of the night, decline invitations to be interviewed, or operate under the radar of participant-observation research, for instance, nonetheless may contribute something to the 'material record'" (Holly and Cordy 2007:347).

Across these different methods, as a researcher I am interested in explaining how characteristics of the setting might influence or otherwise facilitate legend formation or legend tripping. Are there strange features that demand explanation? Are there any features that might contribute to uncanny experiences? Are there signs of past legend trips and, if so, what activities do they indicate? However, I also try to interact with these sites as a legend tripper. I try to establish the proper mood of anticipation and uncanny possibility. I sometimes reenact the behaviors prescribed by the legend to invoke the resident mystery, such as touching cursed gravestones, calling spirits by name, or taking photos of particular locations. I keep an eye out for things that might qualify as supernatural. Thus, when I conduct fieldwork, I try to adopt the perspective of someone expecting supernatural possibilities while simultaneously maintaining an analytical perspective. The interaction of these two perspectives is particularly valuable in achieving my goal of reflexivity.

Throughout this study, I also demonstrate how many of the legend settings themselves can inspire a sort of wonder. They are often distinctive locales with strange characteristics, historical significance, or mysterious allure. Likewise, the journey to legendary places can itself feel like a significant act. Being mindful of the dramatic stories and claims associated with a place, anticipating a visit to that place, actually being there, and later having a tale to tell can produce a subjective feeling of accomplishment akin to what some legend trippers experience even without a supernatural encounter. Other researchers have at times participated in legend trips as a part of their methodology as well. In one well-documented account for instance, Dégh and Elizabeth Tucker visited Step Cemetery in Indiana (McNeill and Tucker 2018). Likewise, Dennis and Michele Waskul visited reputably haunted locations as part of their research on the social experience of supernatural experiences and used a method similar to my own reflexive approach. Contemplating a forthcoming field trip, D. Waskul notes, "In a few days Michele and I will be visiting the location, said to be haunted, and on this night—my eyes peering emptily into the darkness above—I am organizing bits of information in my head, pulling up mental images of old photographs, shaping questions, and perplexing in the sadness of the story"

(Waskul 2016:1). Certain details aside, this brief passage reminds me strongly of my own field notes. It reflects the careful attention to a given legend, the sense of anticipation and possibility, and the overall immersion in the process. It illustrates how ethnographic exploration of a legend is itself a legend trip.

My second contribution to legend-tripping research is to draw on a wider range of data than is typical to supplement my own fieldwork and allow a more robust analysis. This includes textual, televised, and online sources discussing or portraying legend trips to all the sites I conducted fieldwork at as well as additional ones I could not visit in person. These data sources have allowed me to experience legend trips indirectly from the perspectives of other people who have undertaken them and to compare these experiences to my own thoughts and conclusions. First, I read reams of printed material: books, magazines, brochures, and similar items detailing legends and the experiences people have had while investigating them. Given the importance of television and reality TV in particular to the legend process (Koven 2007), I also watched many shows, some of which I have discussed above, for another perspective on the topic. In the process, I suspect I took far more notes than casual viewers do.

Scholarship on legend tripping commenced—and arguably peaked—long before there was such a thing as the internet or reality television. Consequently, much classic work needs to be revisited to see what findings hold up in our digital age. Researchers have been increasingly interested in the online world, which is "a growing setting for a number of contemporary legend trip experiences" (McNeill and Tucker 2018:26). Studies have identified numerous legend-related behaviors online, such as legend formation (Boyer 2013), transmission (Soltero 2016), and discussion (Langlois 2014). Computer-mediated legend trips have begun to receive attention as well. Andrew Peck (2015), for instance, examines how people can go on legend trips in real life looking for Slender Man: a supernatural entity that originally only existed online. Others have made the case that legend trips can occur almost *entirely* online (Kinsella 2011; McNeill 2015).

With this in mind, I make extensive use of online sources, including regular websites, blogs, vlogs, videos, discussion forums, and so forth. Visitors to these sites, as I have found, can read or hear about legends, watch legend trips in action, and access photographs or audio recordings that are presented as proof of supernatural encounters. Indeed, the internet provides unparalleled access to folk processes, including new opportunities to examine the interplay between legends as narratives and legends as actions—that is, the interactive process between legend telling and legend tripping. Researchers frequently only have access to a snapshot of this process offline: the original tale, discussion of the tale, or perhaps conversations with legend trippers after the trip is complete. Online sources provide greater access to all these processes, their interrelationships, and more (Debies-Carl 2021). Any study of contemporary legends would be remiss if it does not include online sources when they are available.

Although I am a sociologist myself, my third contribution is to leverage an interdisciplinary perspective to further develop and promote research on legend tripping. First, scholarship on legend tripping has traditionally been within the purview of the field of folklore. Folklorists first discovered the concept and have consistently developed it over the years. At times, this important work has found its way into other disciplines with similar interests but not as frequently as I think it deserves. In fact, a range of disciplines, including sociology, anthropology, psychology, and even biology, have conducted research on related topics. However, they do not frequently use the term "legend trip," which remains obscure in these fields. Consequently, there has been something of a lack of cross-disciplinary communication. This is unfortunate since research in these other disciplines could benefit from a better acquaintanceship with the important work produced by folklorists. The reverse is true as a well. Thus, part of my task has been to integrate research and perspectives from some of these diverse disciplines into the subject matter to expand our understanding of legend tripping and to show its connections to other key topics like social change and human cognition. Beyond simply taking advantage of the multiple points of view afforded by this approach, I hope this effort will also serve to encourage further interdisciplinary inquiries and dialogue.

My fourth contribution is to expand the scope of legends that are investigated in legend-tripping research. My comparative approach is designed not only to look for patterns or differences across legends but also across various *types* of legends. Most legend-tripping research to date has focused on hauntings or associated curses (e.g., a cursed grave). There is good reason for this since, indeed, these are incredibly popular and widespread objects of discussion. However, there is a great variety of types and topics of legends, many of which are equally capable of inspiring investigation. Similarly, past research has often emphasized adolescent legend tripping, but there is a need for further research that looks at other participants as well.

On account of these considerations, my conceptualization and investigation of legend tripping is generally broader than the traditional emphasis on bored adolescents looking for something to do on a Saturday night: I take into account a wide selection of participants, legend types, and geographic settings. I have found, for example, that adults legend trip too, although they might not do so in the same way as younger folks. While some of the classic destinations— like abandoned cemeteries—are still very much in evidence, a considerable amount of modern legend tripping goes on in locations like haunted hotels, haunted museums, and similar places that market themselves as legendary. Also, although my data collection has indeed turned up a preponderance of legends dealing with the world of ghosts and related entities, I include a range of less frequently considered, modern paranormal interests as well. Legend trippers can hunt for UFOs and Bigfoot just as readily as phantoms and spirits, and as it turns out, the social process is very much the same, as my examples will illustrate. Indeed, legend trips need not involve supernatural claims at all. All that is needed is a legend worth investigating, whatever the nature of that legend might be. I take this fact into consideration as well. Finally, past research has typically concentrated on a small geographic area, such as the researcher's town of residence. Again, this is understandable given the constrains of travel and the use of in-person interviews. Many of my cases are drawn from a fairly broad region, spanning from Washington, DC, to Maine, especially the places I was able to visit in person. However, I include some fieldwork beyond this range as well. More importantly, I was able to greatly expand this range through the use of video and online sources as discussed above.

Again, in all this, my primary goal has been to determine what is true for legend trips in general rather than what is characteristic of a single type of legend trip. I wanted to know how well the concept fit different types of legends and their different contexts. Of course, there are more questions here that deserve closer scrutiny than a single book can afford to answer, so I do not pretend to have addressed these matters completely. There are many opportunities for future research to examine these issues in depth. For example, what differences exist between ghost hunters and Bigfoot hunters? Do adults have different motivations for legend tripping than adolescents? Are there regional differences in what legend tripping entails? What about international differences? In what ways can our understanding of supernatural legend tripping help explain similar activities where the supernatural is not involved at all? This area of research is far from exhausted. On the contrary, there are more areas to explore than ever before.

Finally, the fifth contribution of this book is to provide a comprehensive overview and update of research on legend tripping. I synthesize decades of existing studies in the folklore literature so that readers new to the topic can quickly become acquainted with the vast number of original sources and general themes that make up the existing scholarship without having to read dozens of papers. This material is organized by concept for easy reference. For example, chapter 1 focuses solely on ostension, whereas chapter 4 deals with the ritual behaviors that occur at the site of a legend trip. This organizational scheme should be especially useful to students or those with backgrounds in other areas. For readers keen to fully understand legend tripping, this approach pairs well with a volume like Lynne S. McNeill and Tucker's *Legend Tripping: A Contemporary Legend Casebook* (2018). This important, recent work provides a careful selection of classic and influential studies that represent some of the best examples of research conducted on this topic to date, including several out-of-print works. It also includes insightful introductions that contextualize these works and make them more accessible.

Beyond its utility to readers new to legend tripping, experts should find much of value in the current volume as well. Partly, this is because I simultaneously weave this systematic review of the vast existing literature together with my new findings to extend our understanding of legend tripping as described above. Secondly, I also make connections throughout to research outside of folkloristics to see how this could shed further light on different dimensions of legend tripping. In so doing, I discuss a range of work from other disciplines that provides useful perspectives worth comparing to those long established in this field. Again, I do not claim to have exhausted or included all relevant avenues of work, but by drawing some of these connections, I do hope to encourage interdisciplinary inquiries into the subject and to deepen our understanding of the topic at hand.

A ROADMAP OF THE JOURNEY AHEAD

The journey into legend that you are about to embark on is likely to be a strange one full of bizarre and inexplicable sights—at least on the surface. You will encounter witches and aliens, vampires and cults, and haunted places and haunted people. You will meet those individuals who are eager, or at least willing, to give credence to the possible existence of such things and, stranger still, to go forth and encounter them on their own. As you travel further, you will also find yourself awash in hoaxes, panics, rumors, and bizarre claims. In other words, you will explore the stuff of legend itself. Far from being a realm of childish fairy stories consigned to an earlier, more superstitious age, legends are alive and well. Moreover, they are much more prevalent than most people might imagine and can even influence everyday life.

In the first chapter, I will prepare for this journey by first exploring the concept of "ostension": the means by which legends are told through actions instead of words (Dégh and Vázsonyi 1983). In the process, even something that began as mere fantasy or fiction can take on a sort of reality as people bring it to life through their actions. With this understanding in hand, you will catch the first glimpse of our true quarry with an introduction to legend tripping proper, itself an expression of ostension (Ellis 2003).

The following six chapters will lead you on a legend trip of sorts by tracing the course in steps by which these journeys tend to occur, and I present specimens of each step as we progress. In general, I argue for a more detailed understanding of legend tripping than has previously been available and explore some of its lesser-known characteristics. I hope to provide a concise overview of the concept while also offering interpretations that will make sense of its apparent strangeness and illustrate its significance.

The legend trip begins with the "preliminal stage."[4] This consists of two distinct steps that must occur at the start of the journey. First, participants must engage in "legend telling," as explored in chapter 2. Prospective legend trippers hear a story—a legend—that makes some curious claims. The legend indicates that proof of those claims is available for those who care to search for it. This, along with other compelling characteristics of the legend, may inspire those hearing the tale to do just that. Chapter 3, "Preparations and an Uncanny Journey," explores what comes next, after the legend trippers have made the decision to investigate. The participants make ready whatever they might need for the journey and in the process begin to imagine themselves in the legendary setting where they might experience strange phenomena. They then set forth to find that setting, sharing speculations and reviewing the legend along the way. These activities establish the proper mood, a sense of expectancy, that will enable them to entertain the possibility of a supernatural encounter.

When at last they arrive at their destination, they will also have entered into the "liminal stage" of the legend trip. This too consists of two distinct steps, both characterized by the sense that the participants have left behind the mundane world of everyday predictability and entered into an unknown realm of uncertain possibility. However, that possibility does not manifest on its own. Chapter 4 analyzes the rites and rituals they must conduct in order to invoke the supernatural. Specified or suggested by the legend that initiated the trip, these behaviors allow the participants to enter into the narrative of the legend itself. They take on the role of heroes, villains, or simply prior investigators, and their actions compel the supernatural elements present to act out their role as well. The legend trippers next "encounter" those mysterious entities, as discussed in chapter 5. Something happens that serves as proof of the supernatural—as evidence that the legend is true. This fills the legend trippers with a profound sense of awe but also of terror. The feeling is intense and disorienting, and they cannot endure it for long.

The legend trip concludes in the two steps of the "postliminal stage." The experience of their encounter is so dramatic that the participants must flee the scene. In doing so, they attempt to leave not only the physical place behind but also their sense of the liminal with all of its fascinating—but also unsettling—ambiguity. If successful, they achieve a safe "return," as outlined in chapter 6. However, the unsettling, uncertain, and yet profound nature of the encounter lingers. Having returned to a place of safety and sanity, the legend trippers next discuss their experience with each other and with others who were not there. Chapter 7 examines how in "telling the tale" they are really engaged in a sort of debate. Did the events they thought they experienced really happen? What caused them? What does it all mean? They do not find any sure or stable answers to these questions, especially not answers that society at large will agree with. Nonetheless, they often come to some tentative conclusion that reinforces the overall sense that something significant has happened. Moreover, in concluding their adventure by telling their tale, they simultaneously initiate the legend-tripping cycle anew. Someone hearing their story may become fascinated by it, wonder whether it is true, and embark on a journey of their own to explore that possibility.

In chapter 8, after the legend trippers safely return from this curious process, I take a step back to contemplate the greater significance of legend tripping. What, exactly, is a legend trip? Why would anyone bother to go on one? Why has it become so popular in recent years? The answers to these questions, I argue, are interrelated. Whereas legend trips are similar to classical rites of passage, they have marked differences as well that have not been addressed by prior research. Traditionally, a rite of passage is a mandatory, socially sanctioned ritual process (van Gennep [1909] 1960). Directed by an elder or official of some sort, it provides clear expectations for what participants must do and what the whole affair means. When they have completed the rite, participants are assigned a new social status—such as adulthood—and reintegrated into society. None of these aspects apply so neatly to legend trips. Legend trips are voluntary and operate without institutional oversight or approval. They have no socially sanctioned or legitimated interpretation readily available for participants to draw upon. Participants cannot simply look to the priest, the tribal elder, or some other sort of cultural authority to tell them what has happened and how this will affect their social status. Upon returning home, they similarly cannot assume everyone there will appreciate the significance of what they have endured and treat them in some new, prescribed way. Instead, they must arrive at their own conclusions, compare interpretations, and derive further meaning and some degree of a validating consensus through intense discussion and debate.

I propose that these differences occur not because of some imagined impoverishment of modern ritual but because society itself has changed. Unlike traditional rites of passage, which take place in relatively small, homogenous societies, legend tripping occurs in large, diverse societies. Here, there is no single, agreed-upon institution that can impose a uniform ritual transition or claim a monopoly on truth and meaning. Legend tripping, in its current form, is a reflection of the modern world, revealing both its problems and its virtues. On the one hand, it is characterized by ambiguity, crisis of meaning, and the substitution of debate for social consensus. On the other hand, increasingly, modern societies emphasize individual agency and values, even in spiritual matters. Moreover, traditional institutions that persist—such as formal churches—have lost much of their former influence over even their own denominations. I argue that while the need for meaningful and transformative experiences remains, authoritative, traditional institutions no longer provide this need for most people. Instead, legend trippers voluntarily search for individually meaningful spiritual experiences and actively participate in shaping and interpreting those experiences themselves.

The road ahead beckons. It promises danger and unknown terrors but also excitement, wonder, and discovery. The map is drawn; the course is set. We have packed our bags and heard the claims. Now, let us turn to the next page and take our first step on the path into legend.

Chapter 1

THE VARIETIES OF OSTENSIVE EXPERIENCE

But ancient superstitions, after being steeped in human hearts and
embodied in human breath, and passing from lip to ear in manifold
repetition, through a series of generations, become imbued with an
effect of homely truth. . . . By long transmission among household facts,
they begin to look like them, and have such a familiar way of making
themselves at home that their influence is often greater than we suspect.
—NATHANIEL HAWTHORNE ([1851] 1924:154)

SHOW, DON'T TELL: PRESENTING OSTENSION

A growing fear stalked American communities during the 1980s and 1990s.
The signs were ripe that a dark occult conspiracy was rapidly spreading across
the country, into our schools, our backyards, and even into our families. The
evidence seemed ample: churches and cemeteries were discovered desecrated,
satanic altars were found in the woods, human and other animal sacrifices
turned up by the dozens, the experiences of ritual abuse victims were recounted
under hypnosis, and countless teens were lost to drugs, sex trafficking, and
suicide in the name of the Devil (Bromley 1991; Victor 1993).

In response to these outrages, communities mobilized, experts taught worried parents how to recognize the signs of occult seduction in their teenagers,
and—like a scene ripped from the pages of a gothic horror novel—police and
townsfolk scoured the countryside in search of the monsters hiding in their
midst. Unfortunately, under such intense scrutiny, the culprits of the fiend-
ish acts simply "went even deeper underground" and beyond the reach of
these heroic efforts (Ellis 1989:205). And yet, oddly enough, while all these
things happened, they simultaneously did *not* happen. There was no conspiracy
and no cult (Ellis 1989; Fine and Victor 1994), and thus, these "facts" were

simultaneously both true and not true. This situation, seemingly, is a paradox—but it is a paradox that can be resolved.

In this chapter, I establish the conceptual groundwork needed to understand legend trips and the puzzles, such as this one, that they present. First, I
introduce the concept of "ostension" as an interpretive frame through which
to understand legend trips, and I examine the various forms ostension takes. I
discuss how legends can become reality through ostension, influencing people's
behaviors and society itself. Next, I consider how researchers often compare
legend trips to rites of passage. I present an overview of what this entails, along
with some modifications to this idea that I think are necessary. I also problema-
tize and build on some of these concepts in addition to simply introducing
them. The forms of ostension are overlapping and often misunderstood, and
certain forms of it are sometimes ignored entirely by researchers. Moreover,
legend tripping is complex and does not easily fit into a single mode of ostension. Similarly, although conceptualizing legend trips as rites of passage is
useful, doing so is something of an oversimplification that is not without its
own problems. This is an issue that I return to throughout this study. Unravel-
ling it, I argue, provides important insights into the nature of legend tripping
in the modern world. I conclude by presenting my model for the stages that
comprise legend trips, around which the remainder of the book is organized.

First, let me return to the concept of "ostension," which comes from Latin
"*ostendere*," meaning "to hold out for inspection" or, more simply, "to show"
(Traupman 1995:291). This refers to a form of communication in which instead
of using a sign to represent some concept or thing, one indicates the thing itself.
For example, suppose I want to offer you an apple. Instead of verbally asking
you whether you would like one, I could simply hold the apple out for you to
see. Ostension has been acknowledged as a distinct means of communication
since at least the time of Aristotle (Engelland 2014). However, modern use of
the concept is derived from semiotics.

Umberto Eco's (1979) treatment of ostension is particularly influential.
Beyond indicating specific things, Eco notes that ostension can be used more
generically. For example, you can pick up an object and show it to someone "as
an expression of the class of which it is a member" (Eco 1979:225). Suppose your
friend is heading to the grocery store and asks whether they can pick anything
up for you while they are out. If, in reply, you extend an apple toward them,
as above, you would not be indicating that you want them to bring back that
specific apple, but rather more apples in general. As these examples illustrate,
ostension is imprecise. Here, your friend wouldn't know how many apples
you wanted or, indeed, whether you were really asking specifically for more
apples at all or some other type of food instead. Nonetheless, it is a useful and
important means of communication. Ostension is especially useful for people

who do not speak the same language and for children first learning to speak (Engelland 2014). Ostension might even be used in the absence of spoken language among the other great apes (Moore 2016).

Dégh and another folklorist Andrew Vázsonyi (1983) famously repurpose the concept of "ostension" by applying it to legends. Arguing against an entrenched assumption that folklore and especially legends must be communicated orally, they introduce the idea of "ostensive action" (Dégh and Vázsonyi 1983). Here communication occurs not just by showing an object but through action: "that is, the showing of an action by showing the action itself or by another action" (Dégh and Vázsonyi 1983:8). More broadly and quoting Ivo Osolsobě (1971:35), they note that this sort of legend showing occurs when "the reality itself, the thing, the situation or event itself functions in the role of message." From this perspective, legends can be transmitted through behavior that shows, rather than merely tells, the story. Put another way, ostension "refers to the presentation (as opposed to the representation) of a legend text" (Koven 2007:184).

For example, many people have heard some variation of a legend folklorists call the "Hatchet Man" (Grider 1980) or the "roommate's death" (Brunvand 1981). A young woman is left alone in her dorm room one evening (for one reason or another, depending on the legend variant), waiting for her roommate to return (from a local bar or just from downstairs). She is afraid to go looking for her by herself, sometimes because of warnings that a murderous maniac is on the loose. At one point during the long, nerve-racking course of the night, she hears scratching on her door. Still fearful, she does not open it, thinking it could be the maniac. She remains silent and hides in her closet instead. At last, after many torturous hours have passed, dawn breaks, and she works up enough courage to investigate. She emerges from her hiding place and cautiously opens the door. On the other side, to her horror, she finds her roommate on the floor and covered in blood—dead. The roommate had been attacked by the maniac at some point in the night, and mortally wounded, she desperately crawled her way back to their room. Once there, however, she could only feebly scratch at the door until she bled to death. In some variants, a hatchet is found beside her body or buried in the doorframe.

This story can, of course, be told verbally. It can also be told ostensively, that is, by acting out some meaningful portion of it. Grider (1980) reports on how some female college students did just that in their dormitories after hearing the legend. They left notes for each other, slipped under the door, signed "H. M." (i.e., "Hatchet Man") or, instead of knocking, simply scratched at each other's doors.

Bill Ellis (1982) describes a legend from a summer camp in Ohio.[1] In this tale, campers are told that a man named Ralph—another murderous maniac—is stalking the woods in the area. In a fit of rage one day, so the story goes, he killed his beloved brother, Rudy. Now, he stalks among the trees calling his dead brother's name, and woe unto anyone who strays too far from camp and crosses his path. B. Ellis reports that the campers were very moved by the story and, for some time after hearing it, walked through the woods calling "Ruuuuudy!" And, while shouting the name, they jumped out and scared each other. Actions like these, of course, do not act out their respective legend in its entirety but rather assume that the audience is familiar with the narrative. By performing some specific, key part of it, the action calls the whole legend to mind and plunges both actor and audience briefly into the roles of maniac or potential victim.

LIFE IMITATES LEGEND

Perhaps the most intriguing—or disturbing—characteristic of ostensive action is its capacity to simultaneously be both cause and effect. In other words, as Dégh and Vázsony (1983:29) put it, "fact can become narrative and narrative can become fact." To illustrate this, they discuss the perennial, undocumented rumors of malicious adults contaminating Halloween candy with drugs, poison, needles, or razor blades. These fears, present still today, have proliferated for decades even though there are very few substantiated cases (Best and Horiuchi 1985). Moreover, the few documented accounts seem to have been *inspired* by the legends, *not* to have caused them. There is at least one case of an adult poisoning his own son's candy, seemingly after having gotten the idea from earlier legends (Dégh and Vázsony 1983), and there are cases of children inserting pins or similar objects into their own candy, apparently for attention or excitement (Ellis 1994). The legends also resulted in other related forms of behavior, such as x-raying candy, public-awareness campaigns, parents keeping their children home on Halloween night, and similar signs of a panic. In all these cases, the legends inspired action in that people decided to act some part of them out. In this way, the legend of tainted candy becomes, to some extent, reality.

Activities like these constitute various expressions of ostension. By reacting to the legend, people actually act out part of it: as a villain who harms children, as a victim whose candy has been tampered with, or as heroic defender of children against the alleged threat. They communicate the legend by reproducing it and, thus, make it become true, or they respond to it in such a way that they seem to validate the reality of the legend by behaving as though it is true. These behaviors do not simply result from the preexisting legends. They also contribute to the legend cycle. When adults and children discuss real or alleged "copycat" cases as well as their precautionary activities, they provide further grist for later ostension. Indeed, so ingrained have these precautionary rituals in particular become that they are now, themselves, a part of the Halloween tradition. Again, the belief, however tenuous, in the *possible* reality of a legend can lead to further behaviors substantiating the credibility of its claims that are then incorporated back into the legend cycle only to be ostensively enacted again and so on in perpetuity.

With this conceptual grounding in mind, I can now return to the "satanic panic" (Victor 1993) with which I opened this section and resolve the paradox I introduced along with it: that Devil worship simultaneously did and did not occur throughout the 1980s and early 1990s. The rumors of satanic activity were based on a number of factors like misidentifying and grouping unrelated phenomena and then interpreting them in the light cast by real fears and concerns (Bromley 1991). "Mysterious" animal deaths, local crimes, frightening imagery in role-playing games, and heavy metal music combined with rumor and speculation painted a compelling, frightening, and utterly inaccurate picture of what seemed to be happening. Tellingly, actual occult activity seems to have been largely absent or at least no more prevalent than in prior decades. Nonetheless, the legends ultimately became real in a number of ostensive ways.

The stories we tell, including exaggerated stories about youth activities, can influence the real world even if they start out as false claims (Debies Carl 2020). Hearing these rumors, some teens did indeed play around with satanic imagery and behaviors, but most of this was not serious and was *inspired* by the legend—their actions were not the origin point for it (Fine and Victor 1994). It is even possible that worse actions, including murder, *may* have been the result of people copying the legends they heard, perhaps to mask their crimes and cast suspicion on the red herring of a nonexistent cult (Ellis 1989). In ways like these, legends become life when we act them out through ostension. In fact, the entire episode of fear and reaction to alleged satanic conspiracies in America might itself be an ostensive reenactment of similar but earlier events in Great Britain (Ellis 1993). Legends also become life when people are affected by them, such as when people act toward others in a way that is inspired by a legend or when they change their behaviors in response to a legend that they have heard. Beliefs about Satanism were disseminated not by actual Satanists but by their would-be opponents: "the tireless local police, social workers, school administrators, and members of the clergy" who tried to raise awareness and fight the threat of Devil worship (Fine and Victor 1994:72).[2] Indeed, these attempts to battle with their projected fears probably constitute the bulk of ostensive behavior surrounding this legend cycle, with far more people trying to take action against perceived occultism than trying to emulate it. During the satanic panic, supposed information about Devil worship was widely spread, likely targets became scapegoats and were persecuted for assumed occult involvement, teenagers were diagnosed with satanic seduction and received interventions, and communities took other precautions to combat the imagined threat. For example, various alarmist "awareness" groups formed during this era who offered harsh prescriptions to parents of adolescent fans of heavy metal and punk rock. Darlyne Pettinicchio, cofounder of one of these groups' organizations called Back in Control Training Center, recommends, "If the child won't [give up the music] on his own, the parents have to go into the child's bedroom and remove the posters, the albums and the clothes. . . . Then they have to take him to the barber to get his hair cut, or the hairdresser to get the color changed" and cut off their connections with friends who are into heavy metal or punk (quoted in Benet 1986:n.p.). Meanwhile, one study finds that 83 percent of mental health institutions in southern California recommend that adolescents receive treatment based on displaying punk styles alone, even in the absence of any evidence that these styles actually correlated with dangerous behavior (Rosenbaum and Prinsky 1991).

To the extent that belief in an occult threat caused real consequences, the threat *was* real in a way. When behaviors such as these occur, people are still acting out the legend, but instead of simply identifying with the persona of the legend and acting out their roles, they are behaving as though the legend is true. Here, in addition to all those subsequent behaviors that result from interpreting a legend as real, the mere "act of interpretation is the legend performance, not the actions that actually produced the evidence" (Ellis 1989:208). Note that there can be a degree of overlap between acting out a legend and being affected by it. When one feels they may have been targeted by the plot described in a legend and change their behaviors accordingly, they in fact simultaneously act out a role described in the legend: that of victim. This applies, for example, to individuals who recall false memories of ritual abuse (Bottoms and Davis 1997; Spanos, Burgess, and Burgess 1994) and become involved in further actions to protect themselves or their communities from Satanism.[3]

Ostension can, thus, explain a wide range of seemingly dissimilar behaviors that all share a common origin in being inspired by, or otherwise influenced by, legendary accounts. Sometimes, legend can affect a large number of people across wide geographic areas and persist for decades. Of course, many legends never achieve this degree of influence but might still have dramatic effects on those they do reach. There is perhaps no more compelling, or disturbing, case for the power of legend in this regard than when it motivates ostensive murder or attempted murder. In contrast to those instances referred to by B. Ellis (1989) above, in which a killer might deliberately model a legendary account or copy another homicide reported in the media in the hopes of covering up their involvement, sometimes legends can actually inspire violent acts rather than simply serve as cover stories for them. This was the case for two Wisconsin preteens who stabbed a third girl, their friend, nearly to death in 2014. According to news accounts, the two would-be murderers were motivated by internet legends of a supernatural character called "Slender Man" (Boyer 2013; Tolbert 2013). Apparently, the girls were hoping to attract Slender Man's attention in some way by the attempted murder, but the specific motive remains unclear and varies by account: to be recruited by him as followers, to test his existence, or to somehow dissuade him from targeting their families (Jones 2014).

While cases like these, involving murder and other heinous acts, do on occasion occur as acts of ostension, they are not common. Sociologists have convincingly shown, for example, that copycat crimes, such as those mimicking contaminated Halloween candy legends, are decidedly rare even if the legends themselves are endemic and perennial (Best 1991; Best and Horiuchi 1985). The popular perception that ostension is abnormal or pathological is likely due to a common and understandable human tendency to focus on the rare and dramatic murder or panic instead of more typical behaviors (DeLamater, Myers, and Collett 2015). Many ostensive behaviors, such as x-raying candy in response to a legend, are much more common and much less gruesome. Moreover, positive outcomes are probably just as likely, even if the lion's share of scholarship and media coverage neglects these.[4]

That being said, while the term "ostension" infrequently occurs outside of folkloristic research, significant scholarship exists on related phenomena for which there is considerable support. A famous example is sociologist Robert K. Merton's (1948:passim) "self-fulfilling prophecy." He describes it as "a *false* definition of the situation evoking a new behavior which makes the originally false conception come *true*." Moreover, because of this self-fulfilling quality, this phenomenon presents a "specious validity" that "perpetuates a reign of error. For the prophet will cite the actual course of events as proof that he was right from the beginning" (Merton 1948:195, emphasis original). In other words, this is a situation in which an expectation becomes true precisely because it was so expected and would not have come to pass had expectations not changed anyone's behaviors—a definition that potentially suits ostensive action very well. By way of illustration, Merton describes how a solvent bank may fail if enough investors are convinced that it is actually insolvent and act accordingly. Research has found troubling evidence of the phenomenon in a range of circumstances. Robert Rosenthal and Lenore Jacobson's *Pygmalion in the Classroom* (1968) is a deservedly oft-cited example of the self-fulfilling prophecy, also called the "expectancy effect," at work in the classroom. In this study, the experimenters administer an IQ test to schoolchildren from first through sixth grade. They then randomly select a fifth of the students and inform their teachers that the test results indicate these students are academic "spurters": students who are showing signs of entering into a period of intellectual blossoming for the coming year. Since these students are chosen at random, the chance that there was actually something different about them from the rest of the students is miniscule at best. Nonetheless, when Rosenthal and Jacobson retested the students at the end of the year, they found a significantly greater increase in the IQ scores of the supposed spurters when compared to their less fortunate classmates, particularly the younger children. The likely explanation is that the teachers began to perceive these students differently and then to treat them differently—perhaps encouraging them more, giving them personal attention, or not accepting mediocre performance—now that they had come to believe these children would soon perform better. This explanation is supported by the fact that the teachers, when asked to describe their students, rated the "spurters" as happier, more likely to succeed, and more interesting than their peers. Thus, expectations led to real behavioral changes for both the teachers and the students themselves even though these expectations were based on nothing credible, much like many legends.

A range of studies find similar expectancy effects in other contexts, and the results do not always benefit the people so affected. During job interviews, white interviewers are more likely to convey prejudiced attitudes toward black interviewees using subconscious, nonverbal cues, such as keeping a greater physical distance between themselves and the applicant or failing to lean toward them as they would with a white interviewee (Word, Zanna, and Cooper 1974). The applicants pick up on these cues, which seem to suggest that the interview is not going all that well, and that apprehension has a debilitating effect on the rest of their actual performance. This, in turn, looks to the interviewer like confirmation of their original biased expectations. In a similar vein, a phenomenon called "stereotype threat" influences behavior and performance in response to expectations even when independent of more objective factors. For example, the cultural stereotype that women are inherently worse than men at math may produce a sort of anxiety that actually causes women to perform worse in some situations, even if they are objectively good at math (Spencer, Steele, and Quinn 1999). Likewise, the labeling theory of social deviance (Becker 1963) has inspired a range of research demonstrating how attaching disrepute to someone, even if unearned, can cause others to treat that person unfavorably and, what's worse, even cause that person to actually change their sense of identity and engage in the expected behaviors. Similarly, studies argue that, in mental asylums, even the conventional behaviors of patients are routinely interpreted as signs of illness, and these interpretations can affect the patients' actual identities and behaviors (Goffman 1961) even when those patients are presumably sane, as shown by undercover researchers studying patient experiences through participant observation (Rosenhan 1973). In short, it is clear that ostension is not necessarily an odd or abnormal form of social psychology. It is quite the opposite: there is good reason to assume that ostension is just another face of standard human behavior, even when it manifests in seemingly extraordinary ways.

TYPES OF OSTENSION

Undoubtedly, ostension includes a range of dramatic crimes and hoaxes, but it clearly includes more banal behaviors as well. Dégh and Vázsonyi (1983) suggest that ostension might take the form of one of four theoretically conceivable modes. These are worth considering since they provide a sense of the consistency and variability within this form of behavior.

One mode of ostensive behavior called "quasi ostension" involves the mistaken interpretation of something as evidence of a legend in action. This commonly occurs when people confuse natural occurrences for supernatural ones. Consider the common tales of phantom footsteps and mysterious banging noises in old houses at night. A host of normal sounds ranging from the wind, to rattling heating pipes, and settling foundations cause these very real noises, as can any number of real creatures. In this regard, the author and nature enthusiast John Hanson Mitchell (2014:165) notes that mice, tending to be especially active at night, likely "account for a number of ghosts or poltergeists." Similarly, hearing the call of a screech owl might account "for more ghosts and spirits than any other living creature. Its shivering descending call, echoing through the obscure branches of the night trees, is indeed a somewhat disconcerting sound if you don't know what you are hearing." He recalls how an acquaintance "used to hear them in the orchard outside his house when he was little and would lie in bed too terrorized by the call to even tell his parents" (Mitchell 2014:129). Many years later, this acquaintance eventually learned it was just an owl and "not some hideous monster clamoring among the branches of the apple trees." When I was a child, I had an almost identical reaction to the then unfamiliar calls of screech owls ululating through the woods at night. They did not sound like any animal I was acquainted with, but their cries certainly resembled some Hollywood witch's cackle. Despite the prosaic origin of these sorts of noises, one well versed in ghostly legends and less well versed in the anatomy of a house or the normal activities of animals might understandably attribute these odd sounds to a ghostly presence.

Indeed, such auditory phenomena are so entrenched in ghost lore, particularly as portrayed on television and film, that a phrase like "it's just the house settling" might itself be construed as an attempted rationalization and, thus, a testament to the presence of something spectral when someone utters it. Many people are so familiar with the various phenomena associated with hauntings that they have no trouble recognizing them when they occur. Consequently, they may quickly suspect that a ghost is at large, even when other explanations are more likely. In August of 2013, for instance, a group of Ohio State University students moved into an off-campus rental house where they soon began to notice strange happenings (Haskell 2013; Martini 2013). They found lights switched on that had been off earlier, drawers and cupboards left open that had been firmly closed, and the electricity to the third floor frequently shut off on its own. They heard mysterious noises emanating from the basement, especially when they went down there to reset the breaker for the third floor. One of the roommates even encountered a strange man in the basement one day. When asked his name, the figure cryptically responded "Jeremy" but would answer no other questions and exited the house. Meanwhile, noises continued in the basement. Investigating, the students traced these sounds to a room with a locked door, the secrets beyond it tantalizingly close but out of reach. By this point, unsurprisingly, the students came to believe that they had a ghost on their hands and began to tell people about their haunted house. Eventually, they contacted their landlord and the police who were able to open the mysterious door. What they found shocked the frightened roommates. They did indeed have an unwanted roommate, but it was not a ghost. Rather, it turned out that Jeremy was a very real, flesh-and-blood man who had been squatting for some time in their basement. "He was a really nice guy," noted one of the students about their now-former roommate (Reimold 2013:n.p.).[5]

Fortunately, this story had a humorous ending (except perhaps for poor, evicted Jeremy). The more psychologically traumatic phenomenon called variously "old hag" or "night hag" might similarly qualify as an example of quasi ostension. Earlier, I noted that while the specifics of this experience vary to some degree across accounts, occurrences generally include a remarkably stable set of characteristics, which indeed might be traceable far back in written history to the Norse sagas (Lindahl, McNamara, and Lindow 2001) or even the ancient Greeks (Guiley 1992). Whether antique or modern, generally these accounts include the witness waking up from sleep but being unable to move or speak, feeling a suffocating pressure on their chest, and perceiving some threatening menace approaching their bed. Indeed, sometimes an apparition or form is actually seen or heard lurking nearby. In some more recent accounts, the experience is frequently related to rather contemporary concerns: extraterrestrial visitation and abduction. In his discussion of the phenomenon, the late Carl Sagan (1996:64) summarizes a typical experience: "You're lying in bed, fully awake. You discover you're utterly paralyzed. You sense someone in the room. You try to call out. You cannot. Several small gray beings, less than four feet tall, are standing at the foot of the bed." Apart from the specific appearance of the lurking entities, this experience sounds very much like those that do not invoke alien intruders. Hufford's (1982:ix) influential analysis of this "terror that comes in the night" illustrates that people from diverse cultures with no apparent contact between them recount very similar versions of this tale—with far less variety than one would expect from a typical legend even within a single culture. Modern medical professionals typically consider this phenomenon to be naturally occurring: a sensation sometimes generated as one enters or leaves sleep stages (Sharpless and Doghramji 2015; Terrillon and Marques-Bonham 2001). However, for hundreds of years, disturbed dreamers have attributed the frightening experience to some supernatural agency drawn from familiar folklore, typically a malevolent force, such as a demon or witch.[6]

Unlike quasi ostension, another category of ostensive behavior called "pseudo-ostension" is consciously enacted. It takes the form of a hoax or practical joke in which someone fools others into thinking they are witnessing a real-life manifestation of a particular, preexisting legend by simulating part of it. For example, many people have long believed that the famous Loch Ness in Scotland is the home of some manner of monster. These legends are indeed old, although the most ancient are also fairly vague. One medieval legend, set in the sixth century CE, features St. Columba "confronting a man-killing dragon in River Ness and causing it to flee" (Coleman and Clark 1999:139). Despite this apparently ancient origin of the legend and the fact that it actually occurred a bit away from the loch itself, the modern version of the monster is much more closely linked to alleged sightings that took place in the 1930s. These more recent accounts propelled the formerly obscure Loch Ness to global fame, and monster seekers aplenty continue to scrutinize its shores and waves for the elusive Nessie to this day. Most of these come home empty-handed or with little more than a tale to tell. Others, however, leave the loch with what they claim to be photographic evidence of an encounter with the legend itself. Many of these instances are little more than further cases of quasi ostension in the form of "pareidolia": overactive pattern recognition in random waves' patterns, half-submerged logs, or other natural phenomena (Carroll 2003). However, some are not honest accidents at all, but very dishonest hoaxes staged by those hoping to capitalize in some way on the legend. One of the older and most famous photographs of the "monster" seems to be a case in point. Allegedly taken by Dr. Robert Kenneth Wilson in 1934, the so-called "surgeon's photograph" shows a long, serpentine neck emerging from the water topped by a small dinosaurian head. Countless books and films about the Loch Ness mystery monster have reproduced the image in the decades since. Yet, by the mid-1990s, serious doubts had been raised regarding the photo's authenticity since it was clear that whatever the object was in the photograph, it was much too small to be a dinosaur. Then, one Christian Spurling claimed to have been involved in doctoring the photograph. He and some family members had created "a small model of a sea serpent made of plastic [and] wood attached to a 14-inch toy submarine" (Carroll 2003:200). In this way, they "showed" the legend to the world or, rather, a farcical representation of the legend.[7]

After the 1930s sightings became well publicized, a number of people started to claim that they had also seen the monster, but that they had done so earlier—in some cases much earlier, dating back to the 1850s (Coleman and Huyghe 2003). It is a very real possibility that these individuals also experienced quasi ostension or produced pseudo-ostension. By that time, paleontologists had uncovered and publicized numerous dinosaur fossils, and these, especially the fossils of animals like plesiosaurs, can inspire both types of ostension (Paxton and Naish 2019). However, there is another possibility too: they may have heard stories of the loch and its monster and subsequently claimed the narratives as their own actual experience. Prompted or moved by the sudden fame and significance of monster fever, these "witnesses" might attempt to associate themselves, possibly unconsciously, with the excitement by adding themselves into the story and then sharing the modified legend with others. Dégh and Vázsonyi (1983) call this sort of phenomenon "proto-ostension" in their brief discussion of it. Subsequent treatments have interpreted it somewhat divergently. B. Ellis (2003:164) suggests that people might unwittingly make claims of this sort for something they have not actually experienced as a result of "sincere but false memories." These could stem from fantasy-prone personalities or, in some cases, mental disorders. More mundanely, these memories could be generated through the power of suggestion. This seems to be true in many cases of claimed satanic ritual abuse, alien abduction, and demonic possession. Thanks to the work of researchers like psychologist Elizabeth Loftus (1994), we know that the "recovered" memories of such ordeals are more often than not actually invented and imaginary ones. Regardless of the specific circumstances of any given case, proto-ostension reflects a process where someone has become so moved by a legend or has come to identify so strongly with it that they claim a personal connection to it. Moreover, in the course of the telling, they move the legend from a third-person to a first-person account, breathing new life and credibility into it in the process.

Lastly, there is the possibility that the legend in question is true and demonstrates that truth by showing *itself*. Thus, if a ghost actually exists, it could convey its existence by allowing itself to be seen by some passerby. Dégh and Vázsonyi (1983:19) call this theoretical possibility "pure ostension" and quickly discount its plausibility, suggesting that since ghosts are not real, then no one can have a real experience recognizing one. A witness "would not have recognized the ghost if not already familiar with the necessary ingredients from legend" (Dégh and Vázsonyi 1983:19). This discountenance is perhaps the reason why so many subsequent treatments of their typology have neglected to include this category of ostension from the discussion (e.g., Kinsella 2011) or interpreted it in a different way (e.g., Ellis 2003).[8] This lack of attention is unfortunate since the possibility of a real stimulus being the source of a legend is both intriguing and entirely possible in some cases. Hufford (1982) argues that objective experience was the actual source of the old hag phenomena, for example. He suggests that both cultural and psychological perspectives are inadequate for explaining it in its entirety, although he is careful not to commit to a specific interpretation himself—whether naturalistic or supernatural—to account for the experience. Besides, legends are not exclusively the domain of supernatural phenomena and can, at times, even be based on things that are objectively real and even ordinary (Brunvand 1981). For example, hypothetically, one could imagine that the first person who ever saw a giraffe reported the experience to their friends. By doing so, they created a legend, with the real animal itself having initiated the legend merely by being seen and without any intention on its part to cause a fuss. This hypothetical witness does not need to have had any prior experience with, or cultural knowledge of, giraffes to comprehend that they have seen something interesting and to describe it later—accurately or not—for others.

Sometimes, situations like this do happen. Many stories were once told about a mysterious creature spotted several times in the dense rainforests of Central Africa. Purportedly looking like a cross between a zebra, antelope, and giraffe, the animal sounded quite unfeasible and sparked great curiosity:

> For decades stories circulated about unusual animals in the dark jungle at the center of Africa. Such lore was probably inspired by Phillip Gosse's book, *The Romance of Natural History*, published in 1861. He speculated that those animals yet to be discovered . . . might include the unicorn because natives in the Congo had told him about a horned animal they called "abada." Imaginations were stirred. It would be two decades before this particular mystery would be solved. (Lindsey, Green, and Bennett 1999:2)

And solved it was, but not until many brief episodes and claims of encounter added to the mystery of the legend. Sometime during the 1860s, a physician named Wilhelm Junker came into possession of an unfamiliar animal hide while exploring the Congo. In 1889, the French Captain Jean-Baptiste Marchand spotted strange animals on a riverbank in Central Africa. In 1890, Sir Henry Morton Stanley—famous for his own now-legendary search for Dr. David Livingston—discussed accounts he had heard of a strange donkey-like animal from among the people he called the Wambutti. And so on. Ultimately, a real animal, the okapi, was behind all such tales. It had "showed itself" despite its best efforts to remain elusive and, consequently, became the source of its own legend. The story of this legend come to life was so inspirational that the okapi was chosen as the logo for the International Society of Cryptozoology (Coleman and Clark 1999). In doing so, they continued to "show" the legend itself wherever their logo was displayed.[9]

The typology of various forms of ostension is useful, especially for illustrating the many ways the practice can be enacted to tell a story. However, it is by no means perfect. Even with full information, it can be difficult to determine where a specific incident actually fits into the typology, possibly fitting more than one category or none at all. For any given episode of ostension, multiple forms may be present and reinforce each other (Ellis 1989). Moreover, the sort of information that would allow a confident determination of type is often lacking in real situations: what actually happened and the intentions of the people that reported it (Kinsella 2011). A case in point involves a woman from Puerto Rico, named Madelyne Tolentino, who claimed to have seen the legendary "Chupacabra": a mythical creature blamed for "mysterious" animal deaths. Having followed up on these claims, investigator Benjamin Radford (2010) was able to determine that the "witness" was actually providing an accurate description of a creature from a science fiction film she had recently seen, entitled *Species* (1995). From this, it seems evident that a sort of ostension was at play, but which type? Radford suggests that pure ostension is the least likely possibility since it would require that a real Chupacabra be hanging around to present itself to the witness for inspection *and* that it would happen to look just like the fictional movie monster. Even if this is the case, it still leaves a number of possibilities though. Did Tolentino actually see something that she mistook for a Chupacabra (quasi ostension)? Did she identify with the existing story—either from the film or from existing Chupacabra legends—so strongly that she claimed it as her own tale to tell even though she had no such experience at all (proto-ostension)? Was it simply a hoax and nothing happened in either reality or her imagination (pseudo-ostension)? Or maybe something else entirely happened that the existing typology cannot adequately encompass. Despite all these possibilities, without any hard evidence of the original event, the truth of the matter can never be known with certainty. Nonetheless, it is clearly the case that Tolentino (the witness or hoaxer?) was in some way acting out a legend. That is, she was engaged in ostension.

OSTENSION IN THE TWENTY-FIRST CENTURY

In the years since the publication of Dégh and Vázsonyi's (1983) typology, scholars have continued to explore the concept of "ostension" and to develop new ways to understand it. This is necessary because folklore is not some preserved artifact from the past, but rather an ongoing dimension of human life that persists and changes over time. As an important manifestation of folklore, ostension likewise adapts to the changing times. One such development with important implications for contemporary forms of ostension is the emergence of what Thomas (2015:passim) calls "hypermodern folklore." This refers to folklore that "emerges from, deals with, or is significantly marked by contemporary technology . . . or consumerism" (Thomas 2015:8). Hypermodern folklore spreads quickly and widely through the internet and other new technologies. It exists alongside and in interaction with more traditional methods of transmission but increasingly blends "folk, popular, consumer, and digital cultures" (Thomas 2015:7) to give rise to new forms and practices. After all, people still talk to one another. Sometimes they talk in person, sometimes online, and sometimes they talk in person about something they saw online. These varying and overlapping modes of discourse have implications for folklore.[10]

According to Tucker (2017), the characteristics of hypermodern folklore have likewise infiltrated and altered contemporary ostension. New technologies, popular media, and consumer culture have become integral parts of many ostensive adventures. Fittingly referring to this phenomenon as "hypermodern ostension" (Tucker 2017:26), she documented it in action in her account of a group of Binghamton University students turned temporary ghost hunters as they explored the haunted subbasement of a campus building. They had come prepared for their investigation by downloading a readily available app onto their cell phones specially designed for just this sort of ostension. The app purportedly reveals the presence of supernatural energy through the display of variously colored dots on the screen. It also sporadically shows words on the screen that might be coming from the spirits themselves. Meanwhile, one student recorded the whole event on another cell phone and uploaded it to YouTube soon after it was over. In some ways, this example of hypermodern ostension looks very much like a traditional ghost hunt, but in other ways, the centrality of smart phones and apps makes it very different. The group interacted just as much with software as they did with the haunted subbasement itself. More radically, given that they recorded everything with the intention of sharing it online, "they were aware of performing for an audience" the whole time (Tucker 2017:35). Legend trippers have long expected to share tales of their experiences after the fact, but hypermodern ostension blurs the boundaries between experience and storytelling.

All forms of ostension I have described so far in this chapter start with a narrative: a legend that inspires action. The action, in turn, may lead to apparent encounters with supernatural forces or other strange experiences, which in turn may form the basis for new stories. Jeffrey Tolbert (2013) identifies another contemporary form of ostension that turns this process on its head. Calling it "reverse ostension" (Tolbert 2013:passim), he demonstrates its operation through an analysis of the Slender Man legend. The earliest references to Slender Man appeared in an online forum. These were posted by a user named Victor Surge who had created them in response to a call for users to show off their photo-editing skills by modifying photographs to realistically incorporate supernatural themes and then post them. Each post featured an otherwise normal photograph of children but lurking in the background was a blurry image: a disturbing man in a suit with preternaturally elongated limbs and no face. Vague but suggestive captions implied something horrible had happened to the children shortly after each photo was taken.

Tolbert points out that this at first appears to be a standard case of ostension: the photos and captions seem to be showing a portion of a larger legend narrative. However, in this case, there actually was no legend to which they were referring. Instead, the posts self-consciously invoked established folklore styles and tropes to mislead audiences into thinking they referred to a real legend. Inspired by these posts, other people soon began creating and sharing their own references to Slender Man. Some people even began to claim having encountered Slender Man himself. Eventually, something approaching a traditional legend did emerge, but it did so *after* many of these ostensive acts had already occurred, essentially *reversing* the normal order. Thus, reverse ostension is a collaborative exercise, enabled by the internet, in which a large number of people work together to create a coherent narrative, where none originally existed, out of disparate and otherwise not directly related parts. This creative process knowingly borrows from other folklore tropes and structures in the construction of a given narrative. Moreover, once the narrative takes shape, it can inspire more traditional forms of ostension. In other words, it presents continuity with well-established folkloric processes at the same time as it makes a radical departure from them.

One last example of emerging forms of ostension is what I have called "meta-ostension" (Debies-Carl 2021:passim). Here, an ostensive act directly shows a previous ostensive act, which in turn can also show an even earlier ostensive act. Theoretically, this presentation could continue indefinitely, like staring into the infinite reflections of two or more parallel mirrors. This is enabled by the hybrid nature of the internet and related technologies, which sometimes act like oral traditions, sometimes like text, and sometimes like a confusing mix of the two. In the context of legend tripping, this can manifest in interesting ways.

For example, legend trippers frequently post recordings of their investigations onto social media platforms, like YouTube, an act which in and of itself creates a product that blurs the boundaries between legend telling and legend showing. One such video documents an investigation of an allegedly haunted historic house in Connecticut: the Daniel Benton Homestead (Pudge-Man 2019). The video begins with the narrator standing in front of the house. Facing the camera, he first tells the viewer his location and mentions that it is haunted. Then, he copies *himself*: the video switches to a recording of his previous investigation at the homestead, which provides further details of the legend. It is nighttime now, and the perspective is from the interior of a car as it slowly pulls up to the house. Although neither occupant of the car is in sight, we can hear two voices discussing the legend, one of which clearly belongs to the original narrator. The discussion briefly relates some details of the legend: how former residents of the house fell victim to smallpox and were buried on the property. This sets the scene for the legend tripping that immediately follows. The video returns to the present, and the viewer follows along as the narrator begins walking around the grounds of the homestead. He has a "ghost box" in hand—a device that rapidly scans radio frequencies, which many ghost hunters believe can pick up voices of the dead (Dickey 2016a)—and its rapid-fire static punctuates the scene. The video ends with the narrator apparently back at home. He holds an older newspaper clipping about the haunting up to the camera—literally showing a previous account of the legend to the camera with near perfect fidelity. He does not read the article but rather zooms in and slowly pans across the article's length, suggesting that viewers might want to pause the video to read it.

Taken in total, this video blurs any clear distinctions between copied and original accounts, between fabulates and memorates, and between legend telling and legend tripping. The video presents several perspectives that shift back and forth and inform one another throughout its duration. It provides a sort of meandering conversation by merging presentations of several legend trips and representations of past accounts through a combination of original video, copied video, spoken narrative, and replicated text. As an example of meta-ostension, it amplifies the traditional elements of oral accounts through the provision of new story-telling tools while at the same time enabling novel methods of narration.

While the concept of "ostension" is by no means new, as this discussion has illustrated, it continues to present new surprises. New means of creating, recording, and sharing folklore continue to shift and develop. New means of ostension will continue to develop alongside them as well. As indicators of broader changes in society and everyday life, these emerging forms of ostension need to be continuously tracked and documented and probed by researchers for their deeper significance.

HOW TO HOST A LEGEND TRIP

I began this book by introducing a personal memorate of a legend trip. Returning to it now, I will show how legend tripping can best be understood as a form of ostension. The events I related transpired one evening when I was in college.

I found myself taking part in a curious journey. I did not go very far, nor was I gone for very long, but as far as such things go, it was odd nonetheless in terms of its purpose and content. I had been working as a tutor for the university, spending several afternoons and evenings a week in the peer-tutoring center on campus with a few colleagues. Typically, this was done by appointment during the day, but we also had the occasional evening available when anyone looking for help could just walk in. It was not unusual for several of us to be working on one of these nights when no one came in at all. On these quiet evenings, we had considerable downtime to contend with, and we typically filled it with banter, gossip, and stories.

On one particular night, the conversation turned to ghosts. I don't remember how the subject came up, but, like most university campuses, ours had its share of folklore regarding haunted dorms and the like (Tucker 2007). One of these tales probably made an appearance as we sat around a table, inspired by the gloom gathering outside the windows in the chill night of early spring. Beyond the offices of the tutoring center, everyone else in the usually bustling building had long since departed for home at this late hour. In their absence, an ominous silence filled the darkened halls and corridors throughout the rest of the building. With this backdrop, we were soon swapping rumors and legends when one of our number, Seth, offered his own contribution to the happy exchange.[11]

Seth was a few years older than the rest of us and, unlike us, had grown up nearby in a fairly sparsely populated region of Ohio. He knew something of the lore popular among the local adolescents that we did not. It was a tale drawn from this body of legends that he then shared. He said that somewhere in the woods, not too far from where we were sitting, there was a graveyard. When he was a kid, he used to explore there with his friends, and, while it was fascinating, it was not a pleasant place. According to tradition, it was all that was left of a "home" of some sort for children, presumably an orphanage. When the days of this institution had passed, and the aging edifice was at last torn down, he continued, workers found human remains hidden within the walls. The orphanage, it seems, was the site of numerous abuses, and many of the children who found their way into those graves, or indeed the walls, did not do so as a result of natural causes. The building might be gone, but the gravestones, many of them unmarked, still remain to tell the silent tale. Moreover, over subsequent years, many visitors to the place had seen or heard unnatural things: restless shades of the dead who continued to haunt the site of their untimely demise.

Or so he claimed. I was certainly fascinated by the story, but it was also a bit suspicious. For one thing, although he was a decent and likeable fellow, Seth was also something of a colorful character and not exactly a reliable source of information when it came to anything outside of tutoring. For another, I was not entirely unfamiliar with the concept of urban legends. In fact, during this discussion, we were all sitting mere feet away from the tutoring center's book collection, among the shelves of which sat several copies of Jan Harold Brunvand's classic volume, *The Vanishing Hitchhiker* (1981). So, Seth's story certainly had some familiar dimensions to it despite the fact that I didn't know much about the local folklore beyond the borders of the campus. Indeed, in retrospect, the tale sounds like it might have been lifted from another, relatively famous legend hailing from Northern Ohio, that of the so-called "Gore Orphanage" where children also allegedly died as the result of abuse and a tragic fire (see Ellis 2003). Nonetheless, whether because of its terrible content or the mood of the telling, it was a riveting story, and thinking that some tangible artifact of it might remain in the area to be found made it even more so. It was at this point, as we were debating the merits of the legend, that someone suggested we go have a look for ourselves. That is, of course, exactly what we did.

A few nights later, a handful of us met up outside of the student union and set off to investigate the legend. We loaded into a car—a standard feature of this sort of adolescent behavior (Ellis 2003)—and aimlessly drove around for some time trying to find the location of the cemetery. At length, as the sun dipped below the horizon, we found a part of town that Seth claimed seemed about right. We turned off the main street and headed down a likely looking dirt utility road, parking behind a water tower we found at its end in the woods. We then spent perhaps an hour stomping through the forest in the dark trying to find some evidence of the legend. We never found a graveyard, but at one point we came upon an old, metal fence, and I literally stumbled upon some distinctly untombstone-like masonry (it being made of concrete). We supposed both the fence and the concrete *could* have been the remains of some older orphanage. We never found any ghosts either, but we did experience some odd things that *could* have had a supernatural explanation. At one point, two members of the group simultaneously experienced a strange physical sensation, although one described it as hot, the other as cold. Later, all of us heard but could not see something walking in the forest. We found this especially exciting considering several floodlights from a nearby soccer field provided some otherwise excellent illumination of that particular part of the woods. Yet, like a B-horror movie, the unseen bogie seemed to be making its way closer to us—too close for comfort. This latter development marked the finale of our adventure and prompted an abrupt and panicked flight from the scene. As I will illustrate throughout this book, every feature of this story—from the initial legend telling to the hasty retreat—are typical characteristics of a textbook legend trip. Indeed, as any adolescent legend tripper worth their salt will tell you, we were clearly lucky to have escaped with our lives!

Legends are not simply stories that someone made up or even the historical record—however much in error—of some past happenings. Rather, they serve also as "maps for action" (Ellis 2003:325). In other words, they can tell us as much about the future as (or perhaps more so than) they can tell us about the past. Sometimes that action manifests as legend tripping (Hall 1980). In this form of ostension, a legend inspires people to travel to the alleged site of its occurrence to investigate its validity for themselves. While investigating it, participants enter into the narrative of the legend itself, acting out some part of it and thereby "telling" it through their behaviors rather than through words alone. In this way "experience and performance are integrally connected" (Thigpen 1971:207) during the course of their exploration. Destinations may include "sites of past tragedies, such as murders; otherworldly events, like the appearance of strange objects in the sky; or even locations reputed to have intrinsic magical abilities, such as graveyards where gravestones are said to return if moved or stolen" (Kinsella 2011:28). Was Mercy Brown really a vampire, and can you still hear her scratching or calling from beneath the earth in the small cemetery where she was buried? Many intrepid adventurers make their way to the remote town of Exeter, Rhode Island, to determine just that (Holly and Cordy 2007). Does a mysterious primate, hitherto unknown to science, really stalk the backwoods of North America? Across the country, many dedicated explorers spend their time traipsing through alleged hotspots in the woods "single-minded, focused, and serious in their quest to bring Bigfoot into the light of day" (Bader et al. 2010:122). Is a certain site out in the Mojave Desert an epicenter of extraterrestrial visitations? You can join others in a "night-time sky watch" to find out (Reese 2007:9).

Legends like these, with their associated claims of extraordinary happenings, are not uncommon. Having heard a sufficiently engaging story, those individuals who are interested enough in its potential validity—or its outlandish improbability—may become motivated to explore it further. Not satisfied with the vicarious experience of the "told" tale itself, they visit the alleged scene of the action. Once participants reach such a destination, they literally enter the setting of the respective narrative. They enter further into the story by taking on the role of one of its characters—past victims, villains, or even just previous legend trippers—and ritually acting out the behaviors described in the legend that supposedly brought about a supernatural response in the past. In this way, they are not only testing the veracity of the legend, but they are also hoping to experience it directly for themselves. With the right state of mind and a permeating sense of expectation, against all odds, something may very well occur that seems to confirm the possibility of the extraordinary and, therefore, of the legend itself. In this regard, legend trips can be thought of as a means to achieve "deliberate escapes into altered states of being where conventional laws do not operate" (Ellis 2003:189).

Although I was unfamiliar with the concept of "legend tripping" when I embarked upon my youthful journey to the allegedly haunted "graveyard," which wasn't even there, this is certainly the type of activity I participated in. It is an activity that countless others have taken part in and will continue to engage in as long as legends are told to prompt the journey. In the following chapters, I explore this admittedly strange but equally fascinating practice: its antecedents, form, process, and outcomes. In the course of this exploration, I draw on a number of examples to illustrate the dimensions of legend tripping and show how it can be leveraged to make sense of these seemingly odd experiences. This serves as a foundation for further exploration as I try to understand not only the content of legend trips but also what motivates them and what makes them possible, even believable, to participants. In doing so, I hope to provide a greater understanding of why this behavior is an enduring component of the human experience.

To guide this exploration, a conceptual model of legend tripping will be useful. Folklorists have frequently suggested that legend trips bear a strong resemblance to the anthropological concept of the "rite of passage" (e.g., Ellis 2003; Irving 2016, Kinsella 2011; Koven 2007) in that "to be involved in the legend experience" is to also be involved in an "initiation into adulthood" (Dégh 2001:252). Similarities can be drawn between both the structure and the function of these respective concepts; that is, there are parallels between them in terms of their form and social significance. The comparison has its shortcomings, which I will consider in due course, but it nonetheless provides a useful starting point for understanding and critically interrogating the idea of the "legend trip."

The groundwork for understanding "the rites of passage" was established by the ethnographer and folklorist Arnold van Gennep ([1909] 1960) in his book of the same name. For him, these rites are used to mark and socially facilitate the passage of an individual from one social status to another: the transition from childhood to adulthood or from single to married life, for example. Through formal ceremonies and ordeals, rites of passage provide the individual with a sense that a significant change in their identity and status has occurred, along with all the concomitant privileges and responsibilities that the new status entails. Just as importantly, the rite also explains and legitimates that transition in the eyes of the community. Traditional, small-scale societies have formal, mandatory, and explicit rites of passage, but this is not generally the case for larger, more culturally diverse industrial or postindustrial societies. There is some debate regarding this issue, such as "whether the loss of formal rites of passage is a cause or a symptom of the breakdown of small traditional communities" in places like the United States (C. Bell 1997:101). Activities like legend trips, I argue, provide an experience of a sort that partly fills the space left in the absence of formal rites.

In conceptualizing the cultural logic of rites of passage, van Gennep ([1909] 1960) likens the transition from an old social status to a new one to the act of passing over a threshold—in Latin, "*limen*" (Traupman 1995)—and argues that all rites of passage have a threefold structure in this regard: the preliminal, liminal, and postliminal stages.[12] The preliminal stage involves activities that begin to separate the individual from their previous status. The liminal stage represents an ambiguous period during which one's previous status and identity have been fully stripped away but no new ones have yet replaced them (Turner 1977; Turner and Turner 1978).[13] The individual is without an identity and has no place in the community (Douglas 1966). The final stage, the postliminal, marks their reincorporation into society with their new status and identity. Borrowing, adapting, and expanding upon this basic model sheds light on the legend trip itself.

Any particular legend trip, just like each specific legend that inspires it, is unique in regard to its details, such as the location that serves as its destination and what, exactly, it is you are supposed to do once you reach that place. However, despite this variation, they all share the same basic elements and structure (Bird 1994). This makes them easily identifiable as legend trips when one encounters them, and it also makes them predictable to a certain extent. Researchers usually describe this generic model as consisting of four steps or stages that occur during the standard legend trip: (1) legends are told; (2) an "uncanny journey" is made to the site of the legend; (3) some sort of experience is had at the destination; and (4) the travelers return to safety to tell the tale of what happened (Ellis 2003:167). This series of stages is an elaboration on Kenneth Thigpen's (1971) original model that identified only three steps in the legend trip.[14] This elaboration allows for a greater degree of detail in the conceptualization and analysis of legend trips. Indeed, from the results of my research, it seems to me that even greater elaboration is warranted to allow for a more complete appreciation of the topic. Prior models conflate distinctive moments that occur during legend trips, which merit individualized analysis. I propose an elaborated model consisting of six steps organized into the three larger stages of van Gennep's ([1909] 1960) general conception of the rite of passage as follows:

PRELIMINAL STAGE
    Step 1: Legends are told
    Step 2: Preparations are made for travel and an "uncanny journey" is made

LIMINAL STAGE
    Step 3: Ritual behaviors are enacted
    Step 4: An encounter or experience occurs

POSTLIMINAL STAGE
> Step 5: The travelers flee the site of encounter and return to safety
> Step 6: The tale of all that occurred is told and debated

I examine each step of the legend trip in the following chapters, comparing similar moments from a diverse selection of legend-trip accounts, including well over a hundred I have investigated firsthand (see appendix), as well as many more drawn from online accounts and the reports of previous researchers. While there will certainly be overlap between these steps, each nonetheless represents a distinct moment in the life of a legend trip. Further research might be able to identify or differentiate further steps as well. In particular, I suspect that preparations for travel and the actual travel, itself, are distinctive phases. Currently, the sort of data available that would allow so fine a distinction is not available. After exploring each identifiable step, I conclude by considering what motivates people to participate in a legend trip and what the greater social significance of this phenomenon is.

This chapter has laid the groundwork necessary to make that exploration possible. Having presented the concept of "ostension," its significance, and some of the forms it takes, I illustrated how legend trippers are partly acting out the elements of the legends that motivate their journeys. These legends continue to guide them through the succeeding phases of that journey, influencing their actions and their interpretations of whatever they encounter along the way. Alongside ostension, I also introduced the anthropological concept of the "rite of passage." This, too, is a concept that I return to throughout the remainder of the book, illustrating both the utility and shortcomings of using it to explain legend trips. In particular, the overall structure and spirit of these rites fit legend trips closely, but their place in modern society is not so simple or clear. First, however, I will get our trip started by telling some legends.

Part II

The Preliminal Stage

Chapter 2

LEGEND TELLING

All these tales, told in that drowsy undertone with which men talk in the
dark, the countenances of the listeners only now and then receiving a
casual gleam from the glare of a pipe, sank deep in the mind of Ichabod.
—WASHINGTON IRVING ([1820] 2015:296)

Schoolmaster Ichabod Crane—in Washington Irving's famous tale "The Legend
of Sleepy Hollow"—is not your typical legend tripper. He did not set out into
the night to purposely seek out the famed headless horseman. However, he had
heard the tales about this "commander-in-chief of all powers of the air" (Irving
[1820] 2015:279) at a party just before his ill-fated encounter. These tales, more
importantly, motivated his horrified interest in the matter and made him willing to accept the possibility that such a being might really exist. Stepping out
into the night after the party had ended and making his way home through the
darkened woods, he found his troubled mind very much on this supernatural
folklore, and it shaped all his subsequent experiences. If, upon hearing the tale,
Ichabod had downed his punch and grabbed a few friends before heading out
in search of the spectral horseman, the story might have ended in about the
same way. Indeed, storytelling plays a similar role in legend trips. This process
begins before anyone involved need even step foot outside the front door. That
is, the "legend" component precedes the "trip" component.

Part of the strangeness of these journeys is due to the oddities of the legend genre itself. Folklorists used to define a legend as a narrative that people
believe to be true in contrast to "folktales" that are not believed. The latter "are
not considered as dogma or history . . . and they are not to be taken seriously"
(Bascom 1965:4). More recent consensus suggests that many narratives do not
fit so neatly into this dichotomy. Instead, they occupy the gray area in between,
a hazy demilitarized zone of sorts where belief and disbelief are not necessarily
in a protracted contest and where the concept of "legend" itself is not so clearly
defined by belief status one way or the other. Legends are alleged "accounts of

past happenings" (Ellis 2003:167). They are stories about events that *might* have happened in the past, and while they often contain bizarre and even supernatural elements, people generally consider the events so described as *possible* if not necessarily *plausible* (Brunvand 1981). In this way, they cannot simply be believed or disbelieved out of hand but require a degree of cognitive and emotional engagement from the listener. How, for example, was ice cream invented? One legend suggests that it was an accident. Martha Washington created it when she "left a bowl of cream outside one cold night for a neighborhood kitty and found it frozen solid in the morning" (Ellis 2009:59). The first First Lady proceeded adventurously to taste the frozen morsel and, discovering it was quite good, shared the newly invented treat and the method of its creation with others. Hearing a tale such as this, it is not immediately obvious whether it is true—but it seems like it *could* be true.[1] This is the nature of legends. They are uncertain but generally contain compelling details, some of which might create a sense of engagement sufficient to initiate a legend-tripping episode.

In this chapter, I examine just what it is about legends that makes them so effective at inspiring listener participation through legend tripping. Unlike many other narrative forms, legends tend to be full of characteristics that are especially well suited for capturing a listener's attention and making them feel engaged in the story and its claims. Some of these have to do with the content of the story itself, such as shocking warnings and bizarre claims. Others have to do with the structure of legends, like their ambiguous and open-ended character that require audiences to fill in the gaps on their own. Beyond the narrative itself, the locations where legends are set have an appeal all their own. This is especially true for sites that are forbidden or otherwise mysterious and tantalizing. For all these characteristics, I elaborate on what past scholarship has argued with novel findings from my own research. Next, I explore the meaning of legends. Largely informed by constructionist perspectives, past research has argued that legends are meaningful, regardless of whether they are true in a literal sense, since they reveal people's values and concerns. I build on this perspective by showing how legends change in correspondence with shifts in social concerns and illustrate how future legend cycles might be predictable because of this fact. Finally, I demonstrate that all these factors—legend content, structure, and so forth—can interact with each other to make a legend's appeal even more potent. Provided enough of these characteristics are present, a legend trip can even be conducted within one's own home.

DIRE WARNINGS

First, legends that encourage ostensive responses must contain characteristics that enable them to hold the engaged attention of the listener. Often, this is because they generate a compelling degree of fear or alarm. They provide a plausible warning of some insidious threat and offer a prescription for how to avoid or combat it. Psychological research has long found that this combination offers a potent means of influencing people (Paterson and Neufeld 1987). In this case, not only do fearful listeners enact the legend by taking the steps indicated, but they also helpfully spread the message—that is, the legend—on to friends and family in the hopes of extending the protection it seems to offer. One well-studied example of this function of fear in legends is the "lights out" panic. Warning was spread through faxes and flyers about an alleged form of a gang-initiation ritual that could be deadly to innocent people. The prospective gang members drive at night without their headlights on, and when another motorist flashes their own lights to inform them of the fact, they proceed to kill that person as part of the initiation (Fine and Turner 2001). This claim was without merit, but "the danger from the gang initiation was so dramatic and the story seemed so plausible that many people felt it was 'better to be safe than sorry'" (Fine and Turner 2001:184–85). The legend's warning resonated with concerns over drug violence and gangs and offered a simple course of action: do not flash your lights, but do warn your friends and family.

The panic peaked by 1993 in the United States, and the claim subsequently became recognized as an urban legend, but this did not stop its spread in neighboring Mexico in 2005. Here, the legend was rendered credible despite its prior debunking because it "was preceded by significant criminal activity within the country that caused many to feel unsafe in their own communities" and because it simultaneously "provided participants an illusory means of protection" (Soltero 2016:116). In both episodes, the legend took the form of a threat made potent and feasible by its resonance with existing concerns and the immediacy of the danger it promised. It also included a suggested course of action that permitted a means of defusing the supposed threat while simultaneously transmitting the legend to others. I shared similar examples of this process earlier, as word of the dangers supposedly lurking in Halloween candy or presented by satanic cults engaged audiences and spread rapidly among them.

In cases like these, frightening legends produced ostension, but with possible exceptions, little of this took the form of legend tripping. Legends that do inspire ostension through legend tripping also typically contain one or more warnings to the audience, but these operate in a somewhat different way. These warnings seemingly "appear as caveats against travelling to a site or against performing" particular behaviors once there (Kinsella 2011:30). For example, a given place might be described as cursed or home to a dangerous maniac or vengeful spirit. Simply visiting it, the legend claims, is hazardous to your health and well-being. One cemetery near Weatherly, Pennsylvania, is such a place. According to local folklore, a passersby may happen to see a woman dressed

The Hanging Hills (Meriden, CT): A mysterious black dog prowls here, a harbinger of doom for the unwary. Photo by the author.

all in black. If they are unfortunate enough to do so, woe be unto them, for it means that a friend will die on the following day (Ellis 2003). It is, perhaps, best to just avoid the place altogether. Meriden, Connecticut, has a similar tale to tell, but this time the entity to be wary of is a *dog* in black—black fur, that is (Schlosser 2004). The animal is said to be friendly but leaves no tracks and has a silent bark, belying its true, supernatural aspect. If you should go hiking in the Hanging Hills there and see the dog, be forewarned. The first sighting gives you luck, but the second sighting brings sorrow, while a third encounter brings about, of course, death (Philips 1992). In cases like these, a general atmosphere of threat can hang over places where, according to legend, merely passing through is forbidden or risky.

Beyond general cautions of this sort, legends may articulate more specific behavioral proscriptions. These warn listeners against performing particular behaviors at certain times or in certain locations within the more general setting of the legend. One legend featuring this sort of specificity is Great Hill Cemetery in Seymour, Connecticut, which is more frequently called "Hookman's Cemetery." The nickname originated with the legend that the cemetery is haunted by the ghost of a former caretaker who had a hook instead of a hand. One day, he either hanged himself from a tree here or killed and hanged a young man visiting the cemetery from it.[2] Regardless of who died, you are safe in the cemetery provided you do not park under that specific tree. Unfortunately, the legends are especially vague about which one it is. On my visit, I spent considerable time trying to determine which one was the likely tree, but to no avail. Apparently, it was not the one I parked under since I left the cemetery still very much alive. Dangerously haunted cemeteries are a dime a dozen. Visitors to the Green Mountain Cemetery in Montpelier, Vermont, for example, may come upon a large statue of a seated figure popularly called "Black Agnes" (Gray 2010). Enrobed in a shroud, head tilted back in apparent sorrow or anguish, the statue is said to be cursed, and a number of legends circle around it suggesting slightly different versions of the alleged peril. There are several variants about what exactly you are not supposed to do and what will happen if you do it anyway. None of these, of course, agree with each other except to warn that some *specific* set of behaviors is ill-advised; you are safe if you are just walking by. One version colorfully suggests that you should never sit on the statue's lap while in the light of the full moon. If you do, you will suffer seven years of bad luck or simply die or experience seven years of bad luck and *then* die. This danger is made all the more believable if visitors should happen to be aware that the statue of "Black Agnes" is actually supposed to be Thanatos, the god of death, himself (Citro 2005).[3]

These warnings are always proscriptive in character, but the method of delivery varies. In the examples given above, the warning is explicit and delivered directly to the audience: "never do *x* or else *y* will happen." Implicit forms are also common. Rather than expressly giving a warning, the narrator of the legend simply tells the tale in which the protagonist performs some behavior that results in undesirable consequences. This type of warning tends to follow a standard formula: an "interdiction/violation/death format" (Ellis 2003:124). Here, the protagonist hears a warning of some sort, ignores it and does what he or she is not supposed to, and then finally suffers the consequences for their transgression. This sort of narrative looks like a cautionary tale, fundamentally warning audiences against the same sort of actions by example.

Warnings might understandably be mistaken for what they appear to be on the surface—that is, deterrents, like those involved in the "lights out" or satanic panics. However, in the legend-tripping context, they actually operate in the opposite way: as invitations. The nature of the legendary claims is so compelling or so outrageous that some people are tempted to put it to the test (Kinsella 2011). After all, if it was conceivably possible that a ghost *could* be made to appear by following a simple set of directions, the temptation to try it out could be overwhelming. Likewise, if someone does not believe in this possibility, what better way to disprove it than through firsthand investigation? Warnings can also serve as "dares" (Ellis 2003). When a legend threatens that dangerous things will happen to listeners if they do not heed its warning, then one can prove their bravery by doing just that. Only by engaging in precisely the sort of behaviors that are expressly forbidden can you demonstrate that you are not afraid. Even if the danger turns out to be false, one's courage, one's willingness to confront risk, is still proven. This is often evident in the reports that legend trippers give of their exploits as the following excerpt, detailing a trip to an abandoned house and the dangerous state of its wooden construction, illustrates:

> *Informant*: . . . It's real mushy up there. It's way up in the top of the attic. You'd better not go up in that attic, I'll tell you that. . . .
> *Collector*: Do you ever go around there to see what happens?
> *Informant*: Sure, I go up there all the time. (Thigpen 1971:173)

This short piece of dialogue immediately presents a warning of a nonsupernatural variety: the conditions in the attic of the old house are very dangerous, and you should not risk venturing there. This is immediately contradicted following the researcher's question, when the informant indicates that they nonetheless violate their own warning "all the time." In doing so, they prove that they have the courage to risk these treacherous conditions and implicitly challenge their audience to prove their mettle by doing the same.

A sense of danger can motivate ostension in different ways. In addition to making those who transgress warnings and cautionary notes seem brave, it also gives a sense of gravitas to legend trips. It makes them seem more appealing to engage in and more important precisely because of the potential risks involved. The added value that potential danger brings is perhaps part of the reason why accounts from paranormal-investigative groups tend to emphasize the importance of being careful when looking for spirits and the possible dangers involved. In describing the various roles of the team members of one Rhode Island–based group, the author of *Ghosts of Newport* states (Brennan 2007:88–89, emphasis original), "The only person who can override the team leader is the team *safety*. This person is responsible for the *safety* of everyone involved. The *safety* can cancel an investigation or send someone home if *safety* is compromised for any reason." By way of illustration, the author relates a time when the safety's role was put to the test. One team member, quoted in the text, describes how during an "investigation at Fort Weatherill [*sic*], we had someone lurking around in the woods near the site" (Brennan 2007:89). The tale continues, indicating that the team suspected that this person was merely interested in their activities, but they canceled their hunt out of an abundance of caution just to be safe. They do not seem to have considered the possibility that the presence of another person might have been entirely coincidental, particularly given the fact that Fort Wetherill State Park is open to the public. The person quite possibly bore neither malice for, nor particular interest in, the group. All this is, of course, beside the point. The hint of possible danger involved makes a day at the park seem more significant both for this group and for any subsequent investigators who might follow their example.

A sense of risk and danger can come from a number of sources to cast a sense of importance on the legend-tripping endeavor. Ideally, that risk would be supernatural in character, but as this example of an apparently living man seeming to lurk around Fort Wetherill indicates, this does not have to be the case. Mundane dangers can serve in this capacity, even if the more supernatural ones are disappointingly absent, but the presence of both is not uncommon. Gary Hall (1980) describes how legend trippers to the "Big Tunnel" in Indiana are not just afraid of vengeful spirits said to inhabit the place but are also justifiably concerned by the very real trains that run through it as well. Dark niches in the stone wall provide safe places to take cover when trains speed through the tunnel. Yet these same niches are greatly feared when no train is present, as they are thought to harbor ghosts. Braving both sorts of dangers is an important part of the trip, and each reinforce the other.

There are often less dramatic but more common risks. Many sites that are attractive to legend trippers feature signs stating "no trespassing" or "hazard ahead." Similarly, published and online discussions of these locations typically include their own warnings against trespassing. These are partly disclaimers meant to protect the book publisher or website owner from lawsuit for encouraging illegal acts, but these warnings also serve to enhance the feeling of risk and the sense of significance or adventure involved in going to the places described. This is evident, again, in the tendency these warnings have to overstate the risk. Gunntown Cemetery—a popular legend-tripping destination—in Naugatuck, Connecticut, has an interesting absence of no-trespassing signage. Nonetheless, online discussion advises that "local police patrol the area regularly and frown upon after-dark visits—in other words, *you will be arrested for trespassing at night*" (Bendici 2009:n.p., emphasis original). What

starts out as a slim possibility becomes an inevitability of arrest before the
end of this brief sentence. In fact, this exact choice of words and emphasis
occurs so frequently that it appears to be something of a formula. Compare
this enticing but cautionary tale from another website listing haunted places
in Connecticut: "Middletown—Long Lane—across from Rushford there is a
dirt road and at the end of it there is a cement building underground if [sic
throughout] you go in and be very quiet you can hear the screams of people
being beaten it is apparently the place where the patients were brutally tortured
and murdered.—NO TRESPASSING—you will be arrested" (Shadowlands
2010:n.p., emphasis original). It is unclear whether we should be more concerned about getting arrested or about facing the disincarnate screaming of
spectral murder victims. Both sources of danger seem to contribute equally to
the allure of this legendary place.

Some sites are forbidden and sealed off to visitors. Fences, boarded-up
windows, locked doors, and the like all tend to attract the interest of legend
trippers. Dramatic or unusual barriers are especially likely to inspire speculation. For example, Tucker reports that her students became fascinated with
a forbidden area in the subbasement of a building on the campus of Binghamton University in New York. Here, a custodian "once fainted and fell off
a ladder while cleaning a light fixture [and later] claimed that the spirit of a
young man named Michael had passed through her body" (Tucker 2011:n.p.).
Notably, while students became interested enough to investigate the place
where this occurred, it was actually a nearby locked door that captured and
held their attention. A sign on the door read: "DANGER. NO ADMITTANCE.
FOLLOW CONFINED SPACE ENTRY PROCEDURE BEFORE ENTER-
ING." Of course, what followed were many attempts to gain entry to the
forbidden space despite the fact that they had no real reason to think the
door might be connected to the alleged ghost. As Tucker (2011:n.p., emphasis
original) observed, "any locked door with a 'NO ADMITTANCE' sign offers
a folkloric challenge."

These situations present an interesting problem: any measures taken to
dissuade legend trippers from visiting a site might actually have the opposite
effect and increase their desire to do so. Even very innocuous seals might
provoke supernatural suspicion and theorizing. New England-based author
and ghost hunter David J. Pitkin (2010), a collector of supernatural encounter
stories, includes a typical example in his compendium of New England ghost
tales. In this account, a group of friends was touring an apartment they were
thinking about renting when they encountered a closet with a simple hook
and eye latch on it. This unremarkable discovery inspired some remarkable
speculation. Who put the latch there, they wondered, and why? What possible
reason could a previous tenant have had to install a latch on a closet?

UNFINISHED BUT MEANINGFUL TALES

Warnings are not the only way legends entice would-be explorers into investigating their claims. The very structure of a legend serves the same end. Despite essentially being a story, legends are rarely finished tales. They have a "fragmentary, incomplete form" (Dégh 1971:62), often lacking proper beginnings, character development, motivations for behavior, and so forth. For example, ghosts of female students who commit suicide represent a common motif in college legends, but the stories rarely provide many details regarding why exactly the deed was supposedly committed. Instead, the audience must "fill in the blanks" (Tucker 2007:68). Patrick Mullen elaborates on this inherent problem of incomplete narratives within legends in regard to the perennial accounts of people allegedly finding alligators in New York City sewers. He notes that, for one hearing this legend, the claim "poses a primary question: how did they get there? One traditional variant proposes as a cause that tourists just back from Florida brought live baby alligators with them and tiring of their pets flushed them down the toilets where they proceeded to propagate" (Mullen 1972:109). Incomplete stories capture people's attention as they speculate on how those missing pieces might be filled. The legend begins to draw them in. Moreover, by trying to make reasonable guesses to fill in these blanks, they also make the narrative more believable and more detailed the next time it is told. This incomplete state is perhaps most noticeable or problematic in terms of the fact that legends generally lack a definitive or satisfactory ending. One could interpolate a fitting conclusion through conjecture as well, but when the legend's narrative is implied to continue into the present, it invites listeners to investigate it personally (Ellis 2003). Are there really still alligators in the sewer? Does the ghost still haunt the old manor house? Legend tripping can, seemingly, answer these questions.

Turning from the structure of legends to their meaning reveals a similar lack of completion. Legends are often false in the literal sense. The stories they tell frequently did not really happen in full and maybe not even in part. M. Brown was not a vampire. Washington did not invent ice cream. Simultaneously, there *is* a true dimension to legends in the sense that they resonate with the values and concerns of the people and era in which they circulate: they may "reflect many of our hopes, fears, and anxieties" (Brunvand 1981:2). In doing so, they offer a way to discuss the things that people are too "afraid to speak about in the bright light of day" (Dickey 2016b:2) or simply provide a means of expressing and interrogating these important considerations that are otherwise difficult to grapple with.

Since different social groups have different concerns, it makes sense that legend transmission is especially strong among networks of people with strong social ties (Fine 1992) and demographic similarities or "groups of people who have something in common" (Kinsella 2011:7). Legends about a consumer finding a mouse's tail in a bottle of soda may not be literally true, but they might reflect very real concerns about health, safety, and sanitation that correspond with increasing reliance on industrial production (Brunvand 1981). Tales of ghostly babies crying at night in the basement of an Indiana fraternity house in the early 1970s, likewise, seem to reflect concerns over abortion (Lecocq 1980). After all, the brothers who lived there believed that it was once the home of a doctor who performed these procedures and that he simply threw the remains in a now-bricked-over hole in the cellar wall. A wide range of legends about the restless spirits of murdered Native Americans and enslaved Africans raise obvious concerns about historical abuses and justice deferred or denied (Dickey 2016b; Tucker 2007). Meanwhile, claims about Halloween candy contaminated with razor blades or poison resonate with worries about rising crime and the danger that strangers pose to defenseless children (Best and Horiuchi 1985). Even when a legend is known to be false, the falsehood may triumph over truth in its retelling precisely because it tells the deeper "truth" of cultural expectations and values. The Winchester Mystery House—the sprawling and labyrinthine mansion in San Jose, California—was built by the allegedly crazed Sarah Winchester. Made wealthy as heiress to the Winchester firearms fortune, she supposedly designed the house to keep vengeful spirits at bay. Colin Dickey (2016b) points out that while she did construct the mansion and while it is quite strange, little else about the narrative is true. Regardless of this, the story is too good to ignore, he argues, because it speaks to popular apprehensions about women who live alone, the excesses of the wealthy, and "uneasiness about the gun that won the West and the violence white Americans carried out in the name of civilization" (Dickey 2016b:67).

The idea that legends encode subjective meanings is well established, but in attempting to tease out those meanings, we immediately run into a problem. Earlier in the history of academic folklore, scholars believed that the meaning of a given legend—the values and concerns it reflects—could be simply analyzed and understood based on the content of the tale alone, but more recent work problematizes this idea (Ellis 2003). As Dégh (2001:2) argues, any particular legend "touches on the most sensitive areas of our existence, and its manifest forms cannot be isolated as simple and coherent stories." Instead, "legends appear as products of conflicting opinions, expressed in conversation," doing so by manifesting "in discussions, contradictions, additions, implementations, corrections, approvals, and disapprovals during some or all phases of their transmission, from their inception through various courses of elaboration, variation, decline, and revitalization" (Dégh 2001:2). Whether for scholars or other people who tell and hear these tales, the meaning of a legend is neither clear nor simple. There is no single way to "read" a legend. They do not contain some unchanging and universal Jungian archetype but rather can be understood somewhat differently by different people. Incomplete and sometimes incoherent, they are "subject to varied interpretations depending on how the legend is told, who tells it, the audience, and the social and historical context of the 'telling'" (Holly and Cordy 2007:345). This is because different people bring their own experiences and concerns to bear when trying to make sense of legends, when they retell them, and when they debate them with others. During the course of a legend-telling episode, participants "are free to break into the narration *at any point* to ask questions or make comments" (Hall 1980:249, emphasis original). Legends are not structured lectures or sermons with fixed meanings or well-defined agendas, just manifestations of public discourse. As with all important issues, there is no single, stable consensus to be had so much as there is a stream of interacting arguments. Legends pull listeners in with their incomplete treatment of important values and concerns. People become embroiled in the debate inherent in a legend's form as they try to make sense of them and search for a reflection of their own opinions.

A "deep," abstract reading of a particular legend to determine its meaning is misleading and counterproductive since such an approach overlooks or simplifies the process of debate and interpretation that is necessary for the legend process to unfold. It tells us more about the one doing the interpreting than about the subject matter. However, this is not to say that the meanings of legends cannot be understood at all, merely that there are limitations and dangers in attempting to do so. Additionally, there is complexity involved, and actual interpretations vary from person to person. With this in mind, let me offer some tentative examples of how legends can express deeper concerns.

One common theme that illustrates how legends resonate with concerns or values involves tales of degenerate people living in the woods. While the general motif is common across the world, a specific version of it can be found in the various tales about "Melon Heads." This particular term most commonly appears in parts of the Midwestern United States and Connecticut (Muise 2015). It refers to a supposedly feral population that hides out in the woods, away from prying eyes, despite the fact that their vocation requires that "mostly they terrorize teenagers" (Muise 2015:n.p.). Velvet Street in southwestern Connecticut, which Melon Head aficionados dub "Dracula Drive," is a popular setting for many legend trippers to search for these creatures. It is also a typical example: a long, rural road at the fringes of more densely populated areas that winds its way deep through the forest. Details vary, but legends about these creatures are generally similar regardless of which specific region they are drawn from. Generally humanoid in appearance, Melon Heads are usually described as short of stature, vaguely goblin-like, and sporting bulging eyes as well as disproportionately large, bulbous heads, which likely explains their unlikely appellation (Lamothe 2013).

When they are not chasing teenagers around, they are busily engaged in a full range of activities, like cannibalism and inbreeding. These behaviors are standard taboos but so are some of the circumstances of their origins. These origins are, of course, something of a mystery, but they typically conform to one of several overlapping explanations.[4] The people that would come to be known as Melon Heads were originally patients, prisoners, or orphans in an old asylum, orphanage, or prison or often some mix of these elements. There, they endured abuse, torture, or medical experimentation, which either caused their deformities or were conducted because of them. One day the patients or children escape, sometimes in a fire that they may or may not have set, and many people, including their tormentors, die in the process. They flee into the wilderness where they resort to cannibalism and inbreeding to survive, although these are also sometimes credited with causing their deformities. Though now safe from harm, they have grown feral over time and have come to consider other humans to be their prey.

This legend cycle is bizarre, and, not surprisingly, there is no evidence that there is any sort of truth to it. A survey of online and printed resources indicates that it does not even have the wide range of grainy photographs or video recordings that most paranormal phenomena have to support it. It is certainly not a complete or coherent story. Nonetheless, as with all legends, the fact that it has persisted and flourished over the years suggests that it strikes a chord (Dégh 2001). It seems not only to express but to validate concerns and fears that have persisted across several generations. This is only logical because people pay more attention to and remember things that seem more relevant to them. They retell legends when they find them appealing or relevant in some way and, typically, choose to retell them to others whom they believe will also find the story appealing (Dégh 2001). Additionally, since the overall story is incomplete or does not quite make sense—a hallmark of the legend, bits of it will be modified by people to make it more comprehensible. In the process, people also update the content of the story.

The question remains as to what exactly this legend means. Unfortunately, again, a single or definitive reading misses the point, but a glimpse of its appeal is certainly possible. There are obvious themes that are common across versions of the legend that reflect social values by presenting those things that threaten society, including human cruelty, deformity, inbreeding, and cannibalism. In particular, these themes seem to explore the edges of the human experience without quite crossing into the supernatural. What happens to people cut off from civilization and cast loose in the wilderness? One website begins its introduction to the Melon Heads by comparing them to the backwoods villains in the film *Deliverance* (1972) before launching into its own legend-trip account of a Melon Head-finding expedition (Bendici 2010). What happens to people when they are forced into institutional settings that, although designed and staffed by humans, are nonetheless patently *inhumane*? The Melon Heads, like all legendary entities, provide something of a response to these serious inquiries, but they do not provide firm answers. The legends instead raise questions of their own without putting any worries to rest. They do not reassure listeners regarding their fears so much as they remind them of these. And so, the exact meaning of these legends is unclear or, rather, is up for debate. A general "flavor" is evident, but different listeners do not necessarily focus on the same parts or interpret it in quite the same way. Nonetheless, the fact that a given legend incorporates potentially compelling concerns makes it difficult to ignore entirely, even for those who are not ready to entertain the possible truth of its claims. In many of the sources for this legend I examined, the authors express doubt that these creatures really exist.[5] However, they often suggest *parts* of the legend might be true and seem to be caught up in the part of the narrative that deals with those more plausible components. After all, while the Melon Heads may not be real, human abuses certainly are, and these require discussion over morality and ethics. Debate over meaning then, not just debate over objective truth, further adds to the compelling nature of a legend as long as its contents remain culturally relevant.

Of course, a group's values and concerns can shift over time. As this occurs, sometimes the legends they tell fall by the wayside. This happens when the issues raised by the legend are no longer as immediate or compelling as they once were. Some legends that suffer this fate can fade from folk tradition. They may be told as mere stories that might garner academic interest but not as legends that entertain debate over belief. These expired legends can also be carefully cataloged and preserved in a book or archive, but they are no longer actively told or shared. Legends can also become entirely forgotten and lost forever. These are all possibilities, but legends display a remarkable ability to change with the times. As the values or concerns of the age shift, legends incorporate these changes, reflecting the new issues of the day. This helps them survive to be told again tomorrow. One of the reasons legends change so readily is, again, their incomplete and fragmentary nature (Dégh 1971). They contain gaps that need to be filled and ambiguities that require interpretation. Narrators telling stories or the audiences who hear them readily fill in the missing pieces with hunches or guesses of their own—with things that make sense to them (Mullen 1972; Tucker 2007).

For instance, the Myrtles Plantation in St. Francisville, Louisiana, is famous for supposedly being haunted by the ghost of an enslaved woman named Chloe. No real historical information exists about her, most likely because she did not really exist. This means there are few narrative constraints on her story, and legend tellers are free to interpret the story as they see fit. So depending on what version of the legend you hear, she can be portrayed according to a number of social stereotypes—"Jezebel figure," "mammy," "tragic mulatto," and so forth—as befits the agenda or expectations of the narrator (Dickey 2016b). Interpolations of this sort come from listeners' own presuppositions, which are themselves informed partly by the era and place in which they live. In effect, by engaging in this process, legend tellers update old legends much like a movie producer remakes an old classic for a modern audience.

The resulting revision may borrow heavily from the original version of the legend while simultaneously producing significant differences. A number of popular legends used to warn adolescents, especially teenaged girls, about the dangers posed by strangers. Someone you do not know might murder you if you leave your dorm room at night (Grider 1980) or might murder your boyfriend if he steps out of the car at the local lover's lane (Brunvand 1981). Tucker (2007) observes that more recent legends of this sort link the danger not to strangers, but rather to the boyfriends themselves. These legends are particularly disturbing since they more closely reflect the distressing reality that assaults are more likely to come from intimate partners than shadowy strangers. In a similar vein, these days, no one in America warns young, single, white women to steer clear of ice-cream parlors owned by Italians for fear of corruption and enslavement, but this was once a real concern (Ellis 2009). Popular fear of Italian immigrants has long since subsided, but not the fear of immigration itself. Instead, now legends circulate about different groups, like Latino or Muslim immigrants, and the imagined dangers they supposedly pose to the nation (Fine and Ellis 2010). In these examples, legends have survived over time through relatively small but significant shifts in the messages they communicate. The important element, their resonance with concerns and relevant issues, remains the same and continues to command an interested audience even as the specific nature of those concerns shift.

LEGENDARY PLACES AND MEANING

In addition to the importance of the content of the legend and its presentation, consideration of the types of locations that typically act as legend-tripping destinations is also important. The nature of these settings sheds further light on how the incomplete character of legends serves as an invitation or lure for further investigation. In theory, any place could become the setting for a legend. In actuality, however, certain types of places are more likely to have legends associated with them than others. The folklore literature is full of lists of these sorts of places. According to Dégh (1971:65), legends "cluster around particular cemeteries, as well as abandoned houses, bridges, and objects that have unusual features." Some two decades later, this list remains much the same. For example, S. Elizabeth Bird (1994:193) notes, "It is well-documented that local legends tend to develop around particular types of places—bridges, cemeteries, unusual graves, deserted houses and so on." More recently, Michael Kinsella (2011:33) offers a similar variety of places but adds, "Many European folk customs involve . . . ancient forts, henges, and stone circles" as well. These sorts of places share some similar characteristics.

First, just like legends themselves, the places where these stories are said to have occurred reflect the social values and fears of those who keep the legends in circulation. A survey of the physical environment associated with legends can thus be quite revealing. As Dickey (2016b:2) advises, "If you want to understand a place . . . go straight to the haunted houses. Look for the darkened graveyards, the derelict hotels, the emptied and decaying old hospitals." To examine places like these, where in the darkness legends gather, is to examine "a particular, and peculiar, kind of social memory, an alternative form of history-making in which things usually forgotten, discarded, or repressed become foregrounded, whether as items of fear, regret, explanation, or desire" (Richardson 2003:3). Again, places like these situate the values and concerns that the legends associated with them deal with, sometimes through direct representation and at other times by presenting listeners with things that threaten the ideals they cherish. Just as legends change to accommodate changing concerns, so too do legend *settings* vary over time along with these shifts. Some types of places are ancient and enduring settings for supernatural claims. The belief that old, abandoned, and dilapidated houses play host to ghosts has been with us since at least the time of the ancient Greeks and Romans. While the ghost stories in Pliny the Younger's letters are likely the most famous, the oldest extant story of this sort was written by the Roman playwright Titus Maccius Plautus sometime around 200 BCE (Felton 1999). It, in turn, was based on still older stories that survive in fragmentary form.

Another old and persistent motif is the haunted graveyard. In medieval times, "the cemetery was one of the places most favorable to apparitions" (Schmitt 1998:182). For instance, the Bishop Thietmar of Merseburg writes about the reputed gatherings of spirits within cemeteries in his *Chronicon* (ca. 1009–1018 CE): "According to what I have been told by reliable witnesses, the custodians in the merchants' church saw and heard [supernatural] happenings. . . . Standing some way from the cemetery one evening they saw lights placed upon the candelabra and at the same time heard two male voices singing the invitatory and morning lauds in the usual fashion" (Joynes 2001:17). The bishop notes that the witnesses went to investigate but found nothing. The association of locations like these with ghosts is so familiar that it is by now entirely cliché. That these places have maintained this status for so long highlights their continuing importance. The possibility that a house can be haunted, while familiar, is no less significant on account of mere familiarity alone. The idea that this space, which should be characterized as a home—a place of comfort, safety, and family—can become just the opposite is a particularly disturbing prospect to many people. This is precisely because of the threat it presents to these cherished values and the way that it does so by reversing the everyday, normal order of things (Dickey 2016b).

The association between the supernatural and some settings is thus quite old and resonates with persistent concerns, but other now-familiar haunted locations like mental institutions are fairly recent. In part, this is because mental institutions are themselves a relatively new human invention, but it is also because they did not always represent the concerns they do today. These asylums were intended, as the name originally meant, as a "safe haven" where "one could go to be safe from hurting others and one's self" (Osborn 2009:219). Prior to the availability of an asylum, families had to deal with their own troubled members. This often resulted in unproductive methods, such as simply locking them up in unused parts of the house, like the attic (Dickey 2016b). Consequently, to a certain extent, these professional institutions were initially viewed in a positive light as a modern and humane method of addressing a social problem (Rothman 1971). Of course, this optimism was not to last. Like many other institutional settings with well-intentioned beginnings, such as orphanages or poor farms, they soon became "dumping grounds for the living human waste of society" (Waskul 2016:143) and the breeding grounds for legends.

For example, the architectural style that comes to mind when most Americans think of these facilities is that of the nineteenth-century Kirkbride Plan. Far from a place of nightmares, these buildings were designed to facilitate progressive and humane ideas for treating people suffering from mental disorders (Peloquin 1989), not simply for imprisoning them and hiding them away. The familiar structures featured a central administrative building, flanked by two attached wings arrayed with large windows for housing patients. This allowed fresh air and sunlight to reach the residents, both of which were considered a beneficial part of treatment. The building itself was designed to be beautiful for the benefit of both patients and visitors, as were the grounds. These featured lush gardens, winding trails, and babbling fountains. Facilities to enable a range of activities, like gardening and woodwork, kept patients healthily engaged, experts believed, by occupying themselves with productive and fulfilling labor. Consistent with the principles of a moral approach, "that architecture and landscape had the ability to cure insanity," and this "plan was [intended] to make the hospital look as attractive and impressive as possible to reassure and calm the patients, while bolstering support of family members who committed their loved ones" (Osborn 2009:223). A number of factors led to the decline of the Kirkbride asylums, including the expense of maintaining the elaborate facilities and grounds, the strain of increased demand for housing patients, and a decline in the belief that insanity could be cured through moral treatment (Rothman 1971). Together, stressors like these led to deteriorating conditions, overcrowding, and stories of neglect and abuse (Dickey 2016b). These further hastened the demise of the Kirkbride asylum, and it would not be long before most of these institutions were abandoned by the living only to be occupied by legends of the dead.

Soon a new generation of mental institutions arose, which also optimistically promised reform and advances in how mental health is treated and thought about. History then simply repeated itself. It would not be long before these too took on the aspect of horror that characterized the institutions they sought to displace, and they met the same fate that befell the Kirkbride asylums. One of these was Norwich State Hospital in Connecticut. Locally infamous and legend haunted, only a few decaying buildings remain of what was once a sprawling facility. The site, which is included on the National Register of Historic Places, began to be constructed in 1905. According to the register's documentation, the former hospital straddled the divide between the earlier Kirkbride model and those of its successors both architecturally and philosophically (National Register of Historic Places 1987). In terms of architecture, for example, initially the central building remained administrative in function and was flanked by patient wards, but these were not attached. Many additional, detached buildings connected by tunnels were added over time and it would come to look more like a university campus than the now-classic but defunct asylum plan. Curing rather than simply confining patients remained a concern for the new facility. At first, this followed in the moral tradition through beautiful and tranquil surroundings and by providing patients with plenty of productive activities to keep busy with. Among other facilities, the hospital included carpentry and machine shops, spaces for dances and dramas, and open grounds and a greenhouse for gardening.

Predictably. Norwich State Hospital, like many of the new generation of mental health facilities, was destined to become the subject of horrifying legends made all the more terrifying because of a fairly solid basis in fact. As the times changed, so too did methods of "curing" the mentally ill. In 1920, the Lippitt Building was constructed for use as a psychopathic treatment facility. According to the National Register, it "provided medical and surgical treatment for physical and mental disorders [and] had facilities for x-ray diagnosis, hydrotherapy, and surgery. Frequently performed operations included sterilization and lobotomies." Developments like these loom large in the memory of legend and many modern accounts of the hospital sound much like this example:

> Overcrowded and understaffed, the institution began using extreme measures to control its population, including extended solitary confinement; additionally, reports of physical and sexual abuse abounded. A number of suicides and murders occurred on the property. . . . Norwich State was founded with what's been called a "difficult" population—those classified as "criminally insane"—[but] that still doesn't excuse its descent from care into abuse. . . . The manner in which mental illness has been studied and treated (or "treated," as the case may be) has, I believe, been one of both this country's and, indeed, humanity's greatest shame [*sic*]. . . . [T]he way most psychiatric patients were treated for so long was nothing short of abominable. All patients were treated as prisoners, regardless as to whether or not they were actually criminals, and so-called treatments such as electric shock therapy and pre-orbital lobotomies sought not to understand, but to control. (Peters 2016:n.p.)

The sentiments expressed in a narrative like this, which is itself quite typical of legends dealing with mental institutions in general, are compelling and reflect somewhat more distinctively modern issues than those represented by those more ancient legend settings I have considered. True, the old concerns—death, torture, insanity, inhumanity, and so on—are present, but to these have been added worries about the medicalization, routinization, and institutionalization of horror.

Though closed to visitors, today the crumbling ruins of the hospital remain a popular site for illicit legend tripping because of their dramatic appearance, their disturbing history, and the important issues they represent. Many of the remaining buildings can be seen clearly from along Connecticut Route 12, and there are many places where you can pull over to appreciate the view and think about what may have transpired within these walls. Kinsella (2011) suggests that a legend trip can be conducted entirely online. Since the site is off-limits, in addition to viewing the site from the street, I also attempted to do just that and did indeed experience something suggestive of disturbing activities at the hospital. This was gleaned not so much from legends or even historical accounts but from scholarly publications associated with the hospital. In one study, for instance, researchers report their attempts to better understand the transmission of infectious hepatitis (Havens et al. 1944). The sampling methodology is not entirely clear, but the project included "volunteers" who seem to have come from both Norwich State Hospital and Connecticut State Hospital, both of which are thanked in the paper's acknowledgments. Depending on which experimental group subjects were assigned to, the researchers attempted to infect some of them with hepatitis using "icterogenic materials": in this case, serum, urine, and feces contaminated with the disease. The study reports:

> They were divided into 3 subgroups of 3 men each, with 2 men kept as controls. One subgroup of 3 was *fed* (and given *intranasally*) sera suspected to contain icterogenic agent. Of these, 2 contracted infectious hepatitis with severe clinical jaundice 30 days after feeding and a third developed mild subicteric hepatitis after 84 days. . . . Another subgroup of 3 men was *fed* urine and stool extracts. . . . Of these men, 2 contracted hepatitis 20 and 22 days respectively following feeding. . . . (Havens et al. 1944:207, emphasis original)

Upon reading this, I cannot help but wonder what the circumstances of the subjects' "volunteering" really consisted of and what else went on at the hospital. I do not wonder at all over how practices like these could give rise to legends dealing with the nightmare world of the asylum. The cold, technical character of the writing reflects the portrayal of asylums in legend, as places of clinical horror made all the more terrible by the detached impersonality with which it is administered. The only information provided about the subjects is whether or not they contracted the illness. Their humanity and their suffering are felt only through the apparent neglect of the researchers to even bother taking these into account. Beyond Norwich, the concept of the asylum has become a common cultural motif, much like the stereotypical haunted house: a familiar image in literature (Bailey 1999), film (Curtis 2008), and even Halloween decorations (Grider 2007b). Like the haunted house, this image can be displayed ostensively as a sort of shorthand for equally familiar images of hauntings, which, in turn, reveal the hidden presence of past wrongs.

Extending this argument—that the settings of legends vary over time in response to changing social concerns, I propose that it is possible to predict what sort of new haunted or otherwise legendary settings the future might hold. To do so, it would only be necessary to examine emerging concerns and extrapolate from them onto likely settings. Exploring what happened after the mental hospitals fell from favor and psychiatric patients became outpatients is a useful starting point. Critics observe that the closure of the asylums and the subsequent deinstitutionalization of the mentally ill created many difficulties, including a system that was no more capable of servicing this population than the prior system had been and the subsequent problems that inevitably emerged. The research indicates that optimal outcomes for deinstitutionalized patients are contingent on their receiving suitable care in the community at large, but this was often not what they received (Braun et al. 1981). Instead, deinstitutionalization corresponded with a patient population that would soon "become 'ghettoized' in our inner cities" where the weight of their needs overtaxed an "atrophying service system" and led to "a massive surge in home-lessness among service dependent populations" (Dear and Wolch 2014:4). Consequently, "many groups are being misassigned to inappropriate social settings and reinstitutionalized (for instance, in prisons) because they lack other shelter options" (Dear and Wolch 2014:4). With these developments in mind, might there be a growing legend cycle where the ghosts of psychiatric patients, neglected and abandoned, haunt the streets and alleys of the inner cities to remind society of its unfulfilled obligations to them? Will their spirits call out from jail cells, where they were inappropriately confined, just like the mental patients of old before the asylum? Not only might this sort of analysis predict the future of legends, but it might also predict the future *from* leg-ends. Growing awareness of this problem, both informed by and indicated by such legends, could lead to a new reform movement aimed at another wave of institutionalization. This possibility may not be too far-fetched. The issue is controversial, particularly given the stigma that has long been so closely associated with the institutional environment and its legacy (Goffman 1961). However, some experts suggest that reinstitutionalization might be beneficial, assuming adequate funding and regulation could be procured (Khazan 2018). It seems to me that satisfying these criteria remains as dubious a proposition now as it ever was before.

Values and behaviors are closely associated with the landscape and the built environment (Debies-Carl 2014; Lefebvre 1991). As the former change, the environment that was constructed in response to these concerns becomes obsolete and collects legends reflecting this disjuncture. Just as the Kirkbride asylums became haunted as they became defunct, so too does this process apply to nearly every other environment. The medieval churchyard became a setting closely associated with hauntings partly for this reason. These were replaced by larger, more grandiose, and at the time more modern parklike cemeteries, full of gardens, fountains, and elegant sculptures. While these newer cemeteries reflected a more positive outlook on death and remembrance (Tarlow 2000) with an "emphasis on spiritual uplift, old churchyards, almost out of necessity, came to be seen as their opposite: gloomy, forlorn, dire and dreary" (Dickey 2016b:195). Of course, this corresponded with an increase in alleged phantoms and spirits. The garden cemetery, that grand project of the nineteenth cen-tury (Worpole 2003), has itself since become outdated and filled with ghosts. Its modern descendants too have been giving ground, so to speak, to other practices like cremation (Dickey 2016b). Younger cemeteries are not usually popular legend-tripping destinations, although they are not entirely without their legends. It is only a matter of time before they follow their predecessors.

Finally, dramatic shifts in cultural attitudes might also be linked to new associations between hauntings and particular places. As public opinion turned against slavery, for example, places like plantations that were associated with slavery became famous for being haunted and remain so today (Miles 2017). The modern era is replete with dramatic changes in attitudes across issues ranging from human rights to the environment. One of these issues is growing concern for the welfare of animals other than humans. According to one market report, concern for the treatment of animals has dramatically increased among US consumers in only the past few years (Packaged Facts 2017). The psychologist Steven Pinker notes that this attitude shift represents a significant change in public thought and behavior as evidenced not only by market research but also by dramatic declines in activities like hunting and bullfighting and an increase in practices like vegetarianism and demand for cruelty-free products. Linking this transition to other significant changes, he wonders how far this transformation will go, noting: "People often ask me whether I think the moral momentum that carried us from the abolition of slavery and torture to civil rights, women's rights, and gay rights will culminate in the abolition of meat-eating, hunting, and animal experimentation. Will our 22nd-century descendants be as horrified that we ate meat as we are that our ancestors kept slaves?" (Pinker 2011:473). I agree that the answer to this question remains "maybe, maybe not" (Pinker 2011:472), but evidence that the concern for animals has entered into society's legendry and, thus, also its collective conscience is already becoming apparent and is suggestive of the possibility.

Despite the influence of a religious tradition that teaches that animals have no souls and no true personhood, many Westerners increasingly think of their companion animals as people with personalities and intelligence. Anthropologist Sabina Magliocco (2018:40) documents how these attitudes often result in "vernacular ontologies" whereby humans come to believe that their animals' spirits can survive bodily death, just as they believe human spirits can. She credits a number of reasons for why this shift has occurred. One cause is increasing contact with other religions, such as Buddhism and Hinduism, in which the distinction between humans and other animals is not so pronounced. Another influence is popular culture. Many films and television shows portray nonhuman animals as possessing personhood of some sort. Finally, there is an experiential factor. Many pet owners experience significant social and emotional interactions with their companions. These experiences are difficult to reconcile with an ideology that teaches nonhuman animals are something other than, and less than, people.

If other animals are people too, with personalities and souls that survive death, it follows that they can likewise come back from the beyond. Magliocco's respondents report a wide range of encounters with their deceased pets, ranging from their reincarnation into a new life, communication in dreams, and, of course, ghostly manifestations.

There is certainly nothing new about ghostly animals per se, but traditional folklore generally describes such entities as lacking personality and as serving strictly human interests. For example, according to literary scholar Judith Richardson, ghostly dogs reported in the Jones Folklore Archives in New York State typically take on this sort of one-dimensional role. They "seem primarily to appear in two capacities: first to protect treasure or property; second, to indicate a place that is generally haunted by something else" (Richardson 2003:248). More recent encounters with ghostly animals increasingly portray them as more like humans. For instance, one of Magliocco's (2018:54) respondents reports a visit by the spirit of her beloved dog:

> She and I had a deep connection. . . . It took me a long time after she died to open myself up to another dog. When I finally did, I felt guilty for a while, as if I was betraying Holiday. One night, she came to me in a dream and told me it was okay to love my new dog. She and my new dog played together. The next morning, I found her hair on a blanket she had never been on before. I believe she visited me that night to assure me it was ok to move on with another dog.

Here, a visit from an old friend brings peace and reassurance: the spirit expresses personhood. Visitations from deceased animals whom we knew in life typically bring comfort and a sense of peace.

Conversely, people may also encounter the spirits of animals they do not know who bring no such comfort. Just like human ghosts, these strangers are frequently frightening and possess uncertain but threatening motives (Bennett 1999). They are much more likely to be encountered during the course of a legend trip than in the familiar surroundings of your own home. In Tucson, Arizona, a former slaughterhouse turned theatrical haunted house is believed by some to be the site of supernatural activities. Paranormal investigator and television personality Zak Bagans likens the activities that once took place there to animal sacrifice on an episode of his show, *Ghost Adventures*. He observes that this was "a place where hundreds of thousands if not millions of animals were massacred." Ruminating on this ominous possibility, he continues: "On a daily basis blood was flowing through this building like a water faucet that was never turned off and when you have blood flowing like that, continuously, you wonder—what types of spirits or non-human entities does that attract?" (Breen and Stewart 2018). While not clearly advocating an animal-rights perspective, the shock and horror expressed in this instance seems to express a sort of guilt over the exploitation of animals for food and profit. This guilt manifests in a ghostly tale of haunting, where wrongs once performed have lasting consequences.

In other animal-welfare legends, it may be the vengeful spirits of the animals themselves that are doing the haunting not just evil entities attracted by their suffering. In Stillwater, Pennsylvania, there is a store called The Candle Shoppe of the Poconos that occupies a site said to have formerly been an animal-testing facility. Witnesses claim to see objects flying off shelves and to both hear and smell the monkeys that once lived and died there (Sundra 2016). Animal experimentation also serves as the source of a frightening haunting in nearby Scott Township, Pennsylvania. In an episode of *Ghost Hunters*, the team investigated a structure housing a software company: "The building used to be a poor house for farm workers and also a laboratory for testing animals. When [the owner's] employees see apparitions, hear voices and strange noises or even get touched, they don't know if it's the ghost of humans or animals" (Piligian et al. 2013:n.p.). Again, these tales, like many traditional legends of hauntings, reflect a concern over past tragedies. The fact that those who have been wronged are not human but can come back to remind us of their suffering nonetheless "signal[s] an important shift in attitudes towards animals in Western society" (Magliocco 2018:45).

MYSTERIOUS PLACES

Some places attract legends because of their general characteristics rather than through association with particular concerns. One such characteristic is that are they are typically distinctive: they do not blend into the background like other places. When hiking through the woods, for example, all the terrain you cover may tend to blend together until you reach a peculiar location, like a cave. It will probably stand out in both your immediate awareness of your surroundings and later in your memories. Distinctive features are unusual in some way and do not fit neatly into their environment. Cemeteries are normal parts of the human landscape, but because of their association with death and the dead (Ellis 2003), they feel incongruent next to houses, shops, or other signs of life carrying on. Distinctive places raise questions that may not have immediate answers: What's in that cave? Why is this building abandoned? Why does that particular gravestone look that way? Not just any answer will prove satisfactory. Everyday explanations only explain everyday places, but the more unusual a place is, the more unusual its explanation must be. Features like these suggest that there is a story to be found at the site, but visitors will not generally know what that story is or how it ends. They may instead venture guesses to the implied question—nascent legends that they, or others, may seek to investigate further. In fact, many of these places that serve as the settings for legends are generally part of the "residual landscape" (Debies-Carl 2011). These are spaces that society has either abandoned or largely ignores, like unused buildings or neglected sewers. No strong cultural narrative explains the meaning of these places or any oddities they might contain. In its absence, legends are not only more likely to crop up but more likely to stick as a sort of folk narrative or counternarrative. From a similar perspective, Dickey (2016b:255–56) argues that ghost stories "fester in places unattended to, where the usual patterns of behavior aren't or can't be enforced . . . where it's no longer clear what a building's function was. Where the shadows multiply and nothing restricts your mind from projecting your thoughts and dreams and nightmares."

The grave of Mary Nasson is such a place.[6] It can be found in the Old Parish Cemetery in the center of the quaint town of York, Maine. Many tourists pass through this area for the local beaches and other attractions. They may stop into town for meals, accommodations, or, as I did one summer day, for a visit to the Museums of Old York: a collection of significant, venerable buildings and artifacts curated by the local historical society. I was visiting with friends just up the coast and decided to take a break from the hard work of sitting on the beach to learn about the town's history and, of course, its legends. The Old Parish Cemetery itself is not terribly expansive and largely consists of a number of upright tombstones of the sort you might expect to find in any historic New England cemetery. Nasson's stone, dated 1774, is not so typical. For one thing, it has a portrait of Mary herself on it rather than the more typical cherubs and death's heads.[7] For another, it is the only grave in the cemetery that has a large stone slab placed horizontally on the ground, directly above the deceased. Coming upon this site, some obvious inquiries might come to mind: Who was this person with the unique gravestone? Why is there only a stone slab above *her* final resting place? Local legends provide colorful if questionable answers. These report, not too surprisingly, that she was a witch, and the stone was placed to keep her from rising from the grave (Citro 2005). According to these accounts, visitors may see her ghost roaming the cemetery (I did not), witness an abnormal number of crows lurking about (there were none), and find the headstone strangely warm to the touch (it was about the same as the neighboring stones). Contrary to this explanation, the Old York Historical Society suggests that the stone was simply placed over the grave to keep wandering livestock from doing damage to it. Even this, they note, is simply a "more probable explanation."[8] Not surprisingly, there seems to be no surviving record detailing the purpose behind the stone or carving. The society argues, however, that no one in the town has ever been accused or convicted of witchcraft.

Of course, legendary places are not always so peripheral. If a location is distinctive enough and resonates with cultural expectations, it can attract legends

Belhurst Castle (Geneva, NY): This luxury hotel provides an ideal setting for its ghostly legends. Photo by the author.

of its own. Many businesses have found these tales to be quite profitable (Hanks 2015). For example, Belhurst Castle in Geneva, New York, all but begs for supernatural tales. Looking like something out of a fairy tale, the old stone structure looms high on a ledge, its many windows and towers peering down upon the waters of Geneva Lake. It is no surprise that tales circulate of a ghost or two roaming its storied corridors, chambers, and grounds (Sakmyster 2003), but it is by no means an abandoned or neglected place. In fact, it is a bustling luxury hotel and event venue, complete with two restaurants, a spa, and winery. Not-for-profit organizations can cash in on legends associated with their spooky appearance too. The Mark Twain House in Hartford, Connecticut, is similarly evocative and similarly haunted. It hosts numerous ghost tours around Halloween every year during which visitors can try to meet members of the not-quite-departed Twain family. According to a book about the house's hauntings, published by the organization that operates the establishment, the house is "a brick treasure of the High Victorian Gothic, with Elizabethan chimneys, whimsical carpentry trim, individually designed balconies, a vast porch and a porte-cochère" (Courtney 2013:10). The book also contains a refreshingly frank discussion of how the organization weighed the pros and cons of embracing its haunted reputation before making the decision to do so.

The specific narrative elements of legends are often directly linked to characteristics of their poignant settings. In the town of Trumbull, Connecticut, there is another "witch's grave" in a small cemetery called Gregory's Four Corners. The grave in question belongs to one Hannah Cranna, famed in modern lore as the "Wicked Witch of Monroe." Legend has it that she cursed those who displeased her and blessed those who revered her (Coffey 1974). In the case of the former, for example, she cursed a woman who refused to give her a freshly baked pie. Afterwards, the woman could never bake pies again. In the case of the latter, she granted rain to a farmer whose crops were dying of draught for a bargain price: his immortal soul. No "proof" of these alleged deeds is available on site to modern-day legend trippers. However, they can find odd features of the place that likely gave rise to the legend—in whole or in part—in the first place. First, a good deal of speculation centers on the unusual presence of two death dates on Cranna's gravestone, which reads "1783–1859–60."[9] This likely calls into question the finality of her first death. This interpretation arises on occasion in discussions of the grave. One internet forum poster suggests that, on the evening Cranna died:

> Someone had heard her scream during the night but just shrugged it off i [sic throughout] guess but upon investigated they learned that it must have been her and dug her up only to reveal that she had awoke and tried to claw her way out of the coffin and then they ofcourse reburied her. This is where the 2 dates actuallt come from if i can find the site where it comes from ill post it but it's a pretty know tale around Connecticut. . . .[10]

Other posts suggest that there was some uncertainty regarding the time of her death, for example, because it happened during the winter season and, thus, she was not immediately discovered or because record keeping was not reliable in those days. However, no source is ever cited to support these claims. While more feasible, this too is apparently mere conjecture and underlines an important part of the legend, much of which deals with the difficulty of transporting her body to the grave through the snow. Even if the cited reason for two death dates is true, the frequency of discussion surrounding this uncanny feature of Cranna's grave illustrates how important it is to the legend formation.

Many versions of the legend claim that her ghost haunts the road that runs just past her grave. "At least once a year" a driver swerves to avoid her apparition in the road and soon crashes into her tombstone, and so the "town of Monroe replaces the marker almost annually" (Revai 2006:28). On my visit to the cemetery, it did indeed look like the headstone could have been replaced or repositioned at some point, in part, because it sits in a bed of concrete. This could simply be to deter theft or—given that the stone is perched precariously over the edge of a steep embankment—to combat soil creep. Consistent with

The Grave of Hannah Cranna (Trumbull, CT): Said to be haunted by a witch, the headstone's unusual characteristics fuel speculation. Photo by the author.

many of the legendary accounts, her stone is in fact in much better condition than all the other stones. It is legible and not badly weathered. It is also made of a different material. Nonetheless, its erosion and style are still not consistent with a stone that has been replaced in the past year or even within recent years. In short, it is uncertain why this legend first emerged. However, consistent with folklore scholarship, in all likelihood, at some point, visitors to the cemetery noticed these distinctive features of the gravestone: redundant death dates and a general physical condition incongruent with the surrounding stones. In fact, they may have just been passing by since the stone stands out in other ways: stark white in color and standing close to a well-travelled road. As people attempt to explain these odd features and perhaps having ghosts on their minds on account of the setting, a legend is born. Rather than settling the matter, it invites further speculation and further legend tripping: mystery begets further mystery.

PUTTING THE PIECES TOGETHER

The various factors that contribute to legend formation or legend investigation are not mutually exclusive. They are compatible, interact with each other, and even enhance one another. The more of these characteristics that are present at a given location, the more compelling the legend will be and, therefore, the greater the likelihood that it will attract legend trippers.

For instance, unusual locations, which attract attention and invite specula-tion, often co-occur with and complement sealed-off or otherwise forbidden features. As I discussed earlier, the latter figure prominently in legend trip-ping. Merely boarding up an entryway, locking a door, or erecting a fence can stimulate speculation as to what is being hidden from view, even in the absence of preexisting legends. Whereas an unusual location might project mystery in and of itself, adding an "off-limits" component to it magnifies the effect of each, creating a sense of *forbidden* mystery. The need to explain why the area was sealed off and the dangers—both natural and supernatural—involved in trying to find out heighten the sense of significance in attempting to do so. The Sunken Garden in Rochester, New York's Highland Park is a case in point. It is a formal garden with several levels connected by stairways. It is a distinctive place that is popular to visit but probably wouldn't stimulate much in the way of legends were it not for some additional features. First, in its foundation are two empty rooms with locked metal gates preventing entry. Both are odd but empty. However, inside one of these, just visible if you look carefully, there is a sealed-up doorway in the stone wall that has been the subject of much speculation. Despite the absence of a proper narrative, the distinctive location combined with an apparent secret sealed beneath it conspire together to cre-ate a compelling mystery. Occasionally, it is even linked to legends of a secret Illuminati catacomb system rumored to exist under the city (RocWiki n.d.).

Unusual places that are off-limits are especially potent if they also contain explicit warnings against entry, which the Sunken Garden lacks. As I discussed earlier, these notices function as dares and provide a sense of significance by imparting risk. In Connecticut, the ruins of the former Norwich State Hospital combine all these elements and are enticingly forbidden: "The grounds are

The Sunken Garden (Rochester, NY): This peaceful location would not spark much interest among legend trippers if not for its puzzling features and presumed secrets. Photo by the author.

off-limits to everyone. It is patrolled by a security force in white pickup trucks as the buildings are left to rot and wait for the wrecking ball. . . . The lawns are not maintained, the grounds are littered with 'No Trespassing' signs, and overall, the place feels unwelcome" (Lamothe 2013:24). The hospital looms large in the minds of area ghost hunters, and despite the risks of arrest and roofs collapsing on their heads, many have ventured within the decaying halls of the hospital in search of its presumed secrets.

The combination of these factors can be so compelling that the sense of forbidden mystery they produce can linger even after renovation has removed them from a site. Interesting cases like this often appear in the ghost lore of college campuses, which is full of dorm rooms, tunnels, and other places that have been sealed off and are now forbidden to students because—it is supposed—of a tragic death and subsequent haunting (Tucker 2007). North Hall at Mansfield University in Pennsylvania provides a compelling and enduring example. Due to public interest, the school maintains a website dedicated to the building, which is said to be haunted by a spirit named Sarah (North Hall Library n.d.). Now a library, North Hall was built in 1878 and was originally a women's dormitory. Over time, various parts of the building were boarded up. For many years, the multistory atrium wherein Sarah supposedly plummeted to her death was sealed off but so were the upper floors and later, for a

Norwich State Hospital (Preston and Norwich, CT): Its remains are unusual, off limits, and presumed to have a dark history, making it a compelling destination for legend tripping. Photo by the author.

time, the entire building. While it is unclear whether the ghost lore preceded these changes, sealing off these features certainly ignited speculation and legend tripping. According to the legend, the atrium was boarded up right after Sarah's death, although the same legend claims that the administration denied this was the reason for doing so (Glimm 1983). Interest only increased further when "they closed the upper floors off." As one student notes: "That's when we [students] started 'visiting' her [the ghost]. Kyle would tell us when she wanted to see us and we would sneak into North Hall through an unlocked window" (Glimm 1983:122). Later, the entire building was declared condemned, but official explanations that this was due to its poor condition simply added fuel to the fire of supernatural suspicion. Today, reports of ghostly encounters persist among North Hall visitors. Even though the boards have long been pried up and removed, the sense that something was once hidden remains.

There is a similar case at the Turner-Ingersoll Mansion in Salem, Massachusetts. The mansion is commonly called the "House of the Seven Gables" since some believe it inspired Nathaniel Hawthorne to write his famous novel. Here, however, allure of forbidden mystery is no accident. Rather, management has consciously put this principle of the legend process to profitable use. In the depths of the sprawling house, parts of which date back to the 1600s, one can find the "secret staircase." Many people say that this popular tourist attraction is haunted by the spirit of an enslaved person who has been seen climbing the awkwardly spaced and winding steps—even though the stairway was not constructed until the twentieth century. Given this fact, the author of *Ghosts of Salem* correctly observes that "it's highly unlikely it's a residual haunting of a slave" (Baltrusis 2014:75). Others seem unaware of this problem and continue to perpetuate the belief that it is much older (e.g., Guiley 2011). The "secret" staircase is actually not at all secret and never was. To the contrary, it is part of the tour. On my visit, I did not see any ghosts, but I did see stars. The ceiling in this odd space is very erratic and low in some places, further underscoring the question, Why was it built? Fortunately, we have an answer. It was built specifically to add an odd, mysterious feature to an already odd building in order to attract tourists wondering why it was built (Dickey 2016b). Simply calling something a secret—or even a *former* secret—if it is sufficiently strange, seems to invoke the same curiosity and speculation as an actually sealed or forbidden location.

Of course, the sort of traffic that comes from this compelling combination of legend factors is not always so welcome and can be difficult to deal with. One of the most famous legend-tripping destinations in Connecticut is "a notoriously haunted abandoned village in the woods" called Dudleytown (Lamothe 2013:30). Located in the remote town of Cornwall, this once prosperous settlement is now no more than a series of ruins. Innumerable stories have gathered around it over the years claiming that the town was cursed: "Something—some malevolent spirit, some terrible ill-fortune—dogged the village's every step forward" (Philips 1992:144). Today, many claim that supernatural dangers still lurk here for the intrepid explorer to run afoul of, with some assigning it grandiose titles such as "the most haunted town in the United States" (Kuzmeskus 2006:69). The curse and haunting are regionally famous but so too is the protectiveness or, as some might interpret it, the secretiveness of area residents in their attempts to keep out trespassers. This secretiveness enhances the mystery of what is already a strange and compelling place. One would-be investigator reports that when he first tried to ask for directions to the ruins, locals presented them with nothing but unhelpful responses ranging "from a feigned clueless response of 'What are you talking about?' to a very protective 'You don't go down there!'" (Lamothe 2013:30). The land is privately owned and managed by the evocatively named Dark Entry Forest Association, which does not allow visitors and is reputed to be aggressive in its efforts to keep people out. After writing about the legend of Dudleytown at length—and concluding that, although the idea of a curse is ridiculous, the town was certainly "tainted" or "spoiled" in some mysterious way, one ghost hunter cautions: "I should warn you that trying to visit Dudleytown today can be hazardous—and not because of ghosts. It should be noted that the planners for the Dark Forest Entry Association have forbidden trespassing on their property. In 1999, they announced that they would no longer allow hikers on the land. In spite of this, many still go—now daring not only the spirits, but the authorities as well" (Taylor 2004:n.p.).

Even the Cornwall Historical Society gets in on the action. Their website attempts to dissuade trespassers by warning them that they will be arrested, giving them directions to nearby haunted sites they can go to instead (like the Yankee Peddler Inn in nearby Torrington, which, although closed at the time of writing, would have appreciated the business), and by offering historical facts that they claim debunk various aspects of the legend. The latter statements include many tantalizing arguments, such as the assertion that the Dudley family of Cornwall was not "descended from cursed English royals," that one Mary Cheney Greeley neither grew up in Dudleytown nor committed suicide on account of the curse, that Sarah Swift was not "killed by supernatural forces," and so on (Cornwall Historical Society 2014:n.p.).

Some, upon reading these disclaimers, might think the historical society protests too much. These attempts to discourage legend trippers, combined with the thrill of trespassing, increase fascination with the site and heighten the sense that something important is concealed here. Posting on an internet forum devoted to hiking, one user succinctly states, "Part of my fascination with Dudleytown is that it's 'off limits'" (Hiking New England n.d.:n.p.). Likewise, the investigator discussed above who ran afoul of unhelpful locals was not discouraged from pursuing the matter by the experience. Instead, he doubled down on his conviction that there was something mysterious going on. He reports that while he and his family were "disappointed" they also "felt [their] convictions were reaffirmed by the locals' steadfastness in not letting us know where Dudleytown was located" (Lamothe 2013:31).

I had the opportunity to observe a similar level of conviction and excitement over Dudleytown among a large gathering of people in the autumn of 2017. On the night in question, I attended a presentation at Southern Connecticut State University in New Haven by Tony Spera, a paranormal investigator primarily known for being son-in-law to local ghost hunters/demonologists Ed and Lorraine Warren. They, in turn, made their questionable reputation from the film adaptations of cases they investigated/promoted, such as *The Conjuring* (2013), *The Haunting in Connecticut* (2009), *Annabelle* (2014), and *The Amityville Horror* (1979). Spera, it seems, was attempting to inherit the lecture circuit his in-laws once ruled over and spent the evening presenting pictures and videos that he claimed were proof of the paranormal while simultaneously promoting his own ventures. During his discussion of Dudleytown, he showed the crowd a slide of a roadway in the woods at night with some mist (a ghost?), which he said was the entrance to Dudleytown. He claimed that area residents once threatened his father-in-law, Ed, with a machete and that the Dark Entry Forest Association, acting like a shadowy cabal, threatened Ed with legal action if he ever spoke about the ghost town during his lectures. He said that Ed did so anyway because he was brave. Deploying impressive apophasis, Spera (2017) then went on to declare, to growing laughter and cheers, that:

> I'm not so brave. I don't want to tell you that you can find Dudleytown on Dark Entry Road or that it is right off of State Route 45. I don't want to tell you that they changed the name to Bald Mountain Drive. I don't want to tell you that it *is* really dangerous and you shouldn't go because of the neighbors, the police, or the witch and biker cults. What are they trying to hide?![11]

The crowd burst into enthusiastic applause. It is possible that this location would prove considerably less intriguing to legend trippers if efforts to keep it off-limits did not serve the contradictory end of increasing its mystique. Another ruined and haunted ghost town lies a mere hour and a half away, straddling Hebron and Bolton, Connecticut. Located on public property, Gay City State Park is open to visitors and has all the trappings of a grand legend. It was allegedly the colony of a strange religious sect, torn apart by fighting and murder. Today, it is the site of overgrown ruins and the setting for tales of ghostly skeletons (Philips 1992). While legends circulate about it, they lack the intensity and the sense of mystery that Dudleytown provokes, and legend trippers cause fewer problems when they visit. Thus, if adding compelling legend factors together multiples the allure of a site, it is also possible to reduce the overall effect by neutralizing one or more of these same factors.

LEGEND TRIPPING AT HOME

While an expedition deep into the woods to some remote and ghost-infested ruins in the wilderness certainly sounds compelling, a destination does not have to be very far away or even particularly exotic to inspire a legend trip. Considering this fact gives a better appreciation for the factors I've discussed so far. If these factors are present, a destination can be very mundane and still produce the same fear and excitement as more dramatic ones. These locations can be very close indeed: across the street, next door, or even in your own home.

This is especially likely if the resident is already familiar with legends about the home, but even this is not necessary since most homes have features like those that I have examined that could evoke sufficient discomfort or mystery all on their own. These are typically places that are off the beaten path, so to speak, or peripheral to regular domestic activities. When people come to believe their homes might be haunted and tell others about it, "the action of the ghost story usually takes place in the attic or the basement or on the connecting staircase, locations rich with psychological symbolism of isolation and evil" (Grider 2007b:152). This pattern seems to hold true regardless of the type of home. College dormitories, for example, also have basements and attics that become legend-tripping destinations for similar reasons (Tucker 2007). Strange noises or feelings that seem connected to these places are particularly likely to be attributed to an unnatural source and could provoke an investigation that can be surprisingly similar in mood, tone, and drama to an epic legend trip with its destination in some far-off place.

Pitkin (2010) describes a typical example of this sort of domestic legend trip that took place in Windsor, Connecticut. For years, a family living there in an appropriately spooky Victorian-style home—complete with tower—experienced classic spectral phenomena. These included ghostly footsteps, lights turning themselves on, objects disappearing and reappearing in odd places, and even the manifestation of apparitions. One night, the family "heard a horrific scream" (Pitkin 2010:20), which left an indelible memory. One woman who had lived there as a child returned many years later to visit her mother who had remained in residence over the years. The two decided to go on a legend trip in the house. Pitkin (2010:21) recounts the story she told him:

> She recalled the phantom scream and wondered if something in the dark cellar had prompted the phenomenon. Escorted by her mother, the women went down to "that dark front cellar room, where we were always afraid to go as kids," as Sue Ann called it. The cellar wall clearly showed a different construction pattern at the front corner beyond which lay the base of the house's tower. "I found a loose stone in that wall," Sue Ann told me, "and I pried and pried at it until it came out. Then I moved another and another. Pretty soon, we had a big enough opening to peer into, and I could see the dirt floor inside. I was all for taking down that entire wall, but suddenly, there came more of a feeling than anything we could see from that opening. I suddenly became very afraid and told Mom I was done exploring and hurried upstairs. We'll never know if something or someone's remains were hidden in that room. Dirt floors always make me suspect that someone might be buried there," she grinned.

Here, the destination is not very far away at all given that one of the participants still lives in the house, but the events fit the legend-trip model. Of particular note, nothing in the rest of the story that Pitkin recounts explains why exactly the cellar provoked especial interest. None of the phenomena reported seem to have occurred there, but it is appropriately "dark" and spooky enough to incite interest and to have sustained it for years. The fact that the portion of the basement is apparently below the house's tower seems to lend additional meaning to the setting. It is marked by a "different construction pattern" that further distinguishes the space, making it seem strange and in need of explanation. These features imply that there is a story to tell here and while that story will never be known, some familiar-sounding details are interpolated from the annals of other supernatural legends. This strange place in the basement was sealed off for some reason and is now, presumably, the epicenter of the phenomena. Another "strange" feature, at least to those more familiar with modern basements, is the dirt floor, which evokes thoughts of buried bodies and buried secrets—the expected correlates of hauntings. Standard elements of legend trips I will examine later are also present: (1) a journey to a liminal region where (2) an apparently supernatural experience occurs, which (3) precipitates flight away from the scene. All this, again, is made possible by a simple legend trip down to the basement.

As this chapter has illustrated, many things can interest an audience listening to a legend. Whether it's their content, structure, meaning, location, or some combination thereof, when people encounter these fragmentary accounts called legends, they try to interpret them. The very incompleteness of legendary narratives seems to demand it. They contain suggestions, built-in openings, in which someone could participate further in the story. Warnings, dares, unfinished narratives, unclear meanings, strange settings, and unanswered questions draw the listener in and inspire them to do more than simply hear the story. Listeners may want to test the legend's claims, prove that they do not believe its ridiculous warnings, or at least prove that they are not afraid of it. Then again, perhaps they simply want to find out how the story ends. For this sort of person, legend serves as inspiration for the subsequent behaviors that I turn to next.

Chapter 3

PREPARATIONS AND
AN UNCANNY JOURNEY

All the stories of ghosts and goblins that he had heard in the afternoon,
now came crowding upon his recollection. The night grew darker and
darker; the stars seemed to sink deeper in the sky. . . . He had never
felt so lonely and dismal. He was, moreover, approaching the very
place where many of the scenes of the ghost stories had been laid.

—WASHINGTON IRVING ([1820] 2015:297)

The Finger Lakes region of western New York State is known for many things: its rolling fields of farmland and woods, its remarkable wines, and, of course, the lakes that give the area its name. One cold and gray November morning, my wife and I were driving through this scenic region, but we were not looking for any of these attractions—at least not yet. There was time enough for sightseeing later. The first thing on my agenda that day was to meet the "Lady in Granite." This is a monument for the Bishop and Gillette families, marking their place of everlasting repose within Lakeview Cemetery in the village of Penn Yan, which rests at the northern extreme of Keuka Lake. The monument features a vaguely anthropomorphic discoloration on its side said to be the image of the woman whose spirit haunts it (Wemett 2001). It is surprisingly difficult for an out-of-towner to find. There is no clear guidance and only vague directions available to help locate it, even when using modern technology.

First, there was the matter of locating the cemetery itself. One source—Dwayne Claud's *Haunted Finger Lakes: A Ghost Hunter's Guide* (2009)—gave the wrong town entirely. According to this source, we should go to Interlaken, New York—some sixty miles away by car—where there is indeed another Lakeview Cemetery. Had we done so, we could have visited *Twilight Zone* creator Rod Serling's grave but not the Lady in Granite. In fact, a web search helpfully indicates that there are no fewer than *six* cemeteries with the name

"Lakeview" or "Lake View" around the Finger Lakes region! Fortunately, most sources agreed on the location of Penn Yan, so I checked the route on Google Maps with my laptop and, finding it satisfactory, entered the destination into my wife's smart phone so she could direct us while I drove. Both devices happily and confidently plotted a route that turned out to be very incorrect. We found ourselves in the middle of a typical suburban neighborhood. We could see a cemetery behind the houses, but we had no way to know whether this was the right one or even a way to get to it since we did not want to make a nuisance of ourselves by cutting through people's yards and hopping over their fences. Comparing the map on the phone and the printout from my laptop, there was supposed to be a road directly in front of us leading into the cemetery that would do the trick, except it definitely was not there: just more houses and yards.[1] We eventually circled about and found what looked to be a main entrance.

Once inside, there remained the matter of locating the gravestone itself to contend with. Most of the accounts I had read did not indicate *where* in the cemetery one could find the monument. I was able to find pictures of it online to make identification easier, but given that our visit was scheduled for a cold and windy day, I did not relish the thought of traipsing around longer than necessary. At last, I found a specific set of directions in a back issue of a local publication called *Crooked Lake Review*, which I then reread after pulling the car over: "The monument is not hard to locate. As one enters the cemetery by the Lake Street entrance, the monument is located a short distance up the hill on the left side of the second road to the right" (Wisbey 1994:n.p.). The first problem with these directions is that there *was* no Lake Street entrance. Our point of entry, which it later turned out was indeed the main entrance, was on Elm Street. Further down, this changed names to West Lake Road but certainly not Lake Street. There was, in fact, a Lake Street on my map, but it was in a different part of town and nowhere near the cemetery. We decided to assume this was the correct entrance for lack of a better option. Making our way up the bumpy drive, we soon found a kiosk that contained courtesy maps of the cemetery, but these did not list the Bishop-Gillette marker nor, of course, the Lady in Granite. With no other recourse, I resorted to the directions from the *Crooked Lake Review* article, which, while slightly convoluted, ultimately did the trick. I was soon able to make out the monument on a rise to our right. The distinctive appearance of the monument, which likely gave rise to the legend, made it fairly easy to spot once we managed to get close enough to see it. Pulling the car over, we stepped out from its warm interior and into the chilly air outside where a stiff breeze was blowing. We only had a few more steps to go before the journey was finally over. Soon we would test the legend's claims ourselves.

In this chapter, I will illustrate the importance of the preparatory stage of legend trips, arguably their least-studied and least-understood component. Narratives like the preceding one illustrate some of the unexpected obstacles and challenges that making a legend trip to some mysterious place can entail. Not the least of these are the absence of trustworthy guidance on how to reach the site or, perhaps worse, an abundance of conflicting advice for getting there. So, successfully making the journey, as I will demonstrate, often involves some degree of preparation. This includes carefully reviewing the legend, piecing together its hints, and gathering whatever else you might need along the way or at your destination. The journey itself, as you will see, is also fraught with challenges even for the well prepared. Of course, this cemetery escapade only takes into account some of the potential concerns involved. What if we had been travelling at night, fearfully entertaining the possibility of not only natural but also supernatural obstacles on our journey? All these issues are not *just* circumstantial aspects of a legend trip. I contend that planning ahead, coping with the absence of clear guidance, travelling through physical space, experiencing fear and anticipating the encounter ahead are actually *essential* and interrelated characteristics of the legend trip process. Without them, later stages of the legend trip will not be successful. Many of these characteristics will appear again during the later stages of the trip, but in this chapter, I will explore some of the ways that these factors contribute to the preparatory step of legend tripping and how they set the stage for things to come. While the specific ways in which they operate during this stage vary somewhat, overall, they share a common outcome: they serve as "preliminal rites," which begin to separate legend trippers—initiates—from the everyday world of the mundane so that they will be prepared for the crossing over into a new world or state of being (van Gennep [1909] 1960:21).

DEGREES OF PREPAREDNESS

Legend telling is a necessary but not sufficient precondition for legend tripping proper to occur. Arguably, most legend-telling sessions conclude without participants deciding they need to embark on a journey to test the truth of a legend or otherwise investigate it further. For most, hearing the tale is enough on its own. However, because of the curious characteristics of legends that I examined in the last chapter, some people do become motivated to take up such a journey. For these intrepid souls, the adventure will have only just begun when the legend telling ends. Returning to the *Ghost Hunter's Guide* to the Finger Lakes region of New York State, the author includes a section early on entitled "Preparing for the Journey." This sets the stage for the presumed adventure that is to follow by establishing some preliminaries. It begins by stating: "You're getting ready to embark on your first paranormal investigation. You've seen the television shows. You've heard all the stories growing up. Are you certain that you're ready [to] step over the threshold into another realm? Before you do, there are some important aspects of ghost hunting that you really need to be aware of" (Claud 2009:18). It is true that for those seeking to do more than simply hear the legend, there remains much to do. For them, as they continue on this course, the next step is to "prepare for the anticipated legend in action" (Dégh 2001:253). These preparations include a number of related activities that must be carefully completed if the trip is to unfold properly, illustrating that the "main work of haunting is done by the living" (Richardson 2003:122). The preparations are, themselves, in large part specified or vaguely alluded to by the legend that the participants hope to investigate. In other words, legends serve as both the inspiration for the journey as well as the blueprint upon which to base subsequent behaviors. This is evident not only in this preparatory stage but in most of the subsequent stages as well.

Legend trips vary in terms of how spontaneous or planned they are (Meley 1991). Sometimes, only modest preparation is involved. This is particularly the case for casual or spur-of-the-moment adventures. Ghost walks are typically like this. In these activities, tourist groups follow a guide around some city's streets, stopping outside various locations to hear tales of alleged hauntings and horrific crimes. Generally, the necessary preparation before embarking upon one of these tours consists of little more than buying a ticket earlier in the day (Hanks 2015). Similarly, in many classic studies on adolescent legend tripping, informants indicate that these trips are often fairly spontaneous and involve few preparatory activities. In one such study, an interviewee describes how legend tripping "oftentimes would just be a casual thing. It seemed like you were just plain bored." In this context, a group of friends would typically be "out driving around—been around the square forty times and you had two hamburgers and five cokes—so what else was there to do? And so somebody would say, let's go to Devil's Hollow" (Gutowski 1980:77). Again, in both these examples, formal preparations are relatively lacking, but they do include pre-paratory elements—particularly travel and retelling legends during the course of that travel—that I will consider later.

First, though, to get a better sense of why these sorts of preliminary activi-ties matter at all, let's consider some more explicit and involved examples. For some legend trippers, preparations can be truly extensive. This is generally the case for participants who take the activity more seriously from its very begin-ning. Bigfoot hunters are generally well prepared in this way. The author of an instructional manual for these hunts advises that "a legend trip should never be a spur of the moment thing" (Robinson 2016:242) and offers long lists of equipment that every would-be adventurer should prepare before embarking on an expedition. People who pay money to go on commercial ghost hunts are also often well prepared. Compared to ghost-walk attendees, they might plan for weeks beforehand (Hanks 2015). Paranormal investigators—those who organize their own investigations rather than simply pay admission for one— have a long tradition of perhaps excessive preparedness. Peter Underwood, a famous and controversial figure—well known for his investigations in places like the UK's Borley Rectory—offers an illustrative example of this sort of excess in *The Ghost Hunter's Guide* (1986). He argues that "there is a great deal that prospective ghost hunters should do before they even put a foot inside a haunted house" (Underwood 1986:16). Proving his point, he describes some of his preparations as he got ready to investigate a haunted manor house:

> Three weeks was spent researching the house, the area, the family and everything I could think of that might have some bearing on the case. My first reference, as always, was to my Confidential Files on haunted properties.... I discovered an entry for the house, under Somerset... from a named correspondent ten years earlier and also an intriguing reference to an article in a local Historical Society publication.... I lost no time in writing to request a copy of the relevant issue.... I also dug out the letter referred to from my correspondence files and I contacted my nearest Ordnance Survey Agent ... and ordered a 1:2500 scale (25 inches to 1 mile) large-scale map ... that covered the area of the haunted Somerset mansion.... I was thus able to establish the shape and position of the property in respect of other properties, prevailing winds, the sun, moonlight, proximity of trees, water and so on. I also contacted the Reference Librarian at the Public Library in the nearest large town who put me in touch with a local Historical Society official, who supplied me with a wealth of historical material on the area in general and the manor house in particular, and also pointed out further areas for research. Meanwhile I had been in touch with a Ghost Club member who lived in the vicinity, and he had made extensive enquires in all sorts of places, discreetly and quietly, providing a lot more material for the already growing notebook and file that I had opened on the case. (Underwood 1986:122–23)

These preparations are quite elaborate but not at all out of character for serious legend trippers. Nearly any current television show featuring ghost hunting or similar activities portrays a similar excess of preliminary work, even if the specific techniques and technologies involved have changed since Underwood's time.

So, what is the point of all this work? Briefly put, as preliminal rites, they symbolically and psychologically prepare the legend trippers for the events to come. These activities fill them with a sense of expectancy and a willingness to accept wondrous, otherworldly possibilities that they might not otherwise find easy to entertain. The specific degree of preparation involved varies from person to person and group to group. There is no specific amount that is universally sufficient. Rather, the right amount of preparation is the amount that sufficiently establishes this mindset. To that end, different types of preparatory work contribute to this outcome in different ways and reveal just how this process works.

GETTING PACKED

First, the deeper significance of preparatory activities is evident in the fact that even the most obviously *mundane* tasks that must be completed to prepare for a legend trip matter in meaningful ways. As with any travel, one common preparatory activity is packing—simply gathering together the things you might need during your trip and upon arrival at your destination. For legend trippers, this can include ordinary items, like a lunch, a jacket, or a good pair of walking shoes. These preparations are strictly prosaic or, perhaps, profane (Eliade 1959). That is, they deal with practical concerns, such as travel conditions, length of stay, and so on. They are not directly related to the rituals intended to provoke a supernatural encounter that will occur at the destination. Instead, they help to create a psychological bridge between the participant's current world and their soon-to-be-embarked-on supernatural future. To that end, even these simple acts can help to build a sense of anticipation as participants imagine what the journey and the destination will be like and what they will need in order to be prepared to face it. After all, "packing" implies travel beyond the usual daily round, and doing it properly requires projecting oneself mentally into another place at a future time. Compare this to packing for a day at the beach. By choosing which swimsuit or towel to bring and hunting around for your sunglasses or suntan lotion, part of you is already feeling the surf and the sand. The work you still have to do down at the office and the dirty dishes waiting to be washed in the sink, by contrast, are passing away from awareness for a time. By adopting this sort of mindset, the legend trippers are already taking the first mental step of separation from where they are now. They begin to inch open the door to future possibilities. Like pilgrims preparing for their long trip, they are readying themselves for entrance into "a realm of pure possibility whence novel configurations of ideas and relations may arise" (Turner 1967:97).

If completing these prosaic preparatory activities is an important prerequisite to a successful legend trip, failing to complete them will likely lead to an unsuccessful one. Bigfoot hunter Robert Robinson (2016:56) advises readers: "Monster hunting is not something you should do on a whim. You have to do some research and preparation as there is nothing worse than going on a trip without proper planning." He warns, without proper preparation, "you get there in the woods and end up forgetting something, like a camera. You'll find [that] when you forget something, your adventure comes to an abrupt halt" (Robinson 2016:56). He learned this lesson the hard way during the course of his first expedition in search of cryptozoological curiosities, and his experiences illustrate the problems that plague an improperly prepared legend trip. He had read legendary accounts of Bigfoot, and growing fascinated with the possibilities, he was inspired by these tales to set out in search of the creatures on his own. When he was a senior in high school, he convinced some of his friends to go on a road trip with him to Missouri to conduct a search. However, as he recalls, "we didn't properly prepare ourselves for our excursion" (Robinson 2016:55). They did not know exactly where to go and found that most of the locals were not interested in helping them. They eventually met some teenagers who pointed out where a sighting supposedly occurred but traipsing around the woods with no particular plan and no real idea of what to look for failed to produce an uncanny experience. The young men did not find "anything weird or strange" (Robinson 2016:55). They also spent more time and money than they expected to and had to endure an uncomfortable night in their car. Ordeals like these are not problems in and of themselves. In fact, they are usually necessary for a rite of passage (van Gennep [1909] 1960). In this case, however, they were the consequence of inadequate ritual process rather than part and parcel of it. Therefore, these problems, which were not overcome, detracted from the trip rather than making it feel more like a significant accomplishment. The experience did, however, teach him valuable lessons about the importance of effective preparation for his future, more successful legend trips.

Mundane preparations are clearly important for any sort of travel and have a particular significance for legend trips. They are not the only necessary type of preparation though. *Ritual* preparations are needed too. By this I mean items or activities that are required to complete specific rites at the site of the legend to call forth the supernatural. This includes items that will likely be specified or at least suggested by the legend itself. If the legend requires that visitors leave tribute of some sort, for instance, it is best if the travelers bring the proper sort of offerings with them. Holly and Cordy (2007) list numerous examples of this sort of offering that they found on gravestones serving as legend trip destinations. Some of these may have been improvised on the spot (e.g., pennies, rocks, hairpins, etc.) while others seem to indicate a greater degree of planning beforehand (e.g., pumpkins, bundles of herbs, a paper cutout of an angel, etc.). On a visit to a "witch's grave"—that of the aforementioned Cranna in Trumbull, Connecticut, I observed the usual offerings of coins and stones placed around her headstone. There were also some less typical items, including a key, a candleholder, a pair of plastic sunglasses, and two pairs of women's underwear. Ghost hunters bring a wide range of items to haunted locations in hopes of invoking the spirits there. These might include "trigger objects" that are believed to invoke an interested response from them (Complete Paranormal Services n.d.:n.p.). For example, if a house is haunted by the ghost of a little boy, you might want to pack a toy car for him to play with. If it moves during the investigation, then the object is believed to have provided an experience with the supernatural. Ghost hunters often pack a range of devices—from cameras to electromagnetic field (EMF) meters and more—that they also believe will provide "a certain degree of tangible evidence" of contact with the dead (Sylvia and Boyd 2012:55). The objects selected must fit the legend, so, for instance, Bigfoot hunters might bring plaster mold kits instead of EMF meters or toy cars (Belanger 2011; Robinson 2016). Like these other ritual objects, this equipment will allow them to "detect" the presence of the hairy cryptid by making casts of what might be its footprints. Whatever items they choose to bring will both reflect and reinforce their expectations of the nature of the entity they hope to encounter. You wouldn't bring a toy car to lure Bigfoot any more than you would bring plaster to make castings of ghost tracks.

Other ritual objects might not be used to directly produce or document contact with the supernatural but instead to make them more amenable to showing up in the first place. I found some interesting examples of items like this in Salem, Massachusetts, in a store on Essex Street called Hex: Old World Witchery. One is a small purple candle bearing a label that reads "Ghost Hunt: Salem Spell Candle," and the other is a pack of incense similarly called "Ghost Hunter: Salem Witches' Incense." The latter includes directions on its label advising the user to burn it, either before or while conducting a paranormal investigation, to make the spirits more amenable to a quick chat. It even includes an incantation for the user to recite. Regardless of whether the spirits actually enjoy the aroma, these objects certainly help to establish the mood of expectancy for legend trippers, as they burn quietly and picturesquely in the darkness while filling the air with their exotic perfumes. Stores in the area provide a range of other manifestly ritualistic items for the well-prepared ghost hunter to stock up on before a legend trip as well. These include items ranging from dowsing rods to detect the spirits, should they make an appearance, to "Tituba's Sage Smudge Stick" to make them go away if they overstay their welcome.

I hesitate to describe items like this as "sacred" in comparison to the more prosaic items in the preceding profane category on account of the fact that these lack a clear connection to some divine or holy dimension of belief (Eliade 1965). Nonetheless, some believe, however tentatively, that these have the potential power to invoke the supernatural, so the term would not be inappropriate. I will consider these matters in more depth later. For now, regardless of terminology, much like "mundane" items, objects in this category also tend to require some forethought during preparation for the journey and likewise help build a sense of anticipation. However, since they are not simply prosaic, they have an additional dimension to them. They are symbolic objects with their own meanings that are attached in some significant way to the legend. They matter in and of themselves—not because of their practical utility, but because of their potential power over the supernatural. Thus, they also put legend trippers in the right state of mind to entertain the possibility of the supernatural and the logic through which it might be encountered via ritualistic means.

Many items do not fit so neatly into these categories as either entirely mundane or entirely ritualistic. The type of preparation they provide is *ambiguous*. Many ghost hunters pack protective talismans to bring along on investigations to fend off hostile spirits (Eaton 2015). These could include crosses, Saint Michael medallions, agate stones, and so on, depending on the belief system of each investigator. These are not strictly required for the completion of the forthcoming ritual, but they cannot really be considered mundane objects either. Rather, their usefulness to the legend-tripping endeavor seems to be somewhere in between. Some are considered practical because of the protection they might afford, much like an umbrella might offer protection from the rain, but the mechanism through which they operate is actually more ritualistic—more in line with the magical-psychological process of legend tripping.

Similarly, but less tangibly, legend trippers might engage in various rituals before setting out on their quests. Like these talismans, rituals are believed to offer a degree of protection against the darker facets of the supernatural. Some might say a protective prayer—to God, Saint Michael, the Goddess, a spirit guide, or what have you. Others might engage in positive "visualization." One research participant describes this as trying "to imagine being surrounded by a sphere of protection, and try[ing] to make sure I'm as centered and balanced as I can be" (Eaton 2015:400). At the aforementioned lecture and presentation that I attended by ghost hunter and demonologist Spera (2017), a similar protective ritual was discussed, which blurred Christian and New Age thinking. He spent a considerable portion of his talk outlining the alleged dangers involved in his occupation, especially if you do not know what you are doing. He prescribed a ritual to protect yourself in haunted places so that the dark forces lurking there will not be able to harm you. This requires, he said, that you picture a bright, white light and ask for God's protection. Moreover, you could do this for others too. In fact, he said that, at the beginning of the event, he had scanned the crowd and conferred this protection on all of us so that nothing would follow us home that night.

At first, this seemed somewhat humorous to me since the modern audi-
torium was devoid of any signs or legends of haunting, but it was evident
from the muffled conversations in the audience around me throughout the
evening that this was a real concern for some of those in attendance. A small
group behind me, for example, had been debating who would have to sit on
the ends of their short row of seats when they first entered, semijoking that
the "demons" would get whomever it was since they were more exposed. The
ritual might have afforded them some reassurance, but it is also possible that
preliminary rituals like these could make legend trippers feel *less* safe. The
invocation of protective charms or rituals suggests that there is something
present that you might need protection *against*. This is a bit like having a
friend offer to say a prayer of protection against alligators before you jump
into a swimming hole in their backyard. Maybe you hadn't even thought
about that possibility a moment ago, but it will be weighing very much on
your mind now. Likewise, bearing a Saint Michael medallion or performing
a light visualization might have the contradictory effect of bringing to mind
all the potential dark forces that want to do you harm and further produce
a state of worried expectancy.

In part, then, activities like these, which blur the mundane and the ritualistic,
reemphasize the legend trip's sense of danger and make it seem more compelling and more significant. They can also help provide the confidence to face
the perceived danger, to prove one's bravery, or at least build more confidence
that an encounter with the supernatural will actually happen. Paradoxically,
like all preparations, they also serve to build a sense of fearful expectation for
what is to come and set a tone of both excitement and trepidation. Of especial
note are items legend trippers pack for their expeditions that are simultaneously
prosaic *and* ritually potent. These do not blur the distinction so much as they
combine their dimensions into a single object or action.

One item like this, that you may want to bring with you to a haunted cemetery at night, is a simple flashlight. Ghost-hunting instructional manuals, of
which there are scores available for purchase, frequently include lists of things
to bring along on investigations. They almost always suggest that you pack a
flashlight. Certainly, it's a good idea to have one for the practical or mundane
purpose of seeing where you are going, but flashlights can also serve as a
medium through which to communicate with the supernatural. One way they
can do so is simply by malfunctioning, which could be interpreted as ghostly
interference. A more complicated method is through something variously
called the "flashlight experiment," "flashlight session," or something similar
(e.g., Paranormal School n.d.:n.p.). Popularized by television shows like *Ghost
Hunters* and *Kindred Spirits*, this involves leaving one or more flashlights on
a flat service, asking any nearby ghosts questions, and suggesting they turn

the lights on or off to give responses. Here, the flashlight doubles as both a mundane *and* ritual object.

In addition to recommending that you bring a flashlight, guidebooks rarely fail to spend considerable space encouraging you to think about the batteries you will need for it and for any other electrical devices you might have with you, like the aforementioned EMF meters. The example below, which preserves the capitalization in the original text, is drawn from a standard list of suggested ghost-hunting gear. The entry "batteries" appears in the list between "tape-recorder" and "video camera": "Batteries. ENSURE THAT YOU HAVE ADEQUATE SUPPLIES OF BATTERIES FOR ALL ELECTRICAL EQUIPMENT, EVEN WHERE YOU ARE PROPOSING TO USE A MAINS SUPPLY. IN THE EVENT OF A SUPPLY FAILURE YOU WILL THEN HAVE BACK-UP. YOU WILL ALSO NEED REPLACEMENT BATTERIES. This applies not only to tape-recorders, but also to video cameras, torches [i.e., flashlights] and any other electrical instrumentation" (Spencer and Spencer 1992:370, emphasis original).

It is interesting that batteries appear so near to the top of the list of items to pack and that the authors consider them to be so important to the success of the endeavor that gratuitous capitalization is used to draw the reader's attention to the fact. This is the only place in the entire book, which runs in excess of four hundred pages, where this sort of emphasis occurs. Understanding why this is the case is important for understanding the role of preparation to legend tripping in general.

As mentioned, having a light in the dark is simply a good idea in a practical sense since it allows you to find your way about without tripping over headstones and whatnot. Having extra batteries at first blush is simply more of the same good sense. However, batteries are of particular symbolic importance in legend trips centered on ghost hunting because of the alleged tendency of spirits to draw power from them and, in the process, deplete them. One tour guide notes, for example, that, while leading ghost walks, he and his group typically "lose power in all of our flashlights, despite the fact that we thoroughly check them before each tour, and have new batteries as backup" (Southall 2003:xiii). A flashlight and batteries are not *only* practical tools but ritual tools as well in that they may also allow individuals to determine when they have encountered the supernatural, at least according to these guidelines. By preparing for that encounter—by packing batteries with the knowledge that they might be inexplicably drained by some unseen force, they simultaneously prepare their minds. That is, they begin to expect such an encounter and to think of ways that it might manifest itself. The resulting mindset enables them to interpret a wide range of experiences as indicative of a supernatural presence, including those which they might normally discount as natural in origin or perhaps fail to notice at all.

STOPPING TO ASK FOR DIRECTIONS

As I indicated in the opening vignette to this chapter, legend-tripping destinations can be difficult to find in person. But the journey to a legend's setting is part of the ostensive reenactment of that legend. Therefore, the journey is linked to the narrative. Although it contains directions and hints to guide the trip, all legends are incomplete, vague, or self-contradictory. Trying to assemble their fragmented clues into a coherent whole can be much like piecing together a jigsaw puzzle or participating in a scavenger hunt. Because of this, the journey itself can be quite challenging and confusing. Consequently, another common form of preparatory behavior is simply trying to figure out how to get to your destination in the first place.

By way of example, let us look at a case of aspiring legend trippers trying to plan their journey to one of the locally famous, legendary locations in Connecticut: the Devil's Hopyard. This is a state park in the town of East Haddam. Given its rather evocative name alone, which is actually its official name, it should come as no surprise that a good number of tales are associated with this place. While the park is well known for its waterfalls and the circular holes carved into the rock at their base by erosion, the origin of the name itself seems to be something of a mystery, which attracts legends, and of course, a number of strange things are said to go on here.[2] One of the best-known accounts describes how sometimes the Devil can be seen here, "sitting atop Chapman Falls, tail slung over his shoulder, playing his hellish violin while witches cackle and stir their sinister brews in the potholes below" (D'Agostino and Nicholson 2011:25). This particular story also claims that settlers in the region believed the Devil had made the circular potholes by angrily stomping his fiery hooves into the stone after he accidentally dipped his tail in the water. The tale sounds more like a fable than a legend, but modern legendry, too, is replete with reports of encounters with demons, monsters, and other supernatural entities near the falls and in the surrounding forests.

As part of a discussion of reputedly haunted area parks and forests, Devil's Hopyard predictably came up on a well-used web forum devoted to the supernatural (Ghostvillage 2006). In preparing to visit the park, one legend tripper posted a request for directions—a nearly universal and seemingly mundane preparatory requirement for any sort of travel plans. I include here a brief excerpt of the post and a portion of the discussion that follows. The conversation begins with: "Does anybody know exactly how to get to Devil's Hopyard? I went there once with my boyfriend but we really didn't know exactly where to go and that was almost 2 yrs [*sic* throughout the conversation] ago. We would really like to go back to an exact place, and how to get there." From this we can understand that the poster is actually looking for two separate things: conventional directions to the park in general but also a more specific destination within the park. Reading on reveals more about the role of this discussion and preparatory activities in general within the course of a legend trip. The first response notes: "devils hopyard is a state forest, google it youll find directions its no mystery. Go there at night and get at least escorted out by rangers . . . and according to local police your lucky if he doesnt ticket you for trespassing . . . there are some unmarked paths that are dangerously close to the falls and fast flowing rivers . . . and there are coyotes . . . and its hunting season. . . . not a place you want to go at night. . . ." This response begins with a dismissive tone: the destination is a not a secret place and, thus, may not hold anything of interest. However, this blasé attitude is immediately contradicted by noting the many dangers there, particularly if the original poster goes at night—something that was not actually mentioned in the original inquiry but seems assumed in this response. These are clues that a legend-reviewing session has just begun with their customary warnings, actually serving as dares, lending significance to the place as we saw in the previous chapter. The importance of this will become clear as we read on.

A new participant takes up the implicit challenge in the next response: "If I remember correctly, aren't there campgrounds at Devil's Hopyard? I've been a few times, never had any odd experiences—but by a few, I mean 3 or 4. I plan to go down this summer . . ." (Ghostvillage 2006). By noting the presence of campgrounds, and thus suggesting people are allowed to visit here and do so often, this person seems to contradict the prior poster's warnings about the park's dangers. Simultaneously, they implicitly agree with that individual's conclusion that there is nothing supernatural in character to be found here. In part, this can be interpreted as a normal interaction in the legend-telling process: intense debate (Dégh 2001). As discussed earlier, the legend is vague and incomplete and seems to compel this sort of participation. However, this new participant next demonstrates their bravery by claiming they do not believe there is anything supernatural there while simultaneously implying that there *could* be and that they have already faced this possibility more than once. Their downplayed bravado, their implication that they could be wrong about the dangers, and their stated intention to return despite those possible dangers all contribute to the discussion of that legend in this forum as well as the ongoing life of the legend in general. Yet the original request for directions remains unanswered. We still have no practical information for how to get to Devil's Hopyard ourselves, much less any details on its legendry.

The next reply reads: "Yes, there are campgrounds but I am not exactly sure where they are in conjunction with the activity that has been reported" (Ghostvillage 2006). This brief response confirms one objection to supernatural claims (i.e., that it's just a campground) while also reaffirming the possibility of supernatural occurrences at the park. Importantly, it also shows a tacit under-standing that the original poster was really asking about where to go specifically within the park to encounter the supernatural, not just how to get to the park in general. It is only by getting to the specific sites mentioned in the legend, which include lesser-known areas beyond the recognizable falls themselves, that they can confront legendary claims and put them to the test. While this response then offers little help in terms of practical travel planning, it adds to the whole discussion by allowing for the simultaneous existence of a prosaic campground and a supernatural hinterland somewhere beyond it. It also sug-gests that one might be used as an orienteering point to the other. Rather than serving to disprove paranormal claims, the existence of a banal campground is repurposed to serve as a helpful counterpoint to them.

The discussion thread continues with three more posts, one of which includes reference to an alleged demonic encounter at the park, but analysis of one final reply is sufficient for my purposes here:

> There are definitely campgrounds, I went there two years ago. Noth-ing strange there. The whole thing with Devil's Hopyard, it may or may not be haunted, but it's intersected/laying on an old, dormant fault, and supposedly it's eerily quiet around the fault. No birds, no nothing. It's just completely quiet. Getting there is no mystery, from 395, take exit 80. Most internet directions say 80 West, but 80 West was closed last week and they made 80 East access both sides of the road, now just calling it 80. So take exit 80, take a left onto route 82, and basically, just follow the signs. There are signs that will lead you the whole way, you can't really miss it. (Ghostvillage 2006)

From this, we first receive the now-familiar confirmation of the presence of campgrounds at the site. This is immediately followed by the equally familiar contradiction that there both is and is not something supernatural about the park. The legend is like a ghost itself, "which is neither present nor absent, neither dead nor alive" (Davis 2007:9). It "may or may not" be haunted, there is nothing strange there—except for the preternatural, eerie silence and the inexplicable absence of birds. We receive a hint about where this possible strangeness can be encountered (i.e., near the fault line) but no real informa-tion about how to get there. Finally, at long last, we receive detailed, practical, albeit somewhat convoluted suggestions for how to get to the park itself.

This excerpt makes it clear that getting directions in particular, and mundane preparations in general, are not distinct from the more arcane preparations of legend tripping. By helping legend trippers to imagine making their way to the site of the legend and what it will be like once they get there, taken altogether, these preparations serve to encourage the right state of mind: a sense of expectancy and supernatural possibility in what is to come. Rites of passage and pilgrimages typically feature various ordeals that initiates must contend with as part of the ritual process (Turner and Turner 1978). It is not much of a stretch to think about how some of the challenges facing legend trippers I have considered in this section might qualify as ordeals in this regard: obstacles to be endured and overcome that give a greater sense of significance to the endeavor. Without these challenges, getting to Devil's Hopyard would just be a ride in the car to the park and hardly the stuff of legends. Getting directions was enough of an obstacle, but further ordeals will doubtless face the legend trippers in this account if they manage to reach their destination. Already they are beginning to hear vague and troubling whispers of the things they may face in the woods. Soon they will begin the physical journey itself, and along the way, they will have to face and overcome their growing fears and trepidations as well.

RETOLD TALES

Legend *telling* is a critically important component of legend *tripping*. Not only does it precede and inspire travel, as I outlined in the previous chapter, but it also accompanies it. One of the most typical activities that takes place during the preparatory stage of a legend trip is retelling or reviewing the legend that served as the inspiration for the trip in the first place. Before setting forth, while en route to the destination, or both, participants talk about the legend that has captured their interest and spurred them into action, familiarizing themselves with its details and basking in its possibilities. Hall (1980) describes an example of this process for a group of teens on their way to the "Big Tunnel" in Indiana, a pre–Civil War railroad tunnel notorious for alleged murders and hauntings said to have occurred there. With the total trip taking about half an hour, the teens have plenty of time to discuss its legendry. While there is a certain structure to the legend telling, it is more of a conversation than a formal recitation. At some point early on in the journey, one participant brings up the legends of the tunnel, marking the beginning of the legend-telling session. From there, the group takes turns discussing the various tales they have heard, recounting previous experiences they themselves have had there on prior visits, and filling in gaps in each other's stories. Like most conversations, they might interrupt each other, change the topic, ask questions, and so on as the discussion and the journey proceeds (Ellis 2003). This pattern has held up over the decades, with research on contemporary ghost hunters reporting nearly identical patterns. En route to a haunted destination or upon reaching it, they typically review the details of the legend as they know it and debate its claims (Eaton 2015). Likewise, we see the same pattern on most televised legend trips. After first showing a montage of the team packing equipment excitedly into their vans, shows like *Ghost Hunters* characteristically begin with scenes of the investigators driving to their next case. Along the way, they review the details of the legend and discuss what they might expect to find once they get there while the scenery rolls by.

This illustrates how retelling of the legend can take many forms and need not actually require a traditional setting involving in-person interaction between a storyteller and an audience. Although the cast of the show are partly narrating the legend to each other, they are also doing so for the viewing audience. Modern legend telling often involves mediated transmission like this (Koven 1999; Koven 2007), with films, websites, and books filling in as narrators. In an instructional guide on how to investigate monsters and other mysteries, one author recommends that legend trippers bring along movies or books about the legend because reviewing these helps "to create the right mood" for the participants (Robinson 2016:288). In fact, this capacity of legends to establish a conducive mood and sense of expectation is the key point of retelling them during the preparatory stage. For this reason, regardless of their method of transmission, some of the legends that are reviewed during this step of the journey may not even be topically related to the destination that the participants are steadily making their way toward.

Returning to the legend trippers on their way to the Big Tunnel, Hall (1980:233) reports that in addition to retelling tales about the tunnel itself, they share a number of "local legends, modern migratory legends, horror stories from literature or movies and on occasion someone invents a new story." New technologies allow us to hear this sort of discussion for ourselves because participants are increasingly recording and sharing their adventures online. Listening to an episode of the *Supernatural Occurrence Studies Podcast* (2017), for instance, I found myself along for the ride as a group of friends drives to an allegedly haunted location: Concord's Colonial Inn in Massachusetts. Over the noise of their car's engine in the background, they discuss a number of paranormal claims about the inn. Many of these are related to its association with the opening chapter of the American Revolution and the possibility that the inn served as a hospital during the war's first battle, but they also include stories from previous legend trippers who have visited the site. Looking forward with eager expectation to the experience awaiting them, they discuss their plans for what they will do when they get to the inn: Is there someone at the inn they can talk to about the hauntings? Are there people they can interview? How will they begin their investigation? Just like the legend trippers who visited the Big Tunnel some forty years earlier, this group does not limit their discussion to legends about their destination alone. Nearly anything that creates the right state of mind comes up while they drive. This includes discussion of a scary UFO story someone they met had told them, the mysteries of a place called "America's Stonehenge" in neighboring New Hampshire, how to manipulate pieces of calcite to produce a strange vibration, and an odd childhood memory one of them has that might be supernatural in origin. This involved seeing a half dozen elephants grazing in a vacant lot across from a fast-food restaurant that no one else in the narrator's family, for some reason, seemed to remember.

Another legendary location the travelers discuss during their journey is Dighton Rock in Berkley, Massachusetts. The rock is a large boulder better known for its mysterious petroglyphs than any particular haunting, but it is associated with various strange phenomena. One reason for this is because it is located within a part of the state popularly called the "Bridgewater Triangle." As the name suggestions, this is a triangular area in eastern Massachusetts, marked by Abingdon, Freetown, and Rehoboth at its vertices. "Dead center in the triangle," moreover, "is the largest swampland in all New England—the murky, shadow-infested, quicksand dappled, 6,000 acre Hockomock Swamp . . . a vast primeval horrorscape, unchanged for five hundred years" (Citro 2005:72). In popular lore, all manner of strangeness is associated with the area—UFOs, giant dogs, and winged monsters, to name a few, so it is no wonder that it appears on many legend trippers' bucket lists. As we have just seen, a great variety of spooky topics naturally come up during legend trips, so there is nothing particularly noteworthy about the inclusion of the rock in this legend-retelling session except for one thing: they just came from the place. Before they set off for Concord, they had completed a trip there to examine its supernatural claims first. The experience provided a fresh set of legends to discuss: their own experiences! In fact, there are number of legendary places in Massachusetts, so why choose just one? It turns out the group made a road trip of linking as many of these locations together as possible like a string of outré pearls. These include numerous specific locations in and around the Bridgewater Triangle itself but also other locations within driving distance, like the Lizzie Borden House in Fall River and—a bit further off—Salem, Massachusetts, and its veritable wonderland of bizarre destinations.

This represents a sort of "serial legend tripping." Participants first visit a legendary destination as usual, but this only serves as the appetizer for one or more subsequent destinations, which might even be visited all in the same day. They accumulate experiences and further legends along the way that they can discuss, and these all help to build intensity of mood and expectation as the larger arc of the journey progresses. Serial legend tripping seems increasingly common in recent years. One YouTuber posted a video of her exploration of Union Cemetery in Easton, Connecticut (Crabb 2017a): another allegedly haunted location that paranormal investigators E. Warren and L. Warren popularized (Warren, Warren, and Chase 1992). While strolling among the headstones, the woman reiterates some of the cemetery's legends—about a ghostly lady in white—to the camera. This is especially interesting since she is telling tales to the viewer rather than to anyone there, but the retelling still serves to build excitement and expectation for herself too. She remarks: "I love the feeling here. It feels so spooky. And I think, just because Ed and Lorraine [were here], you know what I mean?" Part of her excitement is due to the location she just came from: "Last night, I was at Eastern State Penitentiary . . . Holy crap! The best investigation. Honestly, I am so amazed, and that place is super haunted." Another part of it is due to anticipation for where she is heading after Union Cemetery: "I'm going to another cemetery after this. . . . It's about the legend of Midnight Mary" (Crabb 2017a:n.p.). Here she is referring to yet another haunted location—Evergreen Cemetery—in nearby New Haven. Located only half an hour down the road, we can watch her next video and learn that she did indeed travel there immediately after visiting Union Cemetery (Crabb 2017c). Incidentally, Union Cemetery served as the starting place for one of my own serial trips as well. After trying unsuccessfully to meet the lady in white there, I also drove to another cemetery. This was Stepney Cemetery in Monroe. The White Lady is spotted here too from time to time, and the Warrens also rest in peace—perhaps—within. Both cemeteries are fairly modest experiences on their own, but spending time in one while anticipating the other certainly adds to the overall experience. Cases like these illustrate how a legend trip can, itself, serve as part of the preparation for *another* legend trip.

Like other preliminary activities, discussing legends—whether related to the destination or not, whether part of a singular or serial trip—is an essential preliminary activity for successful legend tripping. It constructs the proper mood for the activities to come: "affective excitement that translates to expectation" (Kinsella 2011:85). And it mentally prepares legend trippers to accept the potential of supernatural possibilities. This helps set the stage for subsequent encounters with those otherworldly forces.

JOURNEY THROUGH THE BORDERLANDS

Retelling legends is an important preliminary activity during this stage of the journey, but it is also accompanied by *movement*. A good illustration of how these two activities are intertwined can be found in a book by Joseph A. Citro, a Vermont-based author well known for his works documenting the stranger side of New England's history and folklore. In *Cursed in New England* (2004), he describes a hike he took with some friends to show them Vermont's fabled

Union Cemetery (Easton, CT): This graveyard was made famous as a haunted location by Ed and Lorraine Warren and is conveniently located near other legendary locations. Photo by the author.

Brunswick Springs. Many legends accrue to the site and, according to one of these, the springs were cursed by the Abenaki people to protect them from commercial development and exploitation. Recounting these tales provided a sense of atmosphere as the group made its way toward the springs: "As resident ghost expert, it became my job to tell them tales as we moved along the grassy path that had once been a road. Birdcalls and an occasional skittering in the bushes kept us looking from side to side. An intermittent, errant wind lent atmosphere to my stories. 'So, do you believe in the curse?' Lauren asked" (Citro 2004:183). This narrative gives a strong sense of the significance—and the experience—of reviewing legends during the course of the journey. What would normally be experienced as just a walk in the woods becomes something much more ominous but also much more significant. Simultaneously, movement toward the destination makes this more than just a story session too. Those involved start seeing the sights around them in a different light. The possibility arises that something supernatural could occur and expectations begin to build that it *will* occur.

Legend trips might begin with light-hearted banter and legend telling but, as participants move further from their point of origin and approach their destination, something changes. One study on adolescent trips found that "the mood inside the car as the trip begins is often rowdy and excited. The kids laugh and joke about general topics. . . . Once outside the town limits, however, the mood grows serious" and the conversation turns to the legend itself (Meley 1991:14). Something like this seems universal to all successful legend trips. At some point during the journey, things become more tense and frightening, tinged by a growing sense of expectation or even dread.

If the participants are now well prepared, this is because of the growing awareness that they are crossing through something other than mere physical space alone. They have left ordinary lands behind them, with all their banal predictability. Soon, they will enter an entirely different and less predictable realm where the extraordinary and the terrible might occur. This is the very definition of what van Gennep ([1909] 1960:19) calls "a direct rite of passage" whereby "a person leaves one world behind him and enters into another." As they proceed on their journey, the legend trippers draw ever closer to this "other" world and become ever more conscious of its implications. They are not there yet though. Instead, during this stage of the rite of passage they are moving through a sort of "neutral zone" between places (van Gennep [1909] 1960:18). It is an uncertain place, where neither the old rules nor the new rules entirely apply. It is a realm of "not only *transition* but also *potentiality*, not only 'going to be' but also 'what may be'" (Turner and Turner 1978:3).

To fully cross over, they must first find the border: the threshold or limen that symbolically marks the change in realities and possibilities. More accurately, they need to *construct* that boundary by collectively convincing themselves it exists. All the preparatory activities, the *preliminal* rites (van Gennep [1909] 1960:21), that they have engaged in thus far help demarcate that border so that they might complete the passage by stepping over it. According to the historian Johan Huizinga (1955:19), this type of behavior is common to all ritual: "A closed space is marked out for it, either materially or ideally, hedged off from the everyday surroundings. Inside this space the play proceeds, inside it the rules obtain." He compares this ritualism to a game, noting the similarities between both types of imaginative work:

> Just as there is no formal difference between play and ritual, so the "con-
> secrated spot" cannot be formally distinguished from the play-ground.
> The arena, the card-table, the magic circle, the temple, the stage, the
> screen, the tennis court, the court of justice, etc., are all in form and
> function play-grounds, i.e., forbidden spots, isolated, hedged round,
> hallowed, within which special rules obtain. All are temporary worlds
> within the ordinary world, dedicated to the performance of an act apart.
> (Huizinga 1955:10)

In the case of legend tripping, this border might take many forms depending on the nature of the legend and its setting. It might be clearly demarcated, like the fence around a cursed cemetery. It might be vague and abstract, like a dirt road leading into a monster-infested forest. Conversely, it can be very small and finite, like the literal threshold of a haunted house. These variations account for why legend-trip destinations can be far away and take a long time to get to, but simultaneously, it is entirely possible to legend trip in the attic or basement of your own home (Grider 2007b). The boundary's specific form is less important than the consensus-building rituals of the preparatory phase that help to establish its reality for the participants. In this way, stepping across the very border they drew themselves will bear far greater significance than mere motion through space alone would otherwise entail.

The actual crossing will come in the next stage of the legend trip, but there is much work to be done between now and then. In addition to the preparatory activities that I have already considered (packing, reviewing legends, etc.), the activity of movement through space while also telling legends helps to nurture legend trippers' perceptions that they are passing through a borderland, beyond which lies the boundary of the "magic circle" where the ritual to conjure supernatural forces can be performed (Huizinga 1955:10). By way of comparison, the ritual ascent of a mountain is a common motif in many world religions, which reflects an approach to the sacred realm at its summit (Cooper 1978). The climb provides a sense of physical as well as symbolic distance from the regular world below and perhaps even constitutes something of a ritual ordeal or trial in itself. Legend trips likewise make use of this sort of spatial symbolism and, sometimes, even do so with mountains. For example, Mt. Carmel in Hamden, Connecticut, has several legends associated with it. Residents more commonly call it the "Sleeping Giant," claiming that, according to Native American legend, it is in fact a giant in slumber. His name is Hobbomock, a greedy and evil spirit who was put to sleep by the benevolent spirit Kietan to stop his rampages among the people (Sachse 2009).[3] Of interest to many hikers and legend trippers is the one-and-a-half-mile trail that winds its way steeply up the mountain. At its summit looms their destination: a stone observation tower built to resemble a Norman keep. If they make it this far, travelers might feel as though they have indeed entered another realm as they perch high atop the mountain in an apparently medieval tower, gazing out over the New England landscape far below. Properly prepared, they might even experience some strange behavior at the top. One website, paraphrasing oft-quoted local folklore, asks: "Does the ghostly man dressed in black truly exist on this unique area of land? And are the odd happenings in the structure on top of the mountain related to the man?" (CT Paranormal Searchers n.d.:n.p.).

One researcher, Bel Deering, purposely simulated an experience of moving through a symbolic borderland as a method for understanding the power of uncanny places over their visitors. Instead of providing a sense of height and

Sleeping Giant State Park
(Hamden, CT): Visitors will need
to reach the tower at the mountain's summit if they hope to
have a supernatural encounter.
Photo by the author.

distance, however, she went for walks with her research participants at night in a
cemetery to understand how they experienced the place. She reports, "Imagination and storytelling formed a core part of the way in which participants related
their experiences and described how they were feeling both during the interview
and on previous occasions" (Deering 2014:194). Her participants regaled her
"with a variety of tales, including personal legends about spooky experiences,
and even where these were generally mysterious or uncanny and unrelated to
the cemetery, they did serve to heighten the atmosphere that we felt there and
made us alert to every sound and flicker of light that our eyes could pick up"
(Deering 2014:194). This situation, simulated via a field study, sounds very much
like what legend trippers experience during the regular course of their journey.
The situation and their activities produce a state of "physiological arousal," of
heightened alertness or readiness (Duffy 1962), which has long been linked to
alterations in normal human information processing (Zajonc 1965). The air is
thick with possibility and the participants are primed and ready to experience
something strange, but in Deering's account the journey ends while the participants are still wandering in the neutral zone. They feel the sense of possibility
inherent to this borderland, but they never find a threshold to cross over into
the next world and, consequently, fail to experience a supernatural encounter.

Something is missing, which makes it impossible for them to move beyond the preparatory stage of the legend trip. Figuring out what that "something" is will reveal another important requirement of the journey.

I found a clue to that missing element when I experienced something similar to what Deering (2014) describes on an October night during a guided walking tour of Milford, Connecticut. Our tour guide led us up and down the darkened streets of the small coastal town, entertaining us with ghostly legends associated with some of its haunted locations along the way, somewhat like a serial legend trip. At one point, she stopped us and pointed out across the town harbor to the far shore, largely invisible in the murk. She said that, according to legend, one day a group of Native Americans supposedly tortured their enemies to death there. Sometimes, she said, you can see some faint shafts of light out there, across the water. These are really the lost souls of their victims. As we walked further down the street, our group stretched into a long, thin line along the sidewalk and conversations became more hushed. We soon stopped at the corner of Helwig Street and High Street. This would have been a very unassuming corner during the day when you are not on a ghost walk. It is the sort of corner you would drive by without consciously registering that it was even there, the kind of corner that, even when walking, would be the visual equivalent of background noise as you passed on your way. Here in the darkness though, framed by the uncanny situation and the odd topic of conversation, it seemed somehow more significant and filled with possibility—even though her next story had nothing to even do with this corner. Instead, she gestured off into the night again where, somewhere out there beyond our vision, in Long Island Sound, huddled the very cursed Charles Island. In silence, we listened to the story of its tainted past.

This moment of the tour, like many other moments throughout its duration, produced the borderland experience described above. Judging from my fellow tourists' behaviors and the content of their conversations, the combination of travelling and telling stories seemed to make everyone more somber, more aware of possibilities, and very interested and alert when we arrived at each haunted location on the itinerary. The transformation was quite profound considering that only a couple hours earlier many of us, myself included, were happily shopping at stores or eating at restaurants on these very same streets. Despite all this, the experience was limited to expectancy and mood alone, and no one reported an actual supernatural encounter. Several things were missing that could have made this into a successful legend trip. First, with one exception, we never actually crossed a symbolic or physical boundary into a haunted location. Instead, we remained outside these places, hearing about what could happen *within*. Anthropologist Michele Hanks (2015) argues that this is a common characteristic of ghost walks like this one. Participants can see haunted places and hear about

them but seldom get to step foot inside and rarely have a personally transformative encounter with the other world. But another important element that was
missing was a ritual trigger. As I will explore further in the next chapter, this
is an essential component of any legend trip hoping to achieve a supernatural
encounter. True, our guide had distributed several EMF meters to the group, but
she didn't really say much about them, and they were quickly forgotten. On one
occasion, at the end of the tour, we did indeed enter the night-shrouded grounds
of the allegedly haunted Milford Cemetery. There, in the middle of the burying
ground, our guide asked us to extinguish our lights as she told her final tales. Like
Deering (2014) reports in her research, the mood was suitably spooky, standing
there in the darkness and surrounded by headstones for as far as we could see
with imagination filling in the details beyond. The crowd huddled together, more
closely than the temperature required, under an overarching tree. As she spoke,
I gazed upward through its bare limbs and contemplated the distant stars above.
However, the story had nothing to do with the particular part of the cemetery
that we were in, and we did nothing to call the supposed spirits. At length, she
finished her tale and concluded the tour. The group slowly disassembled, apparently unsure what to do next, and wandered off in different directions without
any obvious sense of intention.

Of course, ghost walks don't *have* to end this way. Given just these few minor
modifications, they can provide an experience comparable to a full-blown legend trip. The previous autumn, my wife and I went on a walking tour that
included three buildings at the allegedly haunted Harriet Beecher Stowe Center
in Hartford, Connecticut. We checked in within the first building. This was the
brightly lit and cheery welcome center. Most of the space was utilized as a gift
shop, but there was also a room used for classes and presentations, its walls covered with poster boards and other signs of previous workshops. We wandered
around these comfortable spaces for a while, then all the attendees were asked to
gather outside, in the dark, where the tour guide greeted us and provided a brief
orientation for our small group. He began to tell us stories about what to expect
and what previous groups had encountered inside the first house. This helped
to identify the physical walls of the house as a meaningful, symbolic threshold
to be crossed. He handed us an EMF meter, explaining that if it lit up, it meant
ghosts were nearby, and we would then try to communicate with them. Next,
we set off across the grounds for the first house, which we actually entered, and
tried to talk to the spirits within every time the meter went off, which was often.
We then walked outside toward the second house, hearing more stories along
the way, and repeated the procedure within. In other words, we passed through
the borderland and across the symbolic and literal thresholds twice during this
tour, and the participants were visibly excited by their apparent conversations
with the dead enabled by a ritualistic mechanism.[4] When we were done, he even

guided us away from the site of encounter back to the cheery warmth and safety of the welcome center/gift shop: a standard form of legend-tripping behavior I will consider further in chapter 6. Ironically, I later learned that this building was also supposedly haunted, but the tour was wisely designed to conveniently ignore that bit of folklore, which would complicate and confuse the order of events. In short, a little careful planning can go a long way.

THE SIGNIFICANCE OF PREPARATION

In this chapter, I have argued that preparation is a crucial part of a legend trip and that the journey to a legend's setting is, itself, part of this preparatory stage. Whereas prior researchers often mention the liminal character of legend trips, I have extended their observations by revisiting these concepts in more depth, with an eye toward untangling exactly what it is that enables a sense of liminality and how this contributes to the overall endeavor. Preparation endows the legend trip with a sense of danger, excitement, significance, and supernatural possibility. During the preparatory stage, the legend trippers must themselves construct a liminal boundary through a range of ritualistic, game-like behaviors that I have explored: ordeals, trials, and movement through physical space. Only by successfully establishing this boundary—through shared narratives, social interaction, and psychological expectancy—will they be able to separate themselves from their everyday understanding of the world and proceed to the next stage of the process.

The preparatory phase plays a critical role in legend tripping, but it is not well understood. It also seems to be the least studied part of these journeys and deserves further scrutiny. There are many unanswered questions. What proportion of legend trips are spur of the moment versus well-planned affairs, and what accounts for the difference? How common is serial legend tripping, and who is more likely to do it? Is there any specific ordering of destinations, with the most exciting or frightening places, for instance, reserved as the final destination on the itinerary? Hopefully future work will shed further light on questions like these.

Gaps in our knowledge notwithstanding, the general importance of preparation is clear. The success or failure of a legend trip depends on the successful completion of its preparatory step. Any shortcuts or omissions here may result in a stalled effort. Failure to generate an appropriate mood or sense of expectancy will certainly be a problem, but even accomplishing these alone won't be enough to move the legend trippers beyond this preparatory stage if they cannot construct and cross a meaningful threshold. All their preparatory activities, taken in their entirety, ultimately function to produce an "expectancy effect" or "self-fulfilling prophecy" so that what is initially "a false definition of the situation evok[es] a new behavior which makes the originally false conception come true" (Merton 1948:195). In other words, if the legend trippers can convince themselves that something significant can and will happen, soon they will be sufficiently motivated to interpret nearly anything as validation of that expectation. We will see exactly how this unfolds in the following chapters.

There is a problem, however. Rites of passage are typically fairly regimented and predictable affairs (van Gennep [1909] 1960). This chapter has documented how legend trips approximate the general form of rites of passage in many ways, and later chapters reveal further similarities. However, I have noted many things that can go wrong so far as well. Reflecting on the reasons for these problems highlights the fact that legend trips also display some important differences from rites of passages that have not previously been considered by researchers. I examine these at length later as well, but for now it is worth noting how, unlike rites of passage, there is usually no clear guidance on hand at any point to direct the legend trippers through the proper routes and behaviors. Often, they are fumbling through the journey on their own and cobbling bits of information together as they go. This isn't necessarily because of an absence of guidance per se but because there is no singular, coherent authority and instead a profusion of competing, discordant suggestions. This is likely a major reason why some legend trips never manage to find their destination, establish the right mood, or figure out how to cross over the symbolic threshold.

Despite these issues, many legend trips do achieve success of a sort, and the preliminaries that must be completed before arriving at the site of a legend play an essential role to that end. In a sense, the trip has already begun as soon as the travelers decide that they will go on such a journey and before they have even set foot outside the door. These preparations for travel—whether they include retelling the story, packing, getting directions, or what have you—are similar to the "warnings" inherent in legends themselves in that they have something of a dual nature. On the surface, and to some extent in actuality, they serve the practical purpose of readying the pedestrian dimensions of departure and travel. Digging deeper, we find that they are much more than that. These practical preparations also provide the proper *psychological* preparation for the trip. As the preliminary stage of the rite of passage, these activities together constitute a form of "symbolic behavior signifying detachment" from everyday social life (Turner and Turner 1978:94). They are a way for legend trippers to convince themselves that they are about to depart or separate from the normal world and act as a means of preparing them to enter a realm in which fantastic things are possible. Together, these preparations ready them for that possibility, and the actual travel involved serves to spatially, psychologically, and socially separate them from the constraints of the ordinary world.

Part III

The Liminal Stage

Chapter 4

RITES AND RITUALS

Demons are like obedient dogs; they come when they are called.
—REMY DE GOURMONT (1992:26)

We had been driving for quite some time. The paved road had given up awhile back, and now, we kicked up clouds of dust as we made our way over the crude, dirt road that succeeded it. Other than the road itself, there were few signs of human habitation. There were, however, plenty of trees. Densely packed, they huddled closely together in a sort of arboreal conspiracy that forbid any human gaze from venturing too far within their hidden domain. I had a map to guide us—well, two maps actually, each slightly but significantly different from the other. "It's all part of the experience," I tried to convince myself. One of the few important points of agreement between the two maps was that the abandoned cemetery lay just out of sight in the woods beyond the intersection of the two neglected roads ahead. According to legend, a witch was buried there. All I had to do to invoke her angry spirit and call down her wrath was to find her overgrown grave and foolishly place my hand upon its ancient surface. Pulling over and turning off the engine, I hopped out of the car and into the rapidly darkening woods to find the cursed headstone and do just that. The ritual had begun.

My task in this chapter is to make sense of the wide range of strange behaviors that are distinguishing features of legend trips: vandalism, leaving items on graves, calling names into empty space, and the like. Key to understanding these, I argue, is recognizing their inherently ritualistic character. I identify sets of common, fundamental patterns to these behaviors that reveal their social and psychological logic as a means of invoking a supernatural experience. Some require pleasing otherworldly forces, others angering them—a characteristic peculiar to legend-tripping rituals, but these are variations of the same underlying rationale. I examine other variations of ritual and their relation to legend as well, like verbal incantations and the use of material objects, the

difference between specialized rituals and more generalized ritualistic thinking, and even the importance of maintaining the right mood. Along the way,
I illustrate that while most of these potentially unnerving ritualistic activities
are usually benign, they can easily lead to problems. Sometimes these arise
out of the legend trippers' own volition, but they are especially likely when
nonparticipants become involved.

Rites of passage—whether pertaining to marriage, funerals, coming-of-age
or some other important transitions—commonly involve the ritualistic act of
crossing over a symbolically meaningful boundary in some way. The physical
act of crossing an actual threshold, for instance, historically corresponds to a
symbolic passage as well: "the door is the boundary between the foreign and
domestic worlds in the case of an ordinary dwelling, between the profane and
sacred worlds in the case of a temple" (van Gennep [1909] 1960:20). Many rites
of passage require not only a physical crossing, where the symbolic significance of the threshold or portal is "direct" in this manner, but also an "indirect"
component. In these cases, the gateway is home to some sort of supernatural
"guardians of the threshold" that must be invoked (van Gennep [1909] 1960:21).
Traditionally, this is a deity or monster that protects the way and must be
placated. This is typically accomplished through offering prayers or some sort
of sacrifice to the protector entity. In this way, the "rite of spatial passage has
become a rite of spiritual passage" as well since "a personified power insures it
through spiritual means" (van Gennep [1909] 1960:22).

Legend trips are both like and unlike these traditional rites. In the previous
stage of the legend trip, the participants engaged in a range of preparatory or
preliminary activities. These helped them build a sense of possibility and expectancy, a sense that they were leaving the regular world behind and approaching
a world of new and unknown possibilities. Guided by legend, they passed
through this neutral zone to find and demarcate the border to that other world.
However, no matter how psychologically well prepared they might be, their
arrival at the destination alone is not sufficient to complete the transition. They
have located the border, but in the next step of their trip—the ritual stage, they
will perform the rites that will let them symbolically cross over it at will. At the
alleged setting of the tale, they must engage in peculiar, predetermined behaviors intended to call up the supernatural entities that dwell at the threshold.

I describe something of this sort in this chapter's opening vignette, depicting
my visit to Connecticut Hill Cemetery: an abandoned graveyard in the woods
of Newfield, New York. Passing from the dirt road into the thick forest filled
with dilapidated headstones was very much like crossing a symbolic border.
The legend, however, claimed that I next had to complete a specific rite to
invoke the angry spirit haunting the place. This involved locating and simply
touching the witch's headstone (Scofield 2015).

Although they can vary considerably in their details, rituals like this are standard fare in legend tripping. One place that bears witness to behavior like this is Logan Cemetery in Logan, Utah. It is the destination for many local legend trips, especially for students from nearby Utah State University. They focus their attentions on a monument in the cemetery crowned by the statue of a woman, head bowed and forehead resting on her hand in mourning.[1] Visitors here try to make the statue come to life. Some who claim to have been successful in this endeavor say she will jump down from her pedestal, run across the road, and then return. Others simply try to make her cry. To do so, they must "shine [their] car lights on her and then run around her chanting cry, lady, cry" (Tucker 2007:203). Of course, this is just one of countless legendary destinations. Each location has its own legend as well as its own associated set of equally curious rites.

LEGEND TRIPS AS RITUAL BEHAVIOR

Legend trips are often baffling to outsiders. In large part, this is due to the strange behaviors that legend trippers perform once they reach their destinations. We can make sense of these peculiarities, however, by being mindful of their essentially *ritualistic* character (Ellis 2003). Ritual is a sort of patterned social behavior that is particularly important for those involved because of its symbolic dimensions (C. Bell 1997).[2] Symbols, in general, might also appear to be strange or arbitrary if we merely consider their appearance as objects or images invoking seemingly irrational responses. To anyone unfamiliar with them, the meaningfulness of a national flag or Eucharist wafer would not be obvious. Likewise, to that same outsider, the rituals that correspond with these symbols—the pledge of allegiance, for example, or the Catholic Mass—would seem exceedingly strange. The observer would have a difficult time making sense of the behaviors that take place during these rites without an insider's knowledge of their underlying meanings or at least a willingness to compare them to symbols and rituals with which they *are* familiar. Like the legend that motivates the trip itself, the rituals that occur at legendary locations may serve to express the values and concerns of the groups who carry them out (Durkheim [1912] 1995). The behaviors themselves, whether they look strange or familiar, are not as important for understanding the overall activity as the meanings and intentions underlying them.

Across the documented accounts of legend trips produced by both researchers and by legend trippers themselves, a wide range of possible behaviors is evident. Most of these, according to B. Ellis (1989:202), are relatively benign: "teenagers act out rituals such as honking horns three times, parking on railroad tracks, sitting on stone 'chairs,' or engaging in 'grunch' hunts, all of which are intended to produce supernatural phenomena." Anyone hoping to call up the spirit of M. Brown in Exeter, Rhode Island, just needs to peer "at her grave through an opening in a nearby gravestone while chanting three times, 'Mercy Brown, are you a vampire?'" (Holly and Cordy 2007:345). At a different cemetery—the Old Hill Burying Ground in Concord, Massachusetts, visitors can witness a pair of engraved eyes come to life. To do so, they must make their way to the top of the hill overlooking the town and find the large headstone with a skull and angel carved upon it and an inscription that reads, "All must submit to the King of terrors." Then they simply take a photo and see what develops. To summon up the shade of Mary Johnson, you don't even have to leave your home. Instead, call up some friends and invite them over. Once everyone has arrived, turn off the lights, sit in a circle, and join hands. "Then you repeat together, 'Come, Mary Johnson, come!'" (Langlois 1980:221).

While many ritual activities associated with legend trips, like these, are clearly harmless and perhaps even silly, this is not always the case. At times, the rituals involved can be more problematic and may include theft and vandalism. Investigating these activities, and understanding the meanings behind them, is very revealing. Therefore, I will turn our attention to some of these next. I compare the more problematic elements of legend tripping to their more common, innocuous ones. Through this process, I show that while such activities—destructive or harmless—appear quite dissimilar, there is a shared ritual logic that underlies them.

TRANSGRESSIVE INVOCATIONS

In Loon Lake Cemetery in Jackson, Minnesota, most of the gravestones are "missing and ostensibly have been stolen," and at least one illicit attempt has been made to dig up the body of Mary Jane Terwillegar, who according to legend was a witch (Waskul 2016:108). Unfortunately, thefts like these are often part of legend-tripping rituals. I propose that thinking of stolen items as "mementos" can help explain the rationale behind these acts. Sometimes, individuals steal so that they have some sort of evidence that they actually went to the legendary site and faced whatever dangers lurk there. The ill-gotten object serves as a sort of "memento of proof" that they can show to peers when they later regale them with tales of their exploits. I explore this motivation more thoroughly later, when I consider the latter stages of the legend trip. More immediately, theft can also serve a ritualistic function to call up or otherwise test the existence of the supernatural. The stolen object is not necessarily intended to be proof of the adventure but rather a "memento of invocation." If particular "gravestones are said to return if moved or stolen" (Kinsella 2011:28), for example, you might need to steal one just to see if the supernatural will manifest itself by stealing it back.

Examining the way theft can invoke the dead reveals a more general logic for this sort of transgression. Folklore often warns that those who steal from graves will be punished—often by the dead themselves—for failing to "show proper respect for the dead" (Tucker 2007:157). In fact, warnings against stealing from the dead are so well established that they frequently appear in popular culture, such as in Pixar's *Coco* (Unkrich 2017), in which the theme plays a pivotal role. The film's protagonist, Miguel, steals a guitar from a grave and is transported to the Land of the Dead for his transgression. He soon learns that he is under a curse and will permanently join the dead himself if he cannot find a way to return to the Land of the Living before sunrise. As we have seen, legends often contain warnings like this against things you are not supposed to do lest you risk angering the spirits or some other entity. However, these do not actually inhibit transgressive behavior. Similar to how warnings act as dares to encourage legend trips in the first place, if someone *wants* to experience the supernatural, these same warnings offer a roadmap for how to make it happen. By purposely stealing something belonging to a spirit during a legend trip, you test whether that spirit exists by daring it to do something about the transgression. According to legend, Pere Cheney Cemetery in Roscommon, Michigan, is haunted by a number of entities, including the vengeful spirit of a witch (Haddad 2021). Reminiscing about an adolescent exploit, one legend tripper recalls how he and his friends ran afoul of the witch after stealing from her one fateful night. It was "Devil's Night in 1985" when, along with a number of peers from school, he "went to visit Pere Cheney Cemetery with the intent of getting scared." He recounts, "I had heard tons of stories about the 'ghost train,' the witch and a few other legends and never felt scared one bit . . . until later on." Soon, things took a turn for the worse when "a friend of mine took the top half of the alleged 'witch's' headstone from the cemetery and put it on the floor of his [car]. I did *indeed* have something bad happen to me and I still to this day, strongly believe that because my friend removed the top of that headstone, we suffered consequences" (Liddy n.d.:n.p.). Some of the group, including the narrator, were injured in a freak traffic accident a few weeks after the legend trip.

In addition to theft, many complaints about legend trippers cite vandalism as a cause for concern. A site that serves as the destination for trips can sometimes be identified, even in the absence of any particular knowledge of it, by simply noting the presence of "initials, class symbols, obscene graffiti common to haunted buildings" (Dégh 1971:65). People who engage in vandalism do so for different specific reasons. However, the act is rarely without some sort of meaning, though that meaning may not be apparent to nonparticipants. This fact certainly does not justify destructive behavior, but it does help to achieve an understanding of it. This understanding, in turn, may help efforts to combat it. On one level, vandalism may be a necessary way to symbolically conclude the ritual behavior. Here, legend trippers "leave a mark to show that they've been there. It's their version of writing, 'Kilroy was here.'. . . [T]his mark often takes the form of graffiti, cemetery vandalism, or the remains of campfires or parties" (Fine and Victor 1994:71).

This may be done simply to prove the act was done, much like taking a "memento of proof." More significantly, destructive acts may serve important functions during the climax of the ritual because, like theft, they can potentially cause the supernatural to manifest itself. So familiar is this basic pattern that it frequently makes its way into fictional accounts as well, where it is a common trope. The following example, drawn from a novel set in Mount Hope Cemetery in Rochester, New York, illustrates this traditional pattern from the perspective of a ghost. Hovering out of sight near the grave she shares with her husband, Sam, the shade of the recently deceased Lilla suddenly encounters a small group of apparent legend trippers:

> Three drunken guys staggered up the side of the hill and plopped down on my bench [near our graves]. Some things never change. [When I was alive] I used to pick weeds and beer bottles out of the flowerbeds almost every week. The boys pulled beers out of their pockets, as if they needed more. They weren't the first kids to get drunk in a cemetery, and they certainly won't be the last. I planned to ignore them . . . until one of them smashed a bottle on Sam's headstone. That burned me up. Before I realized what I was doing, I swooped out of the shadows and yelled, "What the hell was that?!" Needless to say, I scared the crap out of them. . . . I'd never seen anyone sober up so quickly. They ran so fast, they didn't even stagger! (Fontaine 2013:27)

While this fictional account does not give us direct insight into the perspective of the teens, it does provide the reader with the imagined ghost's perspective quite well. In empathizing with her, we can understand the cultural logic behind the belief that one can provoke a spirit. Vandalism taunts the ghost and challenges it to show itself (Holly and Cordy 2007). It can also serve to prove that the vandal is not afraid of the supernatural consequences of this ritualized violation—or indeed, the legal consequences (Ellis 2003).

Again, in all these cases, legend trippers steal from the dead or vandalize their graves to somehow compel them to manifest themselves. From an outsider's point of view, these activities are simply destructive to cemeteries and emotionally upsetting to those who have loved ones buried in them. What most of these activities have in common is that they require some sort of ritualized transgression, but transgression does not *have* to be destructive. Many other legend-tripping rituals operate via the same mystical rationale while simultaneously causing little or no damage. In Bonds Chapel Cemetery in West Baden Springs, Indiana, one must not *touch* the image of a chain that can be found on one of the tombstones. While generations of individuals touching the stone might eventually damage it, a single touch is relatively harmless. In Providence, Rhode Island, there is a potentially cursed fountain. One tempts fate here not by damaging it but simply by sipping its waters (Bhargava 2016). Indeed, many legend trips involve simply visiting forbidden places and, by doing so, risking supernatural repercussions. Whenever transgression plays a role, and whatever its specific form, there is the possibility that it will become something other than benign since the point is to cross boundaries and tempt fate. Similar to the Bonds Chapel legend, in Lakeview Cemetery in Penn Yan, New York, one must not touch a stain on the Bishop-Gillette monument if they do not want to risk supernatural punishment. Interestingly enough, other versions of the legend warn you not to throw rocks or cans at the stain instead. This is a much more destructive activity, but clearly it shares a similar underlying logic with the simple touch: both are transgressive, and one can easily substitute for the other.

CONCORDANT INVOCATIONS

Invocation, thus, does not have to be destructive. Notably, it does not even have to be transgressive. In fact, as noted at the beginning of this chapter, traditionally, rites of passage are accompanied by *offerings* to guardian entities—not taunts and challenges (van Gennep [1909] 1960). It is not surprising, then, that sometimes legend trippers perform this more traditional manner of invocation too. Instead of antagonizing the spirits, they can try to achieve contact through concordance: that is, through means that placate them or earn their favor. Casual visitors to graveyards often leave some offering or tribute as a sign of respect or affection for the deceased. For Wiccans hoping to work their craft in cemeteries, showing respect is also important because it helps establish rapport with the dead. To do so, one guidebook suggests, "It's not a bad idea to ask permission [from the spirits] to enter or to bring an offering to show you're not a threat. . . . Picking up trash is almost always a welcome contribution" (Gruben 2018:n.p.). For legend trippers, similar respectful activities take on significance as a potential invocation to call on the spirits of the dead by earning their goodwill (Holly and Cordy 2007). Evergreen Cemetery in New Haven, Connecticut, is allegedly haunted by a witch locally called "Midnight

Mary" who is believed to have the power to kill. This doesn't stop people from visiting her grave, but it does mean that many of these visitors "will leave offerings of coins or candy on her gravestone to placate her angry spirit" (Berry n.d.:n.p.). More famously, people wishing to ask a favor of the spirit of the "voodoo queen" of New Orleans, Marie Laveau, must first make an offering at her grave. This might include "coins, Mardi Gras beads, candles" and so on (Nickell 2011:n.p.). They must also either knock three times or draw three *x*'s on her tomb, depending on which legend variant they have heard. Similarly, many paranormal investigators like to use "trigger objects" to contact the dead. They present the invisible spirit with any sort of object they believe it might like and invite it to interact with that object. For example, "many investigators will use items like toys, i.e., stuffed animals, balls, etc., when dealing with the ghosts of children who have passed on. . . . It is a way of not only drawing the ghost close to you but also gives it confidence that you are not there to harm it, but just to play and contact it" (Complete Paranormal Services n.d.:n.p.).

Something of this sort happens in Savannah, Georgia's Saint Bonaventure Cemetery. Made famous for appearing in John Berendt's best-selling novel *Midnight in the Garden of Good and Evil* (1994), it is haunted by the spirit of a child called "Little Gracie Watson." Her headstone features a lifelike statue of the young girl. According to some accounts, if you give her a quarter by placing it in the statue's hand "and encircle her statue three times, the coin will disappear" (Spiritualized67 2009:n.p.).[3] Many visitors also kindly leave toys at her grave for her to play with. However, presumably others steal them since "some claim [her statue] will cry tears of blood if her playthings are removed" (Spiritualized67 2009:n.p.). This illustrates that, like so many other aspects of the ritual process, despite superficial dissimilarities, concordance and transgression are closely associated sides of the same magical rationale. You can get a reaction from the spirit by either placating *or* antagonizing it. Similar possibilities surround a statue said to be that of "Witch Bonney" in Lowell Cemetery in Lowell, Massachusetts. People sometimes leave offerings to her, "but don't take any of the offerings to the statue—you'll be cursed with bad luck" (Hider 2014:n.p.). Meanwhile, in New York's famed Sleepy Hollow Cemetery, visitors to the resting place of General Samuel M. Thomas have an important choice to make. Facing his mausoleum is the statue of a mourning woman: the "Bronze Lady" (Leary 2000). If you slap her face, take a seat on her lap, and then spit in her eye, she will punish you by haunting you for the rest of your days. If you *just* sit in her lap, however, the nurturing side of the spirit awakens, and she will instead take care of you for the rest of your life.

These last examples again illustrate that the magical logic involved in legend trips is somewhat flexible. A legend requiring that you give tribute to a spirit can easily shift into a version telling you to steal instead. Likewise, while offering a

The Bronze Lady (Sleepy Hollow, NY): Depending on what rituals visitors use, they can either invoke her wrath or her blessing. Photo by the author.

gift should establish concordance with the spirits by placating them, sometimes it actually functions as a transgression and incites punishment. The "10 Penny Bridge" in Charleston, Indiana, illustrates this point: "[It is] haunted by a bum that was killed here. Legend is that if you place 10 pennies across the bridge in a row, turn your car and headlights off, when you try and start your car it acts like it don't [*sic*] want to start and your pennies will be scatterd [*sic*] or missing" (Southern Indiana Ghosts 2004:n.p.). Then again, even this punishment is a sort of reward for the legend tripper if it means the supernatural reveals itself through it. Perhaps this is why transgressive and concordant claims often accompany each other. In Oswego, New York, on the grounds of Fort Ontario, the ghost of George Fikes allegedly prowls the battlements and corridors. He is particularly fond of his grave in the Post Cemetery just outside the fort. If you step on his grave, presumably you will anger him because he will haunt you for the rest of your life. If you jump over it instead, however, he will be pleased and haunt someone else of your choosing (Hirsch 2013).

Sometimes, it is the legend trippers themselves, and not the legend, that confuse transgression and concordance. In one video, we see the familiar pattern of two legend trippers prowling around a cemetery at night.[4] They are looking for ghosts, but they are also engaged in a more unusual pursuit: looking for fallen headstones to upright. They pause every time headlights go by, ducking and whispering frantically in case it is the police, before resuming their efforts. Periodically, they also try to summon the ghosts. They seem to think they are honoring the dead and preserving the historic cemetery and, therefore, placating the spirits who will reward them with an encounter. However, they are not very skilled at this, and it looks like they will ultimately do more harm than good. In one shot, we see the first man heave a headstone upright, mound a small pile of dirt in front of it, and place a rock behind it. The result is a precariously balanced headstone that will fall again sooner than later, possibly incurring more damage in the process. In another scene, we see him aggressively kicking dirt off the front of another headstone. He says to the camera: "It's like out of respect, you know what I mean? If we don't do it, nobody else will." In another scene, he declares: "Alright, let's do an EVP[5] and get the fuck out of here. Our mission's done for the night." He turns on a digital recorder and addresses the spirits, explaining to them that their activities are meant as tribute: "We've been coming here kind of a lot fixing some graves for you guys. As you see, we mean no harm. Will you guys communicate with us?" He pauses, giving the ghosts time to answer before asking some standard, ritual questions: "Will you tell us your name?" Pause. "How old were you when you died?" Pause. Addressing the cameraman, he then indicates a nearby headstone that is leaning backwards: "We could pick that one up a little bit more too." He tries to pull it upright, but discovers it is already leaning against something. He then lifts a second stone upright that was lying flat on the ground and asks the unseen spirits: "Is there anything you wish to tell us?" as a car drives by on the road again. Worried about getting arrested, he remarks, "I'm pretty sure that was a fucking 5-o." His friend replies, "I don't think so." This somewhat bizarre ritual blurs the boundaries of ritual practice. It is both respectful and disrespectful, involving both preservation and desecration, and it illustrates a logic based on both concordance and transgression. Despite this confusion, it ultimately operates in the same way as any other legend trip.

VERBAL AND MATERIAL MAGIC

Another common pattern evident in most of the preceding examples is that legend-tripping rituals—whether based on angering or appeasing spirits—often involve a physical component. Whether an object is given or taken, damaged or preserved, that object has some meaningful connection with the legend and the supernatural, and thus, the rationale behind the associated activity shares that of traditional magical rites (Mauss [1902] 1982). The legend trippers cannot directly affect the invisible and insubstantial entities. Instead, they do so indirectly through the use of "trigger objects" (Koven 2007). By manipulating objects that have come into contact with the deceased, such as their belongings, ghost hunters practice a sort of "contagious" magic (Frazer [1890] 1996). They can also use objects representing the deceased in some way, like a photograph or an object similar to something the person enjoyed in life, which is a form of "imitative" magic. In either case, they believe the association holds some form of metaphysical connection to those entities. This rationale is so prevalent among legend trippers that it is more often than not used to explain why a place might be haunted in the first place.

There is no shortage of stories about places that become haunted because of their association with dead bodies: even if no one actually died there. Most cemeteries are a case in point, but any place will do. Built in 1771, the Publick House in Sturbridge, Massachusetts, has been around long enough to have accumulated numerous strange tales. One theory as to why it is haunted, though, is simply due to a claim that a body was stored here for a short time when the people transporting it had to stop and spend the night (D'Agostino 2007). Despite the short duration, the supernatural association from contact lingers on. A more creative example that uses the same logic of contagion applies to the USS *Con stellation*: a sloop of war docked in Baltimore's Inner Harbor. Critics point out that many of the ghosts that people claim to have encountered on board are actually from a *different* ship that bore the same name (Haunted Places n.d.c). The ghost of Neil Harvey is one such spirit. He was executed for abandoning his post in 1799, but the ship that sits in the harbor was not constructed until 1854. Fortunately, for believers, the new ship did incorporate "a small amount of material salvaged from" the earlier ship (Historic Ships n.d.:n.p.). The ghost must have been included along with the rest of the salvage.

Despite the importance of material contact and contagious association, the magical nature of legend trips is not limited to the use of symbolic *objects* alone. As one would expect from any ritualistic process, *words* can serve a magical purpose as well. Like objects, words can invoke the supernatural through symbolic associations. In Deep River, Connecticut, for instance, visitors to Fountain Hill Cemetery can visit a small headstone with the letters *XYZ* and nothing else engraved on it. By reciting these aloud three times, they can invoke the spirit's wrath.[6] Like those involving a physical component, verbal invocations operate according to a similar dualistic logic. For example, in contemporary ghost hunting, many investigators "call out" to spirits in hopes of getting a response (Hanks 2015). This practice does not require a material component—words alone will do the trick. Calling out can be used in either a concordant or transgressive way, just like the use of physical objects. While typically friendly in intention—asking the spirit its name, telling it you mean no harm, and so forth, it sometimes involves purposely taunting the alleged entity. Like the taboo against stealing from the dead, popular culture and folklore frequently warn that "you shouldn't make fun of supernatural things" (Warren, Warren, and Chase 1992:75). Thus, some ghost enthusiasts suggest taunting could similarly provoke a spirit to such an extent that it reveals itself, possibly by attacking those responsible for invoking its wrath. Verbalizations of either tone—friendly or aggressive, like other components of legend-trip ritualism, appear strange, but they are far from unique in a social context. While most legend trippers are unlikely to use magical terminology to describe their activity, from an anthropological perspective, these ritualistic behaviors are also recognizable as a sort of magic, which "comprises a rite and verbal formula projecting man's desires into the external world on a theory of human control" (Firth [1956] 1970:155).

Given their close relationship to magic and ritual, it should not be surprising to find that legend-tripping activities may unnerve nonparticipants who witness them. It is not unusual to mistake these activities as symptomatic of something more ominous, like when signs of ritualistic play are read as evidence of Satanism (Fine and Victor 1994) or when petty vandalism is misinterpreted as signs of black magic (Ellis 1993). In 1985, the ABC network aired a panicky "exposé" on secret satanic cults supposedly operating in America. As proof, it offered rumor, real crimes with little or no connection to the occult, and adolescent vandalism. The latter included suggestive graffiti, such as crudely scrawled pentagrams and the eye of providence "on public buildings and abandoned buildings, where police suspect secret meetings are being held" (Kunhardt and Wooden 1985:n.p.). One fearmongering mass-market book, coauthored by the infamous Warrens, warns that legend trippers really *are* tampering with satanic powers, even if they don't realize it: "On a lark, people frequently go to nearby graveyards and begin performing all sorts of dark rites that they've read about in books. These people think they're just having a little fun." The Warrens warn, however, that "what they're really doing is inviting satanic forces into the graveyard . . . and into their lives" (Warren et al. 1992:71–72). While there is certainly a serious side to legend tripping, it is likely that many legend trippers find these overreactions entertaining. For adolescents in particular, if "shocking adults" and achieving media notoriety are outcomes of their adventures, this may be "sufficient justification for the activities in the first place" (Fine and Victor 1994:72).

CONFLICT, CONFUSION, AND CRIME

Again, the majority of legend trips and their associated behaviors tend to be relatively benign. Unfortunately, this is not always the case: harassment, damage to property, harm to reputation, physical injury, and even death can occur.

Norma Sutcliffe suddenly found herself the not-so-proud owner of a "haunted" house after her Rhode Island home served as the inspiration for the horror film *The Conjuring* (2013). Soon, she was dealing with unwanted visitors of a different sort: "people trespassing on her property, bothering her neighbors and posting personal information on the internet" (Smith 2014:n.p.). She eventually had to move. In 2000, the remains of a Civil War veteran, General Elisha G. Marshall, were dug up in Rochester, New York's Mount Hope Cemetery. The newspaper accounts are vague regarding the nature of the "satanic symbols" that were "found near the grave," but his bones were scattered, and his skull remains missing to this day (*Chicago Tribune* 2000:n.p.). In 2016, a legend tripper died while looking for the Pope Lick Monster: a sort of half-goat man that roams a railroad trestle bridge in Louisville, Kentucky (Warren 2016). No creature was responsible for the deed; it was a very real train.

Many of the worst problems associated with legend tripping occur not because of the intrinsic character of the activity itself but from confrontations between legend trippers and nonparticipants. The problems that some legend trippers occasionally cause and the tendency to misinterpret what they are up to frequently prompt an overreaction on the part of witnesses or concerned authorities. These reactions might actually pose a threat to the legend trippers or anyone in the wrong place misidentified as one. Even without occult trappings, theft, or vandalism, many legend trips involve harassment or at least trespassing, and this alone can stir up tensions. This is especially so when nonparticipants find their homes or property the destination for repeated legend trips. The clash between these two parties, while again usually mild, can at times get out of control. For example, one August night in 2006, in Worthington, Ohio:

> Tessa [and four of her female friends] drove slowly up Milton Avenue, past the [Walnut Grove] cemetery's entrance and parked the car beside the home. Some of the girls thought it was deserted because of the tangle of trees, winding trails and generally untamed appearance. But others heard it was owned by an old woman whom kids called a witch because of her gray hair and the large black caldron she used as a planter in the front yard. [Four of the girls got out of the car and approached the house.] To make them jump, Una honked the horn. They ran back to the car, giggling and squealing. Awakened by the commotion, Allen S. Davis climbed out of bed and picked up his .22-caliber Marlin rifle. [After repeated incidents of teens attempting to break into his house at night] he and his mother . . . who owns the house, no longer felt safe. . . . Rachel fell into Tessa's lap. The girls thought Rachel was joking until Una saw blood matting her long, blond hair. (Pyle 2007:n.p.)

Sadly, as might have been predicted given the ostensive nature of these activities, the imagined danger that was the inspiration for the legend trip became real precisely because of the legend trip. The ritual intended to provoke spirits instead tormented the homeowners. Rachel survived, but she was badly wounded and, after a long recovery, remained partly paralyzed. The homeowner, Sondra Davis, passed away in 2009 while her son continued to serve his sixteen-year sentence for the shooting (Narciso 2011). The house itself lay empty, overgrown, and abandoned—the property stigmatized—until it was sold at auction for a heavily discounted price to new owners in 2013 who planned to rehabilitate it (Narciso 2013). Doubtless, many potential buyers were put off by the prospect of taking possession of a property that might continue to be haunted—by legend trippers.

The "curious case of St. Ann's Retreat" in Utah, as documented by Lisa Gabbert (2015:147), provides important insight into conflict between legend trippers and nonparticipants.[7] It also illustrates the important role legend plays in both initiating and perpetuating that conflict. As a summer retreat for Catholic nuns, St. Ann's was already out of place in the Mormon-majority area. Its remote setting and increasingly rundown condition did not help matters any. Mormon youth in the area soon began circulating legends, including the claim that nuns who had become pregnant by Catholic priests came here to murder their unwanted babies by drowning them in the facility's swimming pool. The restless shades of these babies haunt the site. Not surprisingly, this motivates many adolescents to visit the retreat to test these claims. The ensuing legend trips "grew into a form of harassment . . . which included nocturnal visits and frequent incidents of vandalism" (Gabbert 2015:157). This had two immediate consequences. First, the destruction caused by vandalism made the place even more difficult to maintain, contributing to its spooky, rundown appearance. Second, it understandably "frightened the sisters" who "acquired guard dogs" to protect themselves (Gabbert 2015:157). The youth soon incorporated the dogs into the legend, claiming that hellhounds prowled the accursed grounds. Encountering the dogs, or hearing them bay in the distance, became a supernatural encounter and encouraged further legend trips. By 1987, matters had become so bad that the diocese decided to sell off the property to a new private owner, but the old legends persisted and so did the legend trips.

This drama reached a crescendo in October of 1997. That night, thirty-eight teens made the trip out to the retreat where they encountered its caretaker and two of his friends:

> [The men] took it upon themselves to protect the property from the continuous stream of young legend questers, who had caused approximately $100,000 worth of damage over the past few years. . . . Armed

with shotguns mounted with flashlights, plastic handcuffs, and the element of surprise, [they] captured the teens by jumping from the bushes,
ordering them to "Hit the ground!" and firing the guns over their heads.
The teens were searched, handcuffed with plastic ties, and led to the
bottom of the empty swimming pool. The men then tied a continuous
nylon rope around the neck of the teens . . . so that when one person
moved, the rope tightened around the necks of the other prisoners.
The teens were told that the ropes were tied to explosives [and that]
they would shoot their legs off if they tried to run. . . . One of the men
put a pistol to the head of an Asian American boy, called him a "gook"
and threated to shoot, and then discharged the pistol into the ground.
(Gabbert 2015:158–59)

This horrifying scenario is the product of both sides—legend trippers and nonparticipants—acting badly. The excesses of each party encourage excess on the
part of the other and escalate until some dramatic incident brings matters to a
head. The teens' interest in the property is understandable and so is the men's
desire to defend it. It is harder to understand how it transformed into such a
potentially deadly situation. Fortunately, it did not come to that. In the end, it
was the men, and not the teens, who faced criminal charges. This conclusion
remained controversial among community members, some of whom felt the
teens were not entirely without blame.

Accounts like these are fortunately rare, but they understandably receive the
lion's share of attention from local news outlets. This, in turn, likely influences
the broader public perception of legend tripping by pushing it in a decidedly
negative direction. However, for others, the media's preoccupation with the
more dramatic incidents in the annals of legend tripping can actually lead
to more problematic outcomes: the accounts serve as models to copy ostensively. In this way, rare "violent or sociopathic acts" (Ellis 1989:202) can become
more common or at least perpetuated by both legend trippers and those who
encounter them. If anything, these dramatic scenarios only increase interest
by adding to the legends of these locations. St. Ann's Retreat remains both a
popular topic for legend tellers and a popular location for legend trippers, with
many recent accounts simply incorporating the events of 1997 into the living
legend. An episode of *Ghost Adventures* set at St. Ann's provides a particularly
irresponsible and sensationalistic example of this continued interest (Frascino
2016). It focuses on the "hostage situation," incorporating it into the older legend cycle by suggesting the two are supernaturally related. For example, the
show depicts interviews with some of the teenagers, now adults, who were
there that night. These witnesses claim to have seen a hellhound before the
incident occurred, a sure sign that something bad was about to happen. In

one of their assailant's eyes, they saw signs of demonic possession. Real-world assault becomes supernatural encounter in the shadow cast by the legend. This incorporation of real events with the legend indicates that both future legend trips and the potential for deadly interactions are quite possible. The case of St. Ann's is far from unique in this respect.

LEGENDS AS BLUEPRINTS

Given the range of unusual behaviors associated with legend trips, it is reasonable to wonder, Where do legend trippers get the idea to do these things? The precise formula for what must be done is typically provided by the legend itself. The plot of the legend, such as it is, inevitably includes one or more protagonists that engage in some sort of behavior that resulted in a fantastic outcome. This can be in the form of a third-person narrative (i.e., a fabulate) or a first-person recollection (i.e., a memorate). As I discussed earlier, this is usually presented in the form of a warning (i.e., do not do *x* or else *y*), which actually functions as a challenge or dare to legend trippers. So, these apparently proscribed actions are actually "*prescribed* actions that, according to legend, have the potential to elicit a supernatural experience" when copied (Kinsella 2011:28, emphasis added). In other words, warnings about what you should *not* do serve the precise opposite end: as a model for what *to* do.[8]

This is because legend tripping is a type of ritual that occurs through reenactment. Those involved are acting out some part of the original legend, which typically describes a "tragic event from the past" (Dégh and Vázsonyi 1983:17). To do so, they must "take on, by turns, the roles of legend villains and victims as they recreate the storied events" (Lindahl 2005:165). This often includes simply taking on the role of previous legend trippers. It is through this ritualized reenactment that they call up the supernatural and, in so doing, "simultaneously expand the tale by adding their experiences to the core narrative" (Lindahl 2005:165). Iowa City's Oakland Cemetery is the site of a locally famous legend that illustrates this point. One of the monuments includes the rather imposing statue of an angel, its patina turned nearly black with age and weathering. The angel looms overhead, arms and wings partly outstretched, face peering down at the grave beneath it. A number of local legends warn that the spirit's wrath will be invoked if a visitor "touches, kisses, or otherwise bothers the angel," variously warning that "the offender will die within 24 hours, seven years, or at an unspecified time" (Bird 1994:199). These same legends tell of previous times when offense and subsequent punishment allegedly occurred. One story recounts, "My sister went there when she was in high school to write an article for the school newspaper, she kissed the angel at midnight on Halloween (gasp!) and set out to prove that she wouldn't die within the year." Fortunately, she did not die. "She was run over by a Good Humor wagon the week after, though" (Bird 1994:199).

In this particular version of the story, kissing the angel serves to call up its supernatural punishment. Those hearing the legend can test it by reenacting it: by placing their own lips upon the forbidden statue just like the original protagonist to see whether anything happens. Again, we can make some sense of this process by comparing it to more orthodox religious rituals. To some extent, for instance, legend-tripping rituals bear similarities to certain elements of rites like the aforementioned Catholic Mass. Here, the priest and parishioners take on the roles of Jesus giving bread and wine to the disciples at the Last Supper: "Bread and wine are consecrated by a priest, and the elements . . . distributed among the faithful . . . [T]he bread and wine become the body and blood of Christ" (Goring 1994:329). Of course, the faithful may feel a sense of divine presence or closeness with God following this ceremony, and so likewise, their own experiential narratives serve as an extension of the original events retold through this ostensive reenactment.

Interesting crossovers can occur, in which the more informal ritualism of the legend trip consciously copies institutionalized religious rituals. One sociologist observed a curious instance of this sort while conducting participant observation with a group of paranormal investigators. He "witnessed investigators blending conventional and paranormal beliefs with a strong faith in science and technology." "One team," for example, "performed a communion service in a Catholic rectory that was supposedly inhabited by demons as well as the spirit of a pedophilic priest. Three team members sat in the parlor, lit a candle, and laid out bread and grape juice." A member of the group who was a practicing Catholic led the ritual, "but in order to provoke an angry reaction by the ghostly priest he also gave communion to Chad, an avowed atheist" (Eaton 2015:403).

There are, of course, limitations to these comparisons, not the least of which is the absence of anything in a proper Mass approaching a "dare" or, more generally, an act intended to provoke the supernatural into revealing itself. Dares and transgression are more in the domain of legend-tripping rituals than institutionalized religion, and this difference is worth future consideration. However, the ritualistic and reenactment characteristics of both legend tripping and proper religious ceremonies are informative, nonetheless.

One important aspect of the ritualistic behavior required for legend tripping that has received little attention is the degree of specificity involved. Some legends are specific in conveying what actions must be performed, the exact location within a place to perform them, as well as the specific time or date for the performance. I think of these as "particularized rituals." One such legend is associated with a certain tombstone in Bonds Chapel Cemetery in the small town of West Baden Springs, Indiana. Here, the image or stain of a chain bisected by a similar image to form something resembling a cross mars the side of Floyd E. Pruett's memorial. The legend surrounding it has remained popular for many years, with various versions attempting to explain the origin of the "chain." One typical version of the legend claims that Pruett murdered his wife for being unfaithful, strangling her with a chain and leaving her in the woods outside town (Green n.d.). However, no one was able to prove he did it. The chain mysteriously appeared on his grave shortly after his death as a supernatural sign of guilt. Various versions of the legend also generally agree that the number of links on the chain have changed over time: "a year to the day after his death, a chain began forming on his tombstone. Year after year, more links appeared until they formed a cross on the side of the tomb" (Schlosser 2012:22). Other accounts claim that the number of links varies depending on when you visit the grave: "At night you can see links forming on the tombstone in the shape of a cross, 13 links up and down and 7 from left to right. The cross is completed at midnight and then disappears by morning" (Gross 2016:n.p.).

The invitation to legend trip is made in part through three claims: (1) that this mysterious image of a chain can be seen if you visit; (2) that you can also witness the number of links vary; and (3) that something will happen to you if you should hazard touching the chain. For the latter two claims to occur, moreover, one must follow specific directions. William Clements's (1980) now-classic study of the chain on the tombstone includes examples of these directions. One of his informants advises that "the links on the chain will vary. I mean, sometimes there'll be seven or eight; sometimes there'll be up to fifteen or sixteen." He warns, "If you touch it when it has thirteen links on it, you will be killed by the chain. . . . But if you touch it during the time of the full moon, you're supposed to go insane or lose your mind, you know." Perhaps even more bizarre, "there's been several incidents of people who touch it, you know, during [the] full moon; and, well, they get chased by a big bright light all the way back to Orleans" (Clements 1980:259).

Overall, this legend offers a fairly detailed set of instructions for prospective legend trippers. It identifies a specific cemetery (Bonds Chapel Cemetery), a particular grave within that cemetery (Pruett's), specific conditions that should be present when you go (at night and during a full moon), and directions on what to do once you get there (touch the chain). Different accounts from different speakers can certainly vary, but any given version of the legend provides specific directions.

GENERALIZED LEGEND TRIPPING

While detailed accounts like the above have received the lion's share of scholarly attention, legends do not always provide this much specificity. In fact, many legends are frustratingly vague, but this doesn't mean that they can't guide ostensive reenactments. To the contrary, sometimes prospective legend trippers are not attempting to investigate a specific legend at all. Instead, they might enact a more generic sort of legend-inspired behavior. Consider the case of the archetypal haunted house. Literary scholars (e.g., Bailey 1999), folklorists (e.g., Grider 2007b), and other experts frequently point out that popular culture conveys a clichéd image of what a haunted house looks like. In discussing this image in film, visual studies scholar Barry Curtis (2008:30) notes that its supernatural character "is instantly recognizable—seen from behind trees, from a moving car, from the road that leads to its gate or from its own garden path." Observers notice that "there is something unsettling about the house's brooding self-possession, its visual complexity and its anthropomorphic façade," suggesting it is "a troubled place, marked by neglect, strange habits and failed rituals of order and maintenance" (Curtis 2008:30). According to Grider (2007b), people might consider a house to be haunted based on its appearance alone. Such a house will typically have predictable features, like "Victorian and Second Empire" architectural styles with "mansard roofs, towers and turrets, multiple stories, and ornate architectural embellishments" (Grider 2007b:146). It might have broken and perhaps boarded-up windows, and it may be located "on an isolated hilltop, surrounded by a high broken fence, with leafless dead trees" (Grider 2007b:147). This image, and its associated meaning, is so familiar that it can be used as a sort of shorthand to communicate the haunted-house motif. It is frequently used as a Halloween decoration (Grider 2007b), for example. Likewise, a flyer in my possession that advertises seasonal ghost tours at the Harriet Beecher Stowe Center in Hartford, Connecticut, does not actually contain any information about what the tour will consist of. It simply portrays an image of the famous author's home—an appropriately Victorian Gothic Revival house—in negative colors flanked by leafless trees. This is sufficient to ostensively communicate the legend theme, and the title of the event, "Spirits at Stowe," is largely superfluous. Indeed, it might be this classic haunted-house archetype that gives rise to legends in the first place for some locations. Even in the absence of specific legends that a particular house is home to ghosts, some people will be inspired to explore such buildings and look for spirits anyway. My research suggests that they can draw on generic haunted-house lore instead. They can ask themselves: What *usually* happens in a haunted house? How do people *usually* get ghosts to appear?

In addition to haunted-looking houses, a similar pattern holds for other suitably spooky-looking places, like cemeteries, old bridges, tunnels, and so on where "the scene itself . . . suggests the horror to be met" (Dégh 1969:80). As Tucker (2007:33) observes in the context of colleges and universities, "If a campus building looks old, creepy, and mysterious, it probably has a ghost."

This likely explains why the most prominent building alleged to be haunted at the Ohio State University, my alma mater, is the dramatic-looking Orton Hall. Built in 1893 in the Romanesque style, the structure is comprised of native stone and features an imposing arched entrance, a main tower complete with gargoyles, and at least two ghosts (Smith 2003). Social scientists have reached similar conclusions about the role appearance plays in determining whether a place might be haunted. Hanks (2015), for example, notes that the British ghost hunters she conducted her ethnographic fieldwork with often became excited about the possibility of a place being haunted based on mere appearance. Again, the effect is not limited to houses but to any place that fits preconceived cultural ideals of what a haunted place looks like, including pubs. She argues: "Haunted-ness alone does not recommend a site as an ideal space for investigation. [The ghost hunters] often pointed to the site's architecture, interior furnishings, and overall management as indicators of its desirability" (Hanks 2015:142). Discussing the case of the Royal Oak in York, England, she describes how, "at first, my investigator friends simply applauded the 'realness' of the pub. It was dark and not entirely well kept." It was for these reasons that "on several occasions, investigators noted that they would 'love to investigate' this pub." Interestingly enough, they had no actual knowledge of a haunting or other paranormal activity in the building. Instead, "the atmosphere, or rather, the aura of the pub served as the primary form of attraction" (Hanks 2015:142).

Similarly, as discussed in chapter 2, a wide range of types of places or even just characteristics of a place are frequently associated with the perception of a possible haunting even in the absence of any specific legend. Places like mental hospitals, cemeteries, or orphanages very frequently give rise to the expectation of a haunting. Legends associated with the University of New Haven's Maxcy Hall consistently link the spirits believed to dwell therein to its previous life as the New Haven County Temporary Home for Dependent and Neglected Children (e.g., Boynton 2013). Characteristics of a place that might cause similar assumptions include abandonment, age, or the knowledge that some tragedy occurred there, such as a murder, suicide, or a disastrous event, like building collapses, explosions, or battles. These calamities often echo among future visitors in the form of supernatural expectation—again, even if there is no known account of previous encounters.

Given that sites of this sort are commonly suspected of being haunted, how might someone proceed if they want to investigate one further? Without a specific legend to guide their behavior—without an existing narrative to copy or reenact, must they give up the ghost, so to speak, and abandon the attempt altogether? The answer is, of course, "no." Consider the case of Gunntown Cemetery in Naugatuck, Connecticut. It is one of the more popular cemeteries to investigate in the region and is often the topic of conversation on discussion

Orton Hall, The Ohio State University (Columbus, OH): Its dramatic appearance justifies its haunted reputation or, perhaps, gave rise to it in the first place. Photo by the author.

boards or in printed collections of local lore. Though people visit it frequently looking for ghosts and other strange phenomena, there is no specific legend about the place to guide them in the attempt (Bendici 2009; Ghostwatcherz 2011). There are no tales of a long-ago tragic suicide that is repeated in spectral form on a certain day at a certain hour. There is no report of a not-quite-dead witch who will return to smite anyone who dares to knock upon her headstone three times on Halloween night. There is no whispered rumor of an ancient curse that will lay low those bold enough to sit on a particular grave while reciting the "Battle Hymn of the Republic." No legends like these exist, but still many people come to experience the uncanny. Given this problem, how do legend trippers invoke the supernatural if they don't know exactly what happened here in the past to guide an attempt to recreate the effect? How does one reenact an unknown event?

Interestingly, while no cohesive legend is available, memorates concerning previous adventures in the cemetery are plentifully available. However, these tend to be fragmentary, and few of them are consistent with one another such that they could serve as a clear guide for ostension. In preparation for my own visit to the site, I reviewed a number of these brief memorates and encountered a bewildering array of disassociated experience claims. Examining a sample of

Gunntown Cemetery (Naugatuck, CT): Despite lacking a coherent legend to guide ostension, it remains a popular destination for legend tripping. Photo by the author.

these, given below, illustrates the problem this poses for anyone interested in investigating Gunntown Cemetery and its associated claims. Here, I summarize some of these claims, drawing from three dissimilar websites.

Damned Connecticut

The longest and most detailed of the three websites, Damned Connecticut (Bendici 2009), consists of a lengthy summary of the location and the author's legend trip to it. Following that, there is a long discussion with numerous users posting comments and experiences. According to this source, you might encounter any of the following:

- Apparitions (a man with a lantern leading a horse, a boy near the rear wall, a black dog in the cemetery or across the street in the woods, a figure in the back seat of your car, a man gliding alongside your moving car, a "dark mass" floating over the hood of your car, "shadowy figures" among the graves, a phantom man being hanged, a crawling ghost, a white ghost at the back of the cemetery, the ghost of a sailor near the gate, or Deacon Osborn—one of those buried there—by the headstone of his wife)
- Other visual phenomena (the vision of a carnival on fire, red eyes peering over the cemetery wall at you, fog on an otherwise clear night, a cat that suddenly appears in a different part of the cemetery than where

you first encounter it, or the lights turning on all at once in the house behind the cemetery and a figure pacing abnormally quickly within)

- Sounds with no source (phantom music, children's laughter, children's singing, children's screams, whistling, voices, chains rattling, rumbling sounds, or disembodied animal noises in the bushes)
- Moving objects (a flag on a grave site moving on its own, losing a phone only to find it placed on a tombstone, or the front gate opening and closing on its own)
- Strange feelings (a sense of creepiness, a sense of presence, or "immense feelings of doom" near the back left corner)
- Visual phenomena appearing only in photographs (orbs, ghostly faces, or the word "run" in the grass)
- Audio phenomena appearing only in recordings (carousel music or voices)
- Physical contact with unseen entities (cold spots, getting scratched, kicked in the groin, or knocked down, having sudden pain in your neck, tugging on your pants, being touched on the posterior, having bruising and handprints on you the next morning, or getting attacked by strange flies)
- Other experiences (anomalous electromagnetic fields, possession by the spirits, or having your car kicked by an unseen entity)

Ghostwatcherz

Ghostwatcherz (2011) gives a shorter overview of the cemetery along with a summary of the author's experiences there, followed by a brief discussion that includes other visitors to the website. According to this source, visitors might experience the following:

- Strange feelings (that you have been there before or odd comfort in the middle of the night)
- Sounds ("old time music" on the right side of the cemetery with no source)
- Moving Objects (the front gate closing and trapping you inside)

Ghostvillage

Ghostvillage (2008) is a web forum discussion in response to a user asking how well supervised the cemetery is after hours, presumably gauging the risk of trespassing. The discussion soon shifts to include claims of the sort of phenomena one might experience there:

- Apparitions ("a small shadow figure [in] the back right corner of the wall" or an apparition near a large tree in the front corner)
- Other visual phenomena (orbs or spectral mist)
- Audio phenomena that appears on recordings (ghostly voices in the field behind the cemetery or near the front gate)
- Moving objects (a self-closing front gate)
- Strange feelings (a certain "feel" to the place "unlike any other cemetery")
- Other experiences ("crazy" electromagnetic field readings near the front of the cemetery)

A comparison of these claims shows there are a few repeated elements, such as the closing gate and mysterious music. Overall, however, there is an incredibly diverse array of possible phenomena to encounter, an equally diverse range of specific locations within the cemetery in which to encounter them when a location is actually specified, and no explicit directions for how to invoke the supernatural like the legend-tripping literature would lead us to expect to find. Of course, there are many more sources for vague and conflicting information than just these three websites to consider as well. Despite all this, the curious come anyway in the hopes of producing their own memorable tale and manage to conduct a legend trip. How do they proceed in this endeavor?

As indicated in this example, legend tripping can still occur in the absence of a specific guiding legend, as it can take on the form of a "generalized ritual" instead. When a guiding legend is absent, participants can enact a more generic understanding of legendry that is appropriate to that *type* of setting. Instead of testing claims that a specific set of behaviors will yield a certain response in a certain place, here legend trippers apply a broader rationale: a general understanding of how certain phenomena are expected to operate in light of a larger, more diffuse legend structure. To provoke a supernatural response, they can engage in any behaviors that they have heard about from other legendary accounts that might be consistent with the current setting and their expectations associated with that type of place. That is, they generalize known folklore to a novel context. This process draws on a shared "belief language" surrounding the phenomenon (Ellis 2003:passim): that is, a culturally or subculturally shared set of expectations for how a given phenomenon is understood to behave.[9] This "convenient cultural language," therefore, not only allows for the discussion of shared uncanny experiences but also for the invocation of them through shared ritual behaviors (Ellis 2003:113). Returning to the example of haunted houses, a known legend may specifically describe who the ghost is, how they became a ghost, and what is needed to make the ghost appear (or speak, or move an object, etc.). In other words, it includes a detailed blueprint for a particular ritual. But in reaction to cases of which there is no specific legend and instead a house simply "looks" haunted based on shared expectations of how a haunted is supposed to look, ghost hunters have developed a range of techniques that are applied to *any* alleged haunting to test its veracity. Likewise, if Gunntown Cemetery *looks* like it is haunted, legend trippers can apply their general knowledge of ghosts and ghost hunting. This body of general lore is so vast that it helps account for the many diverse claims regarding Gunntown. Without the coherence imposed by an overarching legend narrative, different investigators have tried different approaches during their visits there and produced different and conflicting outcomes.

Some places are even more diverse in terms of their legendry. All of Gunntown's claims, diverse though they may be, deal primarily with ghosts of some sort. Many towns have a place where a wider diversity of legends congregate. Spanning the towns of Hamden and Bethany in Connecticut, a street called Downs Road is locally famous in this way. Most of this long street is fairly remote and wooded, with houses spread widely apart between the trees. Another part of it is abandoned and overgrown, closed entirely to vehicular traffic, and blocked off at both ends. This has, of course, encouraged speculation about why it was closed and what can be found there by intrepid explorers. In any case, the entirety of the street is linked to a range of legends. Downs Road has its ghosts, certainly, but it also has a monster (possibly a very short Bigfoot), maniacs, UFOs, Melon Heads, and even Pukwudgies (Nowinski 2012). The latter is allegedly a sort of fairy from Native American lore that can become invisible at will (Muise 2016). In a place like this, legend trippers have even greater license than they do at Gunntown to borrow behavioral cues from nearly any legend they want and to interpret whatever they encounter as something supernatural.

Nearly any paranormal website, televised ghost hunt, or book of ghost stories can serve as source material to learn about these generalized legend-tripping methods. You only need to apply the example set by similar cases to your own investigation. Even better, numerous sources explicitly teach these rituals for application wherever phantoms may be found. Parapsychologist and ghost hunter Loyd Auerbach provides an early example of this sort of approach in his seminal guide *ESP, Hauntings, and Poltergeists: A Parapsychologist's Handbook* (1986). Among many other bits of advice that he gives to aspiring investigators, he suggests, "Try some 'field experiments' if possible (and if appropriate). As best you can, reconstruct the events as they happened, and duplicate any patterns related to the experience . . ." (Auerbach 1986:353). This might require that investigators "put everyone in the same place they were when they saw the apparition and go through the motions of the experience as they reported it." They should also "try to re-create the same conditions as when an apparition was seen or when an object was moved." Here, the author is not presuming to know anything about the specific case his imagined audience is interested in. Rather, he suggests that there are general patterns to such phenomena that can be exploited to make it manifest itself. This involves, once again, reenacting the original events that supposedly led up to the supernatural encounter. This advice presupposes that a previous claim of supernatural encounter is known or at least knowable; it asks that the investigator act as a folklorist and learn more about the tale even as it suggests that a general approach to hauntings can be applied.

Even without this information, when specific claims are unknown, unknowable, or do not yet exist, legend tripping in spooky places is possible. For this, advice of an even more generic nature is available. One of the most common ritual requirements, as illustrated across a vast number of legends, is that one can best encounter the supernatural after dark. As Grider (2007a:135) notes, darkness is a standard expectation even in children's stories where it establishes the proper "legend climate" to tell spooky tales. Of course, it also creates an atmosphere conducive to *performing* legends. As most traditional tales as well as most episodes of any popular "reality" ghost hunting show illustrate, most people expect the spirits to be especially active at night or in unlit places. Legend trips can be conducted in daylight as well, but the conduciveness of darkness to the overall mood and sense of expectation makes night-time excursions the preferred option. And this preference is not limited to ghost hunting. Other legend trips, aimed at achieving contact with other paranormal entities, tend to privilege darkness as well. For example, in Bigfoot hunting and in other cryptozoological legend trips, one can find evidence of the elusive creatures—such as tracks or strangely bent trees—just fine during the day. If you want to encounter an actual creature itself though, you had best seek it at night since "they are said to be mostly nocturnal" (Robinson 2016:15). This includes Bigfoot, which is strange since, as this author correctly notes, all great apes are diurnal.

This expectation does not seem to have any compelling ecological or otherwise naturalistic explanations to support it. Rather, the logic is more ritualistic in character. Darkness, as a prerequisite for encountering the supernatural, might be the clearest example of a factor that *causes* supernatural encounters. From a social perspective, as explored in the previous chapter, this is because it sets the right mood and sense of expectancy. From a legend-tripping perspective, it is because there is something almost magical about the properties of darkness and night that set the right "conditions" for the supernatural to manifest itself. Contemporary ghost hunters have developed a number of explanations for why this might be the case, which tend to bypass psychological explanations. If spirits are luminescent, for example, that light will best be seen in the darkness. Darkness, and nighttime in particular, might also be best because the Earth's natural magnetic sphere is calmer, less affected by solar radiation: "when the electromagnetic environment is calm, it is obviously easier for us to find and follow spectral manifestations [and] it should also be easier for spirits to materialize" (Warren 2003:127).[10]

The use of various devices is another frequently encountered form of ritual behavior that is generic in character rather than specific to any particular legend. Ghost-hunting handbooks almost universally advocate using still and video cameras at nearly any haunted site since these are believed to be capable of seeing things the human eye cannot (e.g., Ellis 2014). EMF meters have become popular as well, and guidebooks generically recommend them for spirit-hunting legend trips because these energy fields "are often associated with ghosts and paranormal activity" (Balzano 2008:32). Or you might hold a "vigil." While the term is little used these days, the method has become popularized by "reality" television shows. It involves an overnight stakeout in a hopefully haunted place with "teams and equipment on site, under controlled conditions, so that there is reliable observation of the paranormal, should it arise" (Spencer and Wells 1995:127). Additional methods, too numerous to list here, are available for consideration. Yet they all share a general ostensive logic toward probing legendary phenomena, even in the absence of a specific guiding legend, because they have all allegedly been used in the past by other legend trippers at other times and under similar circumstances to successfully call up the supernatural.

It is for this reason that, among the numerous aforementioned claims about what can be experienced at Gunntown Cemetery or Downs Road, there are many familiar-looking items that could well apply to any haunted location. To find ghosts there—or anywhere else, you might try using EMF meters, audio recordings to catch disembodied voices, and so forth regardless of the absence of a specific legend to guide the attempt. Many of these activities become transmitted as brief memorates of the sort I have considered, and, fragmentary though they may be, they can serve to inform further legend trips. While the current panoply of divergent memorates might be more overwhelming than informative, the overall message that uncanny events can be found at places like these coupled with the ability to enact generalized ritual behavior ensures that they will remain popular legend-tripping destinations for the foreseeable future. For want of a coherent narrative, the alleged cause or nature of the hauntings remains murky, but, if anything, this absence only adds to the allure and mystery of these places. Already there is abundant speculation in these accounts over the source of the uncanny phenomena. Various historical events and personalities local to both areas have been singled out for consideration as causes. It is possible that, over time, some particular account or set of related accounts will become the dominant narrative and a set of specific ritual behaviors will replace the generalized approach. A simple count of the

locations within the Gunntown Cemetery mentioned in the memorates as paranormal hotspots indicates that some—like the front gate or back corner—are
more popularly cited than others. Perhaps, with time, one of these locations
will serve as the nucleus upon which these nebulous accounts will coalesce
into a more coherent legend.

In summary, two modes of behavior can occur at legend-tripping sites: particularized and generalized ritualism.[11] The latter can occur when no specific
legend is associated with a site—or at least where such a legend is not known
to participants—or in conjunction with a known legend, in which case particular rituals associated with that legend might also occur alongside them.[12]
This distinction broadens the scope of behaviors that are ritualistic in nature
and, more to the point, those that can be classified and understood as forms
of legend tripping. The concept of "legend tripping" itself is greatly expanded
when we consider how legends in general, not just specific legends, can motivate and guide ostensive behavior. This pattern holds when we consider another
little-explored ritualistic element: mood.

SETTING THE MOOD

Beyond the various ritualistic behaviors discussed so far, the proper attitude or
mood often serves as a ritualistic requirement, although, strictly speaking, they
are not behaviors per se. In the previous chapter, I demonstrated how the right
mood prepares legend trippers to entertain the possibility of a supernatural
encounter. In the ritual phase, proper attitude, like proper behavior, also serves
a quasi-magical role as a necessary prerequisite for actually calling forth the
supernatural. Prior scholarship on legend trips largely considers the *normative*
dimension of attitudes. Though such work might hint at possible *ritual* dimensions as well, this seems to be considered an implicit or tacitly understood
requirement. In the traditional adolescent legend trip, for example: "The 'rules'
of the game are that no-one should show undue fear, at least until everybody
else does, and those who show weakness are taunted and tormented. . . ." (Bird
1994:203). Adolescents often display a sort of gendered division of emotional
labor in the endeavor. Boys must "show fearlessness and daring," while girls
should act "appropriately terrified" (Bird 1994:204).

Sometimes, attitudinal requirements are expressed more explicitly but not
necessarily in a straightforward manner. Carl Lindahl (2005:175) summarizes
the feelings expressed by an informant toward the attitudes she and the rest of
her group displayed during a legend-tripping episode during which frightening
events occurred: "They approached the haunted site a little too enthusiastically,
with attitudes a bit too irreverent to suit the tragic circumstances that they

were commemorating in their nighttime ritual." One of D. Waskul's (2016:84) informants likewise believes that a frightening supernatural encounter he had while on a legend trip was "a manifestation in response to this disrespect" one of his friends had displayed by running around a cemetery and laying down on the graves. In instances like these, we see another "warning" ignored: be respectful. Disregarding it and expressing too much ebullience offends the supernatural and invokes its wrath. Of course, this is exactly what is supposed to happen, and so, the necessary attitude is the one that is expressly forbidden. It is not about maintaining the norms of the group, but rather about fulfilling the requirements of the ritual.

Similar suggestions regarding proper mood are prominent among contemporary ghost-hunting legend trips. These vary, as might be expected, instructing that those hoping to see a ghost maintain a mood ranging anywhere from serious to lighthearted. Yet they also tend to be more explicit and straightforward than the examples above. For instance, one set of suggestions advises that "atmosphere is important" (Spencer and Wells 1995:143). This is because "research seems to indicate that when the investigators know each other well, and the witnesses feel comfortable in their presence, then things are more likely to happen." Therefore, in the interest "of making everyone feel comfortable," they recommend "that a sympathetic attitude is more helpful than a suspicious and antagonistic one."[13] This suggestion again clearly indicates that having the right attitude, just as much as performing the right behaviors, is part of a set of ritualistic requirements that must be fulfilled to encounter the supernatural. The correct attitude encourages it to come forth by setting the appropriate, apparently psychic, conditions. Note also that these suggestions fit the distinction I made earlier regarding generalized ritualism: the proper mood might apply to any potentially haunted place. Although I have yet to encounter such a case, it is possible to conceive of a scenario in which a particular legend might call for a specific mood as well.

Just as the right mindset or mood might be specified as a ritualistic prerequisite and conducive for spirit invocation, so might the wrong mindset violate these requirements and cause the invocation to fail. In fact, simply having someone with the wrong mindset present at the ritual is commonly considered to inhibit supernatural encounters. Hall's discussion of legend trips to the haunted "Big Tunnel" in Indiana provides an example of this problem. One informant "glumly" told him of a visit to the haunted railroad tunnel in which the group invited a friend along whose mindset conflicted with the legend-trip requirements. Rather than play along, she harshly criticized the absurdity of the entire endeavor and the legends they told her about the tunnel. This "ruined the trip for everyone" (Hall 1980:255). While it is not necessary for all participants to fully believe in the supernatural in order for a legend trip to succeed, they must at least be willing to play along: to entertain the possibility and keep an "open mind" that is receptive to suggestion and cues from the group. The inclusion of a participant on this particular journey who was openly critical of such possibilities, however, made it impossible for the group to establish the right mindset, and so, the legend trip failed.

This phenomenon seems well known among believers in the supernatural, who are cautious of skeptics being present during their adventures. One legend-tripping author suggests that if you want to have a successful EVP session, in which the spirits decide to talk, you need to have someone running the session who takes it seriously: "If they don't believe in what they're doing, then nothing is going to happen" (Robinson 2016:150). Not surprisingly, even though many believers are aware of the power of belief, they tend to explain it in different terms. They generally argue that there is some unseen or psychic dampening effect that doubting minds have on local conditions. This inhibits mystical forces from manifesting. Psychics are notorious for making such claims when they fail to make a convincing demonstration of their abilities: "their powers diminish markedly whenever skeptics arrive" (Sagan 1996:241). This is especially so under experimental conditions designed specifically to test those powers in part, the psychics and their advocates claim, because of the skeptical mindset of researchers, which is not conducive to their abilities. James Randi (1982:40)—a critical, scientific investigator of paranormal claims—notes that claimants accuse skeptical supervisors of creating "negative vibrations" that adversely affect their abilities. They commonly use this reasoning to explain why their powers fail under rigorous oversight. Beginning with a discussion of two Yorkshire girls who claimed to have photographed fairies in the early twentieth century—a bizarre proposition that was famously promoted by Sir Arthur Conan Doyle in *The Coming of the Fairies* (1922), Randi identifies how this defense has been used by a range of paranormalists. "We are told," he writes, "that subjects do not do well when persons with 'negative vibrations' are nearby." He gives several examples. For instance, "adults were not allowed to be present when Elsie and Frances took the photos. The excuse was that otherwise the fairies would not appear." Meanwhile, "in modern parapsychology, experimenters insist that only persons with a sympathetic attitude (and who therefore believe in the paranormal) be present. The subjects [claiming to possess special powers], too, insist on this." He notes how the psychic, Uri Geller, "has gone so far as to refuse to perform when I am present" (Randi 1982:40). In cases like this, some might interpret the claim of negative vibrations as simply a face-saving excuse for failure. Given the context of legend tripping, however, this sort of critical skepticism can indeed present real albeit not supernatural problems.

I have encountered instances of this sort of wariness several times during my field work. For example, one autumn night my wife and I attended a tour of the

Harriet Beecher Stowe Center in Hartford, Connecticut. Stowe, who famously wrote *Uncle Tom's Cabin* among other influential works, lived in an impressive Victorian Gothic Revival house on the current center's grounds for the final twenty-three years of her life (Harriet Beecher Stowe Center 2008). Today, interested visitors can attend educational events there, consult the research library, and take the aforementioned tours. Usually, these focus on the author's life, the architecture of the house, and so forth. However, we attended one of the themed tours they offer during the Halloween season, called "Spirits at Stowe: An Otherworldly Tour." Advertisements for the tours state that the center allows visitors to wander the center's buildings in the dark while learning about spiritualism in Stowe's time, hearing tales of "unexplained deaths" that occurred in the buildings on the grounds, and hunting for ghosts themselves (Mommy Poppins 2017). A small EMF meter is even provided to guests to help in the endeavor. As our guide led the small group from the visitor center down the darkened path to the first of the houses we were to tour, he asked us various questions. First, he asked how many of us believed in ghosts. There was some hesitation, and then, three or so of the six visitors present raised their hands. It was difficult to count because there was considerable hesitation and not everyone held their hand up high. Perhaps they were concerned about being judged, unsure whether they believed, or both. Many people would likely prefer to include more nuance in their response to a question of belief than a simple "yes" or "no" (Ellis 2003). He then asked how many of us doubted the existence of ghosts. This time, only I raised my hand, doing so with what I hoped was a disarming grin. The guide regarded me silently for a moment with a dubious expression. Then, in a flat tone, he declared that sometimes the presence of skeptics makes it difficult for the spirits to communicate with the living. In any case, he continued, we would try to make contact nonetheless and see what happened. He seemed resigned to inevitable failure. My first thought was that this sort of thinking was a convenient excuse should the ghosts fail to appear. Given what I have discussed here though, it seems just as likely that I really did put a damper on things by expressing doubt, even just by raising my hand in response to a question. For the remainder of the tour, I kept my opinions to myself, and, sure enough, the group became appropriately excited every time the EMF device merrily lit up, indicating, perhaps, the presence of the not quite departed.

Ironically, there are also frequent and contradictory claims that skepticism, rather than dampening uncanny phenomena, actually *incites* the supernatural into making itself known. In one allegedly haunted house, witnesses reported that the ghost would act up whenever visitors "scoffed" at its existence by causing hanging plants there to swing, making noises of shattering glass, and winding or unwinding phone cords (Pitkin 2010:370). A similar thing happens at Captain Grant's Inn of Preston, Connecticut. A frequently retold story deals with a worker who was an "atheist" that "did not believe in the existence of ghosts" (Lake 2011:145–46). When guests at the inn inquired about it being haunted, she would bluntly tell them ghosts were not real. Her skepticism apparently provoked one of the resident entities. One day, the apparition of "a young girl appeared out of thin air and passed right through her," which changed the unbeliever's "view on ghosts" (Lake 2011:146). So, on the one hand, skepticism seems to inhibit the collective accomplishment of a mood or mind-set conducive to supernatural encounters while, on the other, it simultaneously expedites such encounters. It's possible to reconcile these apparently contradictory claims. Whereas a degree of willingness to believe or to entertain belief is typically a ritualistic requirement for spooky encounters, here, expressions of skepticism are reinterpreted as challenges to the alleged supernatural beings that reside in a place. In this regard they still function ritualistically, but as a sort of provocation to those beings. It seems likely that the sort of doubt presented in these cases is more of a ritualistic *performance* of skepticism. Instead of being sincere, one of those present is *acting* in a skeptical manner. It is an expression of disbelief put on display *because* one is hoping for a paranormal punishment and, therefore, proof of experience. These punishments never seem to occur when sincere skeptics are doing the investigating (e.g., Nickell 2007; Radford 2010; Randi 1982). If expressed in the spirit, so to speak, of provocation or transgression rather than actual disbelief, pseudoskeptical challenges may thus actually serve to increase the collective apprehension and expectation of the group rather than inhibit it, just like any other transgressive rite.[14] As it so happens, I had the opportunity to sleep in the haunted room at Captain Grant's Inn one night, where the skeptical employee was scared into a believer. Unfortunately, my own doubts proved inadequate to prod the resident spirit into making an appearance. Clearly, I wasn't doing something right.

THE ROLE OF RITUAL

As I have illustrated in this section, legend tripping is fundamentally magical and ritualistic in character and is intended to invoke a supernatural response. The elements that could potentially qualify for legend-tripping rituals are vast. These include all manner of behaviors ranging from shining car headlights on statues to calling out a specific word or phrase. Whether incorporating verbal elements, material components, or both, the behaviors can be either precisely specified by preexisting legends or extrapolated from an understanding of related legendry in general. Similar to other quasi-magical folk traditions, you do not have to closely follow a strict formulae. A degree of improvisation is

Captain Grant's Inn (Preston, CT): One of its alleged spirits might deign to startle those who scoff at the super-natural. Photo by the author.

permissible or even necessary—abridging previously implemented formula or substituting other components—provided the overall result is in keeping with the spirit of previous models (Firth 1954). Moreover, it is not only behavior, but also less observable elements, like mood, that might fit the ritual requirements of a given legend trip and stir up a supernatural response. No matter how strange or mundane, how well specified or generic, the particular elements involved are not terribly significant in and of themselves. What is important, as with all rituals (Durkheim [1912] 1995), is that the participants believe they have performed the necessary elements correctly. If they do, the legend trip will likely be successful.

Given that previous stages have set the proper level of anticipation and expectation, the ritual serves to trigger that state of mind, that full crossing of the threshold, that will lead to participants interpreting subsequent experiences as confirmation of the legend itself. Rituals—whether intended to anger a spirit, appease it, or both—operate through a similar underlying logic to bring the building sense of tension and expectation to a crescendo. Of course, should nothing occur, should the supernatural fail to make an appearance, this same self-fulfilling expectation can be used to explain that failure. Namely, legend trippers may come to believe that they simply did not execute the ritual prop-erly. Perhaps they came to the wrong cemetery, chose the wrong time, or weren't expressing the proper mood. Given the many challenges I discussed in the previous chapter, this is distinctly possible after all. This sort of explanation, in turn, may serve as an incentive to try again, which increases the likelihood that something—anything—will have a chance to occur that looks like proof of the legend by enlarging the observational window. I will turn to these matters next.

Chapter 5

CLOSE ENCOUNTERS OF THE
SUPERNATURAL KIND

In the deep folds of dream, [he] was conscious that the path from
his father's house had led him into an undiscovered country, and
he was wondering at the strangeness of it all, when suddenly, in
place of the hum and murmur of the summer, an infinite silence
seemed to fall on all things, and the wood was hushed, and for a
moment in time he stood face to face there with a presence, that
was neither man nor beast, neither the living nor the dead, but all
things mingled, the form of all things but devoid of all form.
—ARTHUR MACHEN ([1922] 1948:66–67)

Old Hill Burying Ground sits upon a small but steep hill overlooking the quaint
town of Concord, Massachusetts. From its crest, amid the old headstones,
you can look out over the idyllic town to see the steeples of its churches, its
monument square, and the roadway where, some two and a half centuries ago,
British soldiers engaged Patriot militia in the first clash of what would become
the American Revolution. On this particular evening in March, however, I was
facing away from these sites. I had just entered Old Hill Burying Ground and,
taking in the admittedly spooky ambience, I scanned the old headstones that
littered the hillside rising up steeply before me. There was one in particular I
was hoping to find. It was supposed to be rather distinct from its peers, having been inscribed with the images of both an angel and a skull. According to
legend, there was something uncanny about the skull, and it was this claim that
I had come to investigate. I climbed slowly up the hill, regarding each of the
ancient stones in turn. The sun was sinking, the light fading, and the mosquitos
rallying to the scent of fresh blood. At last, as I crested the summit, I saw it
rise up before me. It was considerably larger than I expected, and it seemed to
loom somewhat menacingly in the gathering dusk. I hesitated for a moment

Old Hill Burying Ground (Concord, MA): What would you do if you saw the monument's dead, stone eyes come to life as legend claims? Photo by the author.

before approaching, wondering whether there was any chance the legends were true. Did the inscription around the skull really bear the ominous and enigmatic phrase "All must submit to the King of terrors"? But that wasn't the strangest claim I had heard. They say that, sometimes—when the conditions are just right, you can take a picture of the grinning face and, upon looking at the photograph, find that its hollow, stone eyes have been replaced with real, living ones. What would I find when I gazed into those eyes? Would I be greeted by mere inanimate stone or by something strange beyond words that would give me cause to question my view of the world and my own place in it?

The primary focus of legend trips is the promise of experiencing something supernatural or uncanny, like the ghostly appearance of real eyes in the stone carving of a skull. All the preparations, travel, and ritual behaviors that have unfolded thus far should lead to this culmination: to actual contact or encounter with something described by legend. It is only through this contact that legend trippers can fully feel as though they have "enter[ed] into the reality" of that legend (Kinsella 2011:103) or that they have succeeded in their attempt "to merge the supernatural realm described [in the legend] with reality" (Thigpen 1971:205). The stories that legend trippers explore are truly fantastic: tales of curses and magic, spirits and monsters, aliens and ghosts. You might expect that a quest for something so extraordinary is doomed to disappointment and failure, but this is not the case. To the contrary, legend trips actually have remarkably high chances of success, though it is success of a certain sort.

During many legend trips, *something* happens that serves as proof of the supernatural: as evidence that there is some truth to the legend. This chapter explores the many things that could count as that proof as well as the numerous factors that help to facilitate the sense of a profound, otherworldly encounter. While something like seeing an apparition will certainly do the trick, a range of environmental, social, and psychological factors can help contribute to a profound experience even in the absence of anything overtly supernatural. Essential to this process, I argue, are two factors. One of these is the proper mindset: a sense of expectation and willingness to entertain possibilities, heightened by fear and excitement. The second is the absence of a single, coherent legend, this absence of which can accommodate almost any experience. I examine the wide range of experiences that can count as a supernatural encounter when these two requirements are met, including natural phenomena, things that have nothing to do with the legend, things that contradict the legend, and even just feelings or mood. The latter are especially interesting since, as I will illustrate, they reveal how mindset can be both requisite for an experience and proof of that experience. I explore other implications of this process as well, such as how proliferating electronic devices play a role in the apprehension of a supernatural experience and how concepts like "ghosts," rather than being coherent ideas with fixed properties, are really residual categories that are useful when more concrete labels are inadequate for classifying an experience.

A LEGEND-TRIP STATE OF MIND

When people put their minds toward finding something, they tend to find it—in their minds if not in the external world. Thus, when witch finders set their minds to tracking down a witch, they typically find one (Levack 2015), and when frightened townsfolk exhume a body in search of a vampire, they usually unearth the desired evidence along with it (Barber 1988). That the so-called witches and vampires in question were only the projections of expectation is perhaps exactly the point. Given the right mindset, evidence can be found in support of even the most bizarre expectations. Something similar happens during legend trips.

Some anomalous phenomena, it has been argued, like the old hag and out-of-body experiences, are fairly consistent across cultural contexts. According to some researchers, this is because witnesses are accurately describing a real stimulus they have experienced (Hufford 1982; McClenon 2001). Whatever the truth of the matter might be, legend trips rarely display this degree of consistency. While this does not entirely rule out external factors, it does require careful attention to the cultural, psychological, and social forces that play an important role in legend-trip-induced experiences. People visit places all the time that are rich with associated legends. Usually when they are unaware of these tales, however, they will not experience anything odd or uncanny.[1] Legend trippers, however, do not venture forth so ignorant and unprepared. They familiarize themselves with the tale, plan their journey, rehearse what is needed to call forth the supernatural, and then perform the necessary rites. These sorts of behaviors "prim[e] the belief pump" (Koven 2007:191) and set the proper mood: one marked by anticipation, excitement, and trepidation (Thigpen 1971). True believers are easily convinced that something they have encountered is supernatural precisely because they *want* to believe it is so. A range of very human cognitive traits can readily explain this. For example, we are all subject to confirmation bias: we tend to place more weight on things we see or hear that agree with what we already believe to be true while discounting or disparaging those troublesome facts that conflict with our beliefs (French and Stone 2014). However, many legend trippers do not wholeheartedly believe in what they are doing. Instead, they entertain the *possibility* of the act and its outcome. They remain open, perhaps even hopeful, that the legend might be true, and so, they actively seek experiences that will verify that truth (Kinsella 2011). A casual visitor to a legendary site generally lacks the proper mindset and sense of expectation that would allow for a fantastical experience and sense of encounter. The legend tripper is prepared—however tentatively or wholeheartedly—to interpret whatever happens there in light of the interpretive framework provided by the legend and their own behaviors up to that point. In this way, they can interpret nearly any experience as support for a legend's claims, even if the actual events that transpire are rather mundane or far removed from what the legend predicted.

Should the legend trippers be unwilling to entertain even this modest degree of tenuous belief, other characteristics of the legend trip encourage them to adopt a supernatural explanation for their encounters anyway. This is because they put themselves into a situation where they will be especially prone to draw on another cognitive trait: an "availability heuristic." This is another basic human tendency in which we "rely strongly on those examples and instances that spring readily to mind" when trying to understand something or solve a problem (French and Stone 2014:126). This commonly operates in everyday life when, for example, we draw on something we just read or watched on TV instead of something we witnessed last year. In our case, the legend trippers immerse themselves in the legend, prepare to investigate it, travel to its source, and engage in many other related activities pertaining to it. After all this, even if it is in jest, their minds are very much on the supernatural when they arrive at the legend's setting. If and when something strange happens—and almost anything can count, as I will demonstrate, this corpus of folklore is more readily available to draw on than alternative explanations that would normally suffice.

My fieldwork experiences made this process abundantly clear to me. Several times, as I prowled around spooky cemeteries and old houses, I observed very minor things that I almost certainly would not have noticed if I didn't have legend tripping on my mind. One of these occurred at the Shelburne Museum in Vermont. This attraction features a number of historical structures on its sprawling grounds that you can enter and tour. These include a church, a train station, a round barn, a lighthouse, a covered bridge, a beached steamboat, and several historic homes. One of the latter is supposedly haunted: the Dutton House. Originally built in 1782, the core of the house is a classic New England saltbox, but generations of occupants expanded it by adding various wings and additions (Shelburne Museum 2022). Wandering around its sprawling rooms and corridors, I eventually found my way into a walk-in attic space that looked familiar. I had seen a picture of it earlier in the day in an article about the haunting, an article of which claimed that the ghost liked to hide out here (Alexander 2011). So, this claim was on my mind as I walked across the attic to the window on the far side. When I got there, I paused to peer through the glass and—while doing so—heard two thumps from somewhere nearby. Was it the floorboards? Someone downstairs? A bird landing on the roof? Or just maybe . . . Okay, it was probably not a ghost, but the possibility readily springs to mind when you are familiar with the legend. On reflection, it occurred to me that I might have heard similar noises throughout the rest of the property that day and simply forgot about them. Without a legend to draw on, my availability heuristic would more readily draw on natural explanations that don't involve ghosts and are, therefore, much less memorable.

I had an even more informative experience in another historic home turned into the headquarters of a historical society in Cheshire, Connecticut: the Hitchcock-Phillips House. The old Georgian-style home, built in 1785 (Romano 2017), certainly looks like it could host a ghost or two. In fact, however, there seem to have been no well-known legends about it until around 2013 when a group of ghost hunters received permission from the town historical society to investigate the house for possible spirits. As it turns out, they were inspired to investigate simply because the house *looked* old and fit the group's expectations for what goes into a haunted house (VanderLek 2013). This is, of course, a pattern I have noted several times so far. The group was especially taken by a room in the house where numerous historical toys are on display for visitors to see. They believe they captured their best evidence here, including the recording of a child's voice and a photograph of a shadowy figure (Rook 2013). My first pass through this room was uneventful. The floor creaked softly as I

Hitchcock-Phillips House (Cheshire, CT): This house is a possible site for encounters with spirits. Photo by the author.

strolled about it, and I thought about how that might sound on a recording to someone listening for disembodied voices. Glancing at the rocking horses, doll house, and various other toys placed around the room, I took a few pictures, wondering whether any reflections or shadows produced by the flash might similarly produce suggestive phantoms. Then, I moved on to other parts of the house, examining artifacts ranging from farm tools to military regalia.

Sometime later, I had to pass back through the toy room to get to another area I had missed, but I stopped dead in my tracks in its entryway. Something was different. At first, I couldn't quite put my finger on it. Then it hit me: the overhead light in the room was on. Hadn't it been off earlier? I consulted with my wife, but neither of us were quite sure. Fortunately, I had the photos on my digital camera to consult, and, sure enough, these revealed that the light had indeed been turned off when we first passed through. Without the ghostly legend on my mind, I doubt I would have noticed this at all, and I certainly would not have been taking so many photos, which allowed me to follow up on the observation. Again, experiences like these were far from the dramatic, ghostly encounters legends promise, but they do technically count as *unexplained* phenomena. This does not mean that they are *unexplainable*. Several *possible* explanations come to mind for this sort of occurrence. In this particular case, I had seen several other fluorescent lights throughout the house flickering and struggling to turn fully on, so they were clearly not in the best shape. Knowledge of the legends at these locations, however, makes it so a supernatural possibility springs readily to mind, in contention with more prosaic explanations.

EXTRAORDINARY EXPERIENCES AND CONFIRMATION

The social and psychological processes of legend tripping predispose participants to interpret a vast range of ambiguous experiences as possibly supernatural, or at least vaguely uncanny, encounters. This is true regardless of whether they really believe in those possibilities outside the context of a legend trip. Primed expectations can transform even relatively mundane occurrences into dramatic experiences for those seeking them. Lindahl provides an illustration of this sort of motivation. He describes a legend trip to "an isolated railroad crossing at the southern extreme of San Antonio" (Lindahl 2005:165). Legend tells that, long ago, a school bus full of children was stuck on the tracks here. Unable to move, it was crushed by an oncoming train, and all the children perished. However, there is said to be a:

> lingering presence of the spirits of the children slain in the crash. [Many] have visited the crossing to test for themselves the validity of the claims that the dead children will reveal themselves to those who seek them. [P]eople who visit the scene by car drive slowly (and at least seemingly) upward along a gradual incline toward the tracks. Stopping short of the rails, the driver shifts the car into neutral, and the car seems to roll uphill and over the tracks in defiance of gravity. (Lindahl 2005:166)

The legend explains the reason for this apparent violation of the laws of physics: the spirits of the children are responsible. Reliving their own tragedy and not wanting it to happen to others, they hasten to push any stopped cars off the fatal tracks to safety—but only if those cars are in neutral. There are natural limits to their supernatural strength. When they come to a stop on the other side, drivers and passengers typically get out to inspect the trunk and rear bumper of their vehicles. They are looking for handprints, signs that the spirits were really there, and they often find them.

These phenomena are all easily explained without resorting to the paranormal. The "gravity hill" or "magnetic hill" effect is a well-known visual trick. The landscape fools people's senses into thinking they are moving uphill when they are, in fact, actually going slightly downhill (Bressan, Garlaschellim, and Barracano 2003). Places of this sort are common. If you drive to "Spook Hill" in Middlesex, New York, you can "be spooked as your car rolls backward up the hill!" (Haunted History Trail of New York State 2022:n.p.). Citro (2005) lists no fewer than three antigravity hills in New England along with one just over the border in Quebec. Similarly, the handprints found after this supernatural ordeal are not unique to this particular legend and have a number of possible prosaic explanations. Bumpers and especially trunks of cars are touched numerous times during the course of an average week. Signs of that contact are likely visible all the time, but, under the conditions of the legend trip, individuals are more likely to notice them and interpret them in terms of the cognitive framework provided by the legend. Interested readers might, right at this moment, find it instructive to consider when the last time they carefully inspected their own vehicle for fingerprints was. Better still, why not take a break from reading and go investigate right now? I dare you.

The likelihood of finding handprints increases if the car in Lindahl's account was covered with dust, which it very well may have been after having driven through the countryside to reach the rails. More tellingly, he notes that many legend trippers purposely bring talcum powder to help them locate handprints. This is another feature common among legends like this. Compare the Gravity Hill in Richfield, North Carolina (OnlyInYourState Staff 2021). The legend here is that a mother and child were killed by a truck while trying to push their car up the hill. They will push your car up the hill too, and you will be able to see their handprints afterwards if you apply baby powder to the vehicle. The reason this claim is so common is because this activity *produces* evidence of supernatural contact rather than simply drawing your attention to evidence that was there all along. It is similar to dusting for fingerprints from living humans or to the traditional prank of writing a scary message on a foggy bathroom mirror with just the oils on your finger. The message itself is invisible, but the oils will repel moisture. The next time someone takes a shower, the message will be revealed as condensation forms more thickly around the text. At this point the unsuspecting victim might mistakenly attribute the message to some supernatural agency, especially if they already have reason to believe the house is haunted. This is a well-known trick, often taught to children,[2] but in the context of the legend trip, participants are preoccupied with finding supernatural explanations that confirm their expectations, not rational accounts. The upward motion against gravity and the mysterious handprints all serve as the sought-after evidence that the legend is indeed true.

Of course, not all legend trips result in such a dramatic outcome. They may sometimes result in the merest suggestion of supernatural possibility. For example, one time while travelling, my wife and I stayed at the Spalding Inn, a small establishment nestled at the edge of the White Mountains in northern New Hampshire. The inn had a reputation for being haunted and used these claims to promote its business. In fact, at the time of our visit, celebrity paranormalists Jason Hawes and Grant Wilson owned it and had featured it on their television show, *Ghost Hunters*. Most of the other guests I spoke to, at breakfast or in the lounge in the evening, seemed well aware of these claims and, in fact, tended to mention them as one of the main reasons they wanted to spend the night there. Upon arrival, thoughts of the supernatural are reinforced in a number of ways.

Flipping through the guestbook at the front desk, I read many claims of ghostly encounters at the inn. For those not inclined to reading guestbooks, there were also several ghost-related objects for sale in the small gift shop on the premises, like T-shirts and beer cozies. The morning before our departure, I was sitting on the front porch, drinking coffee, and writing down some field notes in my journal. Soon, a couple approached me and, after some awkward but friendly preliminaries, they brought up the subject of ghosts. "Did you experience anything weird last night?" they asked. I didn't have much to report except that my wife had heard the doorknob to our room jiggling at one point in the middle of the night, but I slept right through it. The prior evening, I had only seen a brief flash of light outside (which was probably from a car's headlights) and felt some light touches on my face while trying to sleep (which were probably from some unwelcome flies—the room was full of them given the sorry state of the window screens). They, in turn, reciprocated by describing how they had heard a noise from their closet during the night that sounded much like their luggage falling over. Upon investigation in the morning, however, they found it remained standing upright. "It's probably nothing," the man concluded, "but it does make you wonder, doesn't it?"

EXPECTATION PRODUCES EXPERIENCE

Indeed, it does make you wonder. Our experiences were quite minor and most likely mundane. In fact, all of us knew this was the case. Under almost any other circumstances, they might not even have been remarked upon. If we had been spending a night at the Radisson, it is unlikely a bump in the night would have been consciously registered as anything other than someone in the next room. Yet, given the right location and knowledge of legendary claims associated with it, supernatural interpretations readily spring to mind. Even in situations such as this in which those involved do not really believe these explanations, the fact that they occur at all shows how important expectation is for producing experience. As Hall (1973:171) suggests, "A willing suspension of disbelief is crucial to scariness which is so important a part of the legend trip." The events that occur, or seem to occur, are not as important as the mindset that accompanies them: the *desire*, however tentative, for something supernatural to occur. The simple act of choosing to stay at this obscure inn, known only for its ghosts, indicates that desire and mindset.

By way of illustration, one team of sociologists provides an interesting account of a night they spent in an allegedly haunted building with a group of paranormal investigators. For the latter group: "the evening was one of continual and dramatic events. Victoria saw orbs of evil energy in her photographs [and] Gloria was overwhelmed by dozens of ghosts rushing her at once" (Bader et al. 2010:44). The investigators further comment: "[We] talked to ghosts that were standing behind us and conducted rituals to keep us safe. Gloria swooned, gasped, and collapsed at the behest of the pushy spirits." The sociologists observes, "We were able to spend the night, in their view, only through their direct intervention to stave off the evil forces" but they, themselves, experienced nothing and found that "the night passed without incident" (Bader et al. 2010:44). They spent the same time in the same location as the paranormal investigators and observed the latter party's claims, and yet they experienced nothing of a supernatural nature themselves. They describe their orientation toward the subject matter and toward this stakeout in particular as effectively skeptical: they did not expect anything supernatural to occur, and so, for them, it did not.

Given the right mindset, nearly anything can be read as a validation of a legend. In the absence of that mindset, however, these same experiences will be read more routinely. For example, to this day many people have a fascination with the historical vampire panics in New England. Some of these people, after hearing the legendary accounts, drive out to certain cemeteries trying to locate the final resting place of one of the accused vampires. Once there, they hope to experience some sign of their continued presence. All this occurs despite the well-established fact that these unfortunates died of natural causes and despite the fact that, even if they *were* vampires, the same folk beliefs that defined them as such were also put to use long ago to end their undead existences: by exhuming their remains and burning their hearts, for example (Barber 1988). Regardless, one thing that is often encountered at sites like these, which seems to validate the legend for those in the right mindset, is a spooky-seeming epitaph. The gravesite of the alleged vampire Nellie Vaughn was such a popular destination that authorities ultimately removed and hid her tombstone in the hopes of dissuading further visitors to the site. However, she did not receive this undead reputation until perhaps the 1970s when legend trippers looking for vampire graves came upon hers instead.[3] Her subsequent vampire status "may be attributed to a case of mistaken identity" (Holly and Cordy 2007:342). This is because, at some point "in the past, people read her epitaph—'I am waiting and watching for you'—and assumed that she was one of the vampires of legend." Interestingly, although the epitaph could sound spooky if one reads it in the proper frame of mind, it most likely just "suggests that she simply has gone to heaven and is waiting for her family to join her . . ." (Holly and Cordy 2007:342).

Similar scenarios are common for legend trips to the grave sites of alleged witches. Mary Jane Hendrickson died of natural causes in 1898 and was buried in a small cemetery near Butler, Ohio. Despite the absence of witchcraft accusations in life, legend now posthumously claims she was "an evil witch who was hanged," most likely because of her epitaph, which reads: "Not Dead but Sleepth [*sic*]" (Ellis 2004:126). Likewise, New Haven, Connecticut, has its own "witch's" grave in Evergreen Cemetery: that of Mary E. Hart, who is referred to more frequently as "Midnight Mary." Her conceivably ominous epitaph states, "The people shall be troubled at midnight and pass away." Local legends warn of all manner of harm that might befall those passing by her grave—especially, as one might expect, if they go at midnight (Revai 2006:69). All these epitaphs are actually religious in nature—Hart's simply quotes Job 34:20—and fairly conventional for their time. This is the more prosaic interpretation and the more likely one—unless your visit to these graves is informed by a quest to find evidence of supernatural legends. In this case, these inscriptions seem to have more dire meanings that "prove" suspicions that something uncanny occurs there.

Visitors to these graves who have heard the legends don't necessarily have to have any encounters with apparitions, disembodied voices, or other stereotypically spooky manifestations in order to believe that they have experienced something uncanny that validates the legend. If they should find the feature of the physical landscape described so prominently in legend and if this feature is odd enough in its own right, this might be proof enough. During my visit to Concord's Old Hill Burying Ground, which I discussed in the beginning of this chapter, I did not see any ghostly eyes appear in the engraved skull like legend claimed I would. However, I did see the bizarre carvings and the odd epitaph that I had heard about. Features like these seem so strange that the mere experience of seeing them offers excitement of its own. Moreover, the experience suggests that if these unlikely things really exist, then maybe other aspects of the legend are true by association with it. The supernatural explanation for their origins seems validated. Thus, through this circular reasoning, the very features of the landscape that frequently give rise to legend speculation in the first place can, paradoxically, be read as proof of that legend even if nothing else happens.

INCONSISTENT EXPERIENCES

The potency of this phenomenon—where expectation and priming leads to experiences that seem to verify legendary accounts—is most telling when the legend involved is demonstrably false or in error. Consider, for example, the case of the Windmill Tower in Brisbane, Australia. The building, as its name indicates, is a historical windmill constructed in 1828 with forced convict labor (Queensland Government n.d.) According to legend, the spirit of a man hanged inside the windmill still haunts the structure. Many people who have visited in search of a ghostly experience claim to have encountered him. The hanging is in historical record, but, according to one researcher investigating the site, the experiences of legend trippers are at odds with what actually happened (Nickell 2016b). For example, whereas the sightings of a phantom hanging typically occur inside the mill, the deed occurred outside, as you might expect with a public execution. This deviation from history is particularly telling, but other problems with paranormal experiences there raise questions as well. For example, witnesses generally report only seeing one hanged ghost (two men were hanged), descriptions of the corpse are not consistent with someone who was hanged (e.g., tongue protruding or bitten off), and no reported descriptions of the ghost reflect the fact that at least one of those hanged was an indigenous Australian.

Whether these reports are outright hoaxes or given in earnest, they are more a reflection of the legend and the power of expectation than any objective encounters with the supernatural at the old mill. Then again, in cases such as this in which official accounts conflict with eyewitnesses, many paranormal enthusiasts insist that it is the historical record that is in error, not their experiences (Hanks 2015). In one sensationalistic account of a haunted monastery, the authors assert their belief that the land was accursed because a group of Satanists lived there for a time, practicing black magic and animal sacrifice. They admit that "there is no record of these people having been here," but they nonetheless "fee[l] that they did exist, they did stop here, and they did perform necromantic rites on the land" (Warren et al. 1992:40). They believe that the cemetery is haunted by dark forces, and they believe this sort of haunting comes about as a result of cult activity. Therefore, the cult must have been real. The facts must bend to fit expectation.

Not only do supernatural experiences often conflict with historical facts, but they are also frequently inconsistent even with the legendary claims that prompted the search for an experience in the first place. What should legend trippers make of an experience that seems significant and supernatural but was not foretold by the legend? Is it proof of the legend's validity anyway, or is it evidence against it? Since legends are generally not a single, coherent text but a set of diverse and related narratives (Dégh 2001), it is not uncommon to find that a given legend does not make a single experiential promise, but multiple and often contradictory claims instead. "Curse" legends illustrate this problem.[4] These claim that some ill fate will befall anyone that violates some proscription but are often vague or offer numerous possibilities regarding exactly what that fate is. At the University of New Haven in Connecticut, the quad in front of the main administration building, Maxcy Hall, is home to an example of this sort of curse. The university's seal is embedded at the intersection of several walking paths, and, for several years now, students have been warned not to step on it. If they do, *something* "bad" will happen to them. One critical student observes in the university's newspaper, "Those bad things were never really defined. Throughout the year, I heard rumors as to what would happen if I were to step on the letters—I'd fail all my classes, I'd end up transferring out and I'd take more than four years to complete my undergraduate education" and so on (Sanci 2013:n.p.). Essentially, anything bad that happens after stepping on the seal could be interpreted as proof of its potency.

It is not only the outcome of violating the taboo that is vague in many curse legends. Inevitably, the time period within which the unfortunate victim will meet their dire end is also variable; different versions of the same curse legend claim a different expiration date. A cursed statue of an angel in Iowa City's Oakland Cemetery allegedly kills anyone who offends it following a period of "24 hours, seven years, or at an unspecified time" (Bird 1994:199). If, after committing the act, the transgressor can expect to die essentially at any time in the future, it is impossible for the prediction to fail since death comes to everyone and the timeframe is flexible. Given that interpretation of the facts shifts to force accommodation of the expectation, this phenomenon has been called the "Procrustean effect" (Wiseman 2010:20). A somewhat more nuanced curse legend has its setting outside of the Providence Athenaeum, a library in Rhode Island. Here, you can find an old fountain that has similarly contradictory lore associated with it. If you should drink from it . . . Well, the outcome is not entirely clear. According to one account, Edgar Allan Poe placed a curse on it after he was scorned by the poetess Sarah Helen Whitman whom he had been courting. Ever since then, a sip from the fountain will make it so the drinker can never leave the city of Providence (Bhargava 2016). Of course, this can also be interpreted to refer to your spirit as opposed to your body. Poe did not hang around after his alleged malediction in life, but "if we should believe the stories of the guides of the Providence Ghost Tour," his ghost still lingers (Bhargava 2016:n.p.). Other accounts suggest the fountain is blessed, not cursed. A sip will pass its boon on to you: "According to legend, if you [drink], you will one day return to Providence" (Raven 2008:53). Visitors who test their luck, then, should be on the lookout for several possible eventualities. Depending on how they interpret these versions of the legend, and likely there are more, participants face a flexible range of options: they might not leave town, they might not *permanently* leave town, they might come back for a visit someday, they might come back as a ghost someday, they might encounter a ghost or something ghostly from a previous visitor to the fountain, and so forth. I have had the opportunity to visit the fountain twice and, on both occasions, found it to be quite dry and full of litter and dead leaves, so drinking from it would take some effort either way. Other sources have made the same observation, and one even facetiously incorporates it into the legend: "Since the fountain is from 1873, it is not in the best condition and we recommend you don't test this legend out or you may never return to life itself" (Snyder 2013:n.p.). If someone should manage to take a drink from the empty fountain, perhaps they then have one more thing to watch out for.

Because they present so many variations, each making a variety of claims, legends present numerous ways in which they can appear vindicated. However, legend trips in which none of these diverse possibilities occur are common too. Here, nonetheless, legend trippers might still interpret experiences that are truly inconsistent with a particular legend—despite its endless variations—as spooky and, therefore, confirmatory in a vague way. While the legendary claims are slippery and flexible, so too is the process of interpreting experiences in light of that legend. If the ghost is supposed to appear when you repeat its name three times, but instead you hear strange laughter in the distance, does that mean that the legend trip was successful? Usually, it seems, the answer is "yes." Legend-trip reports are full of events like these. Something occurs that is not actually foretold by the legend but that trippers interpret as evidence of its veracity anyway.

Let's return to Gunntown Cemetery in Naugatuck, Connecticut—an uncanny location that has diverse legendary traditions associated with it. As I outlined in chapter 4, visitors here supposedly witness many things, including "random music and the laughter of children . . . , a man carrying a lantern leading a horse . . . , a little boy playing by the back wall who simply vanishes . . . , a black dog that also quickly disappears . . . , spirit orbs and mists, as well as numerous EVPs" (Bendici 2009:n.p.) and so forth. Given the range of possible phenomena associated with this legendary site, it seems like it would be a simple matter to encounter something that could be interpreted as similar to at least one of these claims. Yet this particular written account reveals that none of these turned up during the legend trippers' investigation. However, one event did occur that seemed of possible paranormal significance: the movement of a miniature American flag on one of the graves. Ray Bendici (2009:n.p.) recounts:

> So the visit was fairly uneventful except for one moment. When we were getting ready to take the picture . . . the stick holding the flag on the left moved quite a bit all on its own. Like, it swung around about four to six inches without anyone touching it. Now there was definitely a light morning breeze, and . . . both flags [were] billowing a bit. But it was just weird how much the one flag moved—almost like it was coming to attention!—and the moment it chose to do it. Our hearts stopped for a second, but we realized it was just the wind, right? Right? Hmm. . . .

The author is somewhat skeptical of the event and does not entirely believe it is supernatural in origin. In fact, throughout the remainder of the account, he dismisses a variety of events that others might have interpreted as having paranormal significance. These include some strange audio phenomena that he attributes to the walls of the cemetery and an unusually large number of insects flying around. Nonetheless, his desire to find some verification of the legend is evident, even if it is somewhat restrained. This is especially significant since, again, despite the wide variety of claims about Gunntown Cemetery, none of the prior legends that the investigator seems familiar with—based on his summary of them—said anything about the movement of the flags in particular or of animate objects in general. Regardless of this fact, and regardless of the very real possibility that the movement was caused by the wind, he reads it as at least possible confirmation of the legend.

Again, far from making a legend trip impossible, the absence of a single, coherent legend makes it all but inevitable that the trip will succeed by expanding the range of experiences that can be interpreted as proof of supernatural activity. The sheer quantity of available memorates provides numerous, particular possibilities but also implies that individuals should not feel limited by prior reports. Rather, legend trippers have license to interpret a novel experience as consistent with these past events even if it is quite unrelated. In fact, when too many conflicting claims are present and legend trippers are aware of them, this might actually *require* that they ignore any particular one and instead simply await some event that fits their general expectations. This is because the onslaught of claims is overwhelming, particularly if one wants to reenact them by ostension. In trying to replicate some of the claims during my site visit to Gunntown Cemetery, I had difficulty juggling the various memorates in mind with the materials necessary to reproduce them in my hands. At one point, for example, I was holding my notebook, a pen, a camera, a digital thermometer, an EMF meter, *two* digital recorders,[5] extra batteries, a list of specific locations of interest in the cemetery, and a to-do list reminding me of what I needed all this stuff for based on the accounts I had read beforehand. It would have been much easier to simply look for something—anything—spooky, which is not exactly a tall order in a cemetery.

NATURAL EXPERIENCES

The case of the autonomously moving miniature flag also illustrates another important matter. Sometimes when the specific occurrence predicted by the legend fails to manifest and nothing distinctly uncanny happens, the legend trip can still be considered a success. This is accomplished by simply declaring or at least entertaining the possibility that even very ordinary events—such as the wind—are supernaturally significant. Legend trippers often interpret encounters with normal animals, for example, as spooky when they occur in legendary spaces. Somehow, the presence of these animals is interpreted as abnormal simply by association. Examples include "uncanny" encounters with bees in a haunted house (Pitkin 2010:360) and biting insects or a nonbiting kitten in a creepy cemetery (Bendici 2009). Some of folklorist Patricia Meley's (1991:22) informants report fleeing in terror when they heard a dog: "it sounded like a wolf, it started barking and somebody said that it was . . . midnight, and we started screaming and flipping out."

Most of the classic ghostly phenomena—creaky floors, misplaced objects, and so forth—are essentially normal events that occur under spooky circumstances. Showers and faucets turning on spontaneously are another common experience. Many tales about the allegedly haunted Concord's Colonial Inn in Massachusetts promise you might experience this phenomenon there, and indeed, I did several times while staying there. There are several common and very natural causes for this sort of behavior, including improperly regulated pressure and old packing nuts. Of course, speculation like this doesn't disprove the haunting, but I wasn't about to take apart the plumbing to test these hypotheses. Likewise, it seemed as though a couple items had mysteriously moved on their own during the night: another classic phenomenon associated with hauntings. One morning, I found a pair of errant socks packed in with the food bag, for example, instead of with the rest of my clothing. Unless I had actually seen these float across the room into the bag, it seems much more likely that I simply got my bags confused at some point, but, in the context of a haunted hotel, the mistake gets a lot more interesting. In any case, experiences like these have the advantage of being tangible and objectively observable. However, connecting this sort of thing to the supernatural is a tenuous proposition at best. They offer something of a substitute for a more convincingly anomalous experience: a consolation prize of sorts when something more satisfying cannot be had, but the desire for encounter remains strong.

The attribution of supernatural agency to banal phenomena in the absence of more compelling experiences is increasingly common among supernatural enthusiasts. A contributing factor to this is the growing popularity of using electronic devices during legend-tripping rituals, devices of which often lead to minor and perhaps false significance. As any of the many available accounts of paranormal investigations and countless how-to manuals make clear, ghost hunters in particular tend to deploy all manner of devices in their investigations. At the end of the twentieth century, these ranged from flashlights and walkie-talkies to EMF meters and negative ion generators (e.g., Taylor 1998). Since that time, the number of available devices has only expanded. One online retailer offers a mind-boggling assortment of gadgets (GhostHunter Store n.d.). To name just a few, these include: vibration sensors, infrared motion detectors, laser grids, static-field locators, structured-light-sensor camera systems,

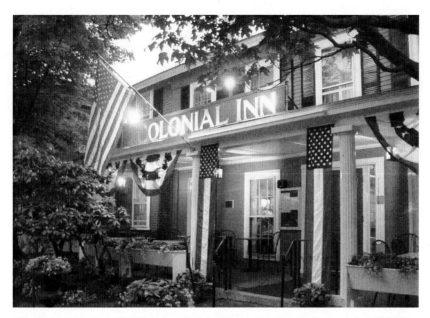

Concord's Colonial Inn (Concord, MA): Its haunted reputation may influence how guests perceive their stay. Photo by the author.

thermal imagers, visual ambient-temperature sensors, ultraviolet floodlights, night-vision camcorders, full-spectrum and infrared dual-switching lights, radio-sweeping "spirit boxes," Faraday-cage pouches, Raudive-crystal-diode receivers, the BooBuddy Interactive Bear, and plush-dog trigger objects (available in fifteen breeds, although sadly, the "Shih Tzu and Cavalier Spaniel are no longer available"). Perhaps not technically devices, they also offer Light of Jerusalem, an anointing oil, evil-eye-protection bracelets (which are both stylish and elastic), Saint Benedict medals (*with* exorcism blessing!), Gifts of the Magi incense sets, Saint Joseph home-blessing kits, olive wood holy oil keychains, and low-interest financing.

When deploying such a wide range of tools, especially for long periods of time, it is likely that one of these—especially the various devices monitoring environmental conditions—will detect some sort of fluctuation, which can be interpreted as supernatural. The same is true for the hours of video and audio recordings ghost investigators collect and later analyze for anomalies. It would be odd if some glitch or weird moment did *not* occur at some point. Even if the chances of a particular anomaly are infinitesimally small for any given moment, adding up the possibilities over the duration of an investigation raises those odds significantly. Statistically, trained readers will readily recognize this problem. For example, in most statistical tests, the level of significance is set at 0.05. This means that the chance of committing a type I error, a false positive result, is 5 percent, and the chance of not committing this type of error is 95 percent. If we conducted three such tests however, "then the overall probability of no type I errors is $(0.95)^3 = 0.95 \times 0.95 \times 0.95 = 0.857$" and "the probability of making a type I error has increased from 5% to 14.3%" (Field 2000:24–25). When one performs too many tests too uncritically, the chances of finding false significance increase quite quickly.

Correctly operating devices, then, can produce false results when uncritically used. They can also malfunction or behave in unexpected ways over long periods of use. This, too, is quite natural, but paranormalists consistently encourage would-be researchers to consider the possibility of *supernatural* causation when these events occur. The author of one ghost-hunting manual advises that "paranormal locations are known for inexplicably draining battery power. On ghost hunts, it's common for a camera display to show more than an hour's battery life remaining, then suddenly terminate" (Warren 2003:141). The aforementioned paranormal investigators Hawes and Wilson, personalities made famous by their television show *Ghost Hunters*, promote this perspective in their book on the subject. In recounting one haunted-house case, they describe how two members of their investigative team were staked out in a bedroom trying to make contact with the spirit believed to be present within. They recall that the two investigators "were there only a few minutes before they noticed that their batteries were losing power precipitously. Was an entity trying to manifest in the room? If so, it would need energy, and the juice in their batteries would be a good source of it" (Hawes, Wilson, and Friedman 2007:197). One of Tucker's (2007:209) informants claims a similar experience: "The video camera had a full battery and was in perfectly good condition, yet it mysteriously turned off during this time. The camera gave no indication that it had stopped recording. . . . Only when reviewing the tape did we realize that it had shut off by itself for no reason."

Tucker's (2007:209) observation regarding the account is quite appropriate: "the solution to this conundrum must be supernatural, not rational." Similarly, I have a small point-and-shoot camera that I carry with me during fieldwork for situations in which a larger camera is too intrusive. Frequently, I found that when I brought it to allegedly haunted locations, the camera would report that the batteries were dead. Later on, after returning home, when I tested the batteries, they would almost always show a healthy charge. In addition to being very annoying, this, at first, seems consistent with supernatural claims of the effects of spirits on batteries. However, this interpretation would really be the outcome of selective observation. The same effect often resulted when I carried the camera to nonhaunted locations. Although there was "no reason" for this behavior, I eventually learned that this particular camera was notorious for a faulty battery connector. Bending the irritating piece of metal improved the camera's performance somewhat and, not surprisingly, also reduced the occurrence of conceivably supernatural interference. Equipment failures like these are certainly not proof of anything supernatural, but, in the right context, they can be interpreted as such. In this case, a tiny piece of improperly bent metal might be mistaken for ghostly activity. Likewise, when the batteries go dead in the remote control in the comfort of my living room on a Sunday afternoon, I rarely blame a ghost. But put these same batteries in my flashlight while I am in the cemetery at night looking for the ghost of a witch who was a vampire, add a dash of fear and expectation, and I may reach an entirely different conclusion.

From an outside observer's perspective, interpreting everyday occurrences as support for a legend's validity may seem strange, especially when that occurrence was not specifically predicted by the legend. The tendency to accept nearly any experience as proof of the legend seems particularly strange when we accept too readily the traditional tendency in much previous research to focus primarily on the specific ritual requirements of a particular legend trip. This tendency implies that legend trips require precise re-creation of events described in legends: careful reenactment of past events that produce a particular, foretold outcome. But as I discussed in chapter 4, specific ritual requirements are not necessarily more important than general ritualism and expectations. Legend trippers not only consider how a particular ghost is expected to behave but also how ghosts in general might behave. Experiences consistent with specific expectations will certainly verify a legend but so will experiences that fit with general expectations. What is important is that the experience is consistent with the "belief language" surrounding the phenomenon (Ellis 2003:94): in this case, those culturally shared expectations for how the phenomenon behaves and how it can be perceived. Using this cultural grammar, it makes sense to say that a ghost moved an inanimate object or drained the batteries from my flashlight because these are consistent with general expectations learned from sources like our friends or television, even if we don't actually believe in ghosts. It would be another matter entirely to say a ghost cooked me breakfast or beat me at chess. This sort of behavior might occur in fiction or fairy tales, but ghosts simply do not behave that way in most legends or in people's experiences.

However, "ghost" constitutes a very broad cultural pattern. I will explore this in more depth later, but a bewilderingly wide variety of sensory experiences can fit the definition of "ghost" even when they have nothing to do with each other (Richardson 2003; Waskul 2016). "Ghost" does not refer to a specific set of phenomena, but rather to a residual category. We have various ideas about the everyday world—how objects are supposed to behave, where certain things are supposed to be found, how we are supposed to feel in a given situation, and anything deviating from those expectations has the capacity to attract disproportionate attention and fill us with unease. When properly cued, we might then conclude there is something supernatural responsible for any discrepancy. The possible realm of experiences is, thus, cast so widely that nearly anything counts as confirmation provided it fits within a set of broad expectations. This is because the legend trip does not just occur in the external environment and with objective occurrences, but because it is very much a social and psychological process. If individuals are motivated strongly enough, any simple occurrence is confirmation for their expectation, particularly if they are accompanied by others who are willing to entertain and support that possibility, providing a sort of social proof (Cialdini 1993). Conversely, if they expect to experience nothing, then very little will persuade them that they have witnessed the supernatural. Having the latter sort of person around during a legend trip, as we saw in the previous chapter, can inhibit others' ability to interpret ambiguous stimuli as signs of a spiritual presence.

SUBJECTIVE EXPERIENCES

The town of Victor, New York, is home to the Valentown Museum. The large wooden structure was built in 1879 with big dreams in mind: the railroad was coming to town, and the numerous businesses housed within it would cater to the increased demand (Historic Valentown n.d.). Unfortunately, the railroad never quite made it, and the venture eventually went bankrupt. Today, you can still visit the quirky place to learn about the town's history. Although the current management does not endorse the idea (Historic Valentown 2019), many people claim the museum is haunted, and it was even featured on an episode of *Ghost Hunters*. One account of an occurrence on the second floor calls into question the nature of supernatural encounter. The witness recounts:

> I didn't actually see her [the ghost] but rather got a mental image. This woman wasn't mean, but meant business. She seemed to be in charge. You definitely got the feeling that she ran a tight ship. . . . Every time I went up there I had a feeling of being watched. With the attitude of, "What are you doing here? Do you belong?" She seems fine once she recognizes that you do belong there and it's okay. You get the feeling she knows the rules and is there to enforce them. (Finch 2006:19)

What should we make of this account? What actually happened, and can we really consider it a supernatural encounter?

All the examples I have examined so far have involved actual experiences. That is, assuming a given story is not simply made up, that the legend trippers in

Valentown Museum (Victor, NY): A historic structure with a storied past and, according to some, resident ghosts. Photo by the author.

question really did objectively experience *something* even if their interpretation of these real experiences as support for the reality of a legend is questionable. They really did hear a bump on the wall or see a blur in the photo. What is particularly interesting, then, is when *nothing* external to the individuals happens at all, and yet, they still interpret this to be proof of a sort. Specifically, legend trippers frequently interpret even subjective feelings or "mood" as having been caused by some supernatural source. In one memorate, an individual went with a friend one midnight to Chapel Island, at Saint John's University in Minnesota, where the ghost of a drowned monk is said to roam. During the course of their investigation, the pair did not actually see or hear anything in particular, but he reports, "The air was charged with possibility. The situation was so scary that we decided not to stick around but leave before anything could happen" (Tucker 2007:191). This is consistent with a conceptualization of "ghosts" as being simply the feeling or the "*the sense of the presence of those who are not physically there*" (M. Bell 1997:813, emphasis original). Although a broad range of phenomena can serve as proof of a supernatural experience, this case of a frightened legend tripper illustrates how even the absence of evidence can be interpreted as the proof: "Feeling a sense of uncanny possibilities has confirmed his belief in the ghost" (Tucker 2007:191).

Substituting subjective impressions for more empirical experiences occurs in many different contexts. Janet Langlois's study of "Mary Whales" or "Mary

Worth" summoning rituals among children provides interesting comparisons. Like the more familiar "Bloody Mary" invocation to which these are related, the ritual generally requires a darkened room and chanting the entity's name a certain number of times, often in front of a mirror or in a circle of one's peers. One of the archival reports that Langlois references describes a ritual that was conducted by several high school girls during a sleepover party. After having decided to try to summon Worth, the group moved to the bathroom and began the ritual. One of the participants later recalls:

> The feeling standing there [in the bathroom] in the dark calling the dead was uncanny. The silence and complete darkness created a sensation of total fright that was unbelievable. We could not have stood there more than a few minutes, though it seemed much longer. Suddenly with one consolidated shriek, everyone headed for the door. It was an unorganized and urgent push on everyone's part to get out as soon as possible. [W]e were uneasy for the rest of the night. (Langlois 1980:220)

Here, the spirit failed to actually show up at all. Nonetheless, the feeling of fear and expectation generated by the setting, the ritualized activity, and the social proof from fellow participants were sufficiently potent that they together served as a supernatural experience in its own right. Just as we saw in the previous account at Chapel Island, the affective "experience" was so compelling that it too prompted flight from the scene of the supposed encounter: one of the hallmarks of the legend trip, which I will examine in the next chapter.

Legend trippers who use psychic or sensitive powers—in cases of which subjective impressions or environmental ambiance are interpreted as supernatural encounters—provide a particularly pronounced form of this phenomenon. Excluding outright frauds, these individuals believe they can perceive information, like the supernatural energy of a place, through extrasensory means (Goode 2000). In doing so, they explicitly conflate subjective feelings and more objective occurrences not only for themselves but for anyone who listens to their tales. For example, Chris Woodyard is an author of allegedly real ghostly occurrences, famous for her books about haunted places in Ohio. In her visit to the Wood County Historical Center and Museum—a former work farm for the poor, sick, and mentally ill in Bowling Green, Ohio, she recounts the following experiences:

> Still in the attic storage area, I paced up the outer aisle past baby carriages, shelves of glassware and past a coffin reeking of formaldehyde only I could smell, wrapped in an avocado-green striped sheet. The sobbing of the phantom boy in the closet was gut-wrenching. I wanted to shriek

and beat the doors down. I got tenser and tenser, stabbing at the paper as I took my notes. It felt like my head was going to explode. I caught a glimpse of military uniforms on racks under sheets and scurried beyond them. [My friend] Linda, following behind me, gestured at the uniforms. "That explains it," she said. Perhaps I was picking up the terrible feelings of aggression and madness from the uniforms. Perhaps not. . . . Then I was drawn to another closet. . . . At the far end, crouching down to make himself as small as possible, was the ghost of a mentally retarded man. He had his hands cocked in front of him like a kangaroo, and he was snuffling wretchedly. The air was getting colder and colder. (Woodyard 2000:191)

To anyone unfamiliar with the author's approach, this account may be some-what disorienting. At first, it seems to be an entirely fictitious account more fitting for the drama of a Hollywood horror film than ghost "stories from the contemporary oral tradition [which] are frequently only *slightly* dramatic" (Thomas 2007:29). The author fails to inform the reader of her peculiar method of investigating allegedly haunted places. It is informed not only by physical sensations but primarily by apparently psychic or "sensitive" ones—terms she does not use in the text until we find them buried in an appendix where she notes that she "is sensitive to seeing and sensing ghosts" without further clarifi-cation (Woodyard 2000:202). This approach is not unique to Woodyard. Other paranormal authors, such as Pitkin (2010:187), similarly substitute "intuitive" impressions that they see in their "mind's eye" for more traditional sensory information. Woodyard, however, is particularly adept at conflating these so that it is not clear which she is referring to at any given moment. Our first hint of this fact is when she reports experiences that no one else who is present shares. Here, for instance, the smell of formaldehyde, which we might under-standably mistake for a physical sensation, is not shared by her friend who is also present. The emotions she feels, apparently, are meant to be understood as having been caused by an external, supernatural force. Likewise, even the sighting of the ghost is not a visual experience, not even a trick of the light, but a psychic impression. Thus, she detects the phantom image of a phantom through phantasmal means. This method of discourse is further disorienting because it becomes difficult to identify which of her experiences actually *are* objective. Her "glimpse" of the uniforms might understandably be mistaken at first for another phantom impression until we learn, through her friend's collaboration, that they are physically present and also possibly *responsible* for those impressions. Regarding the ghostly sobbing and the cold spots, these *could* be things that are physically detected, even if not necessarily due to spirits, or they could be further examples of subjective impressions. We are given no indication one way or the other.

While not always this dramatic, legend-tripping memorates are full of similar accounts: feelings of fear, of foreboding, of not being alone, of being watched by an unseen entity, and of mysterious and otherwise not fully perceived presences. Even apparently physical sensations can be entirely subjective and illusory. Research subjects who are told that a bright green bottle contains a strong mint smell often report the expected odor, even if it is truly odorless (Wiseman 2010). When these subjective impressions are taken seriously by legend trippers, as they often are to varying extents (Hanks 2015), it further increases the likelihood that nearly any trip will find "confirmation" of the legend that inspired it. The significance that some legend trippers place on feelings and mood is particularly fascinating because it conflates the actual order of events. Establishing the proper mood is an essential step in the early stages of the legend trip as it encourages those involved to entertain supernatural possibilities, to take somewhat seriously the rituals that are intended to invoke those supernatural forces, and to interpret whatever experiences they encounter as having been caused by the supernatural. By including mood as one of those supernatural outcomes, cause and effect essentially become one and the same. I am afraid to visit the haunted house because I might experience a ghost there, and simultaneously, the fear I experience at the haunted house is proof that there is a ghost present. State of mind is crucial to the entire legend-trip phenomenon—not just as a preparatory or ritual prerequisite but also as an experiential vindication.

AWARENESS AND FLIGHT

As I have illustrated in this chapter, the experiences that legend trippers usually have during the course of their journeys are not that dramatic or informative in and of themselves. Rarely do people claim to encounter fully formed apparitions or full views of cryptids in excellent lighting. Experiences like these would certainly qualify as remarkable, but more commonly, legend trippers' encounters are ambiguous at best and might not even be noticed outside the context of a legend trip. It could be a natural phenomenon, like the wind, a domestic animal in an uncanny place, or simply an eerie feeling. It could be something totally unrelated to the legend's predictions or even something at odds with those predictions. If the legend trippers, by this point, manage to achieve some sort of experience they find remarkable, this is likely due to their willingness to accept that such experiences *could* happen, their desire to achieve them, and the cultivation of a mindset that makes them possible. It also helps to have a vague legend, flexible enough to accommodate a range of experiences.

Despite all this, when they do first encounter the unknown in whatever guise it might assume, it is typically the case that they do not immediately recognize the uncanny encounter. Instead, there is a period of time in which they might mistake it for something banal or they might recognize it as somewhat odd, but the full strangeness of it is not yet consciously felt. They must draw each other's attention to whatever it is they have noticed and collectively affirm its strangeness through interaction (Ironside 2017). One reason for this lapse between experience and recognition is that those involved are still psychologically ensconced in the liminal stage of the ritual process where such things are possible and expected. However, it is not until they attempt to reconcile the experience with the everyday world from which they hailed, and to which they will soon return, that the weirdness of the encounter can be fully contextualized and therefore appreciated.

As soon as there is true awareness of the uncanny, the full strangeness of the encounter inundates those who experience it, precipitating flight away from the scene as they attempt to reconcile what they have seen or heard with their everyday understanding of the world. This effort is doomed to failure—the two cannot be reconciled. It marks a tipping point in their adventure: the end of the liminal stage and contemplation of a return to normality. Indeed, it is the apprehension of the uncanny that stimulates contemplation of that return, and contemplation further reinforces their apprehension. The achievement of the uncanny is somewhat elusive in this regard but much more so is the interpretation of the experience: the determination of what exactly it might mean. For both of these to be achieved—the definition of an experience as uncanny and the assignation of meaning to it, the participants must pass fully into the concluding stages of their legend trip.

Part IV

The Postliminal Stage

Chapter 6

THE RETURN

He returns to the shadow from which he has emerged,
and leaves the opposing forces of incredulity and belief to
fight the old battle over again on the old ground.
—WILKIE COLLINS ([1885] 2016:72)

The hour had grown late. The sun was long gone beneath the horizon, and the porch lights from some nearby houses did little to illuminate the front lawn. I was still in high school, but it was a weekend, so my parents didn't mind that I was still up, chatting with some friends on the driveway before everyone went home to their beds for the night. There were four of us altogether. Whatever we were chatting about wasn't very memorable, but we spoke enthusiastically anyway, our voices only somewhat louder than the songs of the nocturnal insects resounding in the woods around us as we tried to keep our voices down.

"What is that?" someone asked, interrupting the natural flow of the conversation. Suddenly alert, we all turned to look. At first, I saw nothing interesting as I gazed down the darkened street. Then, I noticed a small light, about two houses down and across an intersecting street where this road terminated. "It's moving," someone observed. "Yeah!" another agreed, "It looks like it's moving back and forth." It was indeed—like a small candle flame swinging on a pendulum. "What *is* that?" another friend asked, repeating the original question with greater urgency. Impulsively, I declared, "Let's go find out." Without delay, we set off down the street to investigate.

As we drew closer, something strange happened: the light stopped moving. We could still see its soft glow however, so we continued our approach, eager to solve this unexpected mystery. Soon, we had spanned most of the remaining distance, crossed the street, and stood on the edge of the lawn on the other side. The light was on the house's porch, just across the yard from us. In fact, it appeared to be no more than the light from an illuminated doorbell button. This made no sense though. Why—and how—had it been swinging only moments earlier? Hesitantly, we started to edge closer to the house to get a better look when, suddenly, we heard a terrific crash come from nearby. It sounded like something very large splashing into a body of water. Enough was enough. We didn't know what exactly was going on. The events, although not particularly dramatic, were just too strange, too inexplicable, so we ran back to the relative surety of the poorly lit driveway to consider these peculiar experiences from a safe distance.

As it turns out, this is a time-honored tradition of sorts when it comes to uncanny encounters. The next step of the legend trip is marked by a process I like to think of as *returning*—usually in a panicked state—from the site of encounter. While there is a consensus among prior researchers that something like this is a common component of legend trips, it has not previously been the subject of directed scrutiny. In this chapter, I explore how this return process is surprisingly consistent across accounts and interrogate why and how it occurs. I begin by reexamining the role of crossing liminal boundaries and consider how the overall process is a sort of mirror image of the preparatory activities that preceded arrival at the legend site. Then, I analyze the subjective experience of encountering an otherworldly force and how, on account of its disorienting characteristics, legend trippers are motivated to flee from its presence across that boundary. Simultaneously, the experience is not entirely negative, but can even present a sense of quasi-religious profundity. I also examine some of the many things that can go wrong during this stage, such as how rituals meant to dispel the supernatural threat might instead exacerbate it or, worse, how it might fail to stay in its domain when legend trippers conduct their retreat. These problems are especially revealing in that they provide further hints regarding the fundamental nature of legend trips—specifically, how their place in modern society might not be the same as that of traditional rites of passage.

THE LIMINAL CHARACTER OF SUPERNATURAL ENCOUNTER

To understand why flight happens, it is necessary to know what those involved are returning *from* and, ultimately, what they are returning *to*. Despite the odds of what a strictly materialist conception of reality might otherwise stack against them, legend trips frequently lead to an experience that seems to validate the legend's claims. This validation, as discussed in the previous chapter, takes the form of an encounter with strange events and uncanny occurrences. Many scholars have commented on this preternatural state of encounter, describing it as a sense of contact with the "numinous" (Ellis 2003), the "interstitial" (Clements 1991), or the "liminal" (Bird 2002; Kinsella 2011). These labels capture how the encounter marks a profound sense of separation from the normal order of everyday social life as well as from the ordinary workings of mundane reality itself. By classifying the experience as liminal in particular, they aptly apply van Gennep's ([1909] 1960) oft-cited conception of a sort of "threshold" phase of a rite of passage. This was later developed and applied to religious pilgrimage by Victor Turner (1977). He argues that this phase follows a "departure from an earlier fixed point in the social structure, from a set of cultural conditions (a 'state'), or from both" (Turner 1977:94)—that is, from a person's preexisting, normal life. It is experienced as a period in which "the characteristics of the ritual subject (the 'passenger') are ambiguous; he passes through a cultural realm that has few or none of the attributes of the past or coming state" (Turner 1977:94). The possibility of this separation and ambiguity first arises during the preparatory stage, but it sharpens acutely as soon as one crosses over the spatial demarcation from normal places where such things cannot occur to uncanny places where they can.

Liminality saturates this stage of the legend trip. Participants have crossed into the liminal setting where they encounter liminal forces. Even reality itself and their place in it are in doubt. To complete the journey, they must cross back over the symbolic threshold—that boundary between worlds—and, in so doing, return to everyday life. It is important to consider these concepts in further depth to understand this stage of the legend trip and some of the challenges it presents.

Houses believed to be haunted are "set apart from mundane, quotidian reality" (Grider 2007b:149) and illustrate the significance of symbolic boundaries well. For example, many legend trippers are eager to visit the "Witch House" in Salem, Massachusetts. With its dark wood siding, tiny latticed windows, and three looming gables facing the street, the house looks very much like a survival from earlier times or another world. In many ways, it is indeed just that. It was the home of Jonathan Corwin, infamous for his role as one of the judges during the gruesome witchcraft trials of 1692, although the house itself is much older than that (Witch House n.d). Legends tell of various presences one can encounter after crossing its formidable threshold (Baltrusis 2014; Guiley 2011). One visitor to the Witch House recalls (*sic* throughout):

> I went with my boyfriend [and] I really did enjoy it but as soon as I walked in a weight came over me and I all of a sudden felt very heavy and then I felt as if something freezing cold was wrapped around my legs[.] I walked through the gift shop into the hallway and all of a sudden I felt extremely sick to my stomach[.] I can't even explain it as I went through I started to feel more and more dizzy and began to feel shaky when I was in the kitchen it felt as though something has brushed

The Witch House (Salem, MA): Its façade signals to observers that the uncanny lies within. Photo by the author.

against my leg. I had to leave as soon as we were done and while walking back through the hallway to the gift shop I felt like something just all of a sudden hit me with even more dizziness[.] I felt like I was going to faint instantly and lost my balance. This place is very haunted. . . . When I finally left I felt normal again[.] I love this place but probably can not handle going back. . . . (Tripadvisor n.d.:n.p.)

The exterior of the Witch House, like all haunted houses, signals to observers that the uncanny lies in wait within but does not provide that experience on its own (Grider 2007b:149). To encounter this supernatural alternative to everyday life, one must cross over the threshold and pass into the unknown, unseen interior of the house and "once the door slams shut after the protagonist has crossed the threshold, whatever takes place inside the house will be other-worldly and surreal, and the laws of logic and physics no longer apply" (Grider 2007b:152).

The beings that reside within places like this are themselves liminal. The most thoroughly discussed entities of this sort are ghosts, which are "neither living nor dead, present nor absent, [functioning] as the paradigmatic deconstructive gesture, the 'shadowy third' or trace of an absence that undermines the fixedness of such binary oppositions" (Weinstock 2004:4). Such entities are unnerving, in part, because of the uncertain and incomplete nature of the encounter. Here, the supernatural "makes its mark by being there and not there at the same time" (Gordon 2008:6). It does not even have the decency to remain a stable, tangible, or at least comprehensible reality. The other things one might encounter during a legend trip express troubling, liminal qualities as well. The maniacs once so popular in American folklore (Brunvand 1981), which are both human and not human, might be found in liminal places. Their motives are unknowable, there movements unpredictable, and they can appear or disappear at unexpected times and places just like ghosts themselves. Or perhaps one might encounter some manner of monster: a confusing hybrid of conflicting characteristics, which down through the ages has come to represent the fears and mysteries beyond the rational, everyday world (Asma 2009). Regardless of the specific details of each situation, the place, entity, and experience encountered all thrust upon the visitor a state that is ambiguous and disorienting.

THE "WHOLLY OTHER"

The liminal state is by necessity disorienting as it calls into question all the familiar assumptions of life and reality. The experience of the numinous or liminal can be understandably shocking or frightening, even for those who were hoping for such an experience. Recalling an encounter with the "Black Angel" in the Oakland Cemetery, a location of which I discussed earlier, one of Bird's (1994) informants describes how one of the boys in their group somehow hit his head on the statue's wing—or perhaps was hit on the head *by the angel*. In the telling, the narrator seems unsure of exactly what occurred at the time. She recalls that "it was kind of strange because nobody really knew how it happened" (Bird 1994:201). This seems to have prompted a sudden awareness of a departure from everyday normality, but this absence is not replaced with a new awareness of some alternative, predictable world. In other words, the legend trippers did not learn something new that corrected an earlier misconception. There is no illuminating discovery or thought-provoking revelation to reorient them. Instead, there is only an uncomfortable feeling of contact with the unknown. This, in turn, arouses a fear response as one "guy took off and [the girls] started running around the cemetery. And so we were running and hiding [and] [e]verybody was just kind of spooked" (Bird 1994:201). The encounter with liminal, supernatural forces characteristic of the legend trip is a novel violation of expected normality as well. It is not something someone can easily make sense of by extrapolating from prior experience or knowledge. However, this is not simply due to mere novelty alone. It is marked by the sense of an intrusive presence that is potentially threatening in unknown and unknowable ways. A subsequent injury, as one of the girls tripped on a gravestone while running away, lent further credence to the perception that something uncanny had occurred. Somehow the legend's claim that the angel can do harm is revealed to be *possibly* true, but even the comfort of certainty is evasive, and the mechanism through which it is able to cause harm remains murky, undefined, and therefore more threatening than mere physical injury alone.

Indeed, it may be that the reaction that the supernatural provokes in those who witness it is more important in defining it, in knowing when it has been encountered, than any specific quality or character of the supernatural concept itself. Ronald Pearsall (2004:162) notes that psychical investigators of the Victorian age reached similar conclusions regarding ghosts: "Probably the most practical way to judge ghosts is by their capacity to frighten . . . the sheeted horrors of Victorian fiction were largely lacking in coherent and corroborated accounts[,] the ghosts reported . . . were for the most part ephemeral, inconsistent, and a little wistful." He notes that "even the most level-headed of percipients found it difficult to convert their vision into experience" (Pearsall 2004:162).

While encounter with the liminal is inevitably disorienting, threatening, and potentially earthshaking, it is not necessarily or exclusively an undesirable experience. To the contrary, this experience with the supernatural at the legend-tripping site can actually produce positive emotions as well. Some of these are fairly predictable, such as the sense of excitement and thrills that are traditionally associated with legend tripping. These are often cited as the main motivation to engage in this activity in the first place (e.g., Bird 1994). In this regard, the bulk of "the extant literature on legend tripping [emphasizes] the exploits of young adults in search of fun in rural and suburban America" (Holly and Cordy 2007:346). Many memorates of legend trips dwell in part on the fun and adventure of it all. The youths whom Thigpen (1971) studies in Indiana, for instance, are somewhat ambivalent toward the supernatural entity they claim to have encountered, called "the Watcher." Their descriptions of it vary, ranging from frightening to almost comforting, but they generally agree on the excitement of the encounters when they purposefully sought it out.

B. Ellis (2003) agrees that legend trips can be enjoyable and that this is part of their appeal but suggests fun is not a sufficient factor on its own to explain the activity. Characterizing them as merely a type of play—despite their game-like characteristics—downplays the fact that there are also serious dimensions involved (Tucker 2007). Lindahl (2005) argues that they can, at times, produce a profound, meaningful, or even spiritual sensation. For some visitors to the haunted railroad near San Antonio, experiencing the apparent presence of the children's ghosts as they push their cars safely off the tracks is experienced with "a sense of pious awe" (Lindahl 2005:174) that validates not only the legend but also their faith in God and the saints. Likewise, Eaton (2015) finds that many ghost hunters, upon encountering something that they define as a spirit, treat it seriously and interpret the experience as proof of the reality of the afterlife and of God or some higher power.

Thus, while some individuals may experience bone-chilling dread, others might feel a sense of religious or at least quasi-religious awe when encountering the supernatural. In fact, they might experience both sensations simultaneously. Illustrating this point, one legend tripper summarizes on her vlog how she felt after an uncanny encounter at Eastern State Penitentiary in Philadelphia. This former prison, turned into a tourist attraction, has become very popular with paranormal enthusiasts and seems to have provided her with a complex experience: "After what happened to me last night at Eastern State. . . . Like I wanted to cry. I was so happy but it was so terrifying, but I was just so excited . . . with what happened" (Crabb 2017a:n.p.). This looks like an irreconcilable contradiction. However, there is really nothing contradictory about these sentiments. To the contrary, both fear and awe are frequently encountered simultaneously in scholarship on conventional religion. The fact that the words "awful" and "awesome" or "terrible" and "terrific" share an etymological stem, despite contemporary distinctions in usage, is no coincidence. Summarizing the work of Rudolf Otto's *Das Heilige* (meaning, "the sacred"), Mircea Eliade (1959:9, emphasis original) captures the essence of this complex sensation well, arguing that, for one who encounters the supernatural, it is a "frightening and irrational experience . . . the *feeling of terror* before the sacred, before the awe-inspiring mystery (*mysterium tremendum*), the majesty (*majestas*) that emanates an overwhelming superiority of power; he finds *religious fear* before the fascinating mystery (*mysterium fascinans*) in which perfect fullness of being flowers." He goes on to note, "Otto characterizes all these experiences as numinous (from Latin *numen*, god), for they are induced by the revelation of an aspect of divine power. The numinous presents itself as something 'wholly other' (*ganz adere*), something basically and totally different." The experience is so immense that it is difficult to handle and incorporate into thought. "It is," Eliade (1959:9–10, emphasis original) concludes, "like nothing human or cosmic; confronted with it, man senses his profound nothingness, feels that he is only a creature, or, in the words in which Abraham addressed the Lord, is 'but dust and ashes' (Genesis, 18, 27)."

The difference between religious and paranormal phenomena does not lay in their characteristics, which are similar if not identical, but in their "cultural boundaries, as created and sustained by interpretive communities" (Baker, Bader, and Mencken 2016:337). In other words, the difference is simply due to the ways in which different groups of believers choose to categorize them. In the preceding passage, Eliade specifically refers to the mystical experience of

God. That is, to a sense of actual encounter, not a philosophy or abstract discourse on God. Yet these words might just as easily apply to some encounters with the supernatural as expressed by legend trips: they are liminal, irrational, disorienting, frightening, yet awe inspiring, and just plain fun all at once. Most importantly, they represent an extreme departure from ordinary life. Taken together, the juxtaposition of terror and the sacred can be expressed as a "confusing sense of two supernatural worlds opening up simultaneously, as if [one] were watching a horror film projected on a church altar screen as mass was in progress" (Lindahl 2005:173).

A HASTY DEPARTURE

Encounter with the supernatural is typically followed by a panicked retreat from the scene: "Something happens, someone sees or hears something, and kids jump into the car, bury their faces, scream, and speed away. The frenzy inside the car generally lasts until the teenagers are back on the main highway; everyone talks at once, in bits and pieces of, 'Oh my god' and 'Did you see?'" (Meley 1991:15). Consider, for instance, some legend-tripping accounts from Duran-Eastman Park in upstate New York. The park, which occupies land in both the city of Rochester and the town of Irondequoit, is allegedly haunted by an entity popularly called the "White Lady." Accompanied by two spectral dogs, she eternally roams its heavily wooded grounds in search of her lost daughter, and woe be unto anyone—especially teenaged boys—who she comes upon (Winfield 2008). Legend trippers are especially enthusiastic about visiting her "castle," which is actually all that remains of a former resort. The following accounts—one a memorate and one a fabulate—describe similar reactions to an apparent encounter with the White Lady:

> I cannot prove anything but, years ago, myself and two others went up there late at night to see what we could see. We definitely saw something there. A white form appeared west (starting out what looked like a porch light) and then continued to move east towards us. My two friends took off quick and ran to the car while I stayed a little longer. It was definitely something moving closer but I did not have the guts to wait until it reached me before I took off too.

> My folks told me their story. One night while searching for worms . . . they were looking down with flashlights . . . , they heard their dog (off leash of course, in those days) utter a very soft whimper. Looking up, they noticed the dog's fur standing up on it's [sic throughout] back, then spotted a white

spectral shape drifting slightly above the ground about 150 feet away from
them. Slowly floating towards them. They looked for dog and saw it running full tilt towards their car, they decided that was probably a good idea
and followed at a run and left in a hurry. (Rochester Subway 2013:n.p.)

Despite being told in very different ways, in these two accounts, supernatural
encounter predictably precipitates flight. Nor is this response limited to this
specific location.

Compare the previous reactions to a memorate from a different location.
This time the legend trippers are at a three-hundred-year-old historic house
that was turned into museum in Tolland, Connecticut. Presumably, the participants are different too, as are some other details, but the overall experience
is so nearly identical that both appear to follow some formula:

The first time I experienced the Benton Homestead was when some
friends of mine wanted to show me a Haunted [*sic* throughout] house
in Tolland. . . . We all piled into the car. . . . It was a dark and chilly night
as we drove down the winding back country roads. We pulled up in
front of the house and dared each other to get out of the car. Of course
none of us had the guts to do it! Now this old house sits really close to
the road as is typical of many old New England farmhouses. We could
plainly see through the bare windows that there were portraits on the
walls in the upstairs bedrooms. With our faces pressed to the car windows we watched the eyes in the paintings glow red! We were freaking
out! "Did you see that?!" we were screaming at each other. "GO, GO!!"
"DRIVE!!" we screamed at the driver. We were scared out of our wits. So
we burnt rubber out of there but as the road was a dead end we had to
once again drive by the house! Our friend who was driving decided to
stop in front of the house on the way back. This time a light came on in
one of the upstairs rooms. We again freaked out and begged the driver
to go. The thing is here folks . . . No one lived in the house. At that time
there was no electric lighting. There were no wires going to that house!
(Shaggyghosts and Seeker 2005:n.p.)

The resemblance across accounts is uncanny, but by no means limited to these
examples alone. Interrogating the experience of supernatural encounter that
occurs during the course of a legend trip is crucial for understanding why this
sort of response is so typical. As I have argued, retreat is partly an escape from
the baffling experiences, but it is also an attempt to *return* to the ordinary world.

First, contact with the supernatural—with the numinous or the liminal—
is disconcerting regardless of what other specific characteristics it presents.

However, it is also a temporary state. The experience is so intense and irreconcilable with daily life that it cannot be sustained. Participants feel compelled
to leave the place—often in flight or hasty retreat—of the encounter and
attempt a return to their normal lives. Achieving this requires both physical
and psychological travel from the site—which is characterized by liminality
and ambiguity—to familiar places marked by normality and, not coinciden-
tally, relative safety and predictability (Thigpen 1971). Returning to Lindahl's
(2005) study, his informant recounts her experiences with entities apart from
the ghostly children at the haunted railroad tracks. She reports that, prior to
her own journey, she had heard some people warn that there were baleful
ghost dogs with red glowing eyes in the area. After her group's experience at
the tracks, where their vehicle had been pushed off the rails by ghostly hands,
they drove down a dirt road to find a place where they could turn around in
their large van. On the way back, she recounts: "[I was] looking out my side of
the window, looking at the trees and *I see these* like glowing things—it was like
[whispering], 'What's that?'" (Lindahl 2005:169). She drew the others' attention
to the lights, to the ghastly eyes in the woods, and a general panic ensued. They
became so frightened that they did not dare get out of the van until they found
a safe place: a service station back on the freeway.

A clear sense of tension permeates this account. Everyone is huddled
together in the darkness of the van while a deeper and more mysterious darkness looms just outside, full of lurking but unknown dangers of a wholly other
nature. What if they cannot find a place to turn around and must instead
continue down this remote dirt path under the malign gaze of these spectral watchers? Worse still, what if, in their attempt to turn around, the vehicle
becomes mired in a ditch or some other obstacle? Even though it is normally
part of the ritual to get out of the vehicle and look for the handprints that
the ghost children are supposed to leave on your car while pushing it off the
tracks, the group decides that they must wait until they escape the site of the
encounter to do so. It is here, under the banal lights of a gas station, far from
the red glowing eyes of the phantom dogs, that they at last find the expected
handprints. The station is safe not just because it is spatially distant from the
site of the encounter but also because it is normal, prosaic. They have crossed
back over the threshold into the everyday world. Conversely, because the legend
is closely associated with its setting (Gabbert 2015), it cannot follow them here
to do harm: the liminal must stay in its liminal setting, "an isolated railroad
crossing at the southern extreme of San Antonio" (Lindahl 2005:165).[1]

This pattern is typical of this sort of legend. Normal creatures, like birds,
can come and go. They can pass through your backyard and be on their way,
they can spend a while in a tree before departing, they can even accidentally
find their way into your house and cause a good deal of havoc before you

show them the door.[2] In many ways, normal creatures are at least potentially roving or migratory, but the supernatural—ghosts and monsters—are more typically thought to be bound to the places in which they reside, even if the migratory nature of legends themselves change the specific location of that place. Traditionally, supernatural beings cannot just pass through or come and go as they please. To haunt, for them, is to dwell. Many people believe that ghosts, for example, are bound to the place where they died on account of suicide or murder (Goldstein 2007a; Waskul 2016). In an episode of the reality ghost-hunting show *Kindred Spirits*, investigators Adam Berry and Amy Bruni (2022b) are investigating a haunted inn. At one point, they are discussing possible ways to trap the resident ghost. Concerned that the invisible entity might overhear their plans, they cautiously continue their discussion outside where they assume the spirit cannot follow. For legend trippers, visiting a place like this, where the supernatural dwells, risks running afoul of the entity. Its territory is liminal but also *limited*—both known and unknown, since we can articulate its boundaries but not understand its content or fundamental "nature." Retreating from the boundaries of these liminal places and back into the quotidian world means returning from the threat of encounter to safety, from the strange to the familiar, from the unknowable to the knowable. The idea that the supernatural is locally bound occurs throughout folklore both old and new. According to one source, for example:

> Most authorities agree that ghosts do not travel. Ghosts will not follow you home, take up residence in your car, or attempt to occupy your body. They are held in a time and space by deep emotional ties to an event or place. Ghosts have been observed on airplanes, trains, buses, and ships; however, it is unlikely that the destination interests them. Something about the journey, some event such as a plane crash or train wreck, accounts for their appearance as travelers. (Dwyer 2008:20)

Statements of this sort offer some reassurance to those who hope—or fear—to encounter supernatural entities. The threat, while seemingly real, can only last as long as the time spent visiting the place wherein it dwells. This offers a degree of control over the unknown at least so far as limiting exposure amounts to control. Just as a border was crossed that marked entry into a realm where supernatural encounters could be had, so too can one cross back over that border when the legend trippers retrace their paths back into the ordinary world.

Just as it did during the preparatory stage, physical distance contributes to the experience, but it is not the distance travelled alone that marks the transition. It is also the *symbolic* distance associated with it: the culturally and psychologically meaningful thresholds that are transgressed. Edith Wharton expresses this fact well in the story "Bewitched." As her protagonists approach a place where uncanny events are occurring, they begin to sense the strangeness of the terrain they have just entered: "'I never knew a place,' Deacon Hibben said, 'as far away from humanity. And yet it ain't so in miles.'" To this, his companion Orrin Bosworth replies, "Miles ain't the only distance" (Wharton [1925] 2016:414). This socio-spatial phenomenon is the reason why legend trippers can achieve safety by returning to a normal place, like a service station, after returning from a haunted rail crossing (Lindahl 2005) or immediately upon crossing a bridge that puts you right "in the main downtown part where it's really well lit" (Waskul 2016:84). This is also why the same sensation can be achieved when one flees their own haunted basement or attic, hurrying through the transitional space of a stairwell and returning safely to the domestic normality of a brightly lit living room or kitchen. Measured in physical distance, the two zones—natural and supernatural—might only be a few feet or even mere inches apart, but the symbolic distance is vast and incalculable, nonetheless.

In one contemporary haunted house legend, homeowner Debra Pickman (2010) describes how much of the supernatural activity she and her husband, Tony, experienced seemed centered in their upstairs nursery. During one incident, they discovered that some unknown agency had moved all the stuffed animals from the room's shelves to the floor. Later, having replaced the toys on the shelves and investigating the room with Debra's sister, Karen, the three tried to come up with some explanation. Failing that, they made their way back downstairs. Once there, Karen looked up the stairs they had just descended and announced with dread:

> "The light in the nursey is back on." [The group w]ent back up the stairs, packed closely to each other like a small herd of sheep. . . . We emerged at the top, peered into . . . what should have been a tranquil room. On the floor in the middle of the room, face up on the floor, lay [a] small scruffy teddy bear. We agreed that for the rest of the evening we would stay as close together as possible. (Pickman 2010:23–24)

What should be a safe, domestic space transformed into an unpredictable place of fear and danger. Later, when the couple had company over, the nursery became a destination for further legend trips. After hearing about the room, two guests went upstairs to investigate. As they stood in the doorway to the room, the hallway light behind them suddenly turned off and back on of its own accord. The two men turned and looked at each other as they tried to process the event, then "without warning, [they] all but trampled each other to get downstairs and away from the ghost they realized was in the area" (Pickman

2010:170). This safe space was mere yards away, just downstairs, but simultaneously worlds removed from the nether realm.

Insights into this process can be gleaned by examining one frequently occurring element typical to these legendary trips: cars. Automobiles are exceptionally meaningful artifacts within American culture (Lewis and Goldstein 1983), and their relevance is maintained even within legend tripping. B. Ellis (2003) in particular has drawn attention to the important role cars play in this process.[3] He points out that the destinations for these uncanny journeys frequently cannot be reached on foot, and this might be precisely the point. This observation, added to the close association of legend tripping with adolescents in the literature, leads him to conclude that the car is both a symbolic and practical expression of the newfound freedom adolescence brings to young people: "the legend trip is an extension of the car's normal function for adolescents—the creation of a personal, mobile territory where they are free to make their own rules" (Ellis 2003:190) and simultaneously challenge the rules of the adult world. The car enables adolescents, and presumably others, to make a journey through space and symbolism, beyond the borders of the everyday to plumb the confusing mysteries of the liminal realm.

Yet the car is also a sort of "refuge from outside threats" (Ellis 2003:190). In addition to allowing travelers to go forth, it also allows for the return journey because, unlike the supernatural, humans do not dwell permanently in interstitial places but are just passing through. Moreover, in most legends involving youths in cars, the danger exists outside of the car and cannot enter it, even while they remain in a liminal place. It is only when some foolish protagonist *leaves* the relative safety of its confines—while parked at a "Lovers Lane" for instance—that the dangerous forces outside can do them harm (see Brunvand 1981). As Lindahl's (2005) legend trippers in their van experienced, the ghostly children left the sign of their presence on the *outside* of the vehicle, and even the ghostly dogs, no matter how frightening, seemed incapable of doing harm while the legend trippers remained within the confines of their vehicle.[4] Likewise, in the account I gave in this book's introduction of my legend trip to the haunted cemetery during my college days, the car played an important role. We drove to the legendary site, building suspense along the way, and returned in the same vehicle. During the final "encounter," when we thought something heard but unseen was making its way toward us, it was by getting hastily back into the car that we were able to feel a degree of relative safety from the perceived threat. Once secure within, this feeling increased as we drove off, putting distance between ourselves and the liminal place. It was not until we returned to campus, with its familiar buildings, glaring lights holding back the dark, and bustling signs of human activity, that we achieved a more complete sense of having returned to the normal world and safety. The car symbolizes and enables both freedom and excitement. However, it simultaneously represents and provides safety and predictability too. The car is, thus, something of a paradox since these outcomes are usually mutually exclusive (Bauman 2001). It is a vehicle, so to speak, for bridging the gap between the mundane and the liminal—between the quotidian and the numinous, a sort of human-made psychopomp for the living.

WHEN THE SUPERNATURAL MISBEHAVES

Contact with the liminal, then, creates a potent but unsettling emotional response, which in turn triggers a desire to flee and seek "safety." Safety can be temporarily achieved by retreating to a sheltered place that the supernatural might not enter, like the interior of a car. A more conclusive form of safety can only be secured by fleeing away from liminal sites entirely and returning to mundane places where the supernatural cannot follow. However, this is only *usually* the case. Many people worry that the liminal will not behave as it is supposed to, and some claim to have experienced just that. This lack of consistency should probably be expected from something that by its very definition frustrates human attempts to understand, predict, and make sense of it. For instance, without being sought, sometimes the supernatural simply shows up in peoples' homes before moving on just as mysteriously. A famous case was written by James Thurber ([1933] 1990), a humorist and cartoonist, in his tale, "The Night the Ghost Got In." While he took literary license in presenting the events that he experienced, the essential elements of his real encounter with the supernatural remain the same as those in the story.[5] It happened one night when he was young and living in his family home in Columbus, Ohio. Thurber was washing up in the second-floor bathroom before bed when he heard heavy footsteps circling the dining room table on the ground floor. Awakening his brother, the two of them stood at the top of the stairs to listen, thinking perhaps a burglar had broken in. Suddenly, the steps quickened their pace, and they heard whoever or whatever it was running up the steps toward them, but they still saw nothing. Whatever it was, it was apparently invisible. Understandably panicked, Thurber's brother beat a hasty retreat back to his bedroom, throwing the door shut behind him. Thurber held out until just before the unseen entity reached him before slamming the bathroom door in its hypothetical face. Despite more recent and ongoing claims that visitors to the house make of ghostly experiences there (Smith 2002), the encounter was a one-time experience for Thurber. In the story, he writes, "After a long minute, I slowly opened [the door] again. There was nothing there. There was no sound. None of us ever heard the ghost again" (Thurber [1933] 1990:475). Unlike most liminal beings, this one does not seem to have been bound to place. It did not exist in the house previously and did not continue to haunt it following this single encounter. In fact, much like more mundane creatures and as the title of the story indicates, it just "gets into the house" one night and is gone the next. Far from being reassuring, the strangeness of the encounter is further exacerbated by its failure to act in predictable ways. Rather than behaving as an enduring presence in a strange, liminal place, this ghost is a temporary presence in a domestic, nonliminal space.

So, while the supernatural *should* stay in its place and usually does, occasions such as this in which it fails to do so are especially troubling and may stick with a person who encounters them. This seems to have been the case for Thurber. The events described are fairly mild as far as legendary encounters go, but they left their mark nonetheless, and he recalls them years later in his writing. The events seem to haunt readers of the tale as well. Interestingly, others have attempted to make sense of his encounter by linking it to place. The not-for-profit foundation that maintains the property as a literary center and museum to this day, called simply the Thurber House (2022), provides an example of this on their website.[6] They suggest that the ghost might be linked to an earlier structure that stood on the site: the Ohio Lunatic Asylum. They claim that a fire at the asylum, which killed seven people, occurred exactly forty-seven years before the date Thurber had his experience. Regardless of whether any of these claims are true, it seems to indicate that we are more comfortable with the idea of tragic deaths haunting a place than unpredictable hauntings appearing more or less at random. By attempting to provide a pseudorational explanation for the ghost, the narrative serves as a type of exorcism, the purpose of which is not so much to banish the supernatural as to make it predictable, subject to the control of human comprehension, and therefore less threatening.

Thurber's account illustrates another important fact. Sometimes it is not the spooky cemetery or the abandoned mansion where the supernatural is encountered but within the walls of one's own home. Sigmund Freud (1919) describes such experiences as *unheimlich*—a word that translators usually express as "uncanny" in English but which literally means "unhomelike" in German. When people suspect that they have a ghost lurking about their house, they will go to great lengths to remove these "quintessential unwanted guests" (Dickey 2016b:70). Encountering the supernatural in distant, liminal places is frightening enough, but suddenly encountering them in a place that is supposed to be mundane and safe, especially your own home, is worse. This is especially true if the encounter does not occur in a liminal area of the home, like the basement or attic, where such things might be expected (Goldstein, Grider, and Thomas 2007), but rather in a central domestic area, like the bedroom. People expect their bedrooms to be characterized by "safety and peace [but] ghosts turn this expectation around" (Tucker 2007:64).[7]

Differences in *how* and *where* one encounters the supernatural can affect the way in which people experience and receive a supernatural encounter. When they encounter it willingly and in an appropriate setting—as on a legend trip, the experience can be simultaneously negative and positive as described above. When the encounter is not voluntary, not expected, and occurs in an inappropriate place, the negative predominates. Legend trips are generally voluntary affairs but spontaneous encounters are not. For instance, as noted earlier, a few decades ago some Indiana youths had encounters with an entity they called "the Watcher" (Thigpen 1971). While, overall, the accounts express ambivalence toward it, the memorates of legend trippers purposely seeking the entity out had a more positive tone overall compared to those who did not try to encounter it but ran into it nonetheless. While both groups had an "immediate reaction" of fear, the former also expressed "curiosity and fascination" (Thigpen 1971:170). The latter group, conversely, experienced the phenomenon by accident and was much less pleased with the encounter. The same pattern holds when considering supernatural experiences in the context of real-estate transactions. Some people may like the prospect of buying a haunted house while others shy away from it. The ability to choose mediates whatever feelings the proud new owner of an old haunted house might express toward the experience: "When buying the ghostly presence is a matter of choice, the ghost is a commodity, but when the ghost is encountered by accident it becomes a liability for both sellers and buyers" (Goldstein 2007a:180). In other words, people who have foreknowledge of a house's reputation but elect to buy it anyway voluntarily expose themselves to the possibility of encounter with the supernatural, just like legend trippers. In making the choice themselves, they experience a degree of agency, exerting some control over the unknown. Subsequent encounters may be frightening, but they will also present positive dimensions. Suddenly and without warning finding yourself beset by unknown ghosts in your home, against your will, is another matter entirely. Even in the absence of actual encounter, the sudden knowledge that *other* people believe your house is haunted is no less unsettling, even if your only concern is for the viability of future resale of the property.[8]

Despite the traditional belief that spirits should stay put, that the supernatural is bound to liminal places, a similar pattern can be traced in the common concern among legend trippers that something they encounter on their journey might disobey expectations and follow them home anyway. This sort of encounter seems to correspond with the highest degree of fear and the least amount of pleasure when compared to other legendary experiences. There are many accounts of people concerned about this possibility. A caretaker at the 1890

House Museum—an historic mansion in Cortland, New York—expresses her worry about entities following her after work during an episode of the television show *Ghost Hunters* (Peebles 2013). A member of the investigating team asks her how she would feel if they discovered that the mansion was indeed haunted. She replies somewhat haltingly as she tries to put her concern into words: "I would think a little differently about my job. I don't want anything . . . haunted, following me. Following me when I go to my car and I leave, going to my house. I don't know if spirits travel. I'd be concerned if they were—with me" (Peebles 2013). She was greatly reassured, later in the show, when the team informed her that while there were likely spirits present in the mansion, they were harmless and probably tied to the place and so, in all likelihood, would not follow her.

Not everyone is so lucky. Ghost lore is full of accounts of people terrorized by the supernatural violating the safety and sanity of their home. The following example, written by a woman who found that the house she and her family moved into was unexpectedly haunted, illustrates the potential severity of this sort of concern:

> It wasn't long before I began to feel ashamed about what was going on in the house. I was frightened that there might be something wrong with me, something almost humiliating. When I lost a night's sleep to unrelenting suffocating dreams, when I lay awake listening to unseen footsteps until the wee hours of the morning, I wondered if perhaps I was under too much stress. Maybe enduring my difficult marriage, attending nursing school, and taking care of my children might be proving too much for me. I didn't *feel* crazy, but I was concerned. My husband thought this was all nonsense. When I tried to bring up the subject with my parents, they just stared at me in disbelief. Except for my brother, Joe, there was no one I felt could understand, never mind explain, what was happening to us. (Mercado 2006:33, emphasis original)

Regardless of the extent to which the attribution of these events to supernatural agents is accurate or not, this excerpt accurately conveys the *fears* of what *could* happen should someone encounter a haunting in their home. This sense of intrusion can threaten their normal lives and relationships, causing some to think they are going crazy or that their lives are falling apart because of an unwanted spirit.[9] It is the fear of supernatural invasion from outside entering the home that is the subject of so much popular discourse, not the fear of going forth and encountering the supernatural, which by contrast is not without its charm.

PRACTICING SAFE LEGEND TRIPPING

Suddenly and involuntarily finding you have been beset by spirits may be a disturbing problem, but it is not the one legend trippers typically worry about. According to one source, "the biggest problem with haunted places is that sometimes you don't come home alone. Here's how to avoid bringing home an unwanted guest" (Wright 2019:n.p.). This is an equally problematic case of the supernatural misbehaving. Legend trippers want to experience it, but they want it to end too. Fortunately, as this source indicates, there are many protective measures one can take. The author suggests saying a prayer, creating barriers that ghosts cannot cross with salt, periodically blessing your house, refraining from buying antiques since these could have spirits attached to them, and so forth. Activities like these qualify as "postliminal rites," which mark reentry from a liminal zone and allow "incorporation into the new world" (van Gennep [1909] 1960:21). Regarding bringing dangerous objects home, one famous incident concerned an allegedly demonically possessed doll that tormented two roommates who brought it home one day (Brittle 1980). This particular case was thoroughly popularized, and the story was featured in the popular films *The Conjuring* (2013) and *Annabelle* (2014). Many other stories of spirits tagging along after the objects they are attached to are brought to one's home are in circulation, albeit few reach this level of fame. The television series *Haunted Collector* focuses entirely on this sort of phenomenon, and books dedicated to the subject are published with surprising frequency. These sport titles like *Possessed Possessions* (Okonowicz 1996), *Haunted Objects* (Balzano and Weisberg 2012), *Haunted Stuff* (Graham 2014), and, of course, *Demonic Dolls* (Harker 2015). While dolls, not surprisingly, seem to be the single most common cause for concern,[10] nearly anything *could* warrant fears of supernatural entities.

One of the most fascinating haunted-object legends I have encountered is in regard to a house called Belcourt in Newport, Rhode Island. Although a mansion by most people's standards, Belcourt was built as a "summer cottage" by Oliver Hazard Perry Belmont, who only occupied the immense structure a few weeks per year (Tinney 2012). Work was completed in 1894, when it joined the ranks of numerous other "cottages" built by families with names like Vanderbilt and Astor, along the famous Bellevue Avenue. Belcourt's reputation as a haunted house did not really take off until after the Tinney family bought the place in 1956. They brought "17 van-loads of glorious furnishings" with them, including piles of antiques from around the world and, supposedly, the numerous spirits attached to them (Tinney 2012:6). Because of these haunted objects,

> there is hardly a room in the mansion that can be said to be specter-free[:] the spirit haunting the sacrificial stone of the Mayan God of

Belcourt of Newport (Newport, RI): Once said to be haunted, this house allegedly held spirits that were banished by removing the antiques they were attached to. Photo by the author.

Gardens; the poltergeist in the English library . . . ; the arm that points through the staircase; the lady in the ball gown in the second floor gallery; the pink lady . . . in the Madame's bedroom; the British soldier, dressed in full regimentals; the samurai warrior . . . ; the white lady who walks through walls in the Grand Hall and gallery; the suit of armor that screams; the swishing battle axe in the weapons cabinet; the ghostly dancers in the French Gothic ballroom; the two spirits who haunt the medieval salt chairs [and] the mysterious monk statue. (Smith 2012:xi)

According to recent additions to the legend, the new owner, Carolyn Rafaelian, got rid of all the ghosts when she bought Belcourt in 2012. She didn't need to burn sage or hire an exorcist, however. All she had to do was remove all the haunted objects (Troost-Cramer 2017). Accounts of the transformation imply that the new owner was probably more interested in exorcising Belcourt's old reputation than she was with actually banishing any lingering spirits.

Most legends about introducing the supernatural into a home through the introduction of haunted objects reflect deeper levels of distress than this account, however, and a harder time dealing with the unwanted supernatural intrusion. In one tale, a family accidentally purchased an antique dresser complete with mirror and resident demon for their daughter's apartment (Okonowicz 1996). The mother received a panicked call from her daughter one day. She was crying and shouting, claiming that the entity was trying to get her. Her mother promptly came over to investigate—an interesting legend trip based on only a few family experiences—and finds her daughter just outside the apartment door, beside herself with fear. The mother reports that upon opening the apartment door to look into the matter further, her daughter suddenly rushed into the room where she "started twirling, spinning around, like she was possessed. . . . Her head jerked back and her eyes rolled up toward the top of her head." Witnessing this unnerving behavior, her "heart was pounding," and then, still watching her daughter, she recounts, "[I] actually saw her starting to rise off the floor, as if something was pulling her up into the air. . . . I pulled her out of there and took her home with me" (Okonowicz 1996:15). Interestingly, it is not only the dresser that is demonically "possessed" but soon the entire apartment and, it appears, its resident as well. These boundaries are transgressed, dissolved. By recklessly bringing the haunted object into the apartment, the safe, domestic space of the home is transformed into a dangerous, liminal one. It is only through bringing her daughter to her own home, free of spirited objects, that they achieve a true return to safety. Subsequent removal of the antique dresser solves the problem, and the apartment is restored to its status as a normal place, but this simple solution is not always characteristic of these stories. It is for this reason that the author advises, "I suggest you be wary of that special piece that now stands unattended—patiently awaiting its resurrection from the locked trunk in your garage or from that cardboard box in the back of your cluttered van" (Okonowicz 1996:5). This warning, like most legend warnings, can also act as a dare to go ahead and do what it seems to be cautioning against. As illustrated in chapter 4, removing items from a haunted location, such as "tombstones and gravesite dirt" (Holly and Cordy 2007:347), is sometimes part of a ritual requirement since it may provoke the dead into showing themselves or act as proof that one braved the frightening location. However, the implication that this danger could be encountered anywhere, whether you purposely seek it out or not, further reflects the tension present when the borders of liminal and everyday spaces collapse.[11]

Because of fears concerning the possibility of bringing dangerous supernatural forces home with them, beyond just leaving antiques well enough alone, many ghost hunters engage in protective rituals (Eaton 2015). As I discussed in chapters 3 and 4, rituals that take place early in the legend-trip process increase fear and expectation, enabling a supernatural encounter. Cleansing or closing rituals, which take place after an encounter, are supposed to reduce fear and symbolically end the encounter. One psychic medium reports that after an investigation, she usually blesses her car with holy water before driving away "to prevent any unwanted visitors" (Wood and Kolek 2009:209). When she gets home, she usually performs an additional closing ritual. This is a "sea salt cleansing," a "method of removing residual energy" by mixing "salt and spring water" and either pouring it over your body or placing it "under the head of the bed" while you sleep (Wood and Kolek 2009:210). After an investigation at the haunted Concord Colonial Inn of Massachusetts, however, she failed to perform these rituals. She remarks, "Intuitively, I knew the [spirit] had followed me home" (Wood and Kolek 2009:211).

Should you believe, as this psychic did, that something followed you home, there are various rituals that can be tried to cast it out. If a priest is not available, you can perform a sort of DIY exorcism. This can be accomplished, for instance, by sprinkling holy water throughout your home, invoking the name of Christ, and sleeping firmly wedged between two Bibles for a month or so (Pitkin 2010:354). Another common ritual of this sort is "smudging," a kind of ceremonial burning of some substance, often sage, believed to have supernatural efficacy. In providing advice on how to deal with evil spirits in the case of possession, one proponent of the practice gives instructions on how to perform the ceremony on an afflicted person. She suggests that you must "start with a prayer of intent: 'You are surrounded and protected by divine energy.'" Once this is done, you should "light a sage or sandalwood incense stick and trace the person's outline with the stick." This is because, "smoke acts as a conduit for the positive intent of clearing energy and will gently clear the auric field," and she advises that "you can also use smudging to clear a hotel room, classroom, or even your home after the stale smoke and negative vibes of a party" (Kuzmeskus 2006:116). At a witchcraft shop in Salem, Massachusetts—where there are many to choose from, I found a range of objects like this for sale. One of these was a smudge stick made of sage and cedar, sporting the brand name Tituba's. The packaging helpfully reminds you that Tituba was one of the first people to be accused of witchcraft during Salem's hysteria and uncritically states that she did indeed teach magic to children. While slightly ominous, this branding seems intended to give credence to the potency of the smudge stick by association. The packaging also tells you how to use it to "cleanse negative or harmful energy" from any space or from your body.

This is all very reassuring for those concerned about unwanted ghosts, but it is not just the spirits of the dead that legend trippers need to worry about. Other supernatural entities can hitch a ride and follow us home too. Not to be outdone by demons and human spirits, there are various faeries and elementals that might attach themselves to you as well if you are not careful. The *bwciod*, for example, is apparently a type of "solitary Welsh goblin" that wanders at night "in wilderness places looking for humans to follow home," and once one occupies your home, "it is very difficult to make him or her leave" (Chauran 2013:30). Fortunately, this author suggests some charms that might do the trick, like wearing a four-leaf clover or planting a mulberry tree by your door.

While examples like these might be humorous from an outsider's perspective, supernatural invasion of the home is a serious concern for many people. Accounts of protective ceremonies in action reveal not only the potency of these concerns but also tend to illustrate a lack of confidence in the rituals themselves. Both folk and popular accounts of supernatural encounters are full of claims of ineffective talismans, failed exorcisms, and similarly ineffective closing rituals. A homeowner demonstrates these concerns well in an episode of *Kindred Spirits* (Berry and Bruni 2022b). She was terrified of the presence haunting her home and refused to enter it alone, especially at night. On previous occasions, she had attempted to burn sage to purify the house and cast the troublesome specter out. Unfortunately, she found that these attempts backfired, and every time she tried the ritual, the activity would only get worse. In an interesting turn of events, the show's investigators then tried smudging themselves. In their case, they weren't trying to get rid of the entity. Instead, they hoped that by replicating the homeowner's actions they could likewise get the ghost to act up since, until that point, they weren't having much luck experiencing anything. Curiously, this too failed. Rather than increasing the intensity of the paranormal activity, the sage did nothing at all.

As illustrated by the homeowner in this example, closing rituals can actually increase fear of supernatural threats rather than help assuage them as they are supposed to. This is partly because they offer a reminder of the threat, reinforcing it and making it seem more real, rather than providing a convincing means of defusing it. In this regard, they are more similar to preliminary rites or the rituals that occur on site to summon the spirts. In fact, this example shows how easily these moments can be conflated or repurposed by other parties and highlight problems with the ritual process. First, smudging *should* serve to close the encounter but only makes it worse. Then, when the legend trippers subsequently try smudging, which in this context *should* call up the supernatural encounter, it fails that purpose as well. In both cases, both the entity and the rituals behave in unpredictable ways. They offer no comfort and no control.

Contextualized as part of the legend-trip phenomenon, all these concerns—of spirits not staying in their liminal domains as they should but instead violating the border of normality by following you home or taking possession of you and of rituals not working as they should—indicate a fundamental problem with the ritual process. Earlier, I showed how failing to complete the proper invocations during the ritual phase and, thus, failing to achieve the proper mindset could result in a failed legend trip with no encounter. Something similar can occur here, except instead of a failed encounter, the participants fail to *end* the encounter. It is not simply the fact that the supernatural has strayed into banal realms that is the main problem. Liminal experiences are supposed to end once one has mentally and physically returned to the everyday world. These spatial definitions are symbolic borders of the psychological conditions of the individual and the socially constructed boundaries established by the group. The experience of the supernatural where and when it should not be marks not only a rupture of the boundary between worlds but also a failure of individuals to return to their normal world. Psychologically, they have not left the liminal behind them at all, regardless of where they find themselves physically. Like the spirit they hoped to encounter, they are trapped betwixt and between. Both haunted and haunting, they have, in effect, not returned from the legend trip at all.

It is worth considering, for comparison, those cases in which instead of the supernatural refusing to stay in its place, it refuses to allow those trespassing in *its* place to leave. It is not uncommon to read legend-tripping accounts where the participants, upon attempting to flee the scene of encounter, find themselves temporarily barred from doing so by the forces they have unleashed. A classic account provided by one of Thigpen's (1971:188) informants describes how she and her friends were briefly frustrated in their attempts to flee a haunted house when they found that "all the doors were bolted" that had previously been open. Similar tales are still told. In a more recent account from the haunted cemetery in Naugatuck, Connecticut, the narrator ran afoul of a comparable obstacle barring flight from the scene: "I have been trapped in this cemetery 2 [*sic*] times already, and by trapped, we mean the iron gate is shut and will not open, even though moments earlier, it opens freely. . . . We found ourselves climbing and jumping over the stone wall to get out" (Ghostwatcherz 2011). Dramatic as such experiences at first appear, they seem to reflect a sense of frightened excitement that adds to the experience more than the more serious concern of permanent, unwilling encounter with the supernatural. Their tone is somewhat brazen, and the supernatural force's attempts to trap these transgressors are consistently ineffective. Being convinced that such occurrences are supernatural in origin should certainly impress those involved, but it is not threatening in the same sense that being followed home by an entity is. Having visited this cemetery myself, I noted that the walls around it are low enough that a fussy gate would be more a source of annoyance than true terror. At this point, the participants are indeed psychologically prepared to depart and need simply, albeit heroically, to overcome some obstacles before they successfully do so. The cemetery walls are more meaningful as symbols demarcating the liminal realm than they are physically significant barriers to movement.

A SAFE RETREAT

As I have argued in this chapter, returning from the site of encounter is an essential component of legend tripping. Assuming participants have completed the previous stages successfully, leading to the culminating experience of a run-in with the supernatural itself, they must next separate from that experience and return to their normal lives. This is compelled by a disturbing but equally awesome experience that is difficult to endure. In their flight, they must cross back over the threshold demarcating the ordinary world from the extraordinary world where the supernatural *should* remain. Yet sometimes it fails to do so. Instead, it follows them past this boundary and creates ruptures in their normal lives. Indeed, sometimes it appears suddenly in their normal lives even when they have not sought it at all. These problems reveal some interesting dimensions of legend trips that are not present in proper rites of passage, such as persistent ambiguity and severe doubt in the process or in its outcomes. They also display contradiction or uncertainty in cultural expectations: the supernatural should behave a certain way—except when it does not. I will return to these matters later when I try to make sense of legend tripping as whole.

Nonetheless, despite any concerns that the supernatural will give chase and follow them and, in fact, in large part because of that fear, at some point following their encounter, legend trippers will feel compelled to hastily depart from the presence of the unknown. Eventually there must come a time when most legend trippers will have well and truly left the encounter behind them and made it to a place of relative safety and normality. For some, there might be lingering uncertainty over whether they really left it behind and further rituals will be needed. For others, the return will be abrupt and definitive. All have traveled through physical space, perhaps running only a few blocks or maybe driving many miles. The actual distance is not important so long as it provides a sense of separation between themselves and the legend site. This physical distance, in turn, provides a sense of symbolic distance in that it provides, or should provide, a barricade of sorts between the travelers and the liminal frontier. They have traversed that boundary, that threshold, to come into the presence of the paranormal. Now, ideally, they have crossed it again to remove themselves from its presence. Once accomplished, the next and final stage of the legend trip can begin and, thus, conclude the whole affair. In the following section, I will explore this ultimate stage and, in the process, come to understand how and why legend trips can and do often go awry.

Chapter 7

TELLING THE TALE

There in seclusion and remote from men
The wizard hand lies cold,
Which at its topmost speed let fall the pen,
And left the tale half told.
—HENRY WADSWORTH LONGFELLOW (1867:22)

I stood in darkness. Again, a small light shone softly, just ahead in the murk. "Look!" I said, indicating the light. "If you watch it long enough, you might begin to see it move. It might even swing back and forth like it's on a pendulum." It was like the past repeating itself, except I was no longer in high school, and I wasn't hanging out on my parents driveway. I was in a classroom, the light projected onto a presentation screen at the front of the room, telling the tale of my experience with the mysterious light to thirty or so undergraduates enrolled in one of my college courses. Today's lesson wasn't about ghosts or the supernatural though. We were talking about social psychology: specifically, how our brains are susceptible to social influences.

You see, when my friends and I witnessed that strange light so many years ago, which I described in the previous chapter, we could not understand or explain it. We had only our senses and each other's perceptions to draw on, and these were not enough. The strangeness of the experience, and our inability to come up with a reasonable explanation for it, caused us to retreat to a safe distance. Once there, we promptly began to exchange guesses regarding what had just happened. I wondered, for example, whether the light was hanging loosely on exposed wires and swinging, but this didn't seem quite right. None of our other guesses were any better. None of us felt it was a ghost or even necessarily supernatural, we were just plain stumped and had to leave the matter at that: unsatisfied and unclear. I can't say it was a particularly meaningful or transformative experience, but every now and then, I'd call it to mind for the simple reason that I wanted an explanation. It wouldn't be until many years later that I accidentally found one.

I was studying social psychology in graduate school when I stumbled upon the answer in a textbook. It was this answer that, back in the classroom, I shared with my students as I turned the lights back on with a click. People have been seeing the same phenomenon for several hundred years at least and, probably, since the dawn of time. The Prussian polymath Alexander von Humboldt discusses the apparent movement of stationary stars in the night sky—which he called "*sternschwanken*"—in his great work *Kosmos* (1850). Researchers soon realized the stars were not really moving because independent observations described entirely different motion. Today, the bizarre phenomenon is fairly well understood. Called the "autokinetic effect" and not limited to stars alone, it is a visual illusion where small lights in the darkness or even small objects against a black background can give the appearance of movement (Guilford and Dallenbach 1928). This concept perfectly explains what we experienced that night.

First, someone had to notice the light and proceed to stare at it. Given that we were just standing around in the dark on the driveway without much else to see, there was plenty of opportunity for this. Next, the conditions were well suited to experiencing the autokinetic effect: a small light in the darkness and therefore no frame of reference to judge its size, location, or (lack of) motion (Guilford and Dallenbach 1928). In this situation, the observer's brain makes random guesses, and the lack of peripheral field plays havoc on eye muscles, whose movements the brain misinterprets as motion of an object (Rucci and Poletti 2009). So, whoever first saw the light soon mistakenly saw motion. They realized something strange was going on and drew everyone else's attention to it, a common preliminary in supernatural encounters (Ironside 2017). Since we all perceived movement, this seemed to validate the claim that something strange was happening. Yet didn't the fact that we all saw the same swinging movement instead of each perceiving our own random pattern at odds with each other's observations prove that the light really was moving?

As it turns out, the answer is "no." Psychologist Muzafer Sherif (1935) studied the effect under laboratory conditions and found that observers influence each other's perceptions of the light's movement. Through discussion, they tend to converge on a consensus, albeit a false one since the light is in fact stable. The "movement" is random because it is really just manufactured by the brain. However, as soon as someone describes what they *think* they are seeing—in our case, a swinging pendulum motion—everyone else will begin to see that as well through the effect of informational social influence. Then, perception altered, we all agree on what we see, and our social consensus looks like proof that this is what really happened. Witnesses to both paranormal and ordinary events often say things like "I know what I saw" and "there were other witnesses who saw the same thing." Intuitively, this social proof sound like good evidence

(Cialdini 1993), but it is only evidence of social psychology. The light was just a stationary doorbell light. That being said, while research continues to unravel the specific mechanisms of the autokinetic effect and similar phenomena, its exact physiology is still not perfectly understood (e.g., Skewes et al. 2013). Come to think of it, I never did figure out what the splash that accompanied the light was either. So, fittingly, some unanswered questions remain.

In this scenario, discussion literally creates the perception of mystery. Afterwards, we also resorted to discussion to try to solve the puzzle, but it did not provide any answers, and we were just left wondering about it. This sort of discussion marks the end of a legend trip: the quest at last approaches its conclusion and soon our weary travelers can rest. They have braved the unknown and returned to tell the tale. But what really happened? Thoroughly ensconced in their place of refuge—the home, a service station on the throughway, or some other comparatively safe and banal place, the legend trippers can now take the time to discuss their experiences without looking over their shoulders in fear of supernatural threats (Thigpen 1971). There, they recount their tale—their individual encounters—and try to make some sort of sense out of the collective experience (Eaton 2018). Afterwards, in the days and years that follow, they will tell the tale to others who were not there. In doing so, they ensure that the legend remains alive in folklore. It evolves through the addition of their tale as a chapter in the ongoing saga and by inspiring others to make similar journeys.

For now, though, there is a problem. As demonstrated in the last chapter and in the preceding vignette, supernatural experiences are characterized primarily through their strangeness and profound inscrutability. Participants will not know for sure what really happened or what it means. Their unanswered questions may haunt them long after the uncanny encounter has passed into memory. This final step of the legend trip consists of more than simply telling stories, however peculiar and compelling they might be. It also comprises an effort to come to terms with the supernatural experience: to make sense of it in some way. This occurs through several interrelated social processes. In addition to providing something of an ending to the legend trip, it also serves as a beginning, because this interpretive process will provide the inspiration for future legend trippers to embark on their own quests in search of the unknown.

The goal of this chapter is to explain this final stage of the legend trip. Throughout, I illustrate how telling the tale of one's adventure is really an interpretative, group process. It is also a very *active* process. Discussants cannot simply apply prepackaged interpretations they heard elsewhere because these do not neatly fit their experience or meet with the consensus of the group. Instead, they draw on these as possible resources as they debate and discuss what happened and what it all might mean. On account of the inherent ambiguity of the experience and the absence of authorities who can explain or legitimate it, a range of discursive peculiarities emerge that I explore as well, such as the use of rhetorical arguments and physical proof that parallel the verbal and material components of the ritual stage. In the end, this discussion does not really settle anything. Instead, it only perpetuates the legend, refueling and updating it, allowing it to stay relevant over time. To illustrate this process, I examine how the introduction of technology has transformed legends that, in turn, then transform subsequent legend trips based on them.

INTENSE DISCUSSION

One's initial conclusions or guesses regarding the meaning of a legend-trip experience, however tentative, might be drawn from any number of cultural or personal sources immediately available to individual participants. They can rack their brains, searching for something they have previously learned or experienced that might fit the encounter. Even though the legend trip is not endorsed by an organized religion (Kinsella 2011), one can certainly draw on religious understandings and try to apply these to the experience (Waskul 2016). Without external validation, this may not be satisfactory to the individual or the institution, but it is a useful first step. Pseudoscientific explanations are increasingly common too (Nickell 2007). Subcultures devoted to paranormal topics can also provide theories and terminology for interpreting anomalous experiences. Even if someone is unaffiliated with one of these, the growing visibility of online sources, television shows, books, and similar materials sampling from these groups provides at least some raw material for interpreting experiences. In short, individuals may draw on whatever sources are available to them.

They may not have much confidence in these initial thoughts given their improvised nature and the inherent ambiguity of what they experienced. They will want to discuss the experience with others to compare impressions (Bird 1994; Lindahl 2005) and, ideally, establish confirmation through social consensus (Cialdini 1993). If anyone else was with them on their legend trip, the initial discussion will occur among this group. Having someone else agree that something happened goes a long way toward alleviating any "self-doubt" individuals would otherwise feel on their own (Waskul 2016), but achieving even this minimal consensus is no simple matter. Unlike some other anomalous experiences (Hufford 1982), much of what occurs during the course of a legend trip is subjective and cannot be easily or impartially corroborated. Not only are participants unsure of each other's experiences, they typically remain uncertain of their own: "They really [are] not sure whether they heard or experienced the facts of their version" of what happened (Dégh 1969:81). Discussion may help to fill in some of these blank spaces, but it is just as likely to lead to disagreement. Just as the first phase of legend telling that sparks the legend trip involves intense debate, so too does this concluding phase of legend telling involve more of the same since "legends normally form part of an ongoing discussion and are continually subject to contributions, corrections, comments, and objections from the other participants" (Ellis 2003:10).

Eaton (2018) provides a detailed analysis of this sort of discussion from a ghost-hunting group he conducted participant observation with. During their investigation of a haunted hotel, one of them fell to the ground. Eaton's (2018:166) analysis details the group's heated discussion as they try to agree on what exactly happened and whether something supernatural caused it:

CHAD: Was she just standing there? Was that not a trip backwards?
MARC: No, that was definitely a push.
SAMANTHA: She got pushed. Didn't you see her chest?
CHAD: I didn't see anything. I was over there. . . .
SAMANTHA: She got pushed. Her chest went back and she landed on her ass.
GABRIEL: Where was Heidi when she got pushed?

And so forth. During this process, "as members of the group fill in details from their own perspectives and confirm one another's accounts, their interpretations coalesce to form a single group narrative that they begin to treat as an objective account of events" (Eaton 2018:169). Overall, the group ultimately favored a supernatural interpretation, but not everyone was convinced. Moreover, members with more status had the most say in this interpretation of the event, independent of the actual accuracy of their perspective or quality of their supporting evidence. Thus, the group's social dynamics and not just objective features of what happened played a significant role in achieving this minimal consensus.

Discussion eventually moves beyond an immediate group of legend trippers as they tell their tale to others who were not there. Reaching a universal consensus among a small group is hard enough, but once the narrative enters into public discourse, a consensus is entirely out of the question. The internet in particular has become an important platform for legend discussion (Blank 2012; Debies-Carl 2021). Some websites anticipate the need for debate and incorporate features to support it. For example, hauntedplaces.org provides information on many spooky locations. For each, it asks users, "What do you think? Is this place really haunted? Voice your opinion here!" Users can then click on either a thumbs up or down button to show what they think: "Click 'thumbs up' if you think its [sic throughout] haunted, or 'thumbs down' if you think its all just a tall tale" (e.g., Haunted Places n.d.c:n.p.). This device is crude and only allows limited, binary responses, but this built-in method nonetheless inspires and facilitates debate. The entry for the allegedly haunted Downs Road in Connecticut—a locale reputedly home to a range of ghosts, monsters, and UFOs—shows 81 percent of an uncertain number of people who voted agree the place is haunted (Haunted Places n.d.a).

This voting system correctly anticipates participants' desire to debate legends. In fact, beneath it on the website is a forum feature where visitors do just that. However, its method of encouraging debate is both artificial and unnecessary. Provided users are allowed to speak their mind, a more organic form of discussion will inevitably emerge. Nearly any webpage reporting a legend—if it includes something like a comments section and has a decent number of users—will spawn a debate. One such website offers a summary of the Downs Road legend and includes an extensive comments section (Schurman 2012).[1] Some visitors are excited about the possibility of supernatural presences, including the website's editor: "I have to admit, having some interesting local lore, true or not, makes [the town of] Bethany feel even more charming for me. . . ." Others find the claims ridiculous: "This is the funniest thing I have ever heard. . . . My grandmother lived on Downs road all her life. Also, I was always at her house [and] I never heard of something so absurd." Some share tales of their own experiences on the road: "One night me and my friend and her brother walked there [and] I kept hearing like faded creepy talking then we heard a gun shot and ran." Still others are ambivalent:

> As a [long-time] resident of Downs Road, I can most assuredly say I've never seen anything remotely yeti-like. Foxes? Yes. Coyotes[?] Absolutely. . . . We did hear screaming one night, but it turned out to [b]e nothing more sinister than a fisher cat. . . . I did have one eery [sic] thing happen to me once back in 1989, but I don't generally think of my neighborhood as "creepy". . . .

She claims not to believe the legend, going so far as to offer naturalistic explanations, before reaffirming it in the same breath by reporting an eerie encounter.

Not everyone who hears a legend will entertain a supernatural interpretation. Excited debate in an attempt to reach an interpretive consensus is one thing, but many of the people who contribute to legend discussions do so in the interest of discrediting the claim. These might include skeptics arguing against the existence of paranormal phenomena in general. Others might have more personal motivations. For example, many people do not appreciate the consequences of having a legend associated with their property. Some legend trippers can be an obnoxious or even destructive presence, and by debunking legendary claims, one might hope to discourage them from coming around.

One resident of the Downs Road area, for example, contributed several critical remarks to the legend discussion of the region, stating that "we are not very happy with the descriptions of 'eerie' or 'spooky' when it refers to our front yard. We are very happy with the peaceful wooded nature of our neighborhood and would appreciate it being respected" (Schurman 2012:n.p.). They conclude, "The only scary things on Downs Road are the people who come looking for scary things." This comment, however, did not succeed in curbing the heated discussion. It is difficult to convince legend trippers that nothing supernatural happened or that a place is not haunted. If people hold on to a belief strongly enough, they inoculate themselves against challenges to that belief (Festinger, Riecken, and Schachter 1956). However, legend trippers do not always have a very strong belief in the phenomena they investigate. Instead, they are often just willing to entertain possibilities while the legend itself invites debate over belief (Dégh 2001). This is a difficult dynamic to transcend. Even people who criticize a legend to put it to rest, in fact, enmesh themselves in this intense discussion. By giving it any attention and joining the discussion, they fuel interest and debate (Noymer 2001), perpetuate the uncertainty that sustains these, and help the legend survive to inspire future action. Just as boarding up a building or sealing a tunnel creates mystery and invites both speculation and legend tripping, as we saw in chapter 2, so too does attempting to metaphorically seal off legends by declaring them to be false. Saying that there is no curse invites fear of the curse while claiming that there is no conspiracy is tantamount to an admission of conspiracy.

DEFENDING THE TALE

Despite the popularity of legends and the supernatural, those claiming to have experienced these can still expect criticism for their efforts. Even neutral agnosticism might be interpreted as a sort of insult, an expression of doubt in the credibility of the legend teller or refusal to take them seriously. It is not surprising then that, when people talk about their anomalous encounters, these accounts typically have a defensive quality. One common defensive technique I have frequently encountered is to include other possible explanations for what they experienced along with a rhetorical attempt to invalidate those alternatives. In the introduction to her book about a haunted house she lived in, for example, the aforementioned homeowner Pickman (2010:2) precedes her tale by informing the reader, "I will discuss how we exhausted every reasonable and logical explanation, theory, and plain common sense to explain each phenomenon." In describing this pattern, Diane E. Goldstein (2007b:70) observes that memorates "are typically told as though one were on the witness stand, detailed and careful, incorporating numerous strategies that outline the nature of the observations, the testing of alternative explanations, and often including an indication of reluctance to interpret what occurred as 'supernatural.'" She argues that this sort of delivery is proof of a rational, not superstitious, mind at work that is unlikely to have simply fallen prey to the sorts of biases, errors, or similar failings that academic observers typically cite to explain such experiences (cf. Waskul 2016).

This argument might be true to a certain degree—certainly the narrators in question are giving thought to these possible naturalistic explanations, but I would argue that in many cases this is less an exercise in reason and more an expression of rationalization. Witnesses mention these alternative explanations but inevitably reject them in favor of supernatural attribution, however reluctant they might appear to do so. This fits well with this stage of the legend trip since, knowing that not everyone who hears their account will be unquestionably sympathetic, narrators prepare for the intense discussion that will likely occur and incorporate it into their tale. That is, they anticipate potential critique, and by building responses to these possibilities into their story, they suggest that they have done some interrogating of their own experience (e.g., "it couldn't have been the wind because there was none that day," etc.). In doing so, they hope to convince their audience that the supernatural origin of the phenomenon they experienced is legitimate since they have already conducted a critical analysis of it, and it has passed muster.

A fairly standard if brief example of this sort of defensiveness Is evident in the account of a woman who believes a ghost wreaked havoc in her home office. One day, the entity's apparent target was her fax machine. She reports that she was on the phone with her husband when the machine, which was downstairs, started spewing out blank paper for no obvious reason: "I have an extra long cord on the phone, so I walked downstairs and could see it happening while I was talking to my husband. But . . . I hadn't turned it on, and, it can only work when I'm not using the phone" (Okonowicz 1996:37). The narrator attempts to establish the validity of her account through several claims. First, the fact that she was not only in another room of the house while the event occurred but also on another floor entirely seems to establish that she herself had nothing to do with the fax machine's behavior. She then legitimates that something was indeed occurring because she was able to directly observe it in progress by going downstairs. She retains hold of the phone as she conducts her investigation, and this provides two further pieces of proof for her. First, however, she must defend her ability to bring it so far with her since, as she already noted, she was not near the machine at the time. The events in this memorate allegedly occurred in 1992 when corded phones were the norm, so mentioning the unusually long cord attached to her phone is unnecessary outside of this context. But for rationalization purposes, having done so means she can then note that her husband stayed on the line. In this way, he is able to serve as an implicit witness to the event. Moreover, his staying on the line also proves that the phone is still in use and further highlights the supernatural character of the event since the machine cannot possibly be operating with the line in use. Finally, of course, she states that the fax machine was not on in the first place, although she offers no proof for this claim. She might, for instance, have strengthened the persuasiveness of her argument by stating that she always turns it off when she goes upstairs or something similar. Technically, these are only a series of claims, but they are presented in a way that expresses a concern for rationality while simultaneously defending a claim of an apparently irrational event. The narrator presents herself as a reasonable person who has considered and preempted several potential objections to the experience from her imagined audience. She has no other recourse than to conclude that the only rational explanation for her fax machine acting up is a ghost.

Beyond validating the experience, defensive devices validate the one telling the memorate as well. Any seeming reluctance that narrators express to define the event as supernatural serves to reinforce their credibility and lends further credence to the conclusion that whatever they experienced really was supernatural. The legend teller presents themselves as a reasonable person who does not believe in ghosts and who has already considered other possible explanations. If, despite all this, they still must conclude it was a ghost, a much more convincing case is made than if someone simply claims they saw a ghost the other day and leaves it at that. One of D. Waskul's (2016:42) informants illustrates this combination of techniques in trying to understand why she keeps finding her kitchen cabinets open: "I try blaming it on my cats, but I don't know how my cats can get into my cabinets. . . . I just don't really believe in ghosts and shit, but I don't know how the fuck this stuff keeps happening." She begins with a rationalization that serves to validate rather than debunk the paranormal nature of the occurrence,[2] then portrays herself as a skeptic who gives little credence to this sort of thing. This is tantamount to saying, "I don't believe in ghosts, but I saw one just now."

One of Dégh's informants uses essentially the same approach. He describes himself as "the type of person who doesn't believe in anything I can't see and only half of what I hear. I have never seen UFO's [sic], ghosts, God or Satan. But, when I was a kid . . ." (Dégh 2001:350). He then relates an account of some spooky doings in the family home that come to a head when his father accidentally blows a hole through the roof in an attempt to shoot the spirit with a shotgun. This sort of testimonial to nonbelief, immediately followed by spectral experience, is a common disclaimer in many third-person fabulates as well, where it serves the same purpose of establishing the credibility of the narrator.

In one ghostly account, Ed Okonowicz (1996:71) begins his tale by telling us a bit about an interviewee before discussing a haunting he experienced: "When it comes to ghosts, Philip would be considered a skeptic, a nonbeliever, a person who would try to find the logical reason behind an action rather than simply 'believe' in the supernatural." Despite this opening, Okonowicz then promptly treats the reader to an account of how, one night, Phillip met a haunted Victrola in his aunt's living room.

Whether there is an actual rational process occurring when individuals try to understand and explain their experiences to others is up for debate, but Goldstein (2007b:78, emphasis original) correctly observes that these arguments do not actually support any "ontological reality" of the experience so much as they show that those involved are "*concerned* with reason." In other words, they are aware that reason is a culturally prescribed persuasive tool, especially when the topic being argued for is controversial and potentially superstitious. As Sagan (1996:184) puts it, they want the "language and credibility of science, but without being bound by its method and rules."

The unconventional is rendered more palatable when it is introduced via conventional narrative techniques. In one legend account, the authors discuss a photograph that appears to contain the apparitions of two children. Their evaluation of the photo is limited to declaring that "the camera couldn't have been double-exposed. Impossible" (Warren et al. 1992:65). They give no reason why exactly it could not be a double exposure, but bringing up the possibility at all and then discounting it out of hand serves as a tip of the hat to critical thinking. Ghost hunters, like most people, have a strong "desire to appear as rational as possible in order to preempt criticism of [their] methodology and motivations" (McNeill 2006:108). Beyond simply claiming to be reasonable, many methods can achieve this goal. They typically portray the devices they use—like EMF meters—as objective tools of science, even when they are not using these correctly or for their intended purpose (Radford 2010). Or, instead of simply claiming their evidence cannot be hoaxed or in error, they might purposely point out the flaws in some of it. They can, for instance, point out the natural causes of some strange photographs they took while claiming that a few remain unexplainable. Thus, by "debunking *some* submitted images, the impact of the remaining images is strengthened" (McNeill 2006:102).

The fact that these preemptive narrative defenses occur so frequently in legend-telling accounts is indicative of the anticipation of debate before a tale is told and, further, shows that this debate starts in the mind of the teller. They are indeed grappling with and attempting to process a strange experience that isn't totally self-evident but which instead begs explanation. Achieving an explanation requires considerable work on their part, as well as if it is to be converted it into something approaching a coherent story that is worth telling and hearing. The end result, if properly achieved, is a strange tale in which the experience of the uncanny is validated as reasonable, while the narrator who experienced it is simultaneously validated as canny. Each claim reinforces and strengthens the credibility of other.

PROOF

Just as ritual invocations to call up supernatural encounters can operate through both spoken and material components, as I outlined in chapter 4, so too can attempts to substantiate these experiences present both verbal argumentation and physical evidence. Earlier, I considered how sometimes legend trippers take things from a site as part of the prescribed behaviors that ritualistically invoke the spirits of a place. Some legends, for example, claim that spirits will manifest to punish those who steal from them (Tucker 2007) or possibly even take back the stolen property (Kinsella 2011:28). In this way, I argued, objects like these can serve as "mementos of invocation": because of their ritual significance and association with the legend, taking them causes the supernatural to reveal itself. These objects can also serve an important but distinct role during the discussion phase of legend trips. Taking into account the often-bizarre nature of the things people claim to have experienced during these journeys, and the not-so-surprising tendency some others have to doubt those claims, objects taken during the course of the ritual might actually serve as a sort of evidence that events actually transpired as described. Here, they become "mementos of proof." They can provide a sort of evidence that the supernatural appeared ("proof of encounter"), or somewhat more mundanely, they can serve to at least prove that the claimant did in fact go on the alleged expedition ("proof of deed"). Whether used to substantiate the encounter or the deed, these mementos of proof can be destructive to the legend location—as when headstones are stolen, but they can also be entirely benign and still fulfill the same purposes (e.g., photos).

Proof of encounter can take a number of forms that all share the same logic. Assuming that the supernatural has not followed you home, your encounter with it is limited to a finite place and time. If you can bring some tangible piece of evidence with you that has somehow captured proof of that encounter, it will serve to crystalize the fleeting experience as an enduring artifact. You can use this artifact, in turn, to substantiate your claim in the face of inevitable skepticism when you tell your tale. For most contemporary legend trippers, perhaps the most popular form of proof is recorded evidence. They can collect videos of alleged UFOs, EVPs of spectral voices, and photographs of elusive monsters. Tucker recounts how a group of legend trippers returned from investigating an abandoned building with more than just a story to tell. They came away with a video recording of a ghostly face peering out of a window that "offers proof of their bravery in confronting supernatural activity" (Tucker 2007:209). Sometimes an indirect approach can work as well. If you run into Bigfoot in the woods, he might not hold still long enough for a photo. In this case, you can opt for a low-tech solution and make plaster casts of the Bigfoot prints he leaves behind (Belanger 2011; Robinson 2016).

Mementos of this sort are compelling and not only because they appear to provide documentation of an encounter. The memento is itself something that has come into contact with the "other" and been transformed in some way: the spirit has manipulated the film or the image sensor on the digital camera, Sasquatch has impressed his footprint into the earth that the plaster has molded itself around, etc. The memento is proof *because* it is the earthly medium through which the unknown has made itself known. In presenting this proof to others, legend trippers do not simply represent the supernatural in uncanny form—they *present* the supernatural itself. In presenting the transformed object, they present their own transformation. All have been changed by their contact with the mysterious.

On occasion, a more visceral sort of memento can serve as a particularly compelling form of proof that a supernatural encounter occurred: injury. One upset parent learned that Gunntown Cemetery in Naugatuck, Connecticut, is haunted because of the visible harm unknown entities there inflicted on their daughter: "My daughter used to go [there] with her friends to take pictures at night looking for orbs. . . . One night they went in after dark . . . and my daughter came out with scratches on her back. I know she didn't have them when she went in [but] there they were all the way down her back. They don't go there anymore" (Bendici 2009). Another legend tripper records an encounter with an angry spirit in Gay City State Park in Hebron and Bolton, Connecticut: "Went here with family and friends, when my mom's friend said 'something has me.' We look to see an unknown force pulling her shirt! . . . [W]e all heard a loud smack and she hit the floor with a red hand print [*sic*] on her face. We all ran" (Haunted Places n.d.b:n.p.).[3] Handprints are a popular form of memento to discuss, perhaps because these invoke an uncanny sense of human agency when no human is to blame for the act. In Lakeview Cemetery in Penn Yann, New York, there is a "stain" on the large Bishop-Gillette monument that some believe resembles the shape of a screaming woman: the aforementioned Lady in Granite. Legend warns that "if you touch the gravestone, you'll wake up with a handprint on your face, like someone slapped you!" (Haunted History Trail of New York State 2014:n.p.). Unfortunately, I woke up handprint-free the morning after I touched the monument myself. Nonetheless, the character of injury as a particular type of memento indicates that the anomalous force is real and

Gay City State Park (Hebron and Bolton, CT): The disincarnate entities that roam the ruins here may express their displeasure in surprisingly visceral ways. Photo by the author.

that the danger of encountering it is real: the angry spirits or vile demons have made visible marks in human flesh with their invisible claws. Injury is also a sort of "reverse vandalism." Rather than the legend tripper causing damage to the cemetery or haunted house to test the existence of the supernatural forces that reside there, the order is flipped around: the supernatural becomes the subject. It asserts its agency by causing harm to the legend-tripper-turned passive object. In doing so, it proves its own existence and leaves lingering evidence of the fact. In cases like these, the injury—as memento of proof—shows that the individual has literally come into contact with the "other." It has left its mark, transformed them in a tangible way, through the medium of their flesh.

If a destination is suitably frightening, off-limits, or otherwise interesting, merely proving that you have been there is almost as impressive as encountering a ghost or UFO there. A memento that provides "proof of deed" is useful to legend trippers narrating these exploits. For example, the "House of Blue Lights," when it stood in Indianapolis, played involuntary host to many furtive, nocturnal legend trips. Several bizarre explanations circulated over why exactly the owner of the house chose to leave blue Christmas lights up year-round.[4] Judging from the literature (Dégh 1980), one popular explanation was that the owner used the lights to illuminate his deceased wife's corpse, which he kept within a glass casket in the living room. Many legend trippers tried to sneak onto the front porch at night to put the legend to the test and catch a glimpse of the body. When the owner died, the executor of his estate held an auction at the house to liquidate his many belongings hoarded there. Some thirty thousand people were reported to have attended the auction and purchased anything they could: a piece of furniture, an article of clothing, or some household good. They did so in large part "to get some curio of no value as proof of their visit to the premises" (Dégh 1980:191). We don't know what happened to these souvenirs following the auction, but most likely, they were hauled out of storage whenever the legend of the House of Blue Lights was told for many years afterwards. In this role, they would not provide evidence of an eerily illuminated corpse, but they would support the claim of the legend teller who wants you to know "I was there."

Auctions at legendary sites are admittedly uncommon, but there are many other ways to acquire mementos serving as proof of deed. As noted above, various types of recordings are very popular among legend trippers. While these are often used to record "proof" of encounter, they can also provide proof of deed. Whether photographic, video, or just audio, as many podcasts are, these recordings can help prove that one visited a particular location by documenting it firsthand. Even if they do not contain evidence of the supernatural, as long as they *do* include or imply inclusion of the legend tripper, they confirm that the individual actually visited the legendary setting. In fact, you have seen several photos serving this purpose throughout this book. In one account of an encounter with an apparition in Louisville's Waverly Hills Sanitorium, the author presents a photo of a dark, empty room. He did not photograph the apparition but explains, "I had my experience and wanted to document where it happened. The experience itself is my trophy" (Belanger 2011:31).

This pattern could explain, in part, why selfies and vlogs have become so popular in discussing legend trips. They provide another medium, beyond the traditional oral account, that allows the storyteller to become the protagonist in their own narrative while also providing a degree of proof that they were really there. Viewers can, for example, virtually accompany legend trippers during the course of their journey via their online videos. One such video begins with a view of the legend tripper herself, a forested view behind her in the frame, as she introduces the location she is about to investigate: Gay City State Park.[5] Formerly a mill town settled in the late eighteenth century by a religious sect, it is now a park full of crumbling ruins. It is also haunted by the spirits of two murdered men, one of whom manifests as a headless skeleton (Philips 1992). After this introduction, the audience follows along as she walks around the park, showing its various sites. She cannot be seen anymore, because she is holding the camera, but she is clearly still there because she continues her narration the whole time. At the end of the approximately ten-minute video, she appears again on camera with the park behind her to offer some concluding thoughts. The video does not show any ghosts, but it does include some interesting ruins and proves that she was there, braving the park and seeing those ruins firsthand.

Sometimes, you can pick up a memento from a legendary site that was specifically made for the purpose of proving you really went there. In Atlantic City, New Jersey, "some people say there are over a dozen spirits haunting" the old and picturesque Absecon Lighthouse (Reeser 2010:27). The place is made all the more imposing by the 228 steps one must climb to reach the top of its tower. Once you finally get all the way up there, however, the lighthouse keeper will hand you a card that says: "I saw the light! Congratulations, you just climbed New Jersey's tallest lighthouse, the third tallest lighthouse in the United States." He even authenticates it with his signature. It does not prove you saw a ghost—indeed, apart from a couple books full of local ghost stories for sale in their gift shop, they make little mention of the haunting, but it does support your claim that you really went there and climbed up to the light. So does the webcam at the top. You can text a web address to your friends so they can watch you wave at them from the comfort of their homes (AtTheShore n.d.).

Then again, a small card is not much to show off. Fortunately, with the growth of businesses catering to the demand for supernatural experiences (Gentry 2007; Hanks 2015; Holloway 2010), mementos of proof are increasingly actual souvenirs purchased in a gift shop (Goldstein 2007a). How can you prove that you visited the notoriously haunted Eastern State Penitentiary in Philadelphia? One vlogger did so by showing off some swag she picked up in the historic attraction's gift shop on her YouTube video: a branded hooded sweatshirt, a reproduction cell key, and even the bag it all came in, which sports an image of the prison (Crabb 2017b). If that is not gruesome enough for you, you can always spend the night at a certain house in Fall River, Massachusetts, made famous for a grizzly double murder that once transpired within its walls. This is, of course, the Lizzie Borden Bed & Breakfast Museum where *someone* killed Borden's father and stepmother in 1892. A court of law found Borden innocent of the deed, but the court of public opinion continues to find her guilty to this day (Chaney 2006). Not surprisingly, many people believe the house is haunted (D'Agostino 2007), and this belief, along with the lingering notoriety of the murders, has made it a popular tourist attraction. More importantly, for our purposes at least, if you are brave enough to spend

Lizzie Borden House (Fall River, MA): Guests may choose from a variety of souvenirs in the gift shop to prove they dared visit the infamous location. Photo by the author.

the night there, you can pick up a memento in the gift shop to prove it to your friends. There are many options, including hatchet-shaped cookie cutters, golf balls sporting Borden's face alongside the slogan "Keep Hacking Away," and a T-shirt that playfully proclaims, "I Survived a Night at the Lizzie Borden Bed & Breakfast."[6] I only took the day tour when I visited the site, so instead of the T-shirt, I opted for a tasteful yet discrete Lizzie Borden bobblehead. It came complete with a hatchet, bloodstained dress, and vacant stare. If I had experienced anything supernatural at the Lizzie Borden House, objects like these would not provide proof of it. However, they can provide some evidence that I really did dare to visit the place. Additionally, they are effective conversation starters and, therefore, useful for telling the tale of a legend trip.

Again, no memento, no matter how interesting, is sufficient to *prove* anything in terms of an actual supernatural encounter beyond the shadow of a doubt. Did the encounter really occur? Photographs are notoriously blurry, plaster casts predictably amorphous, and anything might have caused you to get a scratch in an overgrown cemetery in the dark of night. Moreover, any of these things could easily be faked. Convincing proof that a legend tripper actually visited a particular location, likewise, raises questions. Did you encounter anything there? What was it? How do you know? In other words, while legend trippers present these artifacts as proof, they are really another aspect of debate manifesting in material form. Just like verbal claims, they provoke an array of responses reflecting that debate, ranging from enthusiastic acceptance to cautious consideration to open scorn. Even if everyone agreed that you were scratched by a ghost, it leaves the standard questions: Why did it scratch you? *How* did it scratch you? And, most critically, what exactly is a ghost anyway? Even earnest believers in ghosts propose numerous, competing explanations.[7] These sorts of questions cannot be definitely answered. Indeed, if ever they were, the subject would pass beyond the realm of the legendary into the entirely different domains of simple fact or pure fiction.

Examining a case up close illustrates the point. Earlier, I discussed the Old Hill Burying Ground in Concord, Massachusetts, where there is a large headstone featuring both a skull and an angel, along with a charming inscription: "All must submit to the King of terrors." Some claim that, at times, the engraved eyes of the skull come to life in photographs. At first, this seems to present an ideal opportunity to collect evidence that one can present as compelling proof of a supernatural encounter. One legend tripper attempts to do just that on her website.[8] In reality, we find, the effort only invites debate. She begins by discussing how looking for ghosts has become somewhat routine for her. Having done it for so many years, she has become habituated to cemeteries and the other eerie things one might encounter in the course of that pursuit. This disclaimer legitimates the authenticity of the phenomenon she is about to discuss by suggesting she is not easily spooked or tricked: "It takes a lot to startle me, but this tall, strange headstone did. [E]very time I've visited it . . . I've felt that *something isn't right* about that grave" (Broome n.d.:n.p., emphasis original). She discusses at length how she had taken a photograph of the headstone and, not seeing any orbs or mists, put it aside for a time. Later, intending to use the photo as an illustration, she enlarged the picture. She then noticed that the skull seemed to have real eyes. Increasing the contrast, but otherwise not tampering with it, she found that the effect became even more pronounced and downright uncanny. She presents both photos—original and edited—on her website as tangible proof of her otherwise subjective eerie feelings near the headstone. She also gives directions for how others can follow in her footsteps and experience the anomaly for themselves.

She soon receives several comments in response to her posting. The first, from D, states:

> I live near Concord and have been up to visit this site. I find nothing paranormal or creepy about it. What I do notice is that the back of the carved eye sockets are fairly smooth [and that] this curved surface will reflect back the light from a flash. . . . I haven't experimented with this yet but I would hazard a guess that this phenomena [*sic*] only appears when the camera is pointed directly at the skull. . . . [T]his is a good example of some very nice craftsmanship, but that's it.

This individual is clearly not convinced by the photographic evidence. Instead, he offers some naturalistic theories for the effect. His statement also gives the impression that although D is skeptical, the legend claim may nonetheless motivate him to investigate the possibility himself. The photographer, F, then responds: "Thanks for your comment. . . . When you publish your studies of curved surfaces and their reflections, be sure to let us know. Meanwhile . . . [w]e've never seen this on any other gravestone, including others with [skulls]. Whatever the reason for the eyes . . . we appreciate it as something unusual. . . ." Her response accomplishes several things. First, she attacks her critic by implying he does not have the expertise needed to authoritatively claim that optics, and not ghosts, are at work. She then defends her own claim and her expertise by noting that she has never seen anything like it despite her many years of photographing gravestones. However, she then backs away slightly from that claim by appearing open to the possibility of a natural explanation while still maintaining that the eyes represent something unique and significant, whatever their cause may be. Ultimately, she changes her tone to reflect a more easily defensible position on the matter without entirely stepping away from her original position.

Another user, H, then adds to the debate: "The eyes are convex, no? How, then, could they form focal points? . . . That's a creepy picture." This brief statement defends the original paranormal claim, suggesting that the naturalistic explanation does not fit and, moreover, that the photo is indeed "creepy" and, therefore, noteworthy in some way. D, however, is not without his own defenders, one of whom, J, addresses his comment to F: "There's no need to be rude or sarcastic. [D's] opinion should be taken seriously. It might just be right." This user seems to take issue with F's tone more than anything else. He neither wholeheartedly condemns the paranormal explanation nor fully endorses the naturalistic one.

Two more posts conclude the debate, with one more user supporting the idea of the burying ground being haunted but saying nothing specific about the eyes. This individual uses the validating approach of claiming that they used to be a skeptic until they experienced the graveyard. There is also another very lengthy defense-cum-counterattack by F. She supports her position by claiming to be using the "*scientific method*" (emphasis original), reaffirms her belief in the supernatural, and admits the evidence is not always adequate. She argues that this means there is a need for more investigation (i.e., legend tripping) to get to the bottom of what is really going on in haunted places. F states, "We need more research related to ghost photos, and—in general—we need more *serious* researchers in this field" (emphasis original). Essentially, this amounts to saying that "no one really knows, so let's agree to disagree." The discussion then ceases, with nothing really resolved. More often than not, even when "proof" is presented, this is how debates over legends conclude: without a real conclusion. The legend lives on for others to endorse, criticize, or experience for themselves.

LEGEND TELLING AND SOCIAL CHANGE

In Sudbury, Massachusetts, there is a sprawling historic building called Longfellow's Wayside Inn. Built over three hundred years ago, it was originally called How's Tavern after its proprietor, David How (Plumb 2013). Its name eventually changed to capitalize on the fact that it served as the setting for Henry Wadsworth Longfellow's *Tales of a Wayside Inn*. Today it operates as a museum and interactive educational site. If you should come for a visit, you can still have a traditional New England dinner, spend the night in a well-preserved room, and—maybe—experience ghostly phenomena. These include a piano that sometimes plays by itself on the ground floor, the sounds of phantom fifes and cannons, and encounters with Jerusha Howe (D'Agostino 2007).[9] She perished in 1842 but is apparently still looking for love and is not terribly picky about whom she bestows her favors on, so long as they stay in her old room. The problem with all these claims is that they are all fairly recent. It appears that the only legend that might have some pedigree to it, which may or may not trace back to 1868, pertains to one of the second-floor rooms called the "Hobgoblin Room." The legend tells that a member of the How family "claimed she saw a ghost half floating, half running through this room on a dark night" (Plumb 2013:163). No one seems to have seen it ever since. Guy LeBlanc, a manager at Longfellow's, told paranormal investigator Thomas D'Agostino (2007) that other legends started surfacing only a few decades ago, including those regarding Howe's amorous apparition. Brian E. Plumb (2013), who literally wrote the book on the inn, agrees that legends about Howe started around the 1990s. Yet today the claims continue to proliferate and expand, nonetheless.

Cases like these illustrate how the discussion that follows a legend trip is not without consequences of its own. Legends are not static but change over time as discussion fuels and informs future legend trips. These, in turn, spark further discussion and so on. An important source of change can be linked specifically to the tales told by legend trippers after their return. Earlier, I noted that legend trippers can interpret all manner of experiences had at the site of a trip as support for the legend, even if something fairly mundane occurred and even if the experience is not consistent with the inspiring legend. These inconsistent tales of divergent experiences can be incorporated back into the legend cycle. They are disseminated, discussed, and become the inspiration for subsequent legend trips by others. The originally erroneous experiences are added to the range of possible preparations, expectations, and rituals of the next generation of legend trippers. Longfellow's might likely illustrate this process. Generations of visitors failed to encounter the "hob-goblin," but maybe they heard a mysterious bump or saw a shadow during a visit. Interpreting this as somehow related to the legend and telling their tale to others, the legendary claims quickly expand. All are *inspired* by some earlier claim but otherwise have little to do with it. While it is difficult to illustrate this process through any specific legend-trip records,[10] the overall phenomenon is discernable in the characteristics of various bodies of extant legendry as a whole.

Ghosts are especially prevalent in popular culture and folk belief these days (Goldstein et al. 2007) and serve as an interesting case in point. The concept of "ghost" is much debated, even among believers (Hanks 2015). What a ghost looks like, how it can be experienced, or even what it actually *is* are all matters of ongoing debate, as any good legendary subject should be. Even if there is no consensus, there are still general patterns for what a ghost is like in any particular region or period (Davies 2007). Changes in that conception over time can be partly attributed to the legend-tripping process itself, not just to general cultural change. For example, many discussions of encounters with ghosts in modern times seems to include references to "orbs." Here is a typical description from a ghost-hunting guidebook:

> Lots of ghost photographs show circles, spheres, and ellipses generally called "orbs". . . . These appear especially when photographing, video-taping, or otherwise monitoring the infrared realm. . . . What are these paranormal orbs? Are they spirits? We can't say for sure. But they do seem to be most prevalent at haunted locations. Therefore, there is certainly some connection. Sometimes, one huge orb is lumbering along. At other times, a flurry sweeps by. . . . Could we be taping one aspect of the soul? (Warren 2003:62–63)

While legends of ghost lights, actually seen with one's eyes as they material-ize, are not new, these "orbs" captured on film seem relatively distinct from these and represent a more recent phenomenon. Traditional folklore from around the world is replete with tales of ghostly lights. Those of the British Isles in particular are well documented and have a range of colorful names, like "corposant," "corpse light," "fetch candle," "ignis fatuus," "jack-o'-lantern," and "will-o'-the-wisp."[11] Even a casual comparison with more recent orbs suggests the concepts are not closely, if at all, related. For example, traditional ghost lights are typically seen in motion with the naked eye and often look like flames. Orbs, conversely, tend to be stationary, do not often resemble flames, and appear primarily through various recording devices. They are generally seen *after* the encounter when the recording is reviewed.

Recording devices themselves are fairly new, and the idea that the recorded orbs could be supernatural seems linked to the increasing popularity and accessibility of photography and videography to ghost hunters (Guiley 2008). However, the idea that orbs might be supernatural is relatively recent and utterly lacking in early "spirit photography" until more recently. Perhaps inspired by the tradition of spirit photography, paranormal investigators using cameras were at first hoping to catch actual human apparitions. Primed with expectation and trying to find some evidence of spirits, they captured these orbs instead, which they then interpreted as that desired evidence despite the disparity. As these individuals told others of their experiences and, more importantly, showed them the photographic proof, orbs entered into the legend cycle. In subsequent legend trips, orbs were no longer emergent phenomenon that were accidentally encountered but rather became something people purposely looked for after having heard these earlier accounts: the orbs became ritualized parts of the legend trip.[12] Skeptics argue that these orbs are simply "caused by everything from tiny debris in spider webs to a flash reflecting raindrops to flying insects to dust on a lens" (Radford 2010:156). Even ghost hunters themselves exhibit considerable disagreement over their legitimacy as supernatural phenomena. Exemplifying one perspective in this contested topic, the stars of the *Ghost Hunters* television series reminisce: "So we put up an article on our website that essentially said orbs were trash. Now, orbs were really popular in those days. Hearing they were insignificant was, for some people, a slap in the face. They railed back at us, telling us we were crazy, and the battle was on. The paranormal field was polarized almost overnight" (Hawes et al. 2007:6). Such continuous debate is characteristic of this final stage of the legend-tripping process. Orbs have found a long-term home among the legends of ghostly encounters, even though their exact role remains contested and subject to further revision.[13] It is also easy to see how a process like this can continue to feed back to itself. If legend trippers fail to find orbs while looking for ghosts, they can likewise interpret something else that they do find as worthy of discussion in its place. This new find can then enter into the legend, serving as a quarry for still later investigators.

That legend telling is both the first and last step of the legend-trip process is made clear when considering other new additions to legend cycles. Novel technologies and social change in general are closely related (MacKenzie and Wajcman 1999), and this proves true among legend trips too. New devices are quickly adopted into legend tripping, seamlessly reinvigorating this well-established endeavor while simultaneously transforming it. Many recent devices have been integrated into this pursuit as they have become more widely available.

Technological innovation has been closely linked with efforts to contact the dead for a long time (Sconce 2000). However, the general role technologies play has shifted so that these have moved from a significant albeit marginal element of paranormal interest to the main event. In his 1936 work, *Confessions of a Ghost-Hunter*, famed paranormal investigator Harry Price lists his standard equipment. This includes items for measuring the environment (e.g., measuring tape), recording observations (e.g., notebook), controlling for hoaxers (e.g., "lead seals and sealing tools"), first aid (e.g., bandages), and apparently personal comfort (e.g., "flask of brandy") (Price 1936:31). He includes very little in the way of electrical or otherwise technical equipment and even less in the way of equipment meant to directly indicate the presence of spirits. In terms of the latter, cameras are a partial exception, but he makes it clear that even these are primarily for documenting the scene and catching hoaxers. Many devices that would later be used to directly detect a spirit presence—such as dowsing rods or compasses—were readily available in his day but do not seem to have been of much concern to him.

Sometime after Price's day, an array of books hit the market specifically geared at teaching readers how to investigate ghostly legends. Many older books in this vein barely mention much in the way of technology. Auerbach's (1986) now-classic guidebook for example, while touching on subjects like photography and audio recording, emphasizes interviewing witnesses first and foremost as a means of investigation despite the fact that appropriate devices were readily available at the time. Moreover, even when he mentions other devices, he primarily recommends them as ways to document the physical environment and these interviews. He certainly considers the ability to capture paranormal phenomena on recording devices to be a possibility, but he downplays that possibility. Another famous ghost hunter, the aforementioned Underwood, provides what at first looks like an exception to this general de-emphasis on using technology to detect spirits in his *Ghost Hunter's Guide* (1986). He provides a short chapter on ghost-hunting equipment early in the book, which includes all manner of devices, including cameras, tape recorders, and thermometers along with more prosaic supplies, like tape measures and thermoses. However, apart from a brief treatment of the dubious history of spirit photography and a handful of printed photographs, these same devices are largely absent from the rest of the work. Most of his stories are heavily dependent on witness reports rather than any sort of recorded evidence.

In contrast to these early examples, more recently, technology—and especially technology that promises proof of direct supernatural contact—has become the main event in ghost hunting, monster hunting, and similar endeavors. Its role has shifted from a marginal means of documenting prosaic conditions and events to the primary method of detecting the presence of the supernatural. After the legend trip has concluded, it then serves an equally important role as the primary *proof* of experience. In fact, it would not be an exaggeration to say that, for many contemporary legend trippers, the experiences and proof they seek cannot be achieved without the use of some sort of meter or recording device. Investigating an allegedly haunted location primarily through a wide array of technological gadgets has occupied center stage to such an extent that "one could almost say that ghosts don't exist without the technology that records them" (Dickey 2016b:85). This has partly occurred because of the increasing number of devices available, but this alone cannot explain why they have become crucial. Rather, it is the self-perpetuating nature of the legend process that fuels the change.

Cameras that can detect the infrared spectrum and visually display it to users are a case in point. While these are still relatively expensive, they have become more affordable and increasingly appear in books and television shows about ghosts. Here, they serve as a model for future legend trippers to emulate, and because of this, many ghost seekers hope to be able to afford one someday (Brown 2006). One legend-tripping account set in Freetown State Forest in Massachusetts, for instance, describes how a team of paranormal investigators searched the woods one night in hopes of finding supernatural entities said to live there: "The Wampanoags [Native Americans] call them Puckwudgies [*sic*]. They are troll-like beasties that use balls of light called Tei-Pai-Wankas to lure unsuspecting victims to their doom" (Lake 2011:29). First, the group captures what is described as a "creepy distortion" on their thermal camera while Maureen, their psychic, reports that she is under attack by an incorporeal entity (Lake 2011:30). Later, she seems to be possessed by the entity as she growls and behaves strangely. While the rest of the group tries to restrain her, the author detects something again in the camera: "a strange little light appear[ed] behind the group as they huddled around Maureen on the ground" (Lake 2011:31). The introduction of the infrared camera in part serves as an extension of earlier associations of haunting with temperature fluctuations or "cold spots" as well as an extension of the association between the Pukwudgies and balls of light. However, it simultaneously introduces change into legend cycles by offering new ways in which the paranormal can allegedly be experienced. The group never encounters any trolls or ghost lights, nothing visible to the naked eye at all in fact, as the legend would otherwise suggest they should. By deploying the thermal camera though, they are able to experience additional phenomena that they interpret as evidence for the legend anyway. The experience is then retold to others, in this case through a book, and it should come as no surprise if future legend trippers visiting these woods specifically look for thermal phenomena as evidence of resident trolls.

Similar processes are evident throughout the vast body of lore associated with legend tripping. These illustrate that while discussing a legend and investigating it through legend tripping are traditional behaviors, they are not stuck in the past. Instead, they are constantly updated, constantly revised, kept fresh and relevant to the changing times to suit new generations seeking adventure and mystery. Discussion and debate—telling the tale—allows this procession over the years.

UNANSWERED QUESTIONS

At last, the legend trip comes to its happy conclusion. It is appropriate that it ends where it began: with the telling of past deeds. These exploits will live on as legend. They will be told by word of mouth, on the web, in books, and on television. Of course, they will also live on in actions. For it is inevitable that some of those who hear the new tale may decide to accept its challenge, to take up the cross as it were, and embark on an adventure of their own. From this, they will have their own experiences and their own tales to tell. And so, the ancient cycle begins anew.

This chapter has explained how this process unfolds through active, social interaction. The experiences that legend trippers have do not speak for themselves, but neither are they neatly explained by readily available cultural resources or respected authorities. Instead, I illustrated how participants must try to unravel the mysteries of these encounters together and outlined some of the dimensions of that task. This leads to debate, disagreement, and discussion that only intensify once the conversation expands to include others who were not there to witness the event themselves. All this debate—consisting of defensiveness, criticism, and uncertainty—serves only to reinvigorate the legend and encourage future legend trips to investigate its expanding claims.

Yet something isn't quite right. The quest might be over, and the story of the experience shared, but a final and satisfactory conclusion often proves elusive. There is no real closure to the mystery that prompted the journey. There are ideas and arguments but no real explanation for the events that—maybe— occurred and no definitive interpretation for what they mean. If a legend trip was simply like any other rite of passage, then this final stage should have been accompanied by reincorporation into the community and a new social status (Turner and Turner 1978; van Gennep [1909] 1960), but nothing of the sort really happened. These problems are endemic to legend trips. In the next chapter, I show why.

Part V

At Journey's End

Chapter 8

THE PAST AND FUTURE
OF LEGEND TRIPPING

I am surrounded by unknown things.
—GUY DE MAUPASSANT ([1887] 2012:54)

A funny thing happened to me one winter evening. I wasn't out in some haunted forest or cursed cemetery, but safe at home working on this book. I had spent the better part of the day writing and reading about the supernatural. Sometime after dinner, I was tidying up my handwritten notes from the day's work when I noticed that an important, loose-leaf page of these had gone missing. It had been serving double duty as a bookmark for my manuscript-in-progress and as a handy place to scribble down notes. Assuming I left it in another room, I thought nothing of it but resolved to look for it later. Later came, but I couldn't find the errant page in the likely places: it was not in my office where I type up my notes, not in the spare bedroom where I proofread, not in the living room where I pretend to work while watching TV, and so on. The likely places tapped out, I proceeded to check the *unlikely* ones. Under the desk, behind the couch, down in the basement, and anywhere else I might have absently set it down and then wandered off.

It was during this episode that it occurred to me how amusing it was that I had been working all day on a study of the supernatural and here, not exactly in the flesh but present nonetheless, was a classic example of the sort of phenomenon that is often attributed to that agency. "Wouldn't it be great," I thought to myself, "if I were to walk back into the office and find the missing notes perched in full view on my keyboard as if some playful spirit was trying to teach me something?" Alas, that was not the case. I found the notes sometime later inside a desk drawer. Apparently, I had left the whole stack of work on the open drawer earlier to expand the available surface area on the desk. I simply missed the bottom page when I removed the pile to close the drawer.

Nonetheless, the incident did help me to get into the right mindset and allowed me to briefly wonder, "What if?" Reason, however, prevailed. At least, so I told myself. Finding significance in a misplaced piece of paper seems itself strongly indicative of the mind working after hours. It was a helpful reminder that there is a thin, permeable boundary between reason and its alternative, a boundary any of us can slip past, however briefly, and be granted a glimpse of that liminal realm beyond.

This tendency, or even need, to look for explanation and meaning remains strong in the human mind. What happens, however, when explanation and meaning are not readily available? How do we locate the answers we so badly desire when presented with baffling experiences in situations where our trusted sources of guidance and insight cannot provide satisfactory explanations? What if my page of notes had gone permanently missing or, better, had really turned up in clear view on the keyboard? Understanding situations like this can help establish a better understanding of—and appreciation for—the seemingly odd phenomenon that is legend tripping.

Much like the legend trippers I have examined up to this point, this book has covered quite a bit of ground. However, the journey is not yet over. There are further mysteries to explore. What exactly is legend tripping all about? Why has it become so popular in an age of supposed reason? Given the effort involved and the uncertain award that awaits at the end of it, why would anyone bother going on one? I conclude by offering answers to these questions, based on the findings I have discussed so far and by posing some new ones. Additionally, I consider the bigger picture of why confusion and debate are so prevalent and why the fundamental meaning of the legend trip itself is so unclear. I address two other points as well. Throughout the subsequent pages, I argue that legend trips are imperfect approximations of rites of passage. I will also explain why the popularity of this activity has grown and why this growth is related to legend tripping's imperfect, ritualistic character. These patterns, I argue, reveal not only the significance of legend tripping in the contemporary age but also reflect important changes that have occurred in society itself.

THE LIMITS OF LEGEND-TRIPPING RITES

Many researchers have interpreted legend trips as rites of passage (e.g., Dégh 2001; Ellis 2003). A rite of passage is a ceremonial ordeal, and there are specific things that are *supposed* to happen during one and after its conclusion. Van Gennep ([1909] 1960) argues that the final stage of the ritual is one marked by reconstitution into society. Earlier stages of the rite strip the individual of their original identity as a necessary preliminary to changing that person's place or status in their society. During this time, they have no identity. They undergo tests and are forced to endure challenging circumstances. Then, they return from their trials and ordeals as victorious conquerors. The community celebrates their triumph and awards them with a new status (e.g., adulthood). The experience of the rite of passage changes them for the better. The meaning of the experiences they have undergone are clear and well defined for both the initiates and the community at large.

As well-established and mandatory traditions, rites of passage have institutionalized, clearly defined expectations, interpretations, and social significance. The initiates may or may not know exactly what will happen ahead of time, but they are guided through the process by those who came before them, and the meaning of each act is afforded to them. In western Africa, rites of passage are "controlled by a hierarchy of elders, different in each village, which meets in a sacred grove where the clan founder was buried" (Parrinder 1969:80). Among the Gebusi of New Guinea, the initiatory rites into adulthood are technically supposed to be a secret, as they are for many societies. In practice, most boys will have heard something of what to expect beforehand, having eavesdropped on the adults who seem not to care a great deal about these intrusions (Knauft 2016). Should they have failed to do so, it is of little consequence since an authority figure will be on hand to guide them through the rite anyway. Members of a community who are not directly involved in the ceremonies may not know exactly what activities are involved in the rite, but they nonetheless know what its cultural significance is and what it means for the social status of those who successfully complete it. The sexes typically experience separate activities during rites of passage. This is the case, for instance, for the Barolong boo Ratshidi on the periphery of South Africa (Comaroff 2013). Boys and girls undergo different ordeals and receive distinct instruction as they are inducted into the status of manhood or womanhood, respectively. In other words, while there is intentional ambiguity during a part of traditional rites of passage when initiates experience the liminal stage of the rite, this will be mitigated by the guiding presence of cultural authorities, and all uncertainty should come to a certain end in the final stage of the rite when closure, interpretation, and reintegration are provided.

Although legend trips are similar to rites of passage in many ways, and perhaps even fulfill similar "functions" in society, they also depart from the classical model of the rite of passage in significant ways. Large-scale modern societies tend to experience "deritualization" (Mandelbaum 1959): they have fewer and more poorly defined rituals in general compared to smaller, more traditional societies, and these may not be mandatory or experienced by every member of the group (C. Bell 1997). This includes rites of passage (Moffitt 1983). The relative absence of ritual might, observers often suggest, present a potentially serious social problem. The decline in community, trust, and social capital that many such societies experience (Putnam 2000) could in theory be linked to this social condition of ritual impoverishment (Driver 1991).[1] According to this strain of argument, when formal rituals are lacking, individuals fulfill the need through other, similarly collective means, ranging from participation in "'raves,' rock concerts, stand-up comedy shows, and birthday parties" (Maruna 2011:7). Many argue that this is the case for legend trips, which occur "outside of any institutionally sanctioned sphere" (Kinsella 2011:29). Thus, in the absence of specifically institutionalized rites of passage, but with no decline in the importance of achieving adult status, individuals develop and improvise their own substitutes in the form of, among other things, braving cemeteries and haunted houses.

Interestingly, some research regarding the traditional rite of passage into adulthood suggests that beyond the three stages originally identified by van Gennep ([1909] 1960)—separation, liminality, and reintegration—there is also a phase immediately following separation from the group in which novices receive preparatory instruction from an elder (Delaney 1995). Here too, the legend trip is different, lacking even this element of institutional support. While, as I have argued, it does possess a clear preparatory stage, there is no authority on hand—whether religious or secular—to encourage, guide, clarify, or otherwise approve its activities. Participants receive no instruction from culturally sanctioned authorities, and so, these activities will always have the character of "quasi-improvised rituals" (Ellis 1993:28). Like paranormal beliefs or practices in general, neither established science nor mainstream religion endorse or validate these quests for the supernatural (Bader et al. 2010; Goode 2000). At best, a prospective legend tripper might have access to "an initiate; one who has already had the experience" of the legend trip (Thigpen 1971:204–5) or perhaps impersonal guidance in the form of some textual source whose author claims expertise. Numerous books and websites try to provide such instruction. There are even books dedicated to it, like *Picture Yourself Legend Tripping: Your Complete Guide to Finding UFOs, Monsters, Ghosts and Urban Legends in Your Own Backyard* (Belanger 2011) and *Legend Tripping: The Ultimate Adventure* (Robinson 2016). The former, for some reason, is marketed as a textbook by the major educational publisher Cengage. The latter describes itself "as a guidebook on how to actually conduct and go on a legend trip" (Robinson 2016:9). Sources like these approximate a sort of guidance, but they lack social authority and cultural legitimacy. Moreover, they often disagree with each other, providing conflicting accounts of past happenings, proper ritual behavior, and even the purpose of legend tripping. In this sense, these quasi guides are recognizable as part of the legend-telling process themselves. They inspire action and participate in discussion in the same way as any other source of legend transmission, but they cannot offer anything concrete or authoritative. It remains for the legend trippers themselves to sort through the claims and decide what to make of them.

The preparatory stage illustrates the voluntary and noninstitutionalized dimensions of legend trips.[2] Unlike formal rites of passage, their preparatory phase—such as it is—*precedes* separation from the group and overlaps with the preceding legend-telling stage that motivates the journey to come. No authority dictates that those involved must go on the journey or declares when the candidates are ready to depart. Instead, exposure to the legend itself, heard from peers or others with no formal responsibility, inspires individuals to set out. They make the choice for themselves. Having done so, they must piece together the information necessary to go upon the journey too, deciding for themselves just how much or how little guidance they need and determining when they feel ready to depart. The quasi guidance that is available, noted above, generally acknowledges the primacy of the individual legend tripper in this role as well rather than really claiming authority. For example, Robinson's (2016:172, 175) how-to-legend-trip guide makes it clear that he is only offering suggestions, not prescriptions: "It's up to you. This is just a basic guideline when you're out looking for UFO's [*sic*]"; "Again, you can do it the way you want, because everyone is different." In his how-to guide, Jeff Belanger (2011:216) adopts a similar tone. He claims that the reader's ideas "are as good as any others" and that is why "there aren't any gurus or alpha personalities to dictate how this is supposed to be done" (Belanger 2011:215). The makers of a ghost-hunting app for your smart phone, called "Ghost Radar," say something similar regarding the effectiveness of their software on their website: "You must decide for yourself if the readings are indicative of actual paranormal activity" (Ghost Radar as cited in Tucker 2017:29). Prospective legend trippers can also engage in the preparatory process with peers—that is, with social equals—if they so choose. While such groups might have informal leaders or individuals more experienced with paranormal subjects, neither are legitimate authorities. Alone or among peers, there is no guarantee that those involved will construct the blueprint for a ritual experience that is at all similar to that of some other group of legend trippers.

Just as there is no institutional guidance during the legend-telling or preparatory stages of the legend trip, neither is it to be found during the ritual or encounter stages. These activities might be rehearsed or pieced together from previous legend narratives, but they are not "normative" (Hall 1980:238): they are not ritualized or formalized in any consistent or culturally legitimate sense. So, a comparison of rituals or encounters reveals important patterns but not in terms of specific events or experiences, even when comparing those based on the same legend and concerned with the same site. Legend trippers must infer how to behave from prior accounts, relying on their own interpretations, those of their associates, or other sources of dubious cultural legitimacy, such as oral rumor and internet speculation. There are often many competing versions of exactly what needs to be done once they reach the site of a legend (Dégh 1971), just as there are many versions of the source legend itself. Even directions to the destination might only be vaguely described (Ellis 2003) so that it can be difficult to find exactly the right hill or cemetery in which the legend is set or, more accurately, to convince themselves that they have even reached the correct location.

Even a cursory examination of most legends reveals an incoherent variety of claims regarding what legend trippers are supposed to do if and when they reach their destination and what they might encounter there. In short, just as the absence of a legitimate authority makes it impossible to know what to expect or whether participants are prepared to face it, this also makes it so they can never know for sure whether they have conducted the ritual properly or even what proper conduct requires. Propriety, by definition, is absent. They can only hazard guesses and must content themselves with ambiguity. These problems and uncertainties are significant and may compromise the chances of a successful legend trip: one in which the participants feel they have managed to bring about a significant, uncanny experience. They may fail to achieve a "release from mundane structure" (Turner and Turner 1978:34)—a real sense of separation from everyday life and social order—and might only encounter a mundane setting at the end of their journey no different and no more significant than the one they attempted to leave in the first place. Whatever the goal of the endeavor may have been, they will not have accomplished it.

Of course, many legend trippers achieve a moment of encounter despite the challenges involved. Just as the preparations and ritual activities of legend trippers may vary from group to group or even individual to individual, so might their experiences. Legend trippers who visit Downs Road in Connecticut report a bewildering array of dissimilar paranormal experiences on the partly abandoned road. Depending on what source you read, people have had encounters with ghosts, mutant Melon Heads, UFOs, Pukwudgies, a bear-sized beast with glowing eyes, a miniature Sasquatch, a creepy man with a machete, or nothing at all (e.g., Citro 2005; Nowinski 2012). When examining discussions of legend-trip experiences to the same site, disagreements and arguments are common. A comment posted in an online discussion about legend tripping at Gunntown Cemetery in Naugatuck, Connecticut, reads, "I'm surprised with your findings. . . . We have had many experiences there over the past year however they vary from yours" (Ghostwatcherz 2011). The poster calls out specific phenomena that were reported in the preceding account, like phantom music, which they did not experience during their visits.

While no two formal rites of passage are likely to be completely identical for different participants, there should be some consistency and certainly not disagreements over what happened. Compare your memories of a wedding, baptism, or graduation ceremony you attended with those of others who were there too. What are the chances you will need to argue over what happened that day or what the point of the gathering was? Some of the details may differ, but overall, these should be relatively minor and certainly not call the whole event or its basic purpose into question.

QUESTIONS OF CLOSURE AND MEANING

The inherent ambiguity of legend tipping trails participants through the final stages of their journey and haunts those who have returned to tell the tale. In particular, even though legend tripping might be rooted in extra-institutional quests for meaningful experiences (Kinsella 2011; Tucker 2007), there remains the problem of its fundamental uncertainty to deal with even after the matter is supposed to be concluded and the legend trippers returned safely to their beds. This is another telling departure of legend trips from traditional rites of passage. With no authority to denote or affirm that the rite has reached its end, there is generally a lack of closure, a sense that things may not be fully concluded, and that no resolution to the trip's challenges and mysteries has been achieved beyond the shadow of a doubt. For those participants who have succeeded in leaving the mundane structure of society behind, the challenge now is to complete the return to that very reality and achieve reincorporation with it. Some may never quite be able to retreat from the supernatural experience, even if they leave the site of encounter spatially behind, or at least find that a successful return will be uncertain and long in the making.

The ability of the liminal to, on occasion, follow you home and take on a more persistent presence in your life is another symptom of this problem. The liminal phase of the traditional rite of passage should—and according to the literature, does—only occur in those far-off places and under ritually defined conditions far removed from everyday life. It should not accompany the individual beyond its setting. Instead, individuals either succeed or fail in their passage to adulthood, for example. Either way, their status upon returning is determined, known, and unambiguous. Likewise, in the contemporary legend trip, the supernatural is supposed to stay in its place—the overgrown cemetery, the old house creaking in the wind, the darkened woods under the full moon. It is not supposed to have the capacity to change its setting. Regardless, supernatural intrusions into everyday life *do* occur in the sense that some people believe that the supernatural has followed them or is capable of doing so. This indicates something of a failed legend trip and shows the importance of a successful, well-defined return because for these unfortunate individuals whom have been followed, there *is* no return. They may have left the site of encounter, but that which makes the encounter significant and troubling has left with them. The experience continues to haunt participants, and they can derive little meaning or satisfaction from the persistent encounter. This results from the same cultural ambiguity that marks the legend trip itself. Without some form of collective validation or the authority of backing institutions, the moment in which it has formally commenced or concluded is unclear. There is no mark of adulthood, no induction into the clan, not even a diploma or insignia to officially and symbolically confer the successful completion of the rite and award a new status. The conclusion is inconclusive. This prolonged lingering, this absence of a well-defined conclusion, contributes to the general character of the legend trip as a quasi rite in constant peril of remaining unresolved.

Ambiguity is present in these later stages of the legend trip, then, partly in the absence of satisfactory closure. There is also ambiguity to the fundamental meaning of the whole endeavor. What, participants may ask themselves, did it all mean? There is no ready answer. The meaning of successfully completing high school or college, for comparison, is fairly clear. Once the degree is con-ferred, the individual's new social status, as graduate, is understood in society, and it opens new opportunities for them. Certainly, some disagreement or debate might occur relating to the *precise* meaning of these accomplishments or their exact value in an ever-changing job market, but this disagreement pales in comparison to the ambiguity inherent in a legend trip—even in a successfully completed one.

To begin with, individuals must consider the character of supernatural experiences. Encounters with the paranormal tend to be baffling, fragmen-tary, and unclear in meaning. Those who have these experiences are often left with questions rather than answers to life's mysteries. When they try to tell the story of their encounter to others, they often finish their accounts not with a conclusion, but with questions like: "Did it want something, was there something we were supposed to do? How [were] we supposed to communi-cate with it?" (Okonowicz 1996:12). Encounter with the supernatural is not a simple or uniform experience. People typically experience it as a brief, baffling fragment and not at all as a coherent "something." Hanks (2015), for example, finds that while some tourism sites like to promote themselves by promising that the spirits of historical personalities could be experienced there, people who actually have these experiences usually just hear a strange sound, detect an unusual smell, notice a moving object, or feel an odd presence that they cannot quite make sense of. They tend to describe ghosts "in terms of their vagueness, colorlessness, wispiness, incompleteness; they are most often recognized and defined precisely by their lack of definition or identifiers" (Richardson 2003:26). In interviewing witnesses who had experienced the supernatural, D. Waskul (2016) finds that their experiences were often so fragmentary and uncertain that they did not consider the word "ghost" satisfactory. His respondents were unsure that they really *had* experienced a ghost and tended to use the term, if they used it at all, for lack of a better option to categorize an array of strange experiences that had little in common other than their strangeness. They "were not sure that they had encountered a ghost" but were nonetheless "convinced that they had experience something uncanny . . . and were unsure about how to label it" (Waskul 2016:20–21).

The immediate response to encounter is, thus, uncertainty or bafflement, but for legend trippers, this uncertainty does not simply go away after they have had a chance to step away and digest it. The encounter proves resilient. It resists efforts to defuse its troubling ambiguity by assigning it to a safe and stable category with a comfortingly legible label. Whereas one can turn to a church for interpreting religiously sanctioned supernatural phenomena or science for naturalistic ones, paranormal phenomena have no ready institutional explanation and no recognized authorities one can trust to deliver one (Goode 2000). Considering how religions deal with the supernatural is particularly informative precisely because most religions acknowledge its existence, but they mitigate its ambiguity by providing meaningful interpretations for it. As D. Waskul (2016:7) argues, institutions, religious or otherwise, place a significant role in mediating "between experiences and beliefs." When a member of a faith encounters something anomalous, they can turn to institutional doctrine to both identify and interpret the experience. Religion can, thus, "conventionalize encounters with 'spirits'" (Waskul 2016:7) rather than leave their apparent existence an open question.

This is all well and good for benevolent spirits, for saints and angels and the like, but what about encounters with malevolent forces? Turning to evil spirits, D. Waskul (2016) points out that Christian denominations, for example, feature extensive demonologies. Christians have explanations for what demons are, where they came from, and what they want. They even have names, personalities, and social structures for these entities that the faithful can learn. This is not to say that demons are not frightening. To the contrary, if anything, these interpretations make the demonic more terrifying. Demons, the Devil, possession, exorcism, and so forth remain a major concern for many people (McCloud 2015). However, interpretation dramatically alters the nature of that fear. Rather than a meaning-threatening, confusing encounter, the frightening presence of the demon makes a sort of sense and reinforces the religious doctrine that explains it by serving as proof of that doctrine. While terrifying, the anomaly interpreted as "demon" is also ultimately, if not immediately, comforting in that it validates the master narrative provided by the faith. If there are demons and damnation, then there is also God and salvation. Even as it endorses the reality of the supernatural, institutional doctrine moderates the sense of the uncanny when it is encountered.

QUASI INSTITUTIONS

Legend trips come closest to institutionalization when they take place within a *quasi*-institutional context. There are at least three accessible ways in which this might occur: (1) when legend trippers are members of a paranormal subculture; (2) when they seek help from a paranormal "professional"; and (3) when what I like to call a "para-institution" develops around a particular phenomenon. The term "subculture," like so many other social-scientific concepts, has seen its share of dispute and scholarly drama (Debies-Carl 2013). Without invoking these debates, it is convenient to think of "subculture" as a useful term that simply distinguishes a group in some way from mainstream culture in general (Clark 2003). Christopher D. Bader et al. (2010) observe that we are all members of some subculture or another and that these groups tend to look strange to outsiders because they are unfamiliar. For example: "There are biker subcultures and Goth subcultures. There is a NASCAR subculture and a Twilight subculture; subcultures for hunters and for comic book collectors" (Bader et al. 2010:115). Members of these groups have some interest or concern that they hold more intensely than nonmembers. There are subcultures concerned with paranormal subjects too, including groups organized around topics like ghosts, Bigfoot, or UFOs. These exhibit subcultural indicators—such as norms, fashion, specialized language, or detailed knowledge—that they share and that make members recognizable. Among these cultural elements are ready-made explanations and understandings for various paranormal phenomena. Consequently, members of such groups have access to a range of social and psychological resources, not to mention supportive social networks, that might help alleviate feelings of confusion and uncertainty arising from uncanny encounters. This can approximate the role of religious institutions by interpreting the supernatural for members and, thus, defusing its more threatening aspects.

Imagine that you are walking through the woods one night in search of a supernatural encounter. The stereotypical visual image of a Bigfoot is widely available in popular culture. You have likely seen these images on many occasions and in a variety of contexts, ranging from television shows to product packaging in the grocery store (see Grider 2007b). If you see something that approximates the image of one of these images in the woods, you might be reasonably confident in concluding that you indeed saw a Bigfoot. Many paranormal enthusiasts describe this sort of visual sighting of their quarry as something of a "holy grail"—that is, an elusive but monumentally important goal that few ever achieve. This is true among ghost investigators (e.g., Newman 2011) as well as Bigfoot hunters (Bader et al. 2010) and likely similar groups. Just like ghost encounters (Hanks 2015; Richardson 2003; Waskul 2016), Bigfoot encounters are rarely based on complete visual sightings and more commonly have a fragmentary, confusing character about them. Instead of a Bigfoot, then, imagine that, while delving through those benighted woods, you simply heard some sounds: an unnerving howl and a series of strange knocking noises echoing in the distance as though someone were hitting a tree with a large branch. Assuming you were open to an uncanny explanation, how would you interpret the experience? Is it the work of a ghost? The ravings of a maniac? Is it nothing at all?

For many legend trippers, it would simply have to remain a mystery. However, if you are a member of a Bigfoot subculture, you might reject all of these equally (un)likely explanations and instead have learned to interpret the sounds as coming from a previously undiscovered primate who is actually saying "hello" or, somewhat more ominously, "get off my lawn." Bigfoot believers have a fairly extensive subcultural presence in the United States. They read and write about the cryptid, develop and share theories of its behavior and biology, formulate specialized terminology to describe these ideas, search for it in the wild, and develop organizations and conventions. At a convention, you can "meet Bigfoot celebrities face-to-face,[3] purchase the latest Bigfoot products, trade stories from the field, and hear tips from veteran hunters" (Bader et al. 2010:113). A member of this subculture will not be at a loss when hearing those strange noises in the woods. Likely, there will be some uncertainty and debate, but if those sounds are generally consistent with Bigfoot's behavior—as they have learned it from the subculture and as legitimated by the consensus of at least some of its members, then they will have some ready options for how to interpret it. Members of the subculture often suggest that Bigfoot uses knocks, howls, and other noises to communicate, mark its territory, or—somewhat less popularly—perhaps even navigate via echolocation, like a bat (Brockenbrough 2013). In fact, some members have learned how to make these noises themselves to aid their investigations. They might, for instance, hope to attract a specimen by making their own wood-knocking sounds (e.g., McMillan 2014). Alternately, they could produce blood-curdling howls via "call blasting." This involves playing recorded animal noises, such as previously recorded howls attributed to Bigfoot, with a loudspeaker (Robinson 2016). When engaging in these sorts of activities, not only are they ostensively seeking Bigfoot through their legend trip, but they are also ostensively acting out the legendary role of Bigfoot as learned through the subculture.

What if someone prefers more professional help for their paranormal problems? When you have a crisis of faith, you can call your priest; when you have
a fire, you call the fire department. But "who you gonna call" when you suspect
that a ghost or some other supernatural entity is plaguing you? Although it
treated the matter humorously, the film *Ghostbusters* was partly predicated
on the idea that there is no institutional support for people with paranormal problems. Throughout the film, various institutions—the police, the fire
department, a church, the government, and even the military—are powerless
(and clueless) in the face of supernatural threats. In the absence of authority,
people in real life might do the same thing as those portrayed in the movie:
seek the help of self-styled experts instead. Paranormal subcultures frequently
include individuals who consider themselves, or whom other members of the
subculture consider, to be experts or professionals of sorts. These might be
professional psychic mediums or paranormal investigators (Waskul 2016) or
cryptozoologists (Bader et al. 2010) with some considerable degree of subcultural knowledge about their particular topic.

Even people outside of these subcultures might seek out such an expert to
help explain and interpret an uncanny experience when existing conventional
support is lacking. Dégh once spoke with a young couple who were worried
that an unseen entity was bothering their baby. They were unsure what to
make of the situation, but friends and family urged them to seek help from
a "professional clairvoyant" (Dégh 2001:330). Desperate homeowners can
also get help from professional paranormal investigators. This is a frequent
theme in television shows like *Ghost Hunters*. In one representative episode
from the series, homeowner Adam was experiencing strange phenomena:
disincarnate voices, moving objects, and eerie feelings that had him worried
for his safety and sanity (Piligian and Thayer 2004). After investigating his
home, the team concluded that it was likely the ghost of his grandfather, who
had originally built the house. Far from dangerous, they suggested he was
simply watching over Adam with whom he had had a strong relationship
in life. The episode concludes with Adam summarizing how he felt about
the whole affair: "The results of this investigation: it *did* bring closure to the
subject for me, where I know I'm not crazy. There *is* something there.... It's
most likely a member of my own family" (Piligian and Thayer 2004). His
experience suggests that, under some circumstances, quasi-institutional
professionals like these can provide outcomes that function similarly to
religion proper (Spiro 1966). External confirmation that something strange
is going on relieves his concern about his sanity. An explanation for those
strange phenomena helps him feel like he can understand them. Finally, and
perhaps most importantly, the claim that the unseen entity is simply the
benevolent spirit of his grandfather removes his fear of unknown danger.

Instead, it replaces that fear with the hope and comfort that death has not severed the bonds of love and family (Bennett 1999).

Rather than seeking paranormal professional help to explain a supernatural experience, one can hire a professional to achieve such an experience in the first place. People grieving the loss of a loved one sometimes seek help from professional mediums to put them in touch with the deceased, a practice that might have the potential to help ease the suffering of those who believe in it (Beischel, Mosher, and Boccuzzi 2014–2015). Whereas members of paranormal subcultures already possess explanations for some uncanny experiences, paranormal experts can provide this sort of explanation to people *outside* of paranormal circles. In doing so, they can potentially offer a degree of meaning and closure to an otherwise baffling situation that most people are culturally unequipped to make sense of.

Finally, some paranormal groups adopt the trappings of formal organizations. These might include hierarchical organization, written regulations, specialization and titles, specialized knowledge, and the like (Weber [1921] 1978). By emulating more conventional and more familiar institutional models, these "para-institutions," for lack of a better word, attempt to establish legitimacy for themselves that will grant authoritative interpretive power over the phenomenon that interests them. The extent to which they accomplish this is debatable. The average local ghost-hunting group provides informative examples. Many of these have webpages, and of those I have surveyed, the majority consist of only a handful of members that look more like a group of friends than a formal organization. This does not stop them from attempting to present themselves as something more though. They frequently have an interesting preoccupation with dispensing specialized titles, featuring at least as many titles as actual members. One group, the Eastern Connecticut Paranormal Society (2018)—hereafter ECPS, has five members but includes the titles of cofounder, psychic medium, lead investigator, investigator, Karuna Reiki practitioner, and interviewer. Another group, the Connecticut Paranormal Research Team (CPRT), has six members and includes the following occupational titles: director, senior investigator, investigator, case manager, senior equipment technician, and webmaster (Connecticut Paranormal Research Team n.d.). Sometimes there are formal-looking procedures that individuals must deal with if they would like to join these groups, which reinforce the organizational characteristics of hierarchy, written procedures, and specialized knowledge. To join the aforementioned investigation team, prospective members must pay "a yearly due of $130," "have good knowledge of Paranormal Phenomena and Investigative procedures," "be willing to follow [the group's] protocol and guidelines," and "be willing to participate in ongoing training through [the group]," among other things. New members are typically assigned a title like "trainee" or, in the CPRT's case, "newbie," indicating inferior knowledge and subordinate status.

Para-institutions usually feature attempts to authoritatively explain the paranormal on their websites, generally in incomplete and fragmented ways. ECPS provides an extensive vocabulary of paranormal and related terms, a system for "grading" paranormal evidence, and a section on "Demonology 101," but little else—not even a primer on ghosts. "Investigation files" or "case studies" are common as well and emulate the style of a formal report. One group, Shekinah Paranormal, offers a typical example. They open each case report with boilerplate information (date of investigation, team members present, equipment used, a ranking for how successful the investigation was, etc.) and use a dry, passive-voice style.

For example: "Three digital recorders were utilized. One question session was conducted, with the hopes of recording examples of spirit voice, otherwise known as 'electronic voice phenomena.' Later review would subtract background noise from a nearby wine tasting event. . . . Upon later review of Hi-8 and digital recordings, a few possible examples of 'electronic voice phenomena' were noted. . . ." (Shekinah Paranormal Investigations n.d.:n.p.). The overall effect is like something one might expect from a social worker who deals with the undead and has to write a report for their supervisor, but whose training and methodology is largely informed by popular television. However, the overall desire for an air of legitimate authority is evident. The extent to which the general public might be convinced of their authority is questionable, but this is a potential subject for further investigation.

THE LIMITS OF MEANING

Encounter with the supernatural is disorienting under any circumstances, but this disorientation is *temporary* when it occurs in an institutionalized context (e.g., when interpreted by a formal religion) and partly mitigated within a quasi-institutionalized one (e.g., when interpreted by a paranormal subculture or professional). In these contexts, someone with at least some degree of perceived legitimacy can help by offering an interpretation of what happened, the nature of the encounter, and what it means. Those who have experienced the uncanny need not be left in perpetual uncertainty.

This is less common for extra-institutional legend trips. Although they may try to borrow from formal religion, legend trippers do not usually have this same institutional comfort for their anomalous experiences. Quasi-institutional support is often lacking as well. Most people, including legend trippers, are not members of paranormal subcultures (Bader et al. 2010) and few seek out the help of paranormal professionals (Waskul 2016). They will not be able to draw on whatever sort of consolation these groups might otherwise be able to confer. Even if one does consult subcultures or an expert, they are a far cry from more conventional sources of information. Unless someone seeking their help is also firmly entrenched in that paranormal subculture, they might find the guidance they receive to be questionable and of limited comfort because of that origin. It could even conflict with their preexisting beliefs or background and present more problems than it solves, as when paranormal claims run counter to religious doctrine. This doctrinal conflict is part of the reason why conventional churchgoers are less likely to believe in paranormal phenomena in the first place (Baker et al. 2016), as opposed to institutionalized supernatural phenomena that are specifically endorsed by their faith. Even if they are satisfied with an alleged expert's explanation, friends and family might not affirm the sentiment. They may not recognize the expert, much less acknowledge their authority, even if the individual in question is famous in paranormal circles. If you have a friend who says that they know they have seen a Bigfoot for certain because Loren Coleman or Smokey Crabtree confirmed it for them, these names would likely mean little to you and carry little weight unless you are a member of a cryptozoological subculture (Bader et al. 2010). Again, legend trippers might experience something uncanny and potentially profound, but they have limited options for making sense of that encounter and sharing it with others, unlike those who have more conventional religious experiences.

Without a legitimate framework available, it is difficult to achieve a sense of closure or coherent meaning from supernatural encounters. We can appreciate the scope of this problem by comparing the typical legend-tripping encounter with mysterious forces in real life and the failure to achieve anything beyond confusion from that contact to that typically presented in fictional accounts. In film series like Harry Potter or the Twilight Saga and television shows like *Buffy the Vampire Slayer* or *Supernatural*, there is a sort of dualistic reality. Most of the characters live in a world that approximates the real, normal world. There is no magic, no special powers, or anything particularly strange or unpredictable that one should expect to encounter in everyday life. Just beyond the veil of this world however, hidden from most people's sight, there is another one with supernatural properties. Indeed, the need to shield the existence of this world from the mundane world is often an element in the plot. There is always a moment of revelation, in which the protagonist suddenly learns about the existence of this other world and its wondrous differences from his or her own familiar reality: magic is real, vampires are real, monsters are real, and nothing will ever be the same again. The initial encounter with this world is indeed shocking and troubling. The protagonist is troubled, disoriented, and may initially deny the evidence before them. However, here any similarity with legend tripping ends. Once the initial surprise has passed, they quickly become acquainted with the other world and begin to adapt to its requirements, often with the help of a mentor or some other comforting guide.[4] It becomes just another reality with its own set of predictable expectations—its social rules and natural laws—that can be learned and understood with time and effort. Magic can be taught and controlled, and vampires have stable characteristics and understandable motives, while monsters have knowable properties and predictable habits. In worlds such as these, "magic is a part of everyday life, unseen by the Muggles, but practiced with casual cheerfulness by all those who understand it" (Whited 2002:15).

In other words, these apparently strange things are largely presented as strange simply on account of their novelty, which is not a lasting quality. Unlike many real-life encounters with the liminal or uncanny, these new experiences can be quickly incorporated into one's life and cease to be ontologically threatening. New experiences may threaten one's current worldview, but they never threaten the capacity of worldview itself. After the initial period of acclimatization, what terrors or wonders they continue to present are of the mundane sort, no matter how superficially fantastic. Having faced these novel stimuli and incorporated them into their identity, the protagonist inevitably completes a successful rite of passage. For all the wonder and fascination that they encounter along the way, they have simply entered into a new social status complete with new, but stable and known, rights and obligations. To some extent, it is not that dissimilar to the temporary novelty and disruption of real-life transitions: going to college, getting a job, getting married, or having a child. This characterization is rarely the case with legend trips though. Encounters with liminal forces might be considered a sort of "initiation" into the world of the supernatural (Thigpen 1971:204) but may not yield any real understanding of that other realm nor a fundamental shift in status upon one's returns—if they return. The sense of ambiguity, although it can be ignored with time, cannot readily be resolved and explained away.

Often participants remain uncertain not only as to what exactly happened on their legend trips, they also remain unsure whether it will have any lasting impact on their lives despite the vague sense that it included an experience that seemed somehow significant. As Thigpen (1971:207) observed many years ago, contact with the supernatural, despite its shocking nature, "does not necessarily have a profound or stable influence on one's belief system." One of his informants told him several legends of strange things that were supposed to occur in a local house. When asked whether he believed these stories, the informant replied that he did not—at least he did not believe the legends when he was safely away from that house during the light of day. It was another matter entirely "on dark nights when he had to walk past the house" (Thigpen 1971:207). This is a situation that many people can probably appreciate. What seems impossible and ridiculous when we go about our days at work or at home may seem frighteningly possible when we are alone at night in a strange place: a graveyard under the stars, a remote dirt road in a storm, and so on. Upon returning to the everyday world following flight from a liminal place, it may not just be the possibility of strange things that is left behind but also the importance invested in those things. However, even this insignificance and meaninglessness of the paranormal is neither permanent nor predictable. As Freud (1919:247) puts it, we might believe that "we have *surmounted* these modes of thought; but we do not feel quite sure of our new beliefs, and the old ones still exist within us ready to seize upon any confirmation." Given the right conditions, one can easily be thrust back into the realm of supernatural possibility that calls old experiences or old fears to mind. When asked whether he believed a certain bridge in Indiana was really haunted, another informant once reported, "It could very well be haunted and when I go out there I sure believe it" (Dégh 1969:64). Belief, it seems, is contextual.

Despite these various problems with determining what occurred and what it might mean, it certainly cannot be said that legend trips are entirely meaningless. To the contrary, although there are clearly many challenges and difficulties to overcome, if everything unfolds roughly in the manner described in the previous chapters, participants will in all likelihood achieve the sense that *something* significant has happened and the perception that they, themselves, may have come away from the experience different in some way. The sense of "otherness" provided by the encounter with the supernatural suggests it is significant in some way. As V. Turner (1973:213) might argue, they have underwent a pilgrimage that should have consisted of "beginning in a Familiar Place, going to a Far Place, and returning, ideally 'changed,' to a Familiar Place." The journey has the potential to make a powerful and enduring experience at best, but also a confusing one or even a troubling one at worst since the fundamental meaning of the whole affair is neither self-evident nor clear even after it has been concluded. Like Thigpen (1971), Tucker (2007:64) suggests that experiencing contact with the supernatural is akin to achieving a sort of "initiation into the realm of the supernatural." Indeed, but what exactly does that initiation provide? The effect can be compared to seeing someone appear out of thin air, hand you a blank diploma, and declare "Congratulations! You are now . . ." before trailing off and fading away from view like a ghost. If you could convince yourself of the reality of the experience, it would certainly seem like there should be something potentially meaningful about it. What specifically, though, would you make of it? What would others think if you told them about it?

THE FUTURE OF LEGEND TRIPPING

It is evident from these many complications that making sense of a legend trip is no simple matter. Reconsidering the final stage of the legend trip—intense discussion—in the context of these difficulties helps to explain why this sort of debate must occur. The need for discussion, the intensity of that discussion, and difficulty involved in understanding exactly what happened are certainly related. They can all be linked to those factors I have considered that explain other ambiguities in the legend-tripping process: while the experience feels significant to the participants, its meaning is neither obvious nor intuitive. There is not even a ready script available for them to draw on that can tell them exactly what the meaning of that significance is supposed to be. They are compelled to find meaning and validation of that meaning through discussion with others instead. Just like similar problems with earlier stages of the legend trip, this is partly because the experience of the uncanny is itself ambiguous and because legend trips are not usually affiliated with, or sponsored by, any legitimate institutional authority that can offer competing interpretations. No mainstream, formal religion advocates them, no recognized government or agency promotes them, nor do any institutions provide participants with clear cultural expectations for how they can interpret their experiences, much less a way to reconcile it with others' interpretations. These institutions normally provide ready-made "plausibility structures" (Berger 1967) to their members, a sort of discursive framework that readily identifies, validates, and explains members' experiences in light of, say, church dogma. However, many paranormal phenomena, like ghosts, extraterrestrials, and extrasensory perception more generally—the things encountered on a legend trip—do not conform to institutional doctrine (Baker et al. 2016) nor is the legend trip itself a prescribed activity (Kinsella 2011). For those experiencing these things, there is no such interpretive structure or, if they are a member of an institution that provides one, more likely than not the frameworks they have available condemn rather than interpret the experience.

In his collection of interviews with ghost-hunting organizations, for instance, author Alan Brown (2006) reports that many members have had uncomfortable interactions with religious groups critical of their activities. This sort of condemnation occurs because of doctrinal incompatibilities, even when the ghost hunters consider themselves religious. Illustrating this problem, one angry woman challenged a Kentucky ghost hunter, telling him, "You're messing around with something you really shouldn't be" and demanding, "How can you believe that God would allow an individual to get lost on his way to heaven or hell?" (Brown 2006:146). It is not belief or experience of the supernatural itself that necessarily warrants disapproval from formal religions since these are actually integrated within many religious worldviews (Baker et al. 2016). After all, belief in and experience of supernatural beings, like angels and gods, is a common element in the theology of most religions. Edward B. Tylor (1871:383), the historical founder of cultural anthropology, famously argues that a definition of "religion" should minimally include "belief in Spiritual Beings." While alternative definitions of religion are readily available, this essentialist perspective on supernatural entities remains of concern to religious scholars. Nearly one hundred years after Tylor, for instance, Anthony F. C. Wallace's (1966:5) definition of "religion" similarly emphasizes "belief and ritual concerned with supernatural beings, powers, and forces."

There are two significant reasons for why institutional religions condemn legend trips despite their shared concerns with the supernatural. First, paranormal and religious phenomena are perfectly compatible in the ontological sense. That is, they both endorse supernatural interpretations of reality that do not logically conflict with each other (Goode 2000). However, they *are* incompatible in the doctrinal sense. The supernatural content that serves as the focus of legend trips—things like vengeful ghosts, vampires, curses, and UFOs—are not condoned by the supernatural doctrine of most mainstream religions in America (Bader et al. 2010). Second, like pilgrimages, the grassroots nature of legend trips and their ability to provide unpredictable but potent experiences without this sort of hierarchical oversight might make them appear dangerous or threatening in the eyes of such institutions (Turner and Turner 1978). While one or the other of these factors might be considered harmless or perhaps even susceptible to cooptation by mainstream churches on its own, this combination of the two is particularly unpalatable. This is because "it is in the interest of religious groups to attempt to limit spiritual practice that falls outside of their control," and more strict religious groups often condemn these practices "as theologically suspect, or perhaps even evil" (Baker et al. 2016:336). It is perhaps for reasons of this sort that the visible evidence of completed legend trips is so often interpreted as signs of something more sinister, like Devil worship or serious criminal activity (Bromley 1991; Fine and Victor 1994; Victor 1993). This is a well-established pattern. Throughout Western history, at least, "the Church and the law have never approved of . . . self-appointed experts on the supernatural, and in fact [some were] interrogated in Church courts because of their unorthodox beliefs" (Simpson 1996:13).

The popularity of legend tripping in recent decades might be linked to changes in religiosity across the developed world where many people are disaffiliating with traditional religious denominations (Wuthnow 1998). This does not mean that people are forsaking belief or interest in the supernatural altogether. Rather most people continue to maintain their interest and seek meaning in such matters, but they do so increasingly through *individual* spirituality. These are beliefs and practices that, while personally significant, do not in their entirety conform to a religious orthodoxy. This pattern, which has been in progress since at least the Great Awakening of the 1700s (Deetz 1977), is obviously threatening to established religious institutions. However, it also corresponds with increased interest in the paranormal, that is, supernatural phenomena that are not endorsed by these mainstream religious institutions. Surveys indicate that people less involved in formal church activities or doctrine are much more likely to report witnessing UFOs, having precognitive dreams, experiencing hauntings, and attempting to contact spirits of the dead (Baker et al. 2016). Legend trippers also emphasize the individualized and deeply personal nature of their adventures: "Part of the reason I began legend tripping so many years ago was because I had big questions: Are we alone in the universe? Is there life after death? Who created all of this? Through legend tripping I'm finding answers, but they're my own. I recognize they may not mean anything to someone else" (Belanger 2011:174).

If this process of religious individualization is indeed occurring, there would also be an increase in legend-tripping activities, greater publicity for it in mainstream sources, and a wider range of participants from more diverse demographic backgrounds since a greater number of people would be less bound by institutional restrictions. In fact, this is exactly what has happened. Next, perhaps mainstream and scholarly sources will increasingly treat legend trips with less prejudicial disdain and a greater willingness to try to understand what they are all about before reflexively assuming they are nothing but trivial juvenilia or dangerous Devil worship.

This is not to say, of course, that anyone should necessarily expect to see any cultural consensus emerge as to the meaning or interpretation of legend trips anytime soon. Rather, it seems reasonable to expect that there will be a general increase in perceptions of it being a fairly normal practice or at least not a pathological one. The growth in television (e.g., Koven 2007) and tourism (e.g., Gentry 2007; Hanks 2015; Holloway 2010) centered around supernatural subjects seems indicative of that growing normativity, although this perception is certainly not true among all demographics. Many conservative Christians remain wary of activities like these that seem to flirt dangerously with demonic threats (McCloud 2015) while, at the same time, skeptics critique belief in the supernatural and those who pursue it too as credulous (Nickell 2007; Radford 2010).

As the social context of legend trips change, some of their other characteristics will likely change as well. For example, legend trip destinations may shift proportionately from marginal or residual spaces (Debies-Carl 2011) to more accessible mainstream ones. Again, the rise of tourism featuring haunted restaurants, historic house museums, and other attractions indicates that this shift is occurring even now (Light 2017). Haunted hotels and inns illustrate this point particularly well. Instead of jumping over iron fences to trespass in a cold cemetery in the dark of night only to be chased off by local law enforcement, today's legend trippers can be welcomed by the proprietor of a quaintly spooky inn, spend a comfortable evening in an overstuffed bed, and enjoy a warm breakfast in the morning. The phenomena that mark the supernatural presence in these places are suitably domestic as well. The Kennebunk Inn in Maine has been lodging living guests since the 1790s and the undead somewhat more recently (Mead 1995). Its most famous ghost is called "Silas" or "Cyrus," and he is primarily known for making glassware float about and crash in the inn's tavern. Here, as I experienced one night, a legend trip can amount to coming down to the bar from your room, grabbing a pint (floating or not), and returning to your bed and safety should the encounter be too taxing. If the ghosts of witches are more up your alley, you can do better than prowling around one of the many sorcerous graves I have considered in previous chapters. The Hawthorne Hotel of Salem, Massachusetts, seems to have witches aplenty and perhaps a few other characters roaming about its many floors (Baltrusis 2014; Guiley 2011). In addition to three-star accommodations and period décor, guests might encounter apparitions, cold spots, a bewitched elevator, and all manner of spookiness in a climate-controlled setting. Over dinner, you might even witness the old ship's wheel, housed in the hotel's restaurant, moving about as if some spectral captain thinks he's still on deck and sailing the high seas.

Beyond shifts in setting, some of the social and psychological elements of legend tripping will likely change as well when they occur within a more normative context. The classic legend trip is guided by folklore: by peoples' everyday understanding of how the supernatural might work and under what circumstances. Traditionally, these understandings are passed on in tales told to friends or overheard in the bar. They are not lessons learned in a church or gleaned from a television show. Of course, in modern life this ideal is considerably upset. Subcultural knowledge and popular culture flow smoothly into folklore (Goldstein et al. 2007). Today, many more people can distinguish between "residual" and "intelligent" hauntings while terms like "orb" and "EVP" have, to some extent, entered into folklore from paranormal subcultures as well. They have done so in large part through the conduit of the popular media, which leaves its own mark on the enterprise. The reverse is certainly true as well, with folklore influencing popular culture and paranormal cultures (Goldstein et al. 2007), but it seems likely that the quasi-institutional guidance and interpretation that are made increasingly available through commercial and social media will alter the fundamental character of some important aspects of legend tripping. Most significantly, it is possible that legend tripping will enter the realm of conventional culture and even take on a degree of institutionalized predictability: a "rationalization of irrationality" (Dégh 2001:325). In the

Hawthorne Hotel (Salem, MA): This hotel is a fine place to legend trip, full of hospitality and all the comforts of home. Photograph by the author.

process of this transformation, some of its more emergent and unpredictable characteristics may change. Someday legend trippers may set forth knowing exactly what they are supposed to experience and armed with predetermined, preindoctrinated conclusions about the experience's meaning.

For now, the tales that legend trippers bring back with them from their adventures are fragmentary and unclear in part because the legend trip itself is fragmentary and unclear. It cannot be anything else given the social conditions within which it is undertaken. It has no well-defined beginning, middle, or end; no straight-forward meaning; and no stable body of cultural wisdom to make it conform to. Unlike formal rites of passage in which a deep sense of meaning is conferred, there is confusion. Instead of solidarity and consensus, we see conflict and debate. Understandably, many legend trippers would like to believe that their experiences were significant in some way and to have others to whom they tell their tale affirm that significance. That this will occur, however, is far from a sure thing. Whether the phenomenon involved was really experienced is, itself, put to the question, as is whether and how it matters. Given the overall decline in social rituals in general and considering all of the difficulties and ambiguities involved in improvised rites like legend trips, it is not surprising that many observers have eagerly advocated for the return of formal rites of passage and their reintegration into the social fabric (e.g., Campbell 1988; Eliade 1965). I would caution against this.

We should not unquestioningly accept the wisdom of traditional rites of passage, mourn their loss or modern impoverishment without considerable qualification. Neither should we criticize activities like legend trips on the basis that they appear to be something of a pale imitation of the "real thing." While marking socially sanctioned changes in status is potentially useful for both the individual and for society, many traditional *and* modern practices in this regard are needlessly cruel and traumatic. An oft-quoted description of the traditional rite of passage for Thonga boys in southern Africa provides a fairly representative example of the sort of ordeals children must face in order to be considered adults:

> The initiation begins when each boy runs the gauntlet between two rows of men who beat him with clubs [at the end of which, he is forcibly circumcised]. Afterward he is secluded for three months in the "yard of mysteries," where he can be seen only by the initiated. During the course of his initiation, the boy undergoes six major trials: beatings, exposure to cold, thirst, eating of unsavory foods, punishment, and the threat of death. On the slightest pretext, he may be beaten by one of the newly initiated men. . . . He sleeps without covering and suffers bitterly from the winter cold. He is forbidden to drink a drop of water during the whole three months. Meals are often made nauseating by the half-digested grass from the stomach of an antelope, which is poured over his food. If he is caught breaking any important rule governing the ceremony, he is severely punished. For example, in one of these punishments, sticks are placed between the fingers of the offender, then a strong man closes his hand around that of the novice, practically crushing his fingers. He is frightened into submission by being told that, in former times, boys who had tried to escape or who had revealed the secrets to women or to the uninitiated were hanged and their bodies burned to ashes. (Whiting, Kluckhohn, and Anthony1958:360)

While it is certainly possible that this account is exaggerated—for example, it is impossible for anyone to go three months without drinking unless they are receiving water through some other means (Packer 2014), the general content of the account is not entirely dissimilar from many rites of passage in the anthropological literature (see Comaroff 2013). Moreover, even if the majority of it is the product of exaggeration, the remainder still provides a horrific image of the traditional rite of passage. Those modern rites of passage that most closely resemble traditional ones also include these abuses. Indeed, Ralph Cialdini (1993) draws on the above description of the Thongan rite in his groundbreaking examination of hazing rituals among modern fraternities, which, he

argues, are essentially the same practice. These include similar ordeals: beat-
ings, exposure, thirst, eating unsavory foods, punishments, and death threats.
Only by enduring and accepting these painful and humiliating ordeals can an
individual be accepted as a full member of the tribe/fraternity. Is the decline
of such rituals really something that should be mourned?

Legend tripping, while not without its problems, is at least not institutionally sanctioned cruelty and, to the contrary, need not involve any abuse at all
as many of the examples I have explored illustrate. In practicing them, participants may achieve a degree of meaning, a sense of social transition, even
without the watchful eye of church, state, tribal elder, or fraternity brother. As
Lindahl (2005:165) argues, "Despite scholars' concentration on criminal imita-
tions, there is ample evidence that ostension can transcend horror and inspire
a sense of wonder in those who bring legends to life." Those problems that
do occur—theft, vandalism, underage drinking, trouble with the neighbors,
and the like—may be fairly common, but they are not systematically present
and can be mitigated through other means, like those I have noted in earlier
chapters. The consequences of legend tripping are usually milder than those of
practices like hazing as well. To my knowledge, there are no statistics on rates
of death or injury among legend trippers, but I would predict these are much
lower than comparable figures for hazing.

Finally, even if no meaning is achieved or greater purpose accomplished,
at least most people *enjoy* legend trips. This is not something that can be said
unequivocally about hazing or other similarly imposed practices. As Dégh
(1969:81) argued many years ago: "The exploit is not only a dare but also very
enjoyable fun. Feeling the chill of a 'good scare' is definitely welcome to youths
in this civilized, comfortable and rather uneventful affluent world. To escape
boredom and enjoy adulthood, what could be more exciting[?]"

LEGEND TRIPPING: A MODERN CLASSIC

In this book, drawing on decades of prior scholarship and over a hundred
new cases, I have compared scores of legend trips to see what patterns might
be found rather than extrapolating from a single example. I found remarkable consistencies and interesting variations, which I have examined in depth
throughout the preceding chapters. While legend trips vary in terms of specific
details, their overall structure and content are very similar. For example, the
particular rituals legend trippers conduct or the character of the experiences
they have will never be identical. However, among other commonalities, a successful legend trip always features some ritual and some encounter and there
are typical patterns and characteristics to these, as well as common underlying

rationales. In so doing, I have identified new stages of this activity and refined old ones, suggesting that it can be broken down into six distinct phases. I have also introduced a wide range of specific variants within each of these stages—such as whether a ritual is transgressive or concordant—to help refine our understanding of legend trips. Future research can further examine these stages, perhaps identifying new ones or further exploring the details of existing ones. In terms of the former, for example, I suspect the preparatory stage can further be divided between pretravel preparations and the journey itself. Likewise, further exploration of specific topics like why some legend trippers feel that the supernatural has followed them or how they make sense of their experiences would be invaluable.

While cases of ghosts and curses—the traditional emphasis of research in this field—still predominate, I found that other legends motivate very similar behavior. This is especially true for things like cryptid hunting or UFO watching. These patterns suggest a similar, underlying social and psychological process that facilitates legend tripping. Throughout, I have suggested that legend trips probably do not even have to focus on paranormal phenomena at all provided that other characteristics I have outlined, like a sense of mystery and an apparent threat to values, are intact. Modern concerns like conspiracy-based legends and the potentially dangerous forms of ostension these produce will be particularly important to understand for the foreseeable future (Debies-Carl 2017). Again, there is a need for further inquiry that expands legend-tripping research beyond ghost hunting and, indeed, beyond even the paranormal. What do these various practices have in common and how might they vary? Many other comparative questions remain as well. For example, this could include queries into the differences between age groups who legend trip, differences between commercial and noncommercial legend trips, and perhaps most critically of all, comparisons of legend tripping in other parts of the world (McNeill and Tucker 2018). The latter would be particularly useful in comparing constructionist, perennialist, psychological, and social perspectives on the phenomenon.

While further research is warranted, the current study has revealed important new findings that I hope will help inform that work. The legend trip is certainly comparable to more traditional rites of passage, but it is simultaneously a distinct phenomenon. It provides a similar experience for the individuals involved, separating them from the mundane world, allowing them to encounter strange entities in the liminal land beyond, and come back changed in some way or at least with the sense that something significant has occurred. The various characteristics of the legend trip that I have discussed suggest that its imperfect approximation of a rite of passage is not so much a result of deritualization in developed societies, but rather a consequence of religious deinstitutionalization and the more general, greater emphasis placed on individuals over groups and collectivities in such societies (Bellah et al. 1985). The fact that legend tripping entails a search for meaningful *personal* experiences, likewise, is consistent with the postmaterialist values of contemporary, developed societies as well (Inglehart 1990). Like ritual in general, there is no practical or instrumental dimension involved (Durkheim [1912] 1995). Instead of affirming collective and traditional truths like classical rituals, the legend trip represents a more individualized search for meaning and self-expression. To be sure, many traditional rites that appeal to specific demographic groups can still be experienced by those within those groups today. We still have Catholic baptisms, Latina Quinceañeras, Jewish Bar Mitzvahs, and so on, but the rite of passage, as a collective process made orthodox by widely accepted religious institutions within a homogenous society, has largely passed away. Or, rather, it has changed into forms more consistent with the types of societies within which it is found, like the legend trip. It is no longer mandatory, but voluntary; not formal, but informal; not institutionally approved, but individually validated; no longer uniform in terms of its contents, process, meaning or appeal, but diverse, taking on different forms in response to the needs of the equally diverse individuals and groups that can be found within more heterogeneous social worlds. In other words, as society has changed, so too have many of its rituals and the role of ritual more broadly. Legend tripping is more about the individual as part of a group than it is about teaching them their place in some hierarchical institution. It is not about passively and obediently doing what you are told to do. It requires more agency and creativity as individuals piece together a legend, decide how to investigate it, and interpret its meaning for themselves. Indeed, often these activities and interpretations run counter to what institutions expect or demand of them. In these ways, the legend trip might actually provide a more productive experience than traditional rites of passage and a more appropriate one for the modern age.

The legend trip is not some degenerated half memory of more noble, ancient rites. It is a development or adaptation: a rite fulfilling old desires in the context of modern sensibilities and concerns. Its form and expression will doubtless continue to change along with the times, but it is unlikely to fade away any time soon, despite its critics, given its appeal, its flexibility, and its apparent cultural function.

Tonight, across America, countless people will embark on an adventure. They will prowl through the overgrown headstones in our forgotten graveyards, they will stalk our darkened woods and wildlands, and they will creep through the long-neglected and crumbling corridors of our abandoned buildings. They will come in search of a paranormal experience—for meaning, for a sense of exploration, or for just plain fun, and despite the odds set against them, many will seem to achieve just that. They are legend trippers, and they are part of a growing cultural phenomenon. Will you dare to be among them?

LEGENDARY PLACES VISITED
AND EVENTS ATTENDED

SITE NAME	LOCATION
Absecon Lighthouse	Atlantic City, NJ
Acorn Street	Boston, MA
Algonquin Hotel	New York, NY
American Flatbread	Burlington, VT
Americana Vineyards	Interlaken, NY
Arcade Providence	Providence, RI
Belcourt of Newport	Newport, RI
Belhurst Castle	Geneva, NY
Benefit Street	Providence, RI
Benton Homestead	Tolland, CT
Boston Common	Boston, MA
Boston Public Garden	Boston, MA
Boylston Street Station	Boston, MA
Branford Supply Pond Park	Branford, CT
The Breakers	Newport, RI
Burial Hill	Plymouth, MA
Captain Daniel Packer Inne	Mystic, CT
Captain Grants 1754 Bed and Breakfast	Preston, CT
Central Burying Ground	Boston, MA
Château Ramezay	Montreal, Canada
Chatfield Hollow State Park	Killingworth, CT
Chestnut Hill Baptist Cemetery	Exeter, RI
Concord Colonial Inn	Concord, MA
Connecticut Hill Cemetery	Newfield, NY
Corner of Flamingo Blvd and Koval Ln	Las Vegas, NV

Curtis House Restaurant & Inn	Woodbury, CT
Devil's Hopyard	East Haddam, CT
Downs Road	Hamden and Bethany, CT
Durand Eastman Park	Rochester and Irondequoit, NY
Dutton House, Shelburne Museum	Shelburne, VT
Ebenezer Avery House	Groton, CT
Empire State Building	New York, NY
An Evening with the Spirits	Branford, CT
Evergreen Cemetery	New Haven, CT
"Find the Truth with Eastern Connecticut Paranormal Society" (presentation)	Remote/Danbury, CT
Fort de l'Île Sainte-Hélène	Montreal, Canada
Fort Griswold	Groton, CT
Fort Nathan Hale/Black Rock Fort	New Haven, CT
Fort Ontario	Oswego, NY
Fountain Hill Cemetery	Deep River, CT
Frog Bridge	Windham, CT
Gay City State Park	Hebron and Bolton, CT
"Ghosts and Legends with Jeff Belanger" (presentation)	Seymour, CT
Great Hill Cemetery	Seymour, CT
Gregory's Four Corners Burial Ground	Monroe, CT
Gunntown Cemetery	Naugatuck, CT
Hanging Hills	Meriden, CT
Harriet Beecher Stowe Center	Hartford, CT
Harrison House	Branford, CT
Hawthorne Hotel	Salem, MA
Headless Horseman Bridge	Sleepy Hollow, NY
Hex Old World Witchery	Salem, MA
Hitchcock-Phillips House	Cheshire, CT
Horseman's Hollow	Sleepy Hollow, NY
House of the Seven Gables (i.e., Turner-Ingersoll Mansion)	Salem, MA
Howard Street Cemetery	Salem, MA
International Cryptozoology Museum	Portland, ME
Irving's Legend (event)	Sleepy Hollow, NY
Kennebunk Inn	Kennebunk, ME

Lakeview Cemetery	Penn Yan, NY
"Ouija Boards" (presentation)	Remote/Seymour, CT
Lizzie Borden Bed & Breakfast Museum	Fall River, MA
Longfellow's Wayside Inn	Sudbury, MA
Maxcy Hall, University of New Haven	West Haven, CT
Main Street Antiques	Plymouth, MA
Mark Twain House	Hartford, CT
Miles Wine Cellars	Himrod, NY
Milford Cemetery	Milford, CT
Milford Historic Society	Milford, CT
Mill Hill Historic Park	Norwalk, CT
Mount Hope Cemetery	Rochester, NY
Museum Place Mall	Salem, MA
Nathan Hale Homestead	Coventry, CT
National Aviary	Pittsburgh, PA
Noah Webster House	West Hartford, CT
Norwich State Hospital	Norwich and Preston, CT
Old Burying Point	Salem, MA
Old Dutch Church and Old Dutch Burying Ground	Sleepy Hollow, NY
Old Gaol, Old York Historical Society	York, ME
Old Hill Burying Ground	Concord, MA
Old Manse	Concord, MA
Old Newgate Prison and Copper Mine	East Granby, CT
Old Parish Cemetery	York, ME
Old Salem Jail	Salem, MA
Old Stone House	Washington, DC
Olde Sturbridge Village	Sturbridge, MA
Omen	Salem, MA
Patriot's Park	Tarrytown and Sleepy Hollow, NY
Providence Athenaeum	Providence, RI
Providence Biltmore Hotel	Providence, RI
Publick House Historic Inn	Sturbridge, MA
Rockafellas	Salem, MA
Ruden Street	West Haven, CT
Salem Common	Salem, MA
Savin Rock	West Haven, CT

Saw Mill City Road	Shelton, CT
Sleeping Giant State Park	Hamden, CT
Sleepy Hollow Cemetery	Sleepy Hollow, NY
Snedeker House	Southington, CT
Spalding Inn	Whitefield, NH
Spirits Alive (walking tour)	Cheshire, CT
Spirits of Milford Ghost Walk	Milford, CT
St. Elmo's Crypt, Yale University	New Haven, CT
St. Louis Cathedral	New Orleans, LA
St. Louis Cemetery No. 1	New Orleans, LA
St. Peter's Church	Salem, MA
Stepney Cemetery	Monroe, CT
Stone's Public House	Ashland, MA
Sunken Garden at Warner Castle	Rochester, NY
Sunnyside	Irvington, NY
Union Cemetery	Easton, CT
Union Oyster House	Boston, MA
USCGC Taney	Baltimore, MD
USS *Constellation*	Baltimore, MD
Valentown Museum	Victor, NY
Velvet Street (aka "Dracula Drive")	Trumbull and Monroe, CT
"The Warren Files" (presentation)	New Haven, CT
Wayside Irish Pub	Elbridge, NY
Westminster Burying Ground	Baltimore, MD
Whirlwind Hill Road	Wallingford, CT
White Horse Tavern	Newport, RI
White Springs Manor	Geneva, NY
Winery at Marjim Manor	Appleton, NY

NOTES

INTRODUCTION: OF LEGENDS AND LEGEND TRIPS

1. In addition to those items quoted, the survey also includes the following beliefs: (1) that advanced civilizations like Atlantis once existed; (2) that extraterrestrials visited Earth in antiquity; (3) that some people have telekinetic abilities; and (4) that some people have special powers with which they can see the future. Only 25.3 percent doubted all seven items, although it is possible that they hold other paranormal beliefs not measured by the survey. Many people hold more than one paranormal belief too. For example, 13.8 percent of respondents believed in two of the items, while 5 percent believed in all seven.

2. This emphasis on the individual is also a matter of degree. Multicultural psychology and social psychology, of course, also emphasize cultural and social factors in understanding human behavior. Arguably, however, both still prioritize the role of internal processes more than their respective counterparts of cultural anthropology and sociology.

3. Ethnography is constantly evolving to adapt to new settings and research goals. At present, there are many different, specific forms to choose from with different strengths and shortcomings. For an excellent discussion of some of these in the context of legend research, see Janet Langlois (2008).

4. This term is borrowed from the concept of "liminality" developed by Arnold van Gennep ([1909] 1960), which I will discuss in the next chapter.

CHAPTER 1: THE VARIETIES OF OSTENSIVE EXPERIENCE

1. Ellis (1982) discusses the matter of whether camp tales can properly be considered legends at some length.

2. Patterns like this are not without precedent. For example, a similar outcome was observed in efforts to combat drug abuse among minors. The widespread Drug Abuse Resistance Education (DARE) program was intended to educate students on drugs and reduce their use of them. Subsequent evaluations have indicated that, while the program was largely successful in spreading information about drugs, it generally was ineffective at reducing drug use and may have even increased it precisely because of the information it disseminated (Hanson 2015).

3. A further example of this is provided by B. Ellis (2003) in describing the "AIDS Mary" panics. These involved a series of legends in which a woman was supposedly having sex with men to purposefully infect them with HIV. There was never any proof that these activities actually happened, but some people acted the legend out in the role of culprit or victim. The culprits were hoaxers who, for example, contacted reporters claiming to be the "real" AIDS Mary, while the panic resulted in a number of men fearing they had been victims. This resulted in a dramatic increase in men seeking AIDS education and screening tests, illustrating that the outcomes of legends are not always negative.

4. For examples, see Gary Alan Fine (1986).

5. A similar case was reported in February 2019. When her clothes kept disappearing and mysterious handprints appeared on her walls, a University of North Carolina at Greensboro student initially thought she had a ghost in her apartment. That all changed when she heard a rattling sound coming from her closet. Upon investigating, she didn't find a spirit but instead a very real man, wearing her clothes (Burke 2019).

6. Of course, numerous reports with similar claims need not necessarily be indicative of some common but previously unknown reality. In some cases, it seems more likely that they share a known source: legend. Skeptical researcher Joe Nickell, for instance, wrote about his field investigation of the "Brown Mountain Lights," a series of supposedly anomalous or paranormal lights often seen near the town of Morganton in North Carolina. After a night spent looking for lights with his wife, Nickell (2016a:26) concludes, "We saw, in addition to airplanes, lights that we attributed to automobiles and to Morganton town lights, as well as a distant tower's red flashing light." He notes that other researchers have reached similar verdicts, "conclud[ing] that they were produced by campfires, vehicle headlights, airplanes, and distant town lights" (Nickell 2016a:27). In all these cases, something is actually seen by each of the eyewitnesses, but not only do they mistake a natural occurrence for something more extraordinary, they also individually interpret a wide range of actually quite dissimilar phenomena as being consistent with legend. Unlike in Hufford's case, there can be little doubt that these witnesses were familiar with the same source material or at least some version of it.

7. We should be cautious of people claiming credit for hoaxing famous legends just as we should be cautious of those claiming to have experienced them. Both claims require evidence. Even though a hoax is far more likely here given the absence of evidence for a previously undiscovered, not-quite-extinct dinosaur, this does not itself constitute proof for the claims of any particular person hoping to claim credit for the hoax. In other words, a hoax can be hoaxed.

8. B. Ellis (2003:162) refers to pure ostension as "ostension proper" and describes it as a sincere acting out of a legend as opposed to the insincerity involved in the hoax of pseudo-ostension. He gives the example of some legitimately satanic activity that, while inspired by legends from stories and film, is sincere in its intent and not merely a hoax. This interpretation is particularly useful for taking into account the wide range of behaviors like this that do not fit well into the other categories discussed.

9. This organization no longer exists, but it has been succeeded by the similarly named International Cryptozoology Society (LeBlond 2016). This group has retained the okapi as its logo, and it is affiliated with the International Cryptozoology Museum, located in Portland, Maine, which portrays a different legendary but living animal on its own logo: the coelacanth. This is a prehistoric fish from the Devonian period that was found to be alive and well in the waters near Cape Town, South Africa in 1938. Like the okapi, enthusiasts find this animal to be a

source of inspiration because they believe that "its story demonstrates that unknown, undiscovered, or at least long-thought-extinct animals can still be found" (Coleman and Clark 1999:66).

10. Many researchers have explored these implications. See for example Trevor Blank (2012) and Robert G. Howard (2008).

11. "Seth" is a pseudonym, of course.

12. Victor Turner's (1973; 1977; Turner and Turner 1978) concept of "pilgrimage," which I will also draw on, follows the same structure since it was based on van Gennep's work.

13. V. Turner distinguishes between the "liminal" and the "liminoid" in many ways throughout several of his works. The clearest differentiation between these concepts is, arguably, presented by V. Turner and Edith Turner (1978:254), in which a liminoid phenomenon is "voluntary, not an obligatory social mechanism to mark the transition from one state or status to another within the mundane sphere." This is a significant distinction, but it is not one that I believe necessitates an entirely distinct term. Thus, while the legend trip as I describe it might more properly be termed "liminoid" in Turner's conception, I have opted throughout to refer to it by the more familiar term "liminal" for the sake of simplicity. My discussion should nonetheless make clear how the legend trip varies from obligatory social rituals.

14. Thigpen's (1971) version of this model includes only: (1) an introduction to the possible existence of some phenomenon through legend telling; (2) once at the site, engaging in some required behavior as specified by the legend to experience the phenomenon it describes; and (3) discussion of what happened and dissemination beyond the original group of participants.

CHAPTER 2: LEGEND TELLING

1. In this case, however, it is not. B. Ellis (2009) notes that ice cream definitely preceded Washington, although its origins remain a matter of debate. Moreover, this particular recipe would not have resulted in anything remotely appealing, much less actual ice cream. Like many legends, you can easily test this one yourself.

2. For an example of the first variant, see CT Haunted Houses (n.d.). For the second, see ctsoulseekers (2009). This legend clearly draws on the legend cycle that Brunvand (1981:5) called the "Boyfriend's Death."

3. Thanatos is the personification of death in ancient Greek mythology, brother to Hypnos (god of sleep) and son of Nyx (goddess of the night). He had no father (Seyffert 1995).

4. Most of the more detailed legend accounts include consideration of these various theories and include summaries of them (e.g., Bendici 2010; Citro 2005; Muise 2015). Wikipedia (n.d.) also has a page dedicated to the creatures that provides an informative overview of these origin stories across Michigan, Ohio, and Connecticut. This page is most likely very widely viewed by would-be legend trippers. One variant explanation for the existence of Melon Heads found in these summaries seems understandably limited to the Connecticut legend cycle: that they are descended from a family accused of witchcraft by Puritans and exiled into the wilderness. Once there, however, they promptly initiated their familiar routine of incest, cannibalism, and similar shenanigans.

5. In addition to those texts I have already cited, a number of podcasts provide entertaining treatments of the subject. Interested readers might consider the following examples: *Damned Connecticut* (see Bendici n.d.), *It Gets Weird* (2017), and *Monster Move Podcast* (2017).

6. Tucker (2007:201) notes that the name "Mary" has strong religious connotations (i.e., the Virgin Mary and Mary Magdalene) and that the name often crops up in legends on account of this. Thus, sites with an actual Mary in evidence, like headstones, are more likely to have legends associated with them. Conversely, it might be hypothesized that legendary sites without a known occupant might be more likely to have the name appended to them. Ghosts without "known" identities, for example, might be more likely to be called "Mary" than some other, less culturally significant name.

7. It may sound strange to those unfamiliar with early New England burial practices to suggest that the image of a person on a tombstone is odder than a picture of a death's head—a grinning, winged skull, but this is precisely the case. In the iconography of the era, death's heads were conventional reminders of the mortal condition and the need to lead a moral life whereas even cherubs were originally considered idolatrous, never mind the image of a mere human (Deetz 1977).

8. This interpretation is given on an informational plaque near the cemetery as well as in a pamphlet available from the Museums of Old York, entitled "Set in Stone: A Guide to the York Village Burying Ground." No publication or contact information is provided, but the organization maintains a web presence (Old York Historical Society n.d.).

9. As an informal test of this hypothesis, I often include a photo of this headstone in lectures on research methods in my college classes. I discuss the objects people leave on the grave but not the inscription. Every semester, inevitably, someone asks why there are two death dates. I ask the class what they think, and a lively discussion ensues.

10. Posted on Ghostvillage (2005). Not surprisingly, the author of this claim was apparently unable to find a source to cite for this "well-known" interpretation as neither of their subsequent posts fulfills their initial promise to do so. Interestingly, their last post contradicts the first, stating that no one knows the reason for the second death date but suggesting that maybe it was because Cranna died on New Year's Eve. The urge to engage in further theorizing seems irresistible.

11. Audience members were not permitted to record the presentation. This is a paraphrase of the presentation based on my field notes and memory of the event.

CHAPTER 3: PREPARATIONS AND AN UNCANNY JOURNEY

1. Interestingly, this phantom road is no longer shown on online maps, although I have retained a screenshot of the original map showing its presence to ensure it was not simply my memory in error. Referencing older, printed maps might reveal whether there was in fact a road there at one time.

2. Although they understandably draw considerable attention today, terms like "devil" are common in New England geography and do not seem to necessarily indicate any believed connection with the Devil by those who originally named it. The term "hopyard" would seem to suggest that hops were grown nearby at some point. However, I have not been able to find any reliable sources on the matter. The name seems to be as much the subject of legend and guesswork as the phenomena alleged to occur there. The Connecticut Department of Energy and Environmental Protection (2020) provides a useful description of the park and a summary of some of the dubious claims regarding the origin of its name.

3. I have found no original sources for this alleged legend and suspect that the claim that this is a tale told by Native Americans is, itself, a legend.

4. Visitors report similar experiences on this tour online. One person (Wolak 2014), for example, cites "unsettled" feelings, suggestive results on the EMF meter, and an apparently supernatural cell phone malfunction.

CHAPTER 4: RITES AND RITUALS

1. Many variations of this legend are available. This version is from the archives at Brigham Young University (Christensen n.d.).

2. The topic of ritual, like so many other scholarly subjects, is a matter of some debate. Catherine Bell (1997) outlines a number of competing interpretations of ritual, which may be of interest to those studying legend trips. These include early functionalist and structuralist approaches that emphasize the centrality of society itself in ritual practice, but she also notes, for example, other perspectives that argue that social order is constructed *through* the interaction of rituals, in addition to various other interpretations (e.g., phenomenological, etc.). Again, while no consensus exists, it does not seem necessary to bet on one of the various horses in this race to understand the presence and importance of ritualistic characteristics in legend trips.

3. Another statue in the cemetery called "Bird Girl" appears on the cover of the novel. So many fans of the novel visiting the cemetery broke pieces off it for souvenirs that it had to be removed and placed in a museum (RoadsideAmerica n.d.). This goes to show that legend trippers aren't the only tourists who can cause problems.

4. I have withheld identifying information for this video for obvious reasons.

5. Electronic Voice Phenomenon (EVP) is a method of "modern spirit communication in which the voices of spirits of the dead are recorded directly onto magnetic audio tape" (Guiley 1992:106). Newer technologies, such as digital recorders, have been substituted for earlier cassettes and reels, but the principle remains the same. Typically, the investigators do not hear the voices or other sounds so captured at the time of a recording. Instead, they find these upon reviewing recordings later. The goal is to identify disembodied sounds that can be attributed to supernatural sources, which, presumably, the human ear cannot detect unaided.

6. Interestingly, the concordant version of this ritual involves a physical component *instead* of a verbal one: placing coins on the headstone will appease the spirit, and it will not bother you (Belanger and Auger 2019).

7. St. Ann's is sometimes referred to as "St. Anne's" in accounts of the legend (USU Digital Exhibits 2022).

8. This may seem strange or unique to juveniles, but it is not difficult to find similar examples, even far removed from the realm of legend tripping. Compare the so-called "wine bricks" that were sold by vineyards during Prohibition. Selling wine was illegal, as was selling grapes or grape products that the seller knew would be used for wine production. Some grape growers responded by selling blocks of concentrated grape juice that "included clever instructions that were 'disguised' as warnings, informing the buyer" what not to do lest the concentrate be "accidentally" turned into wine (Petkus 2008:36). This was perfectly legal.

9. B. Ellis (2003) credits his use of the concept of "belief language" to the work of the folklorist Mihaly Hoppal.

10. Interestingly, Joshua Warren (2003) offers similar rationalizations for why autumn and winter might be a better time for ghost hunting. From a social perspective, conversely, these might be considered appropriately "spooky" seasons for such a quest. Also, it should be noted that while darkness is a common ritual expectation among legend trippers in general and ghost hunters in particular, it is by no means universal. Like all legendary materials, the matter is one of some considerable debate. Some ghost hunters advocate that investigating during the day or with the lights on is just as good. One guidebook argues that "perhaps one of the biggest misconceptions in the field of the paranormal is that ghosts must be hunted at night. This is despite the fact that almost every haunted site has reported incidents that occur during daylight hours" (Newman 2011:52). The book goes on to specifically target the more obviously legendary dimensions, stating that the claims of improving one's chances of finding ghosts during the "Witching Hour" or "Dead Time" are "nonsense" (Newman 2011:52).

11. It would be interesting to compare the extent to which different paranormal pursuits might be characterized by a different degree of emphasis on either particularized or generalized ritualism. Bigfoot hunters, for example, might rely more on a generalized set of practices based on the imagined creature's behaviors (e.g., so-called "call blasting" in which ape noises are amplified to attract the animal [Bader et al. 2010]) than any ritual based on a specific place or individual entity, which seems more common among ghost hunters.

12. There is, of course, some middle ground between the two forms of ritualism. The two should not be considered mutually exclusive. "Calling out," the method by which ghost hunters attempt to talk to a spirit (Hanks 2015), is a case in point. It can serve as a generic method for any haunting or it can be tailored to a specific situation. If a place is believed to be haunted, but no guiding legends are known, investigators can simply apply the technique generically by calling out something like "Is anyone here?" or "What's your name?" in the hopes that some entity will respond. However, if there are "known" or suspected spirits on the site, like a previous homeowner, they can try to address the spirit by name or bring up other specific topics that known legends claim will get a reaction out of it.

13. For the sake of fairness, I should note that the authors follow up this interesting proposal by noting that a sympathetic attitude should not preclude being objective. This, however, will be a difficult trick to pull off if the investigators are properly primed with hopeful expectation and excessive "sympathy" for witnesses or alleged phenomena.

14. Incidentally, the word "skeptic" is typically misunderstood and misapplied to anyone who expresses doubt. This is a common problem in the media, for example, in which science deniers are incorrectly identified as skeptics. A statement made by the Committee for Skeptical Inquiry (2014:n.p.) asserts: "Proper skepticism promotes scientific inquiry, critical investigation, and the use of reason in examining controversial and extraordinary claims. It is foundational to the scientific method. Denial, on the other hand, is the a priori rejection of ideas without objective consideration." Interestingly, this would also mean that those expressing doubt in the hopes of provoking a ghost, not because they really doubt its existence, are not properly called either "deniers" or "skeptics." I thus use the term "pseudoskeptic" instead.

CHAPTER 5: CLOSE ENCOUNTERS OF THE SUPERNATURAL KIND

1. That is, unless the location possesses suggestive characteristics of the type described in chapter 2, like a neglected cemetery, which generically invoke legendary associations and expectations.

2. See, for example, Shar Levine and Leslie Johnstone's introduction to scientific thinking for children, *Scary Science* (2010).

3. The story of how this mistake came about is itself seemingly a legend. A common version of the story claims that one day a school teacher told the tale of a local "vampire" to their class. However, to protect the location of the grave from vandalism or other trouble-some student behaviors, this teacher did not tell the class where they could find this final resting place. Instead, he (or she according to other accounts) told them only the age of the girl when she died (later to become a vampire). The students went out looking anyway and found the grave of Nellie Vaughn. The tombstone came from about the right era, contained someone who died around the right age, had a suitably scary inscription, and did not have grass growing on it (Brennan 2007). According to folklorist Michael E. Bell (2001), almost none of these facts can be verified, no original sources can be tracked down, and many of the "facts" seem to change depending on who is telling the tale (such as the sex of the teacher involved). All of these seem to indicate that the story is a legend.

4. Although they demonstrate this issue well, flexible criteria are not unique to curses, but instead are common across different types of legends. One common concern among ghost hunters is the possibility that "something" will follow them home after an investigation. The time frame in which that might occur is so flexible that nearly any odd occurrence *any* time after an investigation can qualify as proof that this happened. One ghost hunter, for instance, notes that this sort of thing is common for his group after they have "cleared" a haunted house of its ghosts: "There is a backlash now and then.... It seems like every time we do a successful clearing, we get bad luck, two weeks later sometimes. We've had electronics in our house blow up and stuff like that, and we're not sure why" (Brown 2006:54).

5. One account claims you will get two different results on them if ran simultaneously. I didn't. However, I did successfully locate some fairly high electromagnetic fields near the front of the cemetery as some reports indicate. Unfortunately, this happened to correspond with the location of some electrical wires overhead.

CHAPTER 6: THE RETURN

1. B. Ellis (2003) provides an interesting example of a ghost that haunts a Pizza Hut restaurant. The legend is strange precisely because, even as far as such stories go, it is unusual. Ghosts rarely haunt chain restaurants or similar places marked by rational modernity. As one paranormal investigator puts it, "Ghosts just don't belong in parking lots" (Pitkin 2010:120). Hanks (2015) similarly notes that the ghost hunters she conducted her participant observation with were rarely interested in chain pubs or other modern buildings, even though they admitted that, in theory, these places should have the capacity to be haunted as far as their conception of ghosts is concerned. These types of places *can* become settings for legends, but I suspect it takes more psychological work and a more compelling story to make them convincing.

2. I was surprised by just such an experience once. The bird in question, a starling, some-how made its way in through the exhaust vent on the hood of my stove. Hearing unusual sounds one morning, I approached the hood to investigate. The bird immediately flew out, buzzed my head, and made straight for the nearest window, which was unfortunately quite closed. I quickly bundled it into a convenient area rug, opened the window, and released it.

Even this sort of banal experience offers interesting contrasts to those reports of unwelcome supernatural entities, which are more difficult to evict, as I will show shortly, and which shock people more severely with their arrival. Having a bird, mouse, or some other wild animal suddenly appear in your home could certainly be disconcerting—or even dangerous in the case of something like a moose or bear, but none of these are *ontologically* threatening. Their behaviors and motives—their very nature—can be understood and predicted.

3. Despite their importance, I am not convinced that cars are indispensable or even that they appear in *most* legend trips. To my knowledge, no scholarship has provided the necessary data to prove these claims. Most research has focused on the US where cars are very important, but legend trips can occur in other parts of the world where this is not the case too (McNeill and Tucker 2018). Indeed, there are many accounts where legend trippers merely walk to the site that they are interested in exploring, including B. Ellis's (1993) own work on legend trips to London's Highgate Cemetery. Legend trips are also conducted by children who do not have the benefit of automobile transportation (Hobbs and Cornwell 1988). I suspect many people, especially young people, use means other than cars for these adventures. For example, I recall bicycles playing an important role in many of my own escapades, not just legend tripping, and those of my peers when I was younger. There might be more accounts of bicycle-enabled legend trips in parts of the world where this form of transportation is more popular and entrenched. Also, bicycles have become more popular in America in recent years too (Pucher, Buehler, and Seinen 2011) and may increasingly appear in legends. Similarly, I suspect that while cars alter the experience (e.g., by providing a more immediate form of refuge than pedestrians or cyclists will have when facing the unknown), they are not essential. Rather, the combined physical and psychological distance travelled to a site, through whatever means of transportation, is the crucial factor.

4. Here, the vehicle provides transportation to the site, refuge from the threat, and a means to escape. However, it also becomes an important ritual element in and of itself since this is where the hands of the children manifest in the form of prints that they leave on its surface. Many legend trips seem to require the use of a vehicle to invoke the supernatural in this way. Dégh's (1969:80) influential analysis of haunted bridges provides an exemplar of this function, wherein she notes, "The parked car seems to be an adequate shelter from which the explorers might urge the ghost to appear: they roll up the windows, honk the horn three times or shine the lights three times." On occasion, the automobile can become an object of danger instead of refuge, and tellingly, this frequently occurs when those involved foolishly leave the safety of the vehicle. In one account, some Connecticut teenagers were driving down the remote road called Velvet Street (aka "Dracula Drive") at night looking for the deformed, cannibalistic Melon Heads when they decided to get out of the car and explore the surrounding woods. This, it turned out, was a bad idea. Before they had gotten too far, the car's engine roared to life behind them, and the girls had to jump out of the way to escape being run down by the errant vehicle. As it turns out, their quest was successful, for as the car passed them, they could see the distorted forms of the creatures who had stolen it illuminated by the interior light. It is not clear how the teens managed to make it home, but according to this legend, the car is still in the possession of the Melon Heads and can on occasion be spotted roaming the back roads and byways (Citro 2005).

5. See, for example, the material provided by the organization that maintains his former house where the tale is set (Thurber House 2022).

6. A similar claim can be found in Robin Smith's (2002) work. Conversely, Woodyard (2000:101) claims that Thurber's own investigation into the background of his house led to a different but no less place-based attempt at explanation: he discovered "that a man, despondent over an unfaithful wife, had shot himself in a second-floor bedroom, after pacing around the dining room table."

7. An important exception to these general rules is the appearance of deceased loved ones. Gillian Bennett (1999) notes that, unlike the spirits of strangers or other odd entities, the dearly departed are believed by many to make themselves known in domestic areas of the house, like the bedroom. When they do so, unlike encounters of other kinds, the experience is generally considered comforting and reassuring.

8. Regardless of their own opinion on the matter of hauntings, this is a reasonable concern real-estate sellers or agents might have given the fear many people have of encountering unwanted entities in their home. Legal scholars have observed similar patterns: "The presence of ghosts or a history of murders might scare away some buyers or lower the market value to those who are willing to buy because of the smaller pool of prospective buyers for a possible resale" (Brown and Thurlow 1996:627).

9. Besides the threat of the supernatural itself, indirect outcomes of experiencing it are very much real. Regarding the fear of losing one's mind, for example, it is noted, "A general diagnosis of mental illness was, in fact, the first conclusion that a significant number of American scientists liked" when it came to dealing with those who claimed to have encountered a ghost (Blum 2006:118). Being perceived as crazy can result in a stigmatized or "spoiled" identity that can be more dangerous and threatening to individuals than anything the "other side" can bring to bear (Goffman 1963).

10. It seems likely that there are specific characteristics of objects that contribute to the likelihood of them invoking supernatural fears comparable to those associated with place that I have discussed. In this case, dolls have a cultural association with legends due to their being the subject of numerous popular films and stories. Additionally, since dolls are representations of humans, they likely invoke a sense of presence, of agency, that could be unsettling because we simultaneously know that they are not actually humans. This uncertainty, according to Ernst Jentsch's ([1906] 1997) early treatment of the subject, can arouse an experience of the uncanny. Although Jentsch's work was not cited, his idea seems to have found support much later in the seemingly unrelated field of robotics. Masahiro Mori (1970:33) proposes that we like and are comfortable with things that have some human traits that are clearly not human (e.g., stuffed animals, cartoon characters, etc.) or things that are identical to humans, but that there is a middle ground—the "uncanny valley"—that we find unsettling because of its ambiguity. Thus, when we see robots that look very much human but are noticeably off (e.g., with unnatural smiles or strange blinking), the feeling of the uncanny can arise. Interestingly, he suggests that corpses and zombies fit this category of the uncanny because they are ontologically uncertain. Debate over Mori's argument continues, but interest in it has increased over the years (e.g., Broadbent 2017).

11. Just as ghosts of passed loved ones, unlike those of strangers, tend to be comforting rather than frightening (Bennett 1999) so too is there a similar pattern with haunted objects. In these stories, when the previous owner is unknown or a stranger, the object tends to take on malign properties, such as the dresser I have described. However, when it belonged to a loved one, the ghostly presence attached to objects tends to be helpful or protective. Another story in Okonowicz's (1996) work, for example, details how one woman inherited

her grandfather's dining room set. The ghost of her grandfather, with whom she was close when he was alive, would violently open and close the doors and make the furniture fly at her husband whenever they got into a fight. Thus, the spirit protected her (a family member) and attacked her husband (a stranger) whom she later divorced.

CHAPTER 7: TELLING THE TALE

1. All comments cited are from this page, although they have since been removed from the site. *Sic* throughout.

2. My own cat, incidentally, is quite adept at getting into cabinets. One wonders why this informant does not think her own cats are capable of it.

3. I have made some minor corrections to punctuation here for the sake of comprehensibility.

4. Incidentally, this provides another example of how strange aspects of the environment require explanation and encourage legend tripping. The case also provides a compelling incentive for taking down your Christmas lights in a timely fashion after the holidays.

5. Since my original viewing, this particular video has been marked as private and is not accessible without permission. I have not cited the source to protect the content creator's privacy.

6. Note especially the "dare"—the implication of danger—suggested in the concept of survival. As discussed earlier, this sort of claim lends gravitas to the experience. This might inspire anyone seeing this shirt to want to learn more (i.e., What's so dangerous?) and possibly embark on their own legend trip to the Borden House. This is, of course, probably intentional.

7. For a classic example, consider Underwood, who was a famous paranormal investigator and avowed believer in ghosts. In one book, he admits that "there was lack of evidence to show exactly what [ghosts] are" (Underwood 1986:12). Instead, he presents numerous theories that remain popular. These include that ghosts are spirits of the dead, psychic impressions, time slips, or even glimpses into another dimension.

8. All quotations in the following discussion are sampled from Fiona Broome (n.d.). I have abbreviated the conversation while keeping essential meanings intact and used only the first initial of each user's handle to distinguish between speakers.

9. According to Brian E. Plumb (2013), the family name and the name of the tavern were primarily spelled "How" for many years. It was not until the time of Adam Howe (1796–1840) that the alternative spelling came into more prominent use.

10. Achieving this could be somewhat complicated but by no means impossible. The first requirement is already present in various folklore archives: a series of dated accounts of legend trips to the same site. We would have to provide evidence that specific experiences in earlier accounts were incorporated into the legends, preparations, and rituals of later accounts. Ideally, a social connection between these accounts—how the legend is dispersed—would also need to be convincingly shown.

11. See the various entries for these related phenomena in Maria Leach's (1972) work.

12. Even the term "orb" is the product of social change. Older sources sometimes apply different names to this phenomenon that did not catch on, such as Warren et al. (1992:59), who refer to orbs with the older term "ghost lights" and seem to conflate the two. They also use the term "sounding" (Warren et al. 1992:60), which never caught on, instead of the now-ubiquitous term "EVP" for recorded audio phenomena.

13. The many interviews with ghost-hunting groups collected in Brown (2006) offer numerous interesting examples of this continued debate over orbs. Each group was asked their opinion of them, and a range of responses is evident.

CHAPTER 8: THE PAST AND FUTURE OF LEGEND TRIPPING

1. C. Bell (1997) argues that this is not established fact. It is just as likely that causation could run the other way: the decline in community causes a decline in communal rites. This begs the question of what, in turn, causes communal decline.

2. According to V. Turner and E. Turner (1978), religious pilgrimages can also be voluntary and can actually be a source of concern for religious authorities. However, unlike legend trips, these pilgrimages are not separate from culturally accepted religion. Rather, it is religion that gives them their meaning, and institutional authorities struggle to exert control over them rather than to simply invalidate them.

3. Meaning, unfortunately, humans famous for their work or experiences with Bigfoot, not an actual Bigfoot.

4. This basic formula is similar to that provided by Christopher Vogler's (2007) interpretation of standard mythic stories as inspired by Joseph Campbell's work, particularly *The Hero with a Thousand Faces* (1961).

REFERENCES

Alexander, William. 2011. "Vermont Haunted House at Shelburne Museum?" Vermonter, August 4. Retrieved July 12, 2022. https://vermonter.com/shelburne-museum-ghosts/.

Appelle, Stuart, Steven Jay Lynn, and Leonard Newman. 2000. "Alien Abduction Experiences." Pp. 253–82 in *Varieties of Anomalous Experience: Examining the Scientific Evidence*, edited by E. Cardeña, S. J. Lynn, and S. Krippner. Washington, DC: American Psychological Association.

Asma, Stephen T. 2009. *Monsters: An Unnatural History of Our Worst Fears*. New York: Oxford University Press.

AtTheShore. N.d. "Absecon Lighthouse at the Top Selfie Cam." Retrieved January 19, 2017. http://attheshore.com/livecam-absecon570#sponsorad.

Auerbach, Loyd. 1986. *ESP, Hauntings, and Poltergeists: A Parapsychologist's Handbook*. New York: Warner Books.

Bader, Christopher D., F. Carson Mencken, and Joseph O. Baker. 2010. *Paranormal America: Ghost Encounters, UFO Sightings, Bigfoot Hunts, and Other Curiosities in Religion and Culture*. New York: New York University Press.

Bailey, Dale. 1999. *American Nightmares: The Haunted House Formula in American Popular Culture*. Bowling Green, OH: Bowling Green University Popular Press.

Baker, Joseph O., Christopher D. Bader, and F. Carson Mencken. 2016. "A Bonded Affinity Theory of Religion and the Paranormal." *Sociology of Religion* 77(4):334–58.

Baltrusis, Sam. 2014. *Ghosts of Salem: Haunts of the Witch City*. Charleston, SC: History Press.

Balzano, Christopher. 2008. *Ghostly Adventures: Chilling True Stories from America's Haunted Hot Spots*. Avon, MA: Adams Media.

Balzano, Christopher, and Tim Weisberg. 2012. *Haunted Objects: Stories of Ghosts on Your Shelf*. Iola, WI: Krause.

Barber, Paul. 1988. *Vampires, Burial, and Death*. New Haven, CT: Yale University Press.

Bascom, William. 1965. "The Forms of Folklore: Prose Narrative." *Journal of American Folklore* 78(307):3–20.

Bauman, Zygmunt. 2001. *Community: Seeking Safety in an Insecure World*. Malden, MA: Polity.

Becker, Howard S. 1963. *Outsiders: Studies in the Sociology of Deviance*. Chicago: University of Chicago Press.

Beischel, Julie, Chad Mosher, and Mark Boccuzzi. 2014–2015. "The Possible Effects on Bereavement of Assisted After-Death Communication During Readings with Psychic Mediums: A Continuing Bonds Perspective." *Omega* 70(2):169–94.

Belanger, Jeff. 2011. *Picture Yourself Legend Tripping: Your Complete Guide to Finding UFOs, Monsters, Ghosts*. Boston: Cengage.

Belanger, Jeff, and Ray Auger. 2019. "XYZ Marks the Spot." October 10 in *Our New England Legends*, podcast, 10:47. Retrieved July 12, 2022. https://ournewenglandlegends.com/podcast -112-xyz-marks-the-spot.

Bell, Catherine. 1997. *Ritual: Perspectives and Dimensions*. New York: Oxford University Press.

Bell, Michael E. 2001. *Food for the Dead: On the Trail of New England's Vampires*. New York: Carroll and Graf.

Bell, Michael M. 1997. "The Ghosts of Place." *Theory and Society* 26(6):813–36.

Bellah, Robert N., Richard Madsen, William M. Sullivan, Ann Swidler, Steven M. Tipton. 1985. *Habits of the Heart: Individualism and Commitment in American Life*. Berkeley: University of California Press.

Bendici, Ray. N.d. "Damned Connecticut Podcast 2: The Melon Heads." *Damned Connecticut*, podcast, 16:05. Retrieved July 11, 2022. https://www.damnedct.com/damned-connecticut -podcast-2-the-melon-heads/.

Bendici, Ray. 2009. "Gunntown Cemetery, Naugatuck." Damned Connecticut, n.d. Retrieved January 16, 2018. http://www.damnedct.com/gunntown-cemetery-naugatuck.

Bendici, Ray. 2010. "The Melon Heads." Damned Connecticut, n.d. Retrieved April 22, 2018. http://www.damnedct.com/the-melon-heads.

Benedict, Ruth. [1934] 2005. *Patterns of Culture*. New York: Mariner.

Benet, Lorenzo. 1986. "Taking Control of a Punk Who Happens to Be Your Kid." *Chicago Tribune*, March 10. Retrieved September 3, 2017. http://articles.chicagotribune.com/1986 -03-10/features/8601180210_1_punk-parents-heavy-metal.

Bennett, Gillian. 1999. *Alas, Poor Ghost! Traditions of Belief in Story and Discourse*. Logan: Utah State University Press.

Berendt, John. 1994. *Midnight in the Garden of Good and Evil*. New York: Penguin.

Berg, Bruce, and Howard Lune. 2012. *Qualitative Research Methods for the Social Sciences*. New York: Pearson.

Berger, Peter L. 1967. *The Sacred Canopy: Elements of a Sociological Theory of Religion*. New York: Anchor.

Berry, Adam, and Amy Bruni [Producers]. 2022a. "The Lurker" in *Kindred Spirits* (Season 6), January 1. Television series episode. New York: Paper Route Production Companies.

Berry, Adam, and Amy Bruni [Producers]. 2022b. "Tripwire" in *Kindred Spirits* (Season 6), January 8. Television series episode. New York: Paper Route Production Companies.

Berry, Kamie. N.d. "The Haunting Tale of Midnight Mary." Blitzlift. Retrieved July 2, 2018. http://blitzlift.com/haunting-tale-midnight-mary/.

Best, Joel. 1991. "Bad Guys and Random Violence: Folklore and Media Constructions of Contemporary Deviance." *Contemporary Legend* 1:107–21.

Best, Joel, and Gerald T. Horiuchi. 1985. "The Razor Blade in the Apple: The Social Construction of Urban Legends." *Social Problems* 32(5):488–99.

Bhargava, Tushar. 2016. "The Fountain's Curse: The Life and Death of Edgar Allan Poe." *Providence Post- Magazine*, April 14, 6–7. Retrieved March 13, 2018. http://post.browndaily herald.com/2016/04/14/the-fountains-curse/.

Bird, S. Elizabeth. 1994. "Playing with Fear: Interpreting the Adolescent Legend Trip." *Western Folklore* 53(3):191–209.

Bird, S. Elizabeth. 2002. "It Makes Sense to Us: Cultural Identity in Local Legends of Place." *Journal of Contemporary Ethnography* 31(5):519–47.

Blank, Trevor. 2012. *Folk Culture in the Digital Age: The Emergent Dynamic of Human Interaction.* Logan: Utah State University Press.

Blum, Deborah. 2006. *Ghost Hunters: William James and the Search for Scientific Proof of Life After Death.* New York: Penguin.

Bohannan, Laura. 1966. "Shakespeare in the Bush: An American Anthropologist Set Out to Study the Tiv of West Africa and Was Taught the True Meaning of Hamlet." *Natural History* 75:28–33.

Bottoms, Bette L., and Suzanne L. Davis. 1997. "The Creation of Satanic Ritual Abuse." *Journal of Social and Clinical Psychology* 16(2):112–32.

Boyer, Tina Marie. 2013. "The Anatomy of a Monster: The Case of Slender Man." *Preternature* 2(2):240–61.

Boynton, Cynthia Wolfe. 2013. "Ghosts of Maxcy Hall." *University of New Haven Alumni Magazine*, Winter, 13–15.

Braun, Peter, Gerald Kochansky, Robert Shapiro, Susan Greenberg, Jon E. Gudeman, Sylvia Johnson, and Miles F. Shore. 1981. "Overview: Deinstitutionalization of Psychiatric Patients. A Critical Review of Outcome Studies." *American Journal of Psychiatry* 138(6):736–49.

Breen, Brittany, and Adrian Stewart [Producers]. 2018. "The Slaughter House" in *Ghost Adventures* (Season 15), January 18. Television series episode. New York: MY Entertainment.

Brennan, John T. 2007. *Ghosts of Newport: Spirits, Scoundrels, Legends and Lore.* Charleston, SC: History Press.

Bressan, Paola, Luigi Garlaschellim, and Monica Barracano. 2003. "Antigravity Hills Are Visual Illusions." *Psychological Science* 14(5):441–49.

Brittle, Gerald. 1980. *The Demonologist: The Extraordinary Career of Ed and Lorraine Warren.* New York: Berkley Books.

Broadbent, Elizabeth. 2017. "Interactions with Robots: The Truths We Reveal About Ourselves." *Annual Review of Psychology* 68:27–52.

Brockenbrough, Martha. 2013. *Finding Bigfoot: Everything You Need to Know.* New York: Macmillan.

Bromley, David G. 1991. "The Satanic Cult Scare." *Culture and Society* 28(4):55–66.

Broome, Fiona. N.d. "Concord: Ghostly Skull with Eyes." Encounter Ghosts. Retrieved May 10, 2017. http://encounterghosts.com/concordghostlyskullwitheyes/.

Brown, Alan. 2006. *Ghost Hunters of the South.* Jackson: University Press of Mississippi.

Brown, Ronald B., and Thomas H. Thurlow III. 1996. "Buyers Beware: Statutes Shield Real Estate Brokers and Sellers Who Do Not Disclose That Properties Are Psychologically Tainted." *Oklahoma Law Review* 49(625):625–50.

Brunvand, Jan Harold. 1981. *The Vanishing Hitchhiker: American Urban Legends and Their Meanings.* New York: Norton.

Burger, Jerry M., and Amy L. Lynn. 2010. "Superstitious Behavior among American and Japanese Professional Baseball Players." *Basic and Applied Social Psychology* 27(1):71–76.

Burke, Minyvonne. 2019. "College Student Finds a Man Hiding in Her Closet Wearing Her Clothes." *NBC News*, February 5. Retrieved March 18, 2019. https://www.nbcnews.com/news/us-news/college-student-finds-man-hiding-her-closet-wearing-her-clothes-n967201.

Bush, Stephen S. 2012. "Concepts and Religious Experiences: Wayne Proudfoot on the Cultural Construction of Experiences." *Religious Studies* 48(1):101–17.

Campbell, Joseph. 1961. *The Hero with a Thousand Faces.* New York: Pantheon.

Campbell, Joseph (with Bill Moyers). 1988. *The Power of Myth.* New York: Doubleday.

Cardeña, Etzel, Steven Jay Lynn, and Stanley Krippner. 2000. *Varieties of Anomalous Experience: Examining the Scientific Evidence.* Washington, DC: American Psychological Association.

Carroll, Robert Todd. 2003. *The Skeptic's Dictionary: A Collection of Strange Beliefs, Amusing Deceptions, and Dangerous Delusions.* Hoboken, NJ: Wiley.

Chaney, Karen Elizabeth. 2006. *Lizzie Borden.* Carlisle, MA: Commonwealth Editions.

Chauran, Alexandra. 2013. *Faeries & Elementals for Beginners: Learn About & Communicate with Nature Spirits.* Woodbury, MN: Llewellyn Publications.

Chicago Tribune. 2000. "Civil War General's Skull Stolen from Grave." June 23. Retrieved July 13, 2022. https://www.chicagotribune.com/news/ct-xpm-2000-06-23-0006240012-story.html.

Christensen, Terry. N.d. "Weeping Lady of Logan Cemetery." William A. Wilson Folklore Archives. Provo: Brigham Young University. Retrieved September 7, 2018. http://sc.lib.byu.edu/.

Cialdini, Ralph. 1993. *Influence: Science and Practice.* New York: HarperCollins.

Citro, Joseph A. 2004. *Cursed in New England: Stories of Damned Yankees.* Guilford, CT: Globe Pequot Press.

Citro, Joseph A. 2005. *Weird New England: Your Travel Guide to New England's Local Legends and Best Kept Secrets.* New York: Sterling Publishing.

Clark, Dylan. 2003. "The Death and Life of Punk, the Last Subculture." Pp. 223–36 in *The Post Subcultures Reader,* edited by D. Muggleton and R. Weinzierl. New York: Berg.

Claud, Dwayne. 2009. *Haunted Finger Lakes: A Ghost Hunter's Guide.* Atglen, PA: Schiffer Publishing.

Clements, William H. 1980. "The Chain on the Tombstone." Pp. 258–64 in *Indiana Folklore: A Reader,* edited by L. Dégh. Bloomington: Indiana University Press.

Clements, William H. 1991. "Interstitiality in Contemporary Legend." *Contemporary Legend* 1:81–91.

Coffey, Edward Nichols. 1974. *A Glimpse of Old Monroe.* Monroe, CT: Monroe Sesquicentennial Commission.

Coleman, Loren, and Jerome Clark. 1999. *Cryptozoology A to Z: The Encyclopedia of Loch Monsters, Sasquatch, Chupacabras, and Other Authentic Mysteries of Nature.* New York: Fireside.

Coleman, Loren, and Patrick Huyghe. 2003. *The Field Guide to Lake Monsters, Sea Serpents, and Other Mystery Denizens of the Deep.* New York: Tarcher/Penguin.

Collins, Wilkie. [1885] 2016. "Mrs. Zant and the Ghost." Pp. 72–94 in *Chilling Ghost Short Stories,* edited by L. Bulbeck. London: Flame Tree.

Comaroff, Jean. 2013. *Body of Power, Spirit of Resistance: The Culture and History of a South African People.* Chicago: University of Chicago Press.

Committee for Skeptical Inquiry. 2014. "Deniers Are Not Skeptics." Center for Inquiry, December 5. Retrieved March 21, 2018. https://www.csicop.org/news/show/deniers_are_not_skeptics.

Complete Paranormal Services. N.d. "Trigger Objects." Retrieved July 2, 2018. http://www.cpsparanormal.com/triggerobjects.htm.

Connecticut Department of Energy and Environmental Protection. 2020. "Devil's Hopyard State Park." Connecticut's Official State Website, n.d. Retrieved July 12, 2022. www.ct.gov /deep/devilshopyard.

Connecticut Paranormal Research Team. N.d. "Meet the Team." Retrieved July 10, 2018. https://connecticutparanormal.com/.

Cooper, J. C. 1978. *An Illustrated Encyclopedia of Traditional Symbols.* London: Thames and Hudson.

Cornwall Historical Society. 2014. "The Truth about Dudleytown." Blog, September 29. Retrieved August 5, 2017. http://cornwallhistoricalsociety.blogspot.com/2014/09/the-truth -about-dudleytown.html.

Courtney, Steve. 2013. *"We Shall Have Them with Us Always": The Ghosts of the Mark Twain House.* Hartford, CT: Paige Compositor Press.

Crabb, Brittney. 2017a. "Exploring Haunted Union Cemetery! (Police Were Watching Me)." Posted May 5. YouTube Video, 7:34. Retrieved June 26, 2018. https://www.youtube.com /watch?v=JfnupSEajTs.

Crabb, Brittney. 2017b. "I Saw a Ghost!!! Reviewing Evidence." Posted June 9. YouTube Video, 36:28. Retrieved June 26, 2018. https://www.youtube.com/watch?v=mb2EINnu-YI.

Crabb, Brittney. 2017c. "Legend of Midnight May! Evergreen Cemetery." Posted May 12. YouTube Video, 9:19. Retrieved June 26, 2018. https://www.youtube.com/watch?v=Ef3dwWDl6IE.

CT Haunted Houses. N.d. "Great Hill Cemetery: Real Haunts in Seymour CT." Retrieved July 11, 2022. https://www.cthauntedhouses.com/real-haunt/great-hill-cemetery.html.

CT Paranormal Searchers. N.d. "Connecticut Investigations." Retrieved September 12, 2019. https://ctparanormalsearchers.weebly.com/ct-buildingsstructures.html.

ctsoulseekers. 2009. "CT Soul Seekers Hookman's Cemetery 7-25-09 A Collection of EVP'S Seymour, CT." Posted September 22. YouTube Video, 3:40. Retrieved July 11, 2022. https:// www.youtube.com/watch?v=86YJk2r7ILA.

Curtis, Barry. 2008. *Dark Places: The Haunted House in Film.* London: Reaktion Books.

D'Agostino, Thomas. 2007. *Haunted Massachusetts.* Atglen, PA: Schiffer Publishing.

D'Agostino, Thomas, and Arlene Nicholson. 2011. *Connecticut Ghost Stories and Legends.* Charleston, SC: History Press.

Davies, Owen. 2007. *The Haunted: A Social History of Ghosts.* New York: Palgrave Macmillan.

Davis, Colin. 2007. *Haunted Subjects: Deconstruction, Psychoanalysis and the Return of the Dead.* New York: Palgrave Macmillan.

Dear, Michael J., and Jennifer R. Wolch. 2014. *Landscapes of Despair: From Deinstitutionaliza- tion to Homelessness.* Princeton, NJ: Princeton University Press.

Debies-Carl, Jeffrey S. 2011. "Mapping the Residual Landscape: Abandonment, Dilapidation, and Ruin." *Environment, Space, Place* 3(2):51–81.

Debies-Carl, Jeffrey S. 2013. "Are the Kids Alright? A Critique and Agenda for Taking Youth Cultures Seriously." *Social Science Information* 52(1):110–33.

Debies-Carl, Jeffrey S. 2014. *Punk Rock and the Politics of Place: Building a Better Tomorrow.* New York: Routledge.

Debies-Carl, Jeffrey S. 2017. "Pizzagate and Beyond: Using Social Research to Understand Conspiracy Legends." *Skeptical Inquirer* 41(6):34–37.

Debies-Carl, Jeffrey S. 2020. "Punk Legends: Cultural Representation and Ostension." Pp. 57–78 in *Researching Subcultures, Myth, and Memory*, edited by B. van der Steen and T. P. F. Verburgh. London: Palgrave Macmillan.

Debies-Carl, Jeffrey S. 2021. "Click 'Here' to Post a Comment: Legend Discussion and Transformation in Online Forums." *Journal of Folklore Research* 58(2):31–62.

Deering, Bel. 2014. "In the Dead of Night: A Nocturnal Exploration of Heterotopia in the
Graveyard." Pp. 183–97 in *The Power of Death: Contemporary Reflections on Death in
Western Society*, edited by M.-J. Blanco and R. Vidal. New York: Berghahn.

Deetz, James. 1977. *In Small Things Forgotten: The Archaeology of Early American Life*. Garden
City, NY: Anchor Press/Doubleday.

Dégh, Linda. 1969. "The Haunted Bridges near Avon and Danville and Their Role in Legend
Formation." *Indiana Folklore* 2(1):54–89.

Dégh, Linda. 1971. "The 'Belief Legend' in Modern Society: Form, Function, and Relationship
to Other Genres." Pp. 55–68 in *American Folk Legend: A Symposium*, edited by W. Hand.
Los Angeles: University of California Press.

Dégh, Linda. 1980. "The House of Blue Lights in Indianapolis." Pp. 179–94 in *Indiana Folklore: A Reader*, edited by L. Dégh. Bloomington: Indiana University Press.

Dégh, Linda. 2001. *Legend and Belief: Dialectics of a Folklore Genre*. Bloomington: Indiana
University Press.

Dégh, Linda, and Andrew Vázsonyi. 1983. "Does the Word 'Dog' Bite? Ostensive Action: A
Means of Legend-Telling." *Journal of Folklore Research* 20(1):5–34.

de Gourmont, Remy. 1992. *The Angels of Perversity*. New York: Hippocrene Books.

DeLamater, John D., Daniel J. Myers, and Jessica L. Collett. 2015. *Social Psychology*. Boulder,
CO: Westview Press.

Delaney, Cassandra H. 1995. "Rite of Passage in Adolescence." *Adolescence* 30(12):891–97.

de Maupassant, Guy. [1887] 2012. *The Horla*. Hoboken, NJ: Melville House.

Dickey, Colin. 2016a. "The Broken Technology of Ghost Hunting." *The Atlantic*, November 14.
Retrieved November 14, 2016. https://www.theatlantic.com/science/archive/2016/11/the
-broken-technology-of-ghost-hunting/506627/.

Dickey, Colin. 2016b. *Ghostland: An American History in Haunted Places*. New York: Viking.

Douglas, Mary. 1966. *Purity and Danger*. Harmondsworth, UK: Penguin.

Doyle, Arthur Conan. 1922. *The Coming of the Fairies*. New York: George H. Doran.

Driver, Tom F. 1991. *The Magic of Ritual: Our Need for Liberating Rites That Transform Our
Lives and Our Communities*. San Francisco: HarperCollins.

Duffy, Elizabeth. 1962. *Activation and Behavior*. London: Wiley.

Durkheim, Emile. [1912] 1995. *The Elementary Forms of Religious Life*. New York: Free Press.

Dwyer, Jeff. 2008. *Ghost Hunter's Guide to Seattle and Puget Sound*. Gretna, LA: Pelican
Publishing.

Earl Babbie Research Center. 2017. *The Chapman University Survey of American Fears,
Wave 4*. Orange, CA: Chapman University.

Eastern Connecticut Paranormal Society. 2018. "About Us." N.d. Retrieved July 10, 2018.
https://www.easternctparanormal.com/aboutus.

Eaton, Marc A. 2015. "'Give Us a Sign of Your Presence': Paranormal Investigation as a Spiritual Practice." *Sociology of Religion* 76(4):389–412.

Eaton, Marc A. 2018. "Manifesting Spirits: Paranormal Investigation and the Narrative Development of a Haunting." *Journal of Contemporary Ethnography* 48(2):155–82.

Eco, Umberto. 1979. *A Theory of Semiotics*. Bloomington: Indiana University Press.

Eliade, Mircea. 1959. *The Sacred and Profane: The Nature of Religion*. New York: Harcourt,
Brace & World.

Eliade, Mircea. 1965. *Rites and Symbols of Initiation: The Mysteries of Birth and Rebirth.* New York: Harper & Row.

Ellis, Bill. 1982. "'Ralph and Rudy': The Audience's Role in Recreating a Camp Legend." *Western Folklore* 31(3):169–91.

Ellis, Bill. 1989. "Death by Folklore: Ostension, Contemporary Legend, and Murder." *Western Folklore* 48(3):201–20.

Ellis, Bill. 1993. "The Highgate Cemetery Vampire Hunt: The Anglo-American Connection in Satanic Cult Lore." *Folklore* 104(1–2):13–39.

Ellis, Bill. 1994. "'Safe' Spooks: New Halloween Traditions in Response to Sadism Legends." Pp. 24–44 in *Halloween and Other Festivals of Death and Life*, edited by J. Santino. Knoxville: University of Tennessee Press.

Ellis, Bill. 2003. *Aliens, Ghosts, and Cults: Legends We Live.* Jackson: University Press of Mississippi.

Ellis, Bill. 2004. *Lucifer Ascending: The Occult in Folklore and Popular Culture.* Lexington: University Press of Kentucky.

Ellis, Bill. 2009. "Whispers in an Ice Cream Parlor: Culinary Tourism, Contemporary Legends, and the Urban Interzone." *Journal of American Folklore* 122(483):53–74.

Ellis, Melissa Martin. 2014. *The Everything Ghost Hunting Book: Tips, Tools, and Techniques for Exploring the Supernatural World.* Avon, MA: Adams Media.

Emerson, Ralph Waldo. [1836] 2008. *Nature.* New York: Penguin.

Engelland, Chad. 2014. *Ostension: Word Learning and the Embodied Mind.* Cambridge, MA: MIT Press.

Felton, Debbie. 1999. *Haunted Greece and Rome: Ghost Stories from Classical Antiquity.* Austin: University of Texas Press.

Festinger, Leon, Henry Riecken, and Stanley Schachter. 1956. *When Prophecy Fails.* Minneapolis: University of Minnesota Press.

Field, Andy. 2000. *Discovering Statistics Using SPSS for Windows.* Thousand Oaks, CA: Sage.

Finch, Carol J. 2006. *The Ghost City of Valentown: Haunting Tales of Valentown Museum.* Phelps, NY: One Feather Press.

Fine, Gary Alan. 1986. "Redemption Rumors: Mercantile Legends and Corporate Beneficence." *Journal of American Folklore* 99(392):208–22.

Fine, Gary Alan. 1992. *Manufacturing Tales: Sex and Money in Contemporary Legends.* Knoxville: University of Tennessee Press.

Fine, Gary Alan, and Bill Ellis. 2010. *The Global Grapevine: Why Rumors of Terrorism, Immigration, and Trade Matter.* New York: Oxford University Press.

Fine, Gary Alan, and Patricia Turner. 2001. *Whispers on the Color Line: Rumor and Race in America.* Berkeley: University of California Press.

Fine, Gary Alan, and Jeffrey Victor. 1994. "Satanic Tourism: Adolescent Dabblers and Identity Work." *The Phi Delta Kappan* 76(1):70–72.

Firth, Raymond. 1954. "The Sociology of 'Magic' in Tikopia." *Sociologus* 4(2):97–116.

Firth, Raymond. [1956] 1970. "Reason and Unreason in Human Belief." Pp. 38–40 in *Witchcraft and Sorcery*, edited by M. Marwick. Baltimore: Penguin.

Fontaine, Tracy. 2013. *Beyond Lilla.* Rochester, NY: Starry Night Publishing.

Frascino, Christopher [Producer]. 2016. "St. Anne's Retreat" in *Ghost Adventures* (Season 13), November 19. Television series episode. New York: MY Entertainment.

Frazer, James G. [1890] 1996. *The Golden Bough: A Study in Magic and Religion.* Abridged ed. New York: Touchstone.

French, Christopher, and Anna Stone. 2014. *Anomalistic Psychology: Exploring Paranormal Belief & Experience*. New York: Palgrave Macmillan.

Freud, Sigmund. 1919. "The 'Uncanny.'" Pp. 219–56 in *The Standard Edition of the Complete Psychological Works of Sigmund Freud*. Vol. 17, *An Infantile Neurosis and Other Works*, edited by J. Strachey. London: Hogarth Press.

Gabbert, Lisa. 2015. "Legend Quests and the Curious Case of St. Ann's Retreat: The Performative Landscape." Pp. 146–69 in *Putting the Supernatural in Its Place*, edited by J. B. Thomas. Salt Lake City: University of Utah Press.

Geertz, Clifford. 1973. *The Interpretation of Cultures*. New York: Basic Books.

Gentry, Glenn W. 2007. "Walking with the Dead: The Place of Ghost Walk Tourism in Savannah, Georgia." *Southeastern Geographer* 47(2):222–38.

GhostHunter Store. N.d. Retrieved July 12, 2022. https://www.theghosthunterstore.com/default.asp.

Ghostvillage. 2005. "Hannah Cranna." February 16. Retrieved September 1, 2016. http://www.ghostvillage.com/ghostcommunity/index.php?showtopic=6768.

Ghostvillage. 2006. "Devil's Hopyard, CT." October 24. Retrieved June 7, 2018. http://www.ghostvillage.com/ghostcommunity/index.php?showtopic=16766.

Ghostvillage. 2008. "Gunntown Cemetery." April 22. Retrieved January 21, 2018. www.ghostvillage.com/ghostcommunity/index.php?showtopic=23664.

Ghostwatcherz. 2011. "Haunted Gunntown Cemetery—Naugatuck, CT." Blog, February 20. Retrieved January 20, 2018. http://www.ghostwatcherz.com/guntown-cemetery-naugatuck-ct/.

Glimm, James York. 1983. *Flatlanders and Ridgerunners: Folktales from the Mountains of Northern Pennsylvania*. Pittsburgh, PA: University of Pittsburgh Press.

Goffman, Erving. 1961. *Asylums: Essays on the Social Situation of Mental Patients and Other Inmates*. Garden City, NY: Anchor.

Goffman, Erving. 1963. *Stigma: Notes on the Management of Spoiled Identity*. New York: Simon & Schuster.

Goldstein, Diane E. 2007a. "The Commodification of Belief." Pp. 171–205 in *Haunting Experiences: Ghosts in Contemporary Folklore*, edited by D. E. Goldstein, S. A. Grider, and J. B. Thomas. Logan: Utah State University Press.

Goldstein, Diane E. 2007b. "Scientific Rationalism and Supernatural Experience Narratives." Pp. 60–83 in *Haunting Experiences: Ghosts in Contemporary Folklore*, edited by D. E. Goldstein, S. A. Grider, and J. B. Thomas. Logan: Utah State University Press.

Goldstein, Diane E., Sylvia Ann Grider, and Jeannie Banks Thomas, eds. 2007. *Haunting Experiences: Ghosts in Contemporary Folklore*. Logan: Utah State University Press.

Goode, Erich. 2000. *Paranormal Beliefs: A Sociological Introduction*. Prospect Heights, IL: Waveland.

Gordon, Avery F. 2008. *Ghostly Matters: Haunting and the Sociological Imagination*. Minneapolis: University of Minnesota.

Goring, Rosemary. 1994. *Larousse Dictionary of Beliefs and Religions*. New York: Larousse Kingfisher Chambers.

Graham, Stacey. 2014. *Haunted Stuff: Demonic Dolls, Screaming Skulls & Other Creepy Collectables*. Woodbury, MN: Llewellyn.

Gray, T. M. 2010. *More New England Graveside Tales*. Atglen, PA: Schiffer Publishing.

Greeley, Andrew. 1975. *The Sociology of the Paranormal: A Reconnaissance.* London: Sage.

Green, Lott. N.d. "The Taletale Tombstone." Lott's Scary Stories. Retrieved February 5, 2018. https://www.angelfire.com/in/lottgreene/hallobond.html.

Grider, Sylvia Ann. 1980. "The Hatchet Man." Pp. 147–78 in *Indiana Folklore: A Reader*, edited by L. Dégh. Bloomington: Indiana University Press.

Grider, Sylvia Ann. 2007a. "Children's Ghost Stories." Pp. 111–40 in *Haunting Experiences: Ghosts in Contemporary Folklore*, edited by D. E. Goldstein, S. A. Grider, and J. B. Thomas. Logan: Utah State University Press.

Grider, Sylvia Ann. 2007b. "Haunted Houses." Pp. 143–70 in *Haunting Experiences: Ghosts in Contemporary Folklore*, edited by D. E. Goldstein, S. A. Grider, and J. B. Thomas. Logan: Utah State University Press.

Gross, Lori. 2016. "Haunted Cemeteries in Indiana Part Two." HubPages, blog, October 19. Retrieved February 15, 2018. https://hubpages.com/religion-philosophy/Haunted -Cemeteries-in-Indiana-Part-Two.

Gruben, Michelle. 2018. "Graveyard Magick: A Witch's Guide." Grove and Grotto, blog, February 28. Retrieved July 2, 2018. https://www.groveandgrotto.com/blogs/articles /graveyard-magick-a-witchs-guide.

Guiley, Rosemary Ellen. 1992. *The Encyclopedia of Ghosts and Spirits.* New York: Facts on File.

Guiley, Rosemary Ellen. 2008. *Ghosts and Haunted Places.* New York: Chelsea House.

Guiley, Rosemary Ellen. 2011. *Haunted Salem: Strange Phenomena in the Witch City.* Mechanicsburg, PA: Stackpole.

Guilford, J. P., and Karl M. Dallenbach. 1928. "A Study of the Autokinetic Sensation." *American Journal of Psychology* 40(1):83–91.

Gutowski, John. A. 1980. "Traditions of the Devil's Hollows." Pp. 74–92 in *Indiana Folklore: A Reader*, edited by L. Dégh. Bloomington: Indiana University Press.

Haddad, Ken. 2021. "Michigan's Most Haunted: The Witch of Pere Cheney Cemetery. Did a Witch Curse the Village of Pere Cheney?" *ClickonDetroit*, October 28. Retrieved July 1, 2018. https://www.clickondetroit.com/features/2016/10/10/michigans-most-haunted -the-witch-of-pere-cheney-cemetery/.

Hall, Gary. 1973. "The Big Tunnel: Legends and Legend-Telling." *Indiana Folklore* 6(2):139–73.

Hall, Gary. 1980. "The Big Tunnel." Pp. 225–57 in *Indiana Folklore: A Reader*, edited by L. Dégh. Bloomington: Indiana University Press.

Hanks, Michele. 2015. *Haunted Heritage: The Cultural Politics of Ghost Tourism, Populism, and the Past.* Walnut Creek, CA: Left Coast Press.

Hanson, David J. 2015. "Drug Abuse Resistance Education (D.A.R.E.)." In *The Encyclopedia of Clinical Psychology*, edited by R. L. Cautin and S. O. Lilienfeld. Online ed. New York: Wiley. Retrieved July 25, 2022. http://onlinelibrary.wiley.com/doi/10.1002/9781118625392 .wbecp084/full.

Haraldsson, Erlendur. 1985. "Representative National Surveys of Psychic Phenomena: Iceland, Great Britain, Sweden, USA and Gallup's Multinational Survey." *Journal of the Society for Psychical Research* 53(801):145–58.

Harker, John. 2015. *Demonic Dolls: True Tales of Terrible Toys.* S.l.: CreateSpace.

Harriet Beecher Stowe Center. 2008. *Harriet Beecher Stowe's Hartford Home.* Hartford, CT: Harriet Beecher Stowe Center.

Haskell, Josh. 2013. "Students Find Mysterious Man Living in Their Basement." *ABC News*, September 19. Retrieved January 31, 2018. http://abcnews.go.com/US/osu-students -thought-house-haunted-find-mysterious-man/story?id=20291683.

Haunted History Trail of New York State. 2014. "Haunted Road Trip—Destination: Finger Lakes Region. Part 2 (Tioga and Yates Counties)." Blog, October 3. Retrieved November 15, 2017. http://hauntedhistorytrail.com/blog/haunted-road-trip-destination-finger-lakes -region-part-2-tioga-and-yates-counties.

Haunted History Trail of New York State. 2022. "Spook Hill." N.d. Retrieved July 12, 2022. https://hauntedhistorytrail.com/explore/spook-hill.

Haunted Places. N.d.a. "Downs Road." Retrieved July 12, 2022. https://www.hauntedplaces .org/item/downs-road/.

Haunted Places. N.d.b. "Gay City State Park." Retrieved July 12, 2022. http://www.haunted places.org/item/gay-city-state-park.

Haunted Places. N.d.c. "USS Constellation." Retrieved July 22, 2022. https://www.haunted places.org/item/uss-constellation/.

Havens, Walter P., Jr., Robert Ward, V. A. Drill, and John R. Paul. 1944. "Experimental Pro- duction of Hepatitis by Feeding Icterogenic Materials." *Proceedings of the Society for Experimental Biology and Medicine* 57(2):206–8.

Hawes, Jason, Grant Wilson, and Michael Jan Friedman. 2007. *Ghost Hunting: True Stories of Unexplained Phenomena from the Atlantic Paranormal Society.* New York: Pocket Books.

Hawthorne, Nathaniel. [1851] 1924. *The House of the Seven Gables.* New York: Houghton Mifflin.

Hider, Anna. 2014. "Meet Massachusetts' Chilling Witch Bonney." Roadtrippers, October 13. Retrieved July 2, 2018. https://roadtrippers.com/stories/witch-bonney?lng=-96.67528&lat =40.80972&z=4.

Hiking New England. N.d. "Haunted Hikes." Retrieved May 9, 2018. http://www.hikingnew england.com/topic/510-haunted-hikes/.

Hirsch, Aimee. 2013. "The Haunted Places of Oswego." *The Oswegonian*, October 29. Retrieved August 23, 2019. https://www.oswegonian.com/2013/10/29/the-haunted-places-of-oswego/.

Historic Ships. N.d. "USS Constellation." Retrieved July 22, 2022. https://historicships.org /explore/uss-constellation.

Historic Valentown. N.d. "America's First Shopping Mall." Retrieved July 12, 2022. http://historic valentownmuseum.org/index.php.

Historic Valentown. 2019. "'Ghost City of Valentown' Story." May 12. Retrieved July 12, 2022. https://historicvalentownmuseum.org/page.php/ghostcityofvalentownstory.

Hobbs, Sandy, and David Cornwell. 1988. "Hunting the Monster with Iron Teeth." Pp. 115–37 in *Monsters with Iron Teeth*, edited by G. Bennett and P. Smith. Sheffield, UK: Sheffield Academic Press.

Holloway, Julian. 2010. "Legend Tripping in Spooky Places: Ghost Tourism and Infrastruc- tures of Enchantment." *Environment and Planning D: Society and Space* 28(4):618–37.

Holly, Donald H., and Casey E. Cordy. 2007. "What's in a Coin? Reading the Material Culture of Legend Tripping and Other Activities." *Journal of American Folklore* 120(477):335–54.

Honko, Lauri. 1964. "Memorates and the Study of Folk Beliefs." *Journal of the Folklore Insti- tute* 1(1–2):5–19.

Howard, Robert G. 2008. "Electronic Hybridity: The Persistent Processes of the Vernacular Web." *Journal of American Folklore* 121(480):192–218.

Hufford, David J. 1982. *The Terror That Comes in the Night: An Experience-Centered Study of Supernatural Assault Traditions.* Philadelphia: University of Pennsylvania Press.

Hufford, David J. 2001. "An Experience-Centered Approach to Hauntings." Pp. 18–40 in *Hauntings and Poltergeists: Multidisciplinary Perspectives,* edited by J. Houran and R. Lange. Jefferson, NC: McFarland.

Huizinga, Johan. 1955. *Homo Ludens: A Study of the Play-Element in Culture.* Boston: Beacon.

Inglehart, Ronald. 1990. *Culture Shift in Advanced Industrial Society.* Princeton, NJ: Princeton University Press.

Ironside, Rachel. 2017. "Discovering Strange Events in Empty Spaces: The Role of Multimodal Practice and the Interpretation of Paranormal Events." *Journal of Pragmatics* 120:88–100.

Irving, Rob. 2016. Legend Landscapes: Sacred Mobilities in the 'Legend Trip' Tradition." Pp. 95–114 in *Sacred Mobilities: Journeys of Belief and Belonging,* edited by A. Maddrell, A. Terry, and T. Gale. New York: Routledge.

Irving, Washington. [1820] 2015. "The Legend of Sleepy Hollow." Pp. 278–303 in *The Legend of Sleepy Hollow and Other Stories.* New York: Fall River Press.

Irwin, Harvey J. 2009. *The Psychology of Paranormal Belief: A Researcher's Handbook.* Hertfordshire: University of Hertfordshire Press.

It Gets Weird. 2017. "Dr. Russell Crowe (Melon Heads)." April 2, podcast, 58:24. Retrieved July 22, 2022. http://itgetsweird.libsyn.com/episode-37-dr-russell-crowes-melon-heads.

Jentsch, Ernst. [1906] 1997. "On the Psychology of the Uncanny." *Angelaki* 2(1):7–16.

Jones, Abigail. 2014. "The Girls Who Tried to Kill for Slender Man." *Newsweek,* August 13. Retrieved January 7, 2019. http://www.newsweek.com/2014/08/22/girls-who-tried-kill-slender-man-264218.html.

Jones, Robert P., and Daniel Cox. 2017. *America's Changing Religious Identity: Findings from the 2016 American Values Atlas.* Washington, DC: Public Religion Research Institute.

Joynes, Andrew. 2001. *Medieval Ghost Stories: An Anthology of Miracles, Marvels and Prodigies.* Suffolk, UK: Boydell.

Kellehear, Allan. 1993. "Culture, Biology, and the Near-Death Experience: A Reappraisal." *Journal of Nervous and Mental Disease* 181(3):148–56.

Khazan, Olga. 2018. "Trump's Call for Mental Institutions Could Be Good: Bringing Back Asylums Isn't Actually the Worst Idea." *The Atlantic,* February 23. Retrieved May 3, 2018. https://www.theatlantic.com/health/archive/2018/02/mental-institutions/554015/.

Kinsella, Michael. 2011. *Legend-Tripping Online: Supernatural Folklore and the Search for Ong's Hat.* Jackson: University Press of Mississippi.

Knauft, Bruce. 2016. *The Gebusi: Lives Transformed in a Rainforest World.* Long Grove, IL: Waveland Press.

Koven, Mikel J. 1999. "*Candyman* Can: Film and Ostension." *Contemporary Legend* N.S. 2:155–73.

Koven, Mikel J. 2007. "*Most Haunted* and the Convergence of Traditional Belief and Popular Television." *Folklore* 118(2):183–202.

Kunhardt, Peter W., and Kenneth Wooden [Producers]. 1985. "The Devil Worshippers" in *20/20,* May 16. Television series episode. New York: ABC News.

Kuzmeskus, Elaine. 2006. *Connecticut Ghosts: Spirits in the State of Steady Habits.* Atglen, PA: Schiffer Publishing.

Lake, Andrew. 2011. *Ghosthunting Southern New England.* Cincinnati, OH: Clerisy Press.

Lamothe, Zachary. 2013. *Connecticut Lore: Strange, Off-Kilter, and Full of Surprises*. Atglen, PA: Schiffer Publishing.

Langlois, Janet. 1980. "Mary Whales, I Believe In You." Pp. 196–224 in *Indiana Folklore: A Reader*, edited by L. Dégh. Bloomington: Indiana University Press.

Langlois, Janet. 2008. "Confessions of a Legend Hunter in the U.S.A." *Cahiers de Littérature Orale* 63–64:185–200.

Langlois, Janet. 2014. "They All See Dead People—But We (Do)n't Want to Tell You About It: On Legend Gathering in Real and Cyberspace." *New Directions in Folklore* 12(1):5–56.

Leach, Maria. 1972. *Funk & Wagnalls Standard Dictionary of Folklore, Mythology, and Legend*. New York: Harper & Row.

Leary, Robyn. 2000. "Ghost Stories: The Other Legend of Sleepy Hollow." *New York Times*, October 29, WC14.

LeBlond, Paul. 2016. "International Cryptozoology Society Founded 2016." January 16. Retrieved January 31, 2018. http://iczsonline.com/.

Lecocq, James G. 1980. "The Ghost of the Doctor and a Vacant Fraternity House." Pp. 265–78 in *Indiana Folklore: A Reader*, edited by L. Dégh. Bloomington: Indiana University Press.

Lefebvre, Henri. 1991. *The Production of Space*. Oxford: Blackwell.

Levack, Brian P. 2015. *The Witch-Hunt in Early Modern Europe*. New York: Routledge.

Levine, Shar, and Leslie Johnstone. 2010. *Scary Science: 24 Creepy Experiments*. New York: Scholastic.

Lewis, David L., and Laurence Goldstein. 1983. *The Automobile and American Culture*. Ann Arbor: University of Michigan Press.

Liddy, Eric D., Sr. N.d. "Don't Steal from the Dead—A Pere Cheney Cemetery Story." *Michigan's Other Side*. Retrieved July 1, 2018. http://michigansotherside.com/dont-steal-pere-cheney-cemetery/.

Light, Duncan. 2017. "Progress in Dark Tourism and Thanatourism Research: An Uneasy Relationship with Heritage Tourism." *Tourism Management* 61:275–301.

Lindahl, Carl. 2005. "Ostensive Healing: Pilgrimage to the San Antonio Ghost Tracks." *Journal of American Folklore* 118(468):164–85.

Lindahl, Carl, John McNamara, and John Lindow. 2001. *Medieval Folklore: A Guide to Myths, Legends, Tales, Beliefs, and Customs*. New York: Oxford University Press.

Lindsey, Susan L., Mary N. Green, and Cynthia L. Bennett. 1999. *The Okapi: Mysterious Animal of Congo-Zaire*. Austin: University of Texas Press.

Loftus, Elizabeth. 1994. *The Myth of Repressed Memory: False Memories and Allegations of Sexual Abuse*. New York: St. Martin's Press.

Longfellow, Henry Wadsworth. 1867. *Flower-de-Luce*. Boston: Ticknor and Fields.

Machen, Arthur. [1922] 1948. *Tales of Horror and the Supernatural*. New York: Knopf.

MacKenzie, Donald, and Judy Wajcman, eds. 1999. *The Social Shaping of Technology*. Buckingham, UK: Open University Press.

Magliocco, Sabina. 2018. "Beyond the Rainbow Bridge: Vernacular Ontologies of Animal Afterlives." *Journal of Folklore Research* 55(2):39–67.

Mandelbaum, David G. 1959. "Social Uses of Funeral Rites." Pp. 189–217 in *The Meaning of Death*, edited by H. Feifel. New York: McGraw-Hill.

Martini, Kathleen. 2013. "Ohio State Students Discover Stranger Living in Basement." *Columbus Lantern*, September 12. Retrieved January 31, 2018. https://www.thelantern.com/2013/09/ohio-state-students-discover-stranger-living-basement/.

Maruna, Shadd. 2011. "Reentry as a Rite of Passage." *Punishment & Society* 13(1):3–28.

Mauss, Marcel. [1902] 1982. *A General Theory of Magic.* New York: Norton.

McClenon, James. 2000. "Content Analysis of an Anomalous Memorate Collection: Testing Hypotheses Regarding Universal Features." *Sociology of Religion* 61(2):155–69.

McClenon, James. 2001. "The Sociological Investigation of Haunting Cases." Pp. 62–81 in *Hauntings and Poltergeists: Multidisciplinary Perspectives,* edited by J. Houran and R. Lange. Jefferson, NC: McFarland.

McCloud, Sean. 2015. *American Possessions: Fighting Demons in the Contemporary United States.* New York: Oxford University Press.

McGuire, Meredith B. 1997. *Religion: The Social Context.* New York: Wadsworth.

McMillan, Blaine J. 2014. *Wood Knocks and Tossed Rocks: Searching for Sasquatch with the Bigfoot Field Researchers Organization.* S.l.: CreateSpace.

McNeill, Lynne S. 2006. "Contemporary Ghost Hunting and the Relationship between Proof and Experience." *Contemporary Legend* 9:96–110.

McNeill, Lynne S. 2015. "Twihards, Buffistas, and Vampire Fanlore." Pp. 126–45 in *Putting the Supernatural in Its Place: Folklore, the Hypermodern, and the Ethereal,* edited by J. B. Thomas. Salt Lake City: University of Utah Press.

McNeill, Lynne S., and Elizabeth Tucker. 2018. *Legend Tripping: A Contemporary Legend Casebook.* Logan: Utah State University Press.

Mead, Robin. 1995. *Haunted Hotels: A Guide to American and Canadian Inns and Their Ghosts.* Nashville, TN: Rutledge Hill.

Meley, Patricia M. 1991. "Adolescent Legend Trips as Teenage Cultural Response: A Study of Lore in Context." *Children's Folklore Review* 14(1):5–24.

Mercado, Elaine. 2006. *Grave's End: A True Ghost Story.* St. Paul, MN: Llewellyn Worldwide.

Merton, Robert K. 1948. "The Self-Fulfilling Prophecy." *Antioch Review* 8(2):193–210.

Miles, Tiya. 2017. *Tales from the Haunted South: Dark Tourism and Memories of Slavery from the Civil War Era.* Chapel Hill: University of North Carolina Press.

Mitchell, John Hanson. 2014. *A Field Guide to Your Own Back Yard.* Woodstock, VT: Countryman Press.

Moffitt, Terrie E. 1993. "Adolescence-Limited and Life-Course-Persistent Antisocial Behavior: A Developmental Taxonomy." *Psychological Review* 100(4):674–701.

Mommy Poppins. 2017. "Haunted Halloween Happenings for Everyone in the Hartford Area." N.d. Retrieved October 1, 2017. https://mommypoppins.com/kids/spirits-at-stowe-an-otherwordly-tour-at-harriet-beecher-stowe-center.

Monster Move Podcast. 2017. "Melon Heads." N.d., podcast, 34:02. Retrieved July 11, 2022. https://player.fm/series/monster-move-podcast/episode-2-melon-heads.

Moore, Richard. 2016. "Meaning and Ostension in Great Ape Gestural Communication." *Animal Cognition* 19(1):223–31.

Moreman, Christopher M. 2013. "On the Paucity of Apparitions in Jewish Contexts and the Cultural Source Theory for Anomalous Experience." *Journal of the Society for Psychical Research* 77(912):129–46.

Mori, Masahiro. 1970. "The Uncanny Valley." *Energy* 7(4):33–35.

Mota-Rolim, Sergio A., Kelly Bulkeley, Stephany Campanelli, Bruno Lobão-Soares, Draulio B. de Araujo, and Sidarta Ribeiro. 2020. "The Dream of God: How Do Religion and Science See Lucid Dreaming and Other Conscious States During Sleep?" *Frontiers in Psychology* 11(555731):1–9.

Muise, Peter. 2015. "Melonheads Part I: A Trip Down Dracula Drive." New England Folklore, blog, August 16. Retrieved April 22, 2018. http://newenglandfolklore.blogspot.com/2015/08/melonheads-part-i-trip-down-dracula.html.

Muise, Peter. 2016. "Pukwudgies in Freetown: Some Fairy Sightings in Massachusetts." New England Folklore, blog, April 25. Retrieved May 11, 2018. http://newenglandfolklore.blogspot.com/2016/04/pukwudgies-in-freetown-some-fairy.html.

Mullen, Patrick B. 1972. "Modern Legend and Rumor Theory." *Journal of the Folklore Institute* 9(2–3):95–109.

Narciso, Dean. 2011. "Worthington Wants to Buy House Where Teen Shot after Prank: Blight Latest Chapter in Property's Ugly History." *Columbus Dispatch*, December 8. Retrieved August 3, 2016. http://www.dispatch.com/content/stories/local/2011/12/08/worthington-wants-to-buy-house-where-teen-shot-after-prank.html.

Narciso, Dean. 2013. "New Owners Plan to Rehab 'Spooky House': Girl Was Shot There During Halloween Incident." *Columbus Dispatch*, February 16. Retrieved August 3, 2016. https://www.dispatch.com/story/lifestyle/home-garden/home-decor/2013/02/16/new-owners-plan-to-rehab/23700389007/.

National Register of Historic Places. 1987. "National Register of Historic Places Inventory—Nomination Form." December 17. Retrieved July 11, 2022. https://npgallery.nps.gov/GetAsset/817e7d75-f2a6-41d7-b294-d209431f8066.

Newman, Rich. 2011. *Ghost Hunting for Beginners: Everything You Need to Know to Get Started.* Woodbury, MN: Llewellyn Publications.

Nickell, Joe. 2007. *Adventures in Paranormal Investigation.* Lexington: University Press of Kentucky.

Nickell, Joe. 2011. "Secrets of the Voodoo Tomb." *Skeptical Inquirer* 11(4). Retrieved July 2, 2018. https://www.csicop.org/sb/show/secrets_of_the_voodoo_tomb.

Nickell, Joe. 2016a. "The Brown Mountain Lights: Solved! (Again!)." *Skeptical Inquirer* 40(1):24–27.

Nickell, Joe. 2016b. "Gallows Ghosts? Mystery at Brisbane's Tower Mill." *Skeptical Inquirer* 40(3):12–13.

North Hall Library. N.d. "Sarah's Page." Mansfield University. Retrieved February 9, 2018. https://lib.mansfield.edu/digitalarchives/sarah.

Nowinski, Jon. 2012. "Urban Legends in a Rural Town." Bethwood Patch, February 27. Retrieved May 12, 2018. https://patch.com/connecticut/bethwood/bp--urban-legends-in-a-rural-town.

Noymer, Andrew. 2001. "The Transmission and Persistence of 'Urban Legends': Sociological Application of Age-Structured Epidemic Models." *Journal of Mathematical Sociology* 25(3):1–98.

Okonowicz, Ed. 1996. *Possessed Possessions: Haunted Antiques, Furniture and Collectables.* Elkton, MD: Myst and Lace.

Old York Historical Society. N.d. Retrieved July 12, 2022. https://oldyork.org/.

OnlyInYourState Staff. 2021. "These 10 Chilling Urban Legends in North Carolina May Terrify You." OnlyInYourState, February 14. Retrieved July 6, 2018. https://www.onlyinyourstate.com/north-carolina/urban-legends-nc-1.

Osborn, Lawrence A. 2009. "From Beauty to Despair: The Rise and Fall of the American State Mental Hospital." *Psychiatric Quarterly* 80(4):219–31.

Osolsobě, Ivo. 1971. "The Role of Models and Originals in Human Communication." *Language Sciences* 14:32–36.

Packaged Facts. 2017. "Animal Welfare: Issues and Opportunities in the Meat, Poultry, and Egg Markets in the U.S." April 10. Retrieved May 4, 2018. https://www.packagedfacts.com /Animal-Welfare-Meat-10771767/.

Packer, Randall K. 2014. "How Long Can the Average Person Survive Without Water?" *Scientific American*, December 9. Retrieved September 30, 2016. http://www.scientific american.com/article/how-long-can-the-average.

Paranormal School. N.d. "Using a Flashlight to Communicate with Ghosts and Spirits." Retrieved August 29, 2020. https://paranormalschool.com/using-a-flashlight-to -communicate-with-ghosts-and-spirits/.

Parrinder, Geoffrey. 1969. *Religion in Africa.* New York: Praeger.

Paterson, Randolph J., and Richard W. Neufeld. 1987. "Clear Danger: Situational Determinants of the Appraisal of Threat." *Psychological Bulletin* 101(3):404–16.

Patry, Alain L., and Luc G. Pelletier. 2001. "Extraterrestrial Beliefs and Experiences: An Application of the Theory of Reasoned Action." *Journal of Social Psychology* 141(2):199–217.

Paxton, C. G. M., and D. Naish. 2019. "Did Nineteenth Century Marine Vertebrate Fossil Discoveries Influence Sea Serpent Reports?" *Earth Sciences History* 38(1):16–27.

Pearsall, Ronald. 2004. *The Table-Rappers: The Victorians and the Occult.* Gloucestershire, UK: Sutton Publishing.

Peck, Andrew. 2015. "Tall, Dark, and Loathsome: The Emergence of a Legend Cycle in the Digital Age." *Journal of American Folklore* 128(509):333–48.

Peebles, Mike [Producer]. 2013. "Permanent Residents" in *Ghost Hunters* (Season 9), February 6. Television series episode. Los Angeles: Pilgrim Films & Television.

Peloquin, Suzanne M. 1989. "Moral Treatment: Contexts Considered." *American Journal of Occupational Therapy* 43(8):537–44.

Peters, Lucia. 2016. "Abandoned: All That Remains of Connecticut's Norwich State Hospital." Ghost in My Machine, blog, January 18. Retrieved February 20, 2018. https://theghostin-mymachine.com/2016/01/18/abandoned-all-that-remains-of-connecticuts-norwich-state -hospital-photos/.

Petkus, Ed. 2008. "Value-Chain Analysis of Prohibition in the United States, 1920–1933: A Historical Case Study in Marketing." *Journal of Business Case Studies* 4(8):35–42.

Pew Research Center. 2018. "When Americans Say They Believe in God, What Do They Mean?" Retrieved July 18, 2018. http://assets.pewresearch.org/wp-content/uploads/sites /11/2018/04/24152307/Beliefs-about-God-FOR-WEB-FULL-REPORT.pdf.

Philips, David E. 1992. *Legendary Connecticut: Traditional Tales from the Nutmeg State.* Willimantic, CT: Curbstone Press.

Pickman, Debra. 2010. *The Sallie House Haunting: A True Story.* Woodbury, MN: Llewellyn.

Piligian, Craig, and Tom Thayer [Producer]. 2004. "The Negative Entity" in *Ghost Hunters* (Season 1), December 15. Television series episode. Los Angeles: Pilgrim Films & Television.

Piligian, Craig, Tom Thayer, Mike Nichols, Alan David, and Rob Katz [Producers]. 2013. "Shock Island" in *Ghost Hunters* (Season 9), October 23. Television series episode. North Hollywood, CA: Pilgrim Media Group.

Pinker, Steven. 2011. *The Better Angels of Our Nature: Why Violence Has Declined.* New York: Penguin.

Pitkin, David J. 2010. *New England Ghosts*. Chestertown, NY: Aurora Publications.

Plumb, Brian E. 2013. *A History of Longfellow's Wayside Inn*. Charleston, SC: History Press.

Price, Harry. 1936. *Confessions of a Ghost-Hunter*. London: Putnam & Co.

Proudfoot, Wayne. 1985. *Religious Experience*. Berkeley: University of California Press.

Pucher, John, Ralph Buehler, and Mark Seinen. 2011. "Bicycling Renaissance in North America? An Update and Re-Appraisal of Cycling Trends and Policies." *Transportation Research Part A: Policy and Practice* 45(6):451–75.

PudgeMan. 2019. "GHOST HUNT!!-Benton Homestead." Posted February 16. YouTube Video, 4:39. Retrieved March 20, 2019. https://www.youtube.com/watch?v=KlbZdZV36YM.

Putnam, Robert D. 2000. *Bowling Alone: The Collapse and Revival of American Community*. New York: Simon & Schuster.

Pyle, Encarnacion. 2007. "The Night That Changed Everything." *Columbus Dispatch*, July 17. Retrieved August 3, 2016. http://www.dispatch.com/content/stories/local/2007/07/15 /rachel1.ART_ART_07-15-07_A1_1V798GI.html.

Queensland Government. N.d. "Windmill Tower." *Queensland Heritage Register*. Retrieved July 25, 2016. https://environment.ehp.qld.gov.au/heritage-register/detail/?id=600173.

Radford, Benjamin. 2010. *Scientific Paranormal Investigation: How to Solve Unexplained Mysteries*. Corrales, NM: Rhombus.

Randi, James. 1982. *Flim-Flam! Psychics, ESP, Unicorns, and Other Delusions*. Amherst, NY: Prometheus.

Raven, Rory. 2008. *Haunted Providence: Strange Tales from the Smallest State*. Charleston, SC: History Press.

Reese, Gregory L. 2007. *UFO Religion: Inside Flying Saucer Cults and Culture*. New York: I. B. Tauris.

Reeser, A. L. 2010. *Ghost Stories of Atlantic City and Other Odd & Ghastly Tales from the World's Playground*. Monocacy, PA: 1stSight Press.

Reimold, Dan. 2013. "Ohio State Students Find Secret Roommate in Their Home." *USA Today*, September 17. Retrieved January 31, 2018. https://www.usatoday.com/story/news /nation/2013/09/17/ohio-state-roommate-secret-basement/2824771/.

Revai, Cheri. 2006. *Haunted Connecticut: Ghosts and Strange Phenomena of the Constitution State*. Mechanicsburg, PA: Stackpole Books.

Richardson, Judith. 2003. *Possessions: The History and Uses of Haunting in the Hudson Valley*. Cambridge, MA: Harvard University Press.

RoadsideAmerica. N.d. "Statue of the Bird Girl." Retrieved July 12, 2022. https://www.road sideamerica.com/story/27535.

Robinson, Robert C. 2016. *Legend Tripping: The Ultimate Adventure*. Kempton, IL: Adventures Unlimited Press.

Rochester Subway. 2013. "Durand Eastman Park and the Lady in White." October 25. Retrieved July 12, 2022. https://www.rochestersubway.com/topics/2013/10/durand -eastman-park-lady-in-white-ghost/.

RocWiki. N.d. "Illuminati Catacomb System." Retrieved May 5, 2017. https://rocwiki.org /Illuminati_Catacomb_System.

Romano, Mitzi. 2017. "A House, A Home, A Home-Away-From-Home: The History of the Hitchcock-Phillips House." Cheshirepedia, May 12. Retrieved July 12, 2022. http://www .cheshirepedia.org/a-house-a-home-a-home-away-from-home-the-history-of-the -hitchcock-phillips-house.

Rook, John. 2013. "Spooky Findings at Hitchcock-Phillips House." *Cheshire (CT) Herald* 32, August 8, 1, 10.

Rosenbaum, Jill L., and Lorraine Prinsky. 1991. "The Presumption of Influence: Recent Responses to Popular Music Subcultures." *Crime & Delinquency* 37(4):528–35.

Rosenhan, David L. 1973. "On Being Sane in Insane Places." *Science* 19(4070):250–58.

Rosenthal, Robert, and Lenore Jacobson. 1968. *Pygmalion in the Classroom: Teacher Expectation and Pupils' Intellectual Development.* New York: Holt, Rinehart & Winston.

Rothman, David J. 1971. *The Discovery of the Asylum.* Boston: Little Brown.

Rucci, Michele, and Martina Poletti. 2009. "Fixational Eye Movements and the Autokinetic Illusion." *Journal of Vision* 9(8):431.

Sachse, Nancy Davis. 2009. *Born among the Hills: The Sleeping Giant Story.* Hamden, CT: Sleeping Giant Park Association.

Sagan, Carl. 1996. *The Demon-Haunted World: Science as a Candle in the Dark.* New York: Ballantine.

Sakmyster, David J. 2003. *The Belhurst Story.* New York: iUniverse.

Sanci, Elissa. 2013. "Step Wherever You Want." *West Haven Charger Bulletin*, October 23. Retrieved January 13, 2022. https://chargerbulletin.com/step-wherever-you-want/.

Schlosser, S. E. 2004. *Spooky New England: Tales of Haunting, Strange Happenings, and Other Local Lore.* Guilford, CT: Globe Pequot Press.

Schlosser, S. E. 2012. *Spooky Indiana: Tales of Hauntings, Strange Happenings, and Other Local Lore.* Guilford, CT: Globe Pequot Press.

Schmitt, Jean-Claude. 1998. *Ghosts in the Middle Ages: The Living and the Dead in Medieval Society.* Chicago: University of Chicago Press.

Schurman, Kathleen. 2012. "There Are Monsters Among Us—On Downs Road, Anyways." Patch, February 23. Retrieved April 21, 2016. https://patch.com/connecticut/bethwood/there-are-monsters-among-us-on-downs-road-anyways.

Scofield, Mikayla. 2015. "The Connecticut Hill Witch." *New Field Press*, April 3. Retrieved July 8, 2018. https://newfieldpress.org/2432/arts-culture/the-connecticut-hill-witch.

Sconce, Jeffrey. 2000. *Haunted Media: Electronic Presence from Telegraphy to Television.* Durham, NC: Duke University Press.

Segal, David. 2007. "Demons of Dark Entry Forest." *Washington Post*, June 7. Retrieved April 22, 2019. http://www.washingtonpost.com/wp-dyn/content/article/2007/06/06/AR2007060602736_pf.html.

Seyffert, Oskar. 1995. *The Dictionary of Classical Mythology, Religion, Literature, and Art.* New York: Random House.

Shadowlands. 2010. "Haunted Places in Connecticut." February. Retrieved February 1, 2018. http://www.theshadowlands.net/places/connecticut.htm.

Shaggyghosts and Seeker. 2005. "Haunted! The Benton Homestead." Seeker: Investigating the Paranormal, July 19. Retrieved July 12, 2022. http://seekerghosts.blogspot.com/2005/07/haunted-benton-homestead.html.

Sharpless, Brian A., and Karl Doghramji. 2015. *Sleep Paralysis: Historical, Psychological, and Medical Perspectives.* New York: Oxford University Press.

Shekinah Paranormal Investigations. N.d. "The Noah Webster House." Retrieved July 10, 2018. http://www.shekinahparanormal.com/page/page/5978606.htm.

Shelburne Museum. 2022. "Dutton House." N.d. Retrieved July 12, 2022. https://shelburnemuseum.org/collection/dutton-house/.

Sherif, Muzafer. 1935. "A Study of Some Social Factors in Perception." *Archives of Psychology* 27(187):1–60.

Simpson, Jacqueline. 1996. "Witches and Witchbusters." *Folklore* 107(1–2):5–18.

Skewes, Joshua C., Lea Skewes, Andreas Roepstorff, and Christopher D. Frith. 2013. "Doing What Others See: Visuomotor Conversion to Informational Social Influence." *Journal of Experimental Psychology* 39(5):1291–1303.

Smith, Andy. 2014. "Owner of R. I. 'Conjuring' House: Movie Has Made Life a Nightmare." *Providence Journal*, January 30. Retrieved May 6, 2017. https://www.providencejournal.com /story/entertainment/2014/01/31/20140131-owner-burrillville-house-attacks-accuracy -movie-about-haunting-that-conjured-nightmare-ece/35368473007/.

Smith, Robin. 2002. *Columbus Ghosts: Historical Haunts of Ohio's Capital.* Worthington, OH: Emuses.

Smith, Robin. 2003. *Columbus Ghosts II: More Central Ohio Haunts.* Worthington, OH: Emuses.

Smith, Virginia L. 2012. "Foreword." Pp. xi–xii in *The Ghosts of Belcourt Castle*, edited by H. H. Tinney. Bloomington, IN: iUniverse.

Snyder, Paige. 2013. "13 Uniquely Rhode Island Superstitions." *Providence Monthly*, December 12. Retrieved March 13, 2018. http://providenceonline.com/stories/13-Rhode-Island -Superstitions-Haunting-Friday-the-thirteenth-ghosts-legends-witches,10765.

Soltero, Gonzalo. 2016. "The Mexican Transmission of 'Lights Out!'" *Journal of Folklore Research* 53(3):115–35.

Southall, Richard. 2003. *How to Be a Ghost Hunter.* Saint Paul, MN: Llewellyn Publications.

Southern Indiana Ghosts. 2004. "10 Penny Bridge—Charleston Indiana." Retrieved July 2, 2018. http://www.angelfire.com/in4/believe/tenpenny/bridge.html.

Spanos, Nicholas P., Cheryl A. Burgess, and Melissa Faith Burgess. 1994. "Past-Life Identities, UFO Abductions, and Satanic Ritual Abuse: The Social Construction of Memories." *International Journal of Clinical and Experimental Hypnosis* 42(4):433–46.

Spencer, John, and Anne Spencer. 1992. *The Encyclopedia of Ghosts and Spirits.* London: Headline Book Publishing.

Spencer, John, and Tony Wells. 1995. *Ghost Watching: The Ghosthunter's Handbook.* London: Virgin Books.

Spencer, Steven J., Claude M. Steele, and Diane M. Quinn. 1999. "Stereotype Threat and Women's Math Performance." *Journal of Experimental Social Psychology* 35(1):4–28.

Spera, Tony. 2017. "The Warren Files: Night of the Haunted." Presentation at Southern Connecticut State University, Hamden, October 27.

Spiritualized67. 2009. "The Haunted Tale of Little Gracie Watson." Daniel Stainer Photography, blog, August 31. Retrieved July 1, 2018. https://danielstainer.wordpress.com/2009 /08/31/the-haunted-tale-of-little-gracie-watson/.

Spiro, Melford E. 1966. "Religion: Problems of Definition and Explanation." Pp. 85–126 in *Anthropological Approaches to the Study of Religion*, edited by M. Banton. London: Tavistock.

Stace, Walter T. 1961. *Mysticism and Philosophy.* London: MacMillan.

Sundra, Cheri. 2016. "The Haunted Monkey Candle Shoppe." Abandoned Places and Urban Exploration, October 23. Retrieved May 4, 2018. https://cherisundra.com/2016/10/23/the -haunted-monkey-candle-shoppe/.

Supernatural Occurrence Studies Podcast. 2017. "Live from Haunted Concord's Colonial Inn."
     N.d., podcast, 199:08. Retrieved July 12, 2022. https://www.spreaker.com/user/supernatural
     occurrencestudies/episode-27-live-from-haunted-concords-co.

Swami, Viren, Rebecca Coles, Stefan Stieger, Jakob Pietschnig, Adrian Furnham, Sherry
     Rehim, and Martin Voracek. 2011. "Conspiracist Ideation in Britain and Austria: Evidence
     of a Monological Belief System and Associations between Individual Psychological
     Differences and Real-World and Fictitious Conspiracy Theories." *British Journal of Psy-
     chology* 102(3):443–63.

Sylvia, Shannon, and Katie Boyd. 2012. *Paranormal Unwrapped.* Atglen, PA: Schiffer
     Publishing.

Tarlow, Sarah. 2000. "Landscapes of Memory: The Nineteenth-Century Garden Cemetery."
     European Journal of Archaeology 3(2):217–39.

Taylor, Troy. 1998. *The Ghost Hunter's Handbook: The Essential How-To Guide for Investigat-
     ing Ghosts & the Paranormal.* Alton, IL: Whitechapel Productions Press.

Taylor, Troy. 2004. "The Curse of Dudleytown: The Story Behind One of the Most Infamous
     Lost Towns in American History." Prairie Ghosts, n.d. Retrieved February 19, 2017.
     https://www.prairieghosts.com/dudleytown.html.

Terrillon, Jean Christopher, and Sirley Marques-Bonham. 2001. "Does Recurrent Isolated
     Sleep Paralysis Involve More than Cognitive Neurosciences?" *Journal of Scientific Explo-
     ration* 15(1):97–123.

Thigpen, Kenneth. 1971. "Adolescent Legends in Brown County: A Survey." *Indiana Folklore*
     4(2):141–215.

Thomas, Jeannie Banks. 2007. "The Usefulness of Ghost Stories." Pp. 25–59 in *Haunting Expe-
     riences: Ghosts in Contemporary Folklore,* edited by D. E. Goldstein, S. A. Grider, and J. B.
     Thomas. Logan: Utah State University Press.

Thomas, Jeannie Banks, ed. 2015. *Putting the Supernatural in Its Place: Folklore, the Hyper-
     modern, and the Ethereal.* Salt Lake City: University of Utah Press.

Thomas, Jeannie Banks. 2018. "On Researching the Supernatural: Cultural Competence and
     Cape Breton Stories." Pp. 35–53 in *The Supernatural in Society, Culture, and History,* edited
     by D. Waskul and M. Eaton. Philadelphia, PA: Temple University Press.

Thurber House. 2022. "What Is Thurber House?" N.d. Retrieved July 12, 2022. https://www
     .thurberhouse.org/about-thurber-house.

Thurber, James. [1933] 1990. "The Night the Ghost Got In." Pp. 474–79 in *Haunted America:
     Star-Spangled Supernatural Stories,* edited by M. Kaye. New York: Barnes and Noble Books.

Tinney, Harle H. 2012. *The Ghosts of Belcourt Castle.* Bloomington, IN: iUniverse.

Tolbert, Jeffrey A. 2013. "The Sort of Story That Has You Covering Your Mirrors: The Case of
     Slender Man." *Semiotic Review* 2(November):n.p.

Traupman, John C. 1995. *The Bantam New College Latin and English Dictionary.* New York:
     Bantam.

Tripadvisor. N.d. "Witch House." Retrieved July 22, 2022. https://www.tripadvisor.com/Show
     UserReviews-g60954-d107580-r417172596-Witch_House-Salem_Massachusetts.html.

Troost-Cramer, Kathleen. 2017. "Haunted No More?" *Newport (RI) Daily News,* October 24.
     Retrieved February 9, 2019. https://www.newportri.com/7433c0cc-224c-505d-b06c
     -46fdd37f5f82.html.

Tucker, Elizabeth. 2007. *Haunted Halls: Ghostlore of American College Campuses.* Jackson: University Press of Mississippi.

Tucker, [Elizabeth] Libby. 2011. "Down to the Depths." *Voices: The Journal of New York Folklore* 37(3–4). Retrieved February 1, 2018. http://www.nyfolklore.org/pubs/voic37-3-4 /gspirits.html.

Tucker, Elizabeth. 2017. "'There's an App for That': Ghost Hunting with Smartphones." *Children's Folklore Review* 38:27–38.

Turner, Victor. 1967. *The Forest of Symbols: Aspects Ndembu Ritual.* Ithaca, NY: Cornell University Press.

Turner, Victor. 1973. "The Center Out There: Pilgrim's Goal." *History of Religions* 12(3):191–230.

Turner, Victor. 1977. *The Ritual Process: Structure and Anti-Structure.* Ithaca, NY: Cornell University Press.

Turner, Victor, and Edith Turner. 1978. *Image and Pilgrimage in Christian Culture.* New York: Columbia University Press.

Tylor, Edward B. 1871. *Primitive Culture: Researches into the Development of Mythology, Philosophy, Religion, Art, and Custom.* London: Bradbury, Evans, and Co.

Underwood, Peter. 1986. *The Ghost Hunter's Guide.* London: Javelin Books.

Unkrich, Lee [Director]. 2017. *Coco.* Motion picture. Burbank: Disney/Pixar.

USU Digital Exhibits. 2022. "St. Anne's Retreat: History and Naming." Utah State University, n.d. Retrieved July 12, 2022. http://exhibits.lib.usu.edu/exhibits/show/stannesretreat /history.

VanderLek, Joy. 2013. "Paranormal Group to Investigate at Hitchcock-Phillips House." *Cheshire (CT) Citizen*, July 4, 7.

van Gennep, Arnold. [1909] 1960. *The Rites of Passage.* Chicago: University of Chicago Press.

Victor, Jeffrey S. 1993. *Satanic Panic: The Creation of a Contemporary Legend.* Chicago: Open Court.

Vogler, Christopher. 2007. *The Writer's Journey: Mythic Structure for Writers.* Studio City, CA: Michael Wiese Productions.

von Humboldt, Alexander. 1850. *Kosmos.* Vol. 3. Stuttgart: J. G. Cotta.

von Sydow, Carl Wilhelm. 1948. *Selected Papers on Folklore.* Copenhagen: Rosenkilde and Bagger.

Vyse, Stuart A. 1997. *Believing in Magic: The Psychology of Superstition.* New York: Oxford University Press.

Wallace, Anthony F. C. 1966. *Religion: An Anthropological View.* New York: Random House.

Warren, Beth. 2016. "Tourist Dies on Search for Pope Lick Monster." *Louisville (KY) Courier-Journal*, April 24. Retrieved May 29, 2018. https://www.courier-journal.com/story/news /local/2016/04/24/tourist-dies-search-pope-lick-monster/83470646/.

Warren, Ed, Lorraine Warren, and Robert David Chase. 1992. *Graveyard: True Hauntings from an Old New England Cemetery.* New York: St. Martin's Press.

Warren, Joshua. 2003. *How to Hunt Ghosts: A Practical Guide.* New York: Fireside.

Waskul, Dennis (with Michele Waskul). 2016. *Ghostly Encounters: The Hauntings of Everyday Life.* Philadelphia, PA: Temple University Press.

Webb, J. Eugene, Donald T. Campbell, Richard D. Schwartz, and Lee Sechrest. 1973. *Unobtrusive Measures: Nonreactive Research in the Social Sciences.* Chicago: Rand McNally and Company.

Weber, Max. [1921] 1978. *Economy and Society: An Outline of Interpretive Sociology*. Berkeley: University of California Press.

Weinstock, Jeffrey Andrew. 2004. "The Spectral Turn." Pp. 3–17 in *Spectral America: Phantoms and the National Imagination*, edited by J. A. Weinstock. Madison, WI: Popular Press.

Wemett, Laurel C. 2001. "The Spooktacular Finger Lakes." *Life in the Finger Lakes*, Fall. Retrieved November 15, 2017. https://www.lifeinthefingerlakes.com/the-spooktacular -finger-lakes/.

Wharton, Edith. [1925] 2016. "Bewitched." Pp. 413–26 in *Chilling Ghost Short Stories*, edited by L. Bulbeck. London: Flame Tree.

Whited, Lana A. 2002. *The Ivory Tower and Harry Potter: Perspectives on a Literary Phenomenon*. Columbia: University of Missouri Press.

Whiting, John W. M., Richard Kluckhohn, and Albert Anthony. 1958. "The Function of Male Initiation Ceremonies at Puberty." Pp. 359–70 in *Readings in Social Psychology*, edited by E. E. Maccoby, T. M. Newcomb, and E. L. Hartley. New York: Henry Holt.

Wikipedia. N.d. "Melon Heads." Retrieved April 22, 2018. https://en.wikipedia.org/wiki /Melon_heads.

Winfield, Mason (with John Koerner, Tim Shaw, and Rob Lockhart). 2008. *Haunted Rochester: A Supernatural History of the Lower Genesee*. Charleston, SC: History Press.

Wisbey, Herbert A., Jr. 1994. "The Lady in Granite." *Crooked Lake Review*, October. Retrieved November 20, 2017. http://www.crookedlakereview.com/articles/67_100/79Oct1994 /79wisbey.html.

Wiseman, Richard. 2010. *Paranormality: Why We See What Isn't There*. S.l.: Spin Solutions.

Wiseman, Richard, Caroline Watt, Paul Stevens, Emma Greening, and Ciarán O'Keeffe. 2003. "An Investigation into Alleged 'Hauntings.'" *British Journal of Psychology* 94(2):195–211.

Witch House. N.d. Retrieved July 12, 2022. https://www.thewitchhouse.org/.

Wolak, Chris. 2014. "Spirits at Stowe: An Otherworldly Tour of Harriet Beecher Stowe's House." Stay Curious, October 26. Retrieved August 28, 2020. https://chriswolak.com /2014/10/26/spirits-at-stowe-an-otherworldly-tour-of-harriet-beecher-stowes-house/.

Wood, Maureen, and Ron Kolek. 2009. *The Ghost Chronicles: A Medium and a Paranormal Scientist Investigate 17 True Hauntings*. Naperville, IL: Sourcebooks.

Woodyard, Chris. 2000. *Ghost Hunter's Guide to Haunted Ohio*. Dayton, OH: Kestrel Publications.

Word, Carl A., Mark P. Zanna, and Joel Cooper. 1974. "The Nonverbal Mediation of Self-Fulfilling Prophecies in Interracial Interaction." *Journal of Experimental Social Psychology* 10(2):109–20.

Worpole, Ken. 2003. *Last Landscapes: The Architecture of the Cemetery in the West*. London: Reaktion.

Wright, Mackenzie. 2019. "How to Keep Ghosts from Following You Home." Anomalien, January 8. Retrieved July 12, 2022. https://anomalien.com/how-to-keep-ghosts-from -following-you-home/.

Wulf, David M. 2000. "Mystical Experience." Pp. 397–440 in *Varieties of Anomalous Experience: Examining the Scientific Evidence*, edited by E. Cardeña, S. J. Lynn, and S. Krippner. Washington, DC: American Psychological Association.

Wuthnow, Robert. 1998. *After Heaven: Spirituality in America Since the 1950s*. Berkeley: University of California Press.

Zajonc, Robert B. 1965. "Social Facilitation." *Science* 149(3681):269–74.

INDEX

Abenaki, 107

Absecon Lighthouse, 217

Africa, 9, 39, 231, 251, 260n9

AIDS rumors, 260n3

alien abduction experiences, 12, 36, 38

alligators in sewers (legend), 61

America's Stonehenge (New Hampshire), 105

Amityville Horror, The (film), 84

animals, ghosts of, 56, 73–75, 130–31, 138–39, 164, 188

animal welfare, 73–75

Annabelle (film), 84, 196

architecture: Georgian, 155; Kirkbride Plan, 68–72 (*see also* legend locations; mental hospitals); moral, 68–71; Romanesque, 136; saltbox, 155; Second Empire, 135; Victorian, 77, 86–87, 135, 147

Arizona: Tucson, 74–75

Australia: Brisbane, 161–62

autokinetic effect, 203–5

automobiles. *See* legend trips: automobiles in

availability heuristics, 154–56, 157–59

Back in Control Training Center, 32

backmasking, 13

Bagans, Zak, 74. See also *Ghost Adventures* (television show)

Belcourt of Newport, 196–97

Belhurst Castle, 77

belief language, 140, 169, 263n9

Belmont, Oliver Hazard Perry, 196

Berry, Adam, 98, 189, 200

"Bewitched" (Wharton), 189–90

Bigfoot, 22, 46, 92–93, 95, 96, 141–42, 214, 234, 238–39, 264nn11–12

"Big Tunnel" (legend), 59, 103, 104, 145–46

Binghamton University, 41, 60

"Black Agnes" (legend), 57

"Black Dog of West Peak" (legend), 56–57

"Bloody Mary" (legend), 120, 171–72

Bonds Chapel Cemetery (Indiana), 123

Borden, Lizzie, 105, 217–18, 268n6

"boyfriend's death" (legend), 261n2

Bridgewater Triangle, 105

Brigham Young University, 263n1

Brown, Mercy, 46, 120

Brown Mountain Lights, 260n6

Bruni, Amy, 98, 189, 200

Buddhism, 73

Brunswick Springs (Vermont), 106–7

Buffy the Vampire Slayer (television series), 243–44

California: San Jose, 62

call blasting, 239, 264n11

cameras, 96

camp tales, 29–30, 259n1 (chap. 1)

Candle Shoppe of the Poconos, 75

candy, contaminated (legend), 30–31, 62

cannibalism, 64, 261n4, 266n4

Captain Grant's Inn, 148

Chapel Island (Minnesota), 171–72

Chapman University (Earl Babbie Research Center), 7–8

Charles Island (Connecticut), 111

Cheshire Historical Society, 263n4 (chap. 3)

Chestnut Hill Baptist Cemetery, 46, 120

Chronicon (Thietmar of Merseburg), 67

Chupacabra, 40

Civil War, American, 129

Coco (film), 121

coelacanth, 260n9

Coleman, Loren, 243

Columba, Saint, 37

Coming of the Fairies, The (Doyle), 146

Committee for Skeptical Inquiry, 264n14

Confessions of a Ghost Hunter (Price), 224

confirmation bias, 154

Congo, 39

Conjuring, The (film), 84, 129, 196

Concord's Colonial Inn, 104–5, 166, 199

Connecticut, 261n4; Bethany, 141, 208–9,
     234; Bolton, 85, 214, 216–17; Cheshire,
     155, 263n4 (chap. 3); Cornwall, 6, 83–85;
     Deep River, 127; Easton, 105–6; Haddam,
     100–102, 262n2; Hamden, 109, 141,
     208–9, 234, 263n3 (chap. 3); Hartford, 77,
     112–13, 135, 147; Hebron, 85, 214, 216–17;
     Meriden, 56–57; Middletown, 60, 70;
     Milford, 111–12; Monroe, 77–78, 95–96,
     106; Naugatuck, 59–60, 136–41, 143–44,
     164–65, 201, 214, 234; New Haven, 84–85,
     106, 161; Norwich, 69–71, 80–81; Preston,
     69–71, 80–81, 148; Seymour, 57; Tolland,
     42–43, 187; Torrington, 84; Trumbull,
     63–64, 77, 96, 262n9, 266n4; West Haven,
     136, 163–65; Windsor, 86–87

Connecticut Department of Energy and
     Environmental Protection, 262n2

Connecticut Hill Cemetery, 117–18

Connecticut State Hospital, 70

conspiracy theories, 6, 10, 27–28, 209, 253.
     See also satanic panic

contemporary legends. *See* legends

copycat crimes, 30–31, 32–33, 131

Cornwall Historical Society, 85. *See also*
     Dudleytown

Corwin, Jonathan, 181–82

Crabtree, Smokey, 243

Cranna, Hannah, 77–78, 95–96, 262n9

Crooked Lake Review (magazine), 90

cryptozoology, 39, 95, 141–42, 183, 189, 240,
     243, 253, 260n9. *See also specific cryptid
     names*

Cursed in New England (Citro), 106–7

curses: debate and, 209; folklore research
     and, 17, 21, 253; fountains, 123, 163; grave-
     stones, 19, 21, 117; islands, 111; monastery,
     162; religion and, 247; springs, 106–7;
     standard characteristics, 162–63, 265n4;
     statues, 57; stealing and, 121, 124, 213;
     towns, 83–84; warnings as, 55–56; witches
     as, 78

darkness, 110, 142–43

Damned Connecticut (podcast), 261n5

Daniel Benton Homestead (Connecticut),
     42–43, 187

Dark Entry Forest Association. *See*
     Dudleytown

Das Heilige (Otto), 185

Davis, Allen S., 130

Davis, Sondra, 130

Deliverance (film), 65

Demonic Dolls (Harker), 196

demons, 37, 98, 100, 102, 133, 197–98, 237–38,
     242, 248. *See also* possession: demonic

Devil's Hopyard State Park, 100–102, 262n2

Devil worship. *See* Satanism

Dighton Rock, 105

dinosaurs, 37–38, 260n7

discussion of supernatural experience,
     24–25, 45, 234, 246; defensiveness,
     209–13, 219; group consensus, 145–46,
     170, 175, 203–5, 206–8, 250; group debate,
     14; group disagreement, 145–48, 170,
     206–9, 219–21; inspiring legend trips,
     205, 221–26; interpretation, 175, 205–6,
     206–7, 212; mementos of proof, 120, 122,
     206, 213–21; nonparticipants and, 205,
     207–9, 210, 219–21, 226; online, 207–9;
     participants and, 203–6, 206–7, 226; per-
     petuating legends, 205–6, 209; proof as,
     218–21; proof debated during, 218–21; so-
     cial status, 15, 207; transforming legends,
     205–6, 221–26; trustworthiness during,
     210–12; verbal arguments, 209–13

Downs Road (Connecticut), 141, 208–9, 234

Doyle, Arthur Conan, 146

"Dracula Drive" (legend). *See* Melon Heads

dread. *See* fear

dreams, lucid, 12
Drug Abuse Resistance Education (DARE), 259n2 (chap. 1)
drugs, 27, 30, 259n2 (chap. 1)
Dudleytown (Connecticut), 6, 83–85
Durand Eastman Park, 186–87

Eastern State Penitentiary (Pennsylvania), 106, 185, 217
Eaton, Marc, 5
1890 House Museum (New York), 195
electromagnetic fields (EMF), 96, 112, 139, 140, 143, 147, 165–66, 212, 265n5
electronic voice phenomenon (EVP), 13, 126, 139, 140, 155, 164, 213, 242, 249, 263n5, 265n5, 268n12
Emerson, Ralph Waldo, 3
ESP, Hauntings, and Poltergeists (Auerbach), 141
ethnography, 18–19, 20, 259n3
Evergreen Cemetery (Connecticut), 106, 161
EVP. See electronic voice phenomenon
exorcism, 199, 200, 238
expectancy effect, 24, 33–34, 113–14, 149, 153–57, 159–61, 174, 223; producing supernatural experience, 153–56, 157–59, 159–61; ritual requirement, 172

fairies, 146, 199
fairy tales, 3, 132
fake news, 6. See also conspiracy theories
false memories, 32, 38
fear (dread, terror): AIDs, 260n3; closing rituals and, 200, 265n4; crime, 31, 55, 62; cults (see Satanism); defused by interpretation, 237, 241–42; domestic space, 85–86, 190, 198–99, 267n8; expressed through legends, 6, 31, 59, 61, 64–65, 67, 183, 185; immigrants, 66; insanity, 267n9; legend trip, during, 59, 91, 98, 103, 144, 159, 169, 183, 194; legends generating, 55; objects, 267n10; poisoned candy (see candy, contaminated); religious, 185; strangers, 62, 66, 74–75, 267n7, 267n11; supernatural, 172, 194, 195, 196, 202, 205, 209, 245; as supernatural experience, 171–72, 174; survey of American fears, 7

Fikes, George, 125
Finding Bigfoot (television show), 5
flashlights, 98–99
folklore: changing over time, 40–43, 226; college, 29, 44, 61, 62, 66, 81–82, 86, 135–36; hypermodern, 40–41; online, 41–43
Fort Ontario, 125
Fort Wetherill State Park (Rhode Island), 59
Fountain Hill Cemetery (Connecticut), 127
Freetown State Forest, 225

Gay City State Park (Connecticut), 85, 214, 216–17
Geller, Uri, 146
Geneva Lake (New York), 77
Georgia: Savannah, 124, 263n3
ghost (concept), 153, 169–71, 182–83, 184, 189, 268n7
Ghost Adventures (television show), 5, 74–75, 131–32
ghost box (device), 43, 167
Ghostbusters (film), 240
Ghost Club, 93
Ghost Hunters (television show), 5, 75, 98, 104, 158, 168, 170, 195, 223, 240
Ghost Hunters Guide (Underwood), 224
ghost lights, 222–23, 225, 268n12
"ghost radar" (application), 233
ghosts of loved ones, 74–75, 267n7, 267n11
Ghosts of Newport (Brennan), 58–59
Ghosts of Salem (Baltrusis), 83
Gore Orphanage, 45
Gosse, Phillip, 39
gravestone motifs, 76, 262n7
gravity hills, 157–58
Great Awakening, 248
Great Hill Cemetery (Connecticut), 57
Greece, ancient, 27, 67
Greek mythology, 57, 261n3
Green Mountain Cemetery (Vermont), 67
Gregory's Four Corners Cemetery (Connecticut), 77, 95–96, 262n9
Gunntown Cemetery (Connecticut), 59–60, 136–41, 143–44, 164–65, 201, 214, 234

Halloween, 31–32, 33, 62, 77, 132, 135, 147
hallucination, mass, 16

Hanging Hills, 56–57

Harriet Beecher Stowe Center, 112–13, 135, 147

harassment, 129–30

Harry Potter film series, 243–44

Hart, Mary E., 106, 161

Harvey, Neil, 127

"hatchet man" (legend), 29

Haunted Collector (television series), 196

Haunted Finger Lakes (Claud), 89, 91–92

Haunted Objects (Balzano and Weisberg), 196

Haunted Stuff (Graham), 196

Haunting in Connecticut, The (film), 84

Hawes, Jason, 158–59, 168. See also *Ghost Hunters* (television show)

Hawthorne, Nathaniel, 82–83

Hawthorne Hotel, 249

hazing, 251–52

headless horseman, 53

heavy metal music, 31, 32

Hendrickson, Mary Jane, 160–61

hepatitis, 70–71

Hex (store), 96

Highgate Cemetery (UK), 266n3

Highland Park (New York), 80

Hinduism, 73

Hitchcock-Phillips House, 155, 263n4 (chap. 3)

hoaxes, 37–38, 40, 162, 212, 224, 260n3, 260nn7–8

Hobomock (legend), 109

Hockomock Swamp (Massachusetts), 105

Holocaust denial, 10. See also conspiracy theories

Hookman's Cemetery (legend), 57

Hoppal, Mihalyi, 263n9

House of Blue Lights, 215–16, 268n4

House of the Seven Gables, 82–83

Howe, Jerusha, 221

Humboldt, Alexander von, 204

Hypnos, 261n3

hypnosis, 27

Icelandic culture, 9

Indiana, 62, 194; Big Tunnel, 59, 103, 104, 145–46; Bloomington, 59; Charleston, 125; Indianapolis, 215–16; West Baden Springs, 123

individualism, 25–26

institutional distrust, 64–65, 68–71, 230, 237

International Cryptozoology Society, 260n9

International Society of Cryptozoology, 39, 260n9

internet (as data source), 17, 18, 20–21, 104

Iowa: Iowa City, 132, 162–63, 183–84

It Gets Weird (podcast), 261n5

Japanese culture, 9

Jewish culture, 9

Jones Folklore Archive, 74

Junker, Wilhelm, 39

Kennebunk Inn, 249

Kentucky: Louisville, 129, 216

Keuka Lake, 89–90

Kietan (legend), 109

Kindred Spirits (television show), 98, 189, 200

Kirkbride Plan, 68–72. See also legend locations: mental hospitals

Kosmos (Humboldt), 204

"Lady in Granite" (legend), 89–90, 123, 214

Lakeview Cemetery (New York), 89–90, 123, 214

land of the dead, 121

landscape, residual, 76, 248

Laveau, Marie, 124

legend locations, 46, 54, 66, 155, 255–58, 265n1; abandonment, 21, 58, 67, 71, 75–76, 83, 85, 141, 214; animal testing facilities, 75; attics, 58, 68, 86, 109, 155, 172–73, 190, 193; bridges, 67, 125, 135, 155, 219, 245, 266n4; cellars and basements, 36, 41, 60, 62, 86–87, 109, 190, 193; cemeteries and graveyards, 57, 67–68, 72, 75–76, 123–24, 127, 135–36, 219 (*see also specific location names*); churches, 67, 258; dilapidation and ruins, 58, 70, 135–36, 216–17; distinctive features, 67, 75–80, 80–85, 86–87, 90, 100, 215–16, 268n4; environmental characteristics, 13–14, 18–19; forts, 59, 67, 125, 256; forbidden places, 6, 54, 60, 80–85, 141, 162–63, 209; hotels and inns, 21, 77, 84, 104–5, 147–48, 158–59,

166, 189, 199, 207, 217–18, 221, 248–49;
interacting characteristics, 54, 80–87;
mental hospitals, 64, 68–72, 80–81, 136;
orphanages, 44–45, 64, 68, 136; Pizza Hut,
265n1; plantations, 6, 65–66, 73; poor
houses and farms, 68, 75, 172; prisons,
64, 72, 106, 185, 217; providing proof of
legend, 78–80; pubs and taverns, 136, 221,
249; remote, 63; sewers, 61, 76; slaughter
houses, 74–75. *See also* architecture
"Legend of Sleepy Hollow, The" (Irving), 53
legends: ambiguous meaning, 4–5, 61–66,
250; ambivalence of belief in, 4–5, 65, 147,
157; bizarre content, 4, 54, 63–64; change
over time, 65–66, 67–75, 268n10; dares
(*see* legends: warnings; ritual behavior:
warnings as directions for); defined, 4,
53–55; engaging character, 54, 65; incomplete structure, 54, 61–66, 143–44, 153;
inconsistent claims, 132–34, 138–44, 153,
162–65; influencing behavior, 28, 30–34,
46, 49, 54–60, 92, 130–34, 137–42, 219,
225–26; nonsupernatural, 6, 10, 22, 39,
58, 253; plausibility of, 4, 54–55, 65; ritual
character, 119–20, 148–49 (*see also* ritual
behavior); social concerns and values
in, 6, 54, 61–66, 67–75, 254; warnings, 54,
55–60, 80–85, 101
legend telling, 24; debate during, 62, 101–2;
dichotomous structure of, 4; inspiring
legend trips, 25, 226, 234; mood during,
44–45
Legend Tripping (Robinson), 232
legend trips: authority, problematic,
206, 219–20, 232–34, 235–37, 242–43;
automobiles in, 45, 157–58, 186–88, 189,
191–92, 266nn3–4; autonomy, 232, 254;
bravery test, 58, 98, 101, 122, 144, 214;
case studies, 16–17, 20; close to home, 54,
85–87, 190–91; comparative perspective
on, 16–17, 20, 22, 144, 153, 233–35, 252–53;
compared to fiction, 243–44; conflict between participants and nonparticipants,
129–32, 208–9, 246–47, 252 (*see also* theft;
trespassing); danger, sense of, 58–60,
97–98; defined, 5; ethnography as legend
trip, 20; fieldwork, 18–19, 20; guidance

during, 141–42, 143, 232–34, 238–42, 252
(*see also* preparatory activities: guidance,
conflicting); individual agency, 25–26,
233, 253–54; interdisciplinary perspective
on, 17, 21, 23; lack of closure, 226, 235–38,
265n4; legend testing, as, 45, 46, 58, 61,
157–59; liminal character, 113; motivations, 17, 25; noninstitutional character,
25, 206, 232, 235–36, 238, 240–42, 246–48,
253–54; online, 5, 70; perceived as
trivial, 5; popularity of, 5, 25, 248, 254;
preparatory phase (*see* preparatory
activities); public panic over, 5, 128–29;
reincorporation, problematic, 235–38,
244–45, 253; as rites of passage, 25, 47–49,
114, 118, 202, 226, 231–35, 253–54; ritual
phase (*see* ritual behavior); role playing,
24, 30, 46, 49, 132–33; stages of, 48–49,
252–53, 261n14; tourism as, 248–50 (*see
also* souvenirs); transforming legends,
131–32, 246–54; voluntary character, 25,
194, 233, 254, 267n7. *See also* discussion of
supernatural experience
"lights out" (legend), 55, 58
liminoid, 260n9
litter, 18, 122, 123, 163
"Little Gracie Watson" (legend), 124
Lizzie Borden Bed & Breakfast Museum,
105, 217–18, 268n6
Loch Ness monster, 37
Logan Cemetery (Utah), 119
Longfellow, Henry Wadsworth, 221
Longfellow's Wayside Inn, 221, 268n9
Loon Lake Cemetery (Minnesota), 5, 120
Lowell Cemetery (Massachusetts), 124
Louisiana: New Orleans, 124; St. Francisville, 65
lucky objects, 13. *See also* supernatural expe-
rience: superstition

Magdalene, Mary, 262n6
magic. *See* ritual behavior
magic circle (concept), 108–9
Maine: Kennebunk, 249; Portland, 260n9;
York, 76, 262n6
maniacs, 29–30, 55, 141–42, 183, 234
Mansfield University, 81–82
Marchand, Jean-Baptiste, 39

Mark Twain House, 77

Marshall, Elisha G., 129

Mary, Virgin, 262n6

Mary Magdalene, 262n6

Maryland: Baltimore, 127

Massachusetts: Berkley, 105; Bridgewater, 105; Concord, 104–5, 120, 151–52, 161, 166, 199, 219; Fall River, 105, 217–18, 268n6; Freetown, 105; Freetown State Forest, 225; Lowell, 124; Rehoboth, 105; Salem, 82–83, 96, 105, 181–82, 199, 249; Sturbridge, 127; Sudbury, 221, 268n9

media effects, 12, 16

mediums. See psychics

Melon Heads (legend), 63–65, 141–42, 234, 261n4, 266n4

memorates (defined), 4, 132

mental hospitals, 32, 34. See also legend locations: mental hospitals

Mexico, 55

Michigan, 261n4; Roscommon, 121

Midnight in the Garden of Good and Evil (Berendt), 124, 263n3

"Midnight Mary" (legend), 106, 161

Milford Cemetery (Connecticut), 112

Minnesota: Chapel Island, 171–72; Jackson, 5, 120

Missouri, 95

modernity, 25, 28, 231–32, 250, 253–54, 269n1

Mojave Desert, 46

Monster Move Podcast, 261n5

MonsterQuest (television show), 5

monsters. See specific monster names

Most Haunted (television show), 5

mountains, sacred, 109

Mount Carmel (Connecticut), 109

Mount Hope Cemetery (New York), 122, 129

Museums of Old York, 76, 262n6

Myrtles Plantation (Louisiana), 65

mystical experiences, 11, 14, 185–86

myth, 269n4

Nasson, Mary, 76

National Register of Historic Places, 69–70

near-death experiences (NDEs), 12

negative ion generators, 166

New Hampshire: Salem, 105; Whitefield, 158–59

New Jersey: Atlantic City, 217

New York: Binghamton, 41, 60; Cortland, 195; Geneva, 77; Irondequoit, 186–87; Interlaken, 89; Middlesex, 157; Newfield, 117–18; New York City, 61; Oswego, 125; Penn Yan, 89–90, 123, 214; Rochester, 80, 122, 129, 186–87; Sleepy Hollow, 124; Victor, 170

night hag (phenomenon). See sleep paralysis

"Night the Ghost Got In, The" (Thurber), 192–93

nonbelievers. See skeptics

Norse sagas, 37

North Carolina: Morgantown, 260n6; Richfield, 158

Norwich State Hospital, 69–71, 80–81

Nox, 261n3

Oakland Cemetery (Iowa), 132, 162–63, 183–84

offerings. See ritual behavior: tribute

Ohio, 29–30, 44–45, 261n4; Bowling Green, 172–73; Butler, 160–61; Columbus, 35–36, 136, 192–93, 267n6; Worthington, 129–30

Ohio Lunatic Asylum, 193

Ohio State University, 35–36, 136

okapi, 39, 260n9

old hag (phenomenon). See sleep paralysis

Old Hill Burying Ground (Massachusetts), 120, 151–52, 161, 219

Old Parish Cemetery (Maine), 76, 262n6

Old York Historical Society, 76, 262n6

operant conditioning, 13

orbs, 139, 140, 159, 164, 214, 219, 222–23, 268n12, 269n13

ostension: defined, 28; folklore as performance, 29–30; hypermodern ostension, 41; legend tripping as, 28, 43–49, 239; meta-ostension, 42–43; positive outcomes, 33, 260n3; problems with typology, 40; proto-ostension, 38, 40, 260n8; pure ostension, 38–39, 40; pseudo-ostension, 37–38, 40 (see also hoaxes); quasi ostension, 35–37, 40; as reenactment, 100, 132, 141–43, 165; reverse ostension, 41–42;

role playing and, 30; self-fulfilling character, 30–31, 33–34; typology, 35–43
Otto, Rudolf, 185
out-of-body experiences (OBEs), 11, 14, 153

paranormal: defined, 7; para-institutions,
  238, 241–42; professionals, 238, 240–41;
  rate of belief in, 7–8, 259n1 (intro.);
  religion and, 7, 185–86, 243, 246–48; science and, 220; subcultures, 206, 238–39,
  243–43, 249–50. See also supernatural
  belief
pareidolia, 37
participant observation, 15, 19
Pennsylvania: Mansfield, 81–82; Philadelphia,
  106, 185, 217; Scott Township, 75;
  Stillwater, 75; Weatherly, 56–57
Pere Cheney Cemetery (Michigan), 121
personality, fantasy-prone, 38
Pettinicchio, Darlyne, 32
petroglyphs, 105
Pew Research Center, 7
Picture Yourself Legend Tripping (Belanger),
  232
Pixar, 121
phantom hitchhikers, 78–80
physiological arousal, 110
Plautus (Titus Maccius Plautus), 67
Pliny the Younger, 67
Poe, Edgar Allan, 163
"Pope Lick Monster" (legend), 129
popular culture, 12, 16, 41, 249–50
Possessed Possessions (Okonowicz), 196
possession: demonic, 38, 132, 198, 199, 238;
  spirit, 225
Post Cemetery (New York), 125
postmaterialist values, 254
practical jokes. See ostension:
  pseudo-ostension
prejudice, 34
preparatory activities, 24, 108, 181, 232–33,
  237, 253; ambiguous preparations, 94–95,
  98–99; anticipation building, 91, 93–94,
  96–97, 99, 102–3, 105–7, 113, 118; degrees of
  preparation, 92–93; demarcating threshold, 108–13, 118, 201; flashlights, 98–99;
  guidance, conflicting, 91, 114, 232–34, 246

(see also legend trips: guidance during);
  insufficient preparation, 95; legend reviewing, 91, 101, 103–6, 106–8, 112, 114, 233;
  mood, 19, 96, 104, 105–6, 107–8, 110–12,
  113–14, 174; mundane preparations,
  94–95, 98–99, 114; ordeals, 95, 103, 109,
  113, 217; packing, 91, 92–93, 94–99, 114;
  rites, preliminary, 91, 200; ritual preparations, 95–97, 98–99, 113, 114; serial legend
  tripping, 105–6, 113; significance of, 94,
  113; travel, 19, 91, 106–13, 114, 253; tribute,
  95–96; wayfinding, 100–103
Procrustean effect, 163–64
Prohibition era, 263n8
Providence Athenaeum, 123, 163–64
psychics, 146, 172–73, 198–99, 240–41
Publick House (Massachusetts), 217
Puckwudgies, 141–42, 225, 234
Puerto Rico, 40
punk rock, 32
Puritans, 261n4
psychopathology, 13
Pygmalion in the Classroom (Rosenthal and
  Jacobson), 33–34

quasi-institutions, 238–42, 242–43, 249–50
quasi ostension, 35–37, 40

Rafaelian, Carolyn, 197
real estate industry, 194, 267n8
reincarnation, 74
religion and supernatural belief, 7, 185–86,
  243, 246–48
religiosity, American, 7, 26, 237–38, 247–48
residual landscape, 76, 248
Revolution, American, 104, 151
Rhode Island, 19, 265n3; Burrillville, 129;
  Exeter, 46, 120; Jamestown, 59; Newport,
  196–97; Providence, 123, 163–64
rites of passage (traditional), 25, 47, 103, 181,
  230–31, 235; authority in, 231, 232; direct
  rite of passage, 108, 118; guidance during,
  231, 232; indirect, 118; institutional character, 231; meaning of, 231; ordeals, 231;
  problems with, 251–52; reincorporation,
  181, 196, 214, 215, 226, 230; social status,
  230–31, 251; stages, 230–31, 232; tribute, 123

ritual behavior, 19, 22, 24, 108–9, 233–34; absence of in modern society, 47, 231–32; calling out, 117, 127, 148; darkness, 110, 142–43, 172, 264n10; defined, 119; expression of group culture through, 118; invocation of supernatural, 112, 117, 118–19, 149, 172, 198–200, 238; invocations, concordant, 123–26, 127–28, 149, 253, 263n6; invocations, transgressive, 117, 121–23, 127–28, 132–35, 145–49, 162–63, 198, 200, 253; magic, contagious, 127, 214; magic, defined, 128; magic, material, 117, 126–27, 148, 206, 213, 263n6; magic, sympathetic, 127; magic, verbal, 117, 148, 206, 213; mementos of invocation, 120–21, 122, 213; as mood, 142, 144–48, 149, 154, 174, 264n10; as play, 108–9, 110; problems caused by, 118; rites, postliminal, 199, 200, 196–201, 265n4; rituals, generalized, 118, 134–44, 148, 155, 165, 169, 264nn11–12; rituals, particularized, 118, 133–34, 140–41, 144, 148, 169, 264nn11–12; rituals, protection, 160; rituals, religious, 133; rituals, scholarly interpretations of, 263n2; rituals, social functions of, 254; smudging, 199, 200; threshold, symbolic, 118; threshold crossing by participants, 118, 149, 181, 188–92, 201–2, 253; threshold crossing by supernatural, 190–91, 192–95, 196–201, 235–38, 253, 265n4 (chap. 5), 265n2 (chap. 6); tribute, 95–96, 117; trigger objects, 96, 124, 127, 167; warnings as directions for, 121, 131–32, 134, 143, 147–48, 259n2 (chap. 1), 263n8. *See also* preparatory activities: ritual preparations; vandalism
role-playing games, 31
Romance of Natural History, The (Gosse), 39
Romans, 67
"roommate's death" (legend), 29
Royal Oak Pub (UK), 136

Saint Bonaventure Cemetery (Georgia), 124
Saint John's University (Minnesota), 171–72
Sasquatch. *See* Bigfoot
satanic panic, 27, 31–32, 55, 58
Satanism, 27, 31–32, 38, 128–29, 162, 247–48, 260n8
self-fulfilling prophecy. *See* expectancy effect
Serling, Rod, 89

sewers, New York City, 60
Shelburne Museum, 155
skeptics, 164–65, 213; performative, 147–48, 211–12, 220, 248; sincere, 7, 146–48, 208, 219–20, 223, 264n14
slavery, 62, 65–66, 73, 83
Sleeping Giant State Park, 109, 263n3 (chap. 3)
sleep paralysis, 11, 36–37, 38–39, 153
Sleepy Hollow Cemetery (New York), 124
Slender Man, 32–33, 41–42
smallpox, 43
social capital, 232, 269n1
social influence, 55, 170, 203–5, 206–8
social media, 42–43, 249. *See also* YouTube
South Africa: Cape Town, 260n9
Southern Connecticut State University, 83–85
souvenirs, 217–18
Species (film), 40
Spera, Tony, 83–85
Sperling, Christian, 37
spirit box (device), 43, 167
Spook Hill (New York), 157
Stanley, Henry Morton, 39
St. Ann's Retreat (Utah), 130–32, 263n7
status, social, 15, 25, 207, 230–31, 235–36, 244, 251
Stepney Cemetery (Connecticut), 106
stereotype threat, 34
stigma, 267n9
stimuli, ambiguous, 8–9, 15–16
Stowe, Harriet Beecher, 112–13, 135, 147
subcultures, paranormal, 206, 238–39, 241–43, 249–50
Sunken Garden (New York), 80
Supernatural (television series), 243–44
supernatural belief: ambivalence of, 24–25, 209; culture and, 8–10, 12, 54; religion and, 7
supernatural experience, 24, 233–34; academic debate over, 8; ambiguous character of, 15, 202, 219, 222–23, 236–38, 239; ambiguous meaning, 25, 203, 205, 206, 226, 235–38, 242–46, 252; attitude requirements, 153–56, 174; batteries draining as, 99, 168–69; bound to place, 188–89, 192–93, 194–95, 196–201, 213; constructionist perspective (cultural

source theory), 8–10, 12, 54, 253, 260n6; cross-cultural comparisons, 8–9, 11–12, 36–37, 153–54; culmination of legend trip, 152–53; cultural expectations of, 35–36, 140, 169, 206, 238–39, 263n9; debate (*see* discussion of supernatural experience); environmental factors, 13–14, 161; feelings as, 139–40; flight from, 45, 171, 175, 180, 186–92, 202, 245; group process, 15–16 (*see also* discussion of supernatural experience); inconsistency with history, 161–62; inconsistency with legends, 153, 161–62, 174, 221–26; injured by, 139, 214–15; interpretative process, 15; involuntary, 190–91, 192–95, 196–201, 202, 213, 265n2; malfunctioning equipment as, 99, 168–69, 263n4 (chap. 3); mood as, 19, 153, 171–72, 174, 219; natural phenomena mistaken as, 35–37, 153, 165–70, 171, 174, 209–10, 220, 260nn5–6; objective perspective, 9–10; perennialist perspective (experiential source theory), 6, 11–12, 16, 38–39, 253; photographs as proof of, 20, 37, 42, 64, 155, 212, 213, 216–18, 219–21, 222–26; plaster casts as proof of, 96, 214, 218; positive experience, 184–86, 194; profundity of, 24; proof of deed, 213–18; proof of encounter, 213–15, 218–20, 224–25; protection from, 97–98; psychological perspectives, 12–14, 253, 259n2 (intro.); psychological phenomena as, 153; returning from, 24, 113, 187, 201–2; safety from, 24, 113, 188–92, 193, 203, 245, 250; social perspectives, 14–16, 253; social phenomena as, 153; subjective experiences, 170–74, 199, 214–15, 219; subtlety of, 173, 174; superstition, 9, 13; symbolic meaning of, 6, 8–9, 14; uncanny character, 175, 180–86, 188, 193–94, 200, 202, 235–37, 242–45; verbal arguments as proof of, 209–13; video recordings as proof of, 20, 216–17, 222–26. *See also* electronic voice phenomenon

Surge, Victor, 41–42
Sutcliffe, Norma, 128
synesthesia, 14

Tales of a Wayside Inn (Longfellow), 221
talismans, 97, 200

television: as data source, 17, 18; reality TV, 5, 20. *See also specific program names*
"Ten Penny Bridge" (legend), 125
Terwillegar, Mary Jane, 5, 120
Texas: San Antonio, 157, 184–85, 188, 191, 266n4
Thanatos, 57, 261n3
theft, 120–21, 124, 127–28, 124, 129, 252
thermal imaging, 167, 225
Thietmar of Meresburg (Bishop), 67
Tinney family, 196–97
Tituba, 199
Tiv culture, 9
Thomas, Samuel M., 124
Thonga, 251
Thurber, James, 192–93, 267n6
Thurber House, 192–93, 267n6
Tolentino, Madelyne, 40
trespassing, 6, 59–60, 84–85, 129–30
trigger objects, 96, 124, 127, 167
trust, social, 232, 237, 238. *See also* institutional distrust
Turner-Ingersoll Mansion, 82–83
Twain, Mark, 77
Twilight Saga (film series), 243–44
Twilight Zone (television show), 89

UFO Hunters (television show), 5
UFOs, 16, 22, 105, 141–42, 213, 233, 234, 253
uncanny valley, 267n10
Uncle Tom's Cabin (Stowe), 147
unicorns, 39
Union Cemetery (Connecticut), 105–6
United Kingdom: Borley Rectory, 93; London, 266nn3; Somerset, 93; York, 136; Yorkshire, 146
university folklore. *See* folklore: college
University of New Haven, 136, 163–65
unobtrusive research methods, 18–19
urban legends. *See* legends
USS *Constellation*, 127
Utah: Logan, 119, 130–32, 263n7
Utah State University, 119

Valentown Museum, 170
vampires, 19, 46, 120, 153, 160, 265n3
vandalism, 5, 18, 27, 117, 120, 121–23, 126, 128, 129, 130, 213, 252, 263n3; reverse, 215

Vaugn, Nellie, 160, 265n3. *See also* vampires
Velvet Street (Connecticut). *See* Melon
    Heads
Vermont: Brunswick Springs, 106–7;
    Montpelier, 57; Shelburne, 155
vigils (in ghost hunting), 143
violence, legend-inspired, 30, 32–33
voodoo, 124

walking tours, 92, 93
Wampanoag, 225
Warren, Ed and Lorraine, 84–85, 106, 128
Washington, DC, 6, 22
Washington, Martha, 54, 61, 261n1
"Watcher, The" (legend), 184, 194
Waverly Hill Sanitarium, 216
Wharton, Edith, 189–90
"White Lady" (legend), 186–87
Whitman, Helen, 163
Wicca, 123
"Wicked Witch of Monroe" (legend), 77–78,
    95–96
Wilson, Grant, 158–59, 168. See also *Ghost
    Hunters* (television show)
Wilson, Robert Kenneth, 37
Winchester, Sarah, 62
Winchester Mystery House, 62
Windmill Tower (Australia), 161–62
Wisconsin, 32
Witch Bonney (legend), 124
witches, 76, 77–78, 95–96, 106, 120, 121, 124,
    129, 153, 160–61, 261n4
Witch House (Massachusetts), 181–82
witch trials, 153, 181–82, 199, 249
Wood County Historical Center and
    Museum, 172–73

XYZ grave, 127

Yankee Peddler Inn (Connecticut), 84
YouTube, 5, 41, 42, 105–6, 217

zombies, 267n10

ABOUT THE AUTHOR

Jeffrey S. Debies-Carl, PhD, is associate professor of sociology in the Department of Psychology and Sociology at the University of New Haven. His research examines the social significance of physical, digital, and hybrid environments. His work has appeared in a number of scholarly journals, such as the *Journal of Contemporary Ethnography* and the *Journal of Folklore Research*, and he is the author of *Punk Rock and the Politics of Place* (Routledge, 2014).

Made in United States
North Haven, CT
23 January 2024

47795849R00188